DESERT
WALKER

DESERT

WALKER

DESERT WALKER

My adventures relived

Denis Charles Bartell OAM

"Every journey starts with a dream – and then that vital first step"

Published in 2012
by Denis Bartell
www.desertwalker.com.au

Book cover design and layout
by Publicious Pty Ltd
www.publicious.com.au

ISBN: 978-0-9872810-2-9

Also available in paperback colour
ISBN: 978-0-9872810-0-5

Catalogue-in-Publication details available
from the National Library of Australia

Also available in ebook
ebook ISBN: 978-0-9872810-1-2

Non-fiction — Adventure

Dedicated to:

The Bush and its people
and
Explorers long gone

My wife Jeanne, a soul mate who I would be
lost without and who puts up with so much

My ex wife Rotha who sacrificed so much to help
me achieve my dreams. I am forever grateful.

and

my wonderful children
David, Susan and Richard
and my stepson Damien

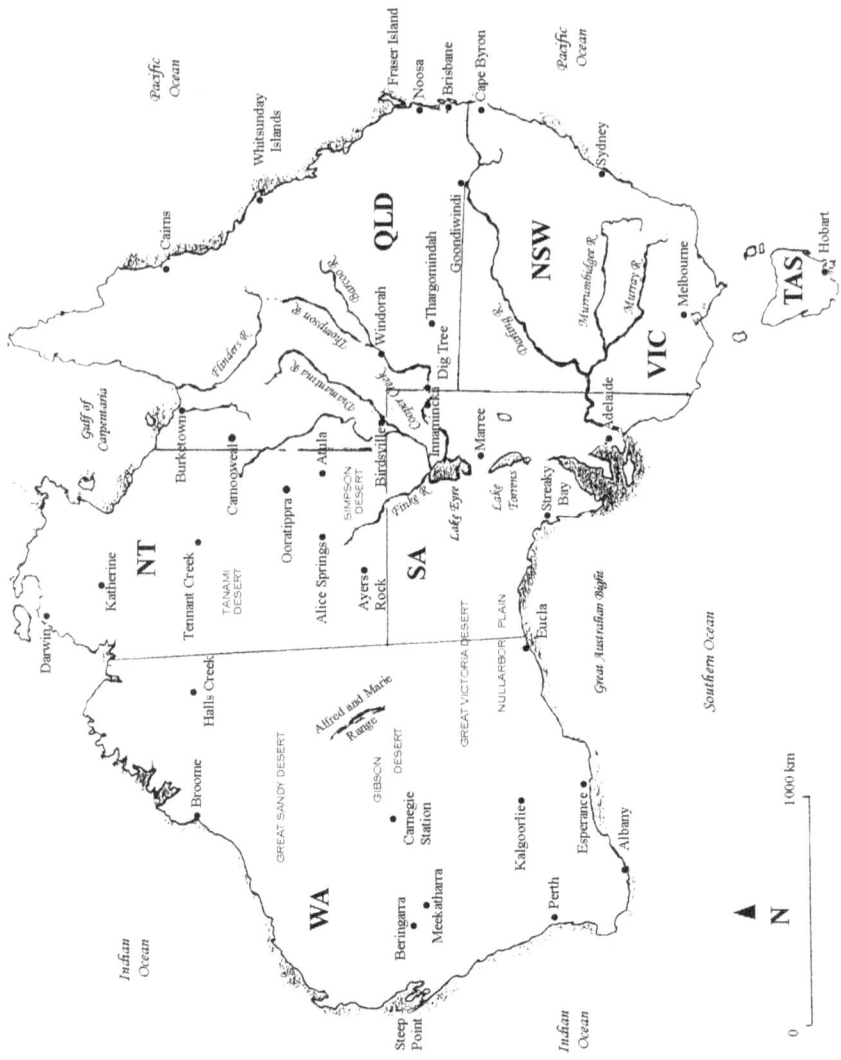

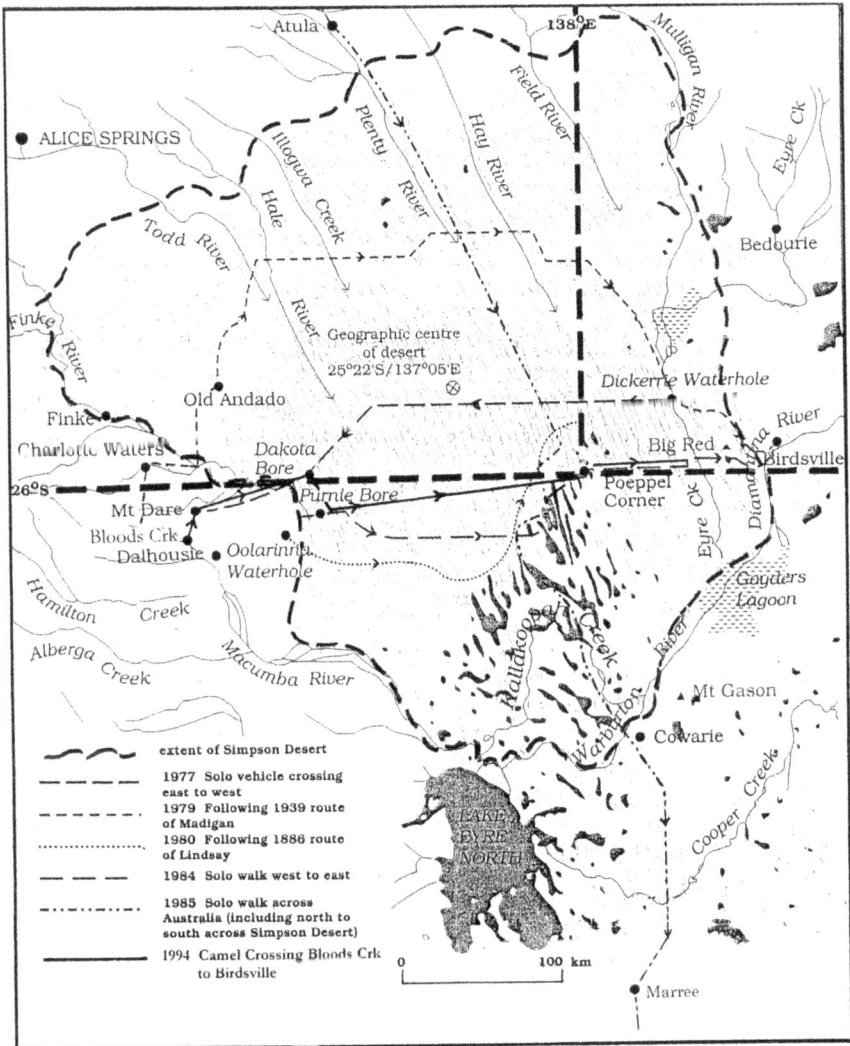

Of seventy plus Simpson Desert crossings, these are
my six most memorable

BIG RED

It is late afternoon as
I stagger to the top of this red dune
It is a journey I've made many times before
and hopefully will continue to make for many years to come

It's a special place, my high perch
where I sit cross-legged facing the setting sun

To the north and south of me
domes of windswept sand
protrude like pimples above the ridge line
each one fired like a glowing poker.........
while below me
the shadow cast by the westerly dune
inches its way across the interdunal flat
intent on extermination.

The eagle makes a long low graceful run to view the intruder
then catches an updraught and rises effortlessly into the sky
How I envy him his range of visibility, his perspective, his freedom

The sun, now a fiery ball
makes a mockery of the colour chart
as its light dances over the scattered clouds to the west

An artist is at work here splashing, dabbing, continually changing,
working his paints on the largest canvas in the world
Then in a frenzy, the final burst .... and it's finished
A masterpiece has been wrought by the fire of life

Sadly I watch this moment of art, this original
as it struggles in its death throes
to be obliterated forever by the curtain of night

Darkness falls on Big Red

Denis Bartell 1980

(Nappanerica sand dune near Birdsville dubbed "Big Red"
by Denis Bartell in 1980).

Contents

1. The Challenge..1
2. Early Days..29
3. Making a Quid..48
4. The Day of the Gecko...66
5. In the Footsteps of Lindsay.................................87
6. Bushmen and Heroes...107
7. Murray River Solo Marathon................................121
8. Darling River Solo Marathon...............................135
9. Solo West–East Simpson Desert Crossing...........149
10. Desert Walker — Gulf to Gulf............................174
11. The Spirit of Adelaide.....................................218
12. Gold Fever..234
13. Journey to an Inland Sea.................................241
14. Jeanne..269
15. Desert of Dreams...273
16. Ghost of Sturt...300
17. Retirement..312
18. The Desert Mums..315
19. My Mate Ron..334
20. One Last Camp...338
21. Post Script...347
22. Outback Adventures DVD Combo.................349
23. Acknowledgements.......................................351
24. Bibliography...353

Foreword

Contemporary Australian explorer? One of the quintessential characters of Australia's inland? Australian adventurer? Outback legend? That's how the press describes Denis Bartell.

Self-employed from an early age, his varied careers took him all over Australia, working on the land as windmill expert, irrigation and farm machinery salesman, agricultural and poultry farmer, hovercraft manufacturer, jade miner, gold prospector, shark fisherman, tourism operator, author and historian.

By the age of 40 he was finally able to more fully indulge his passion – exploring our great Outback. Denis has traversed the Australian continent on foot, in four-wheel drive vehicles and a solar car, boated down mighty rivers, canoed the flood waters of the Cooper Creek, and ridden camels, walked or navigated almost every square kilometre of the Simpson Desert.

Aged 53, he took a five-and-a-half month solo walk across Australia north to south passing through the centre of the Simpson Desert. In one section he covered 450 kilometres cross-country: no roads, no tracks, just a compass to guide him. The greatest distance between towns, a beer or an icecream was a massive 1450 kilometres – a journey of true isolation. This walk raised some $70,000.00 for the Royal Flying Doctor Service.

He has endeavoured through his stories, television interviews and news media to encourage everyone to seek their own personal goals and for all of this, he was recognised by the Australian Government when he was awarded the Order of Australia Medal. A few years later he was again honoured, this time with the Australian Geographic Adventurer of the Year Gold Medallion.

Denis has always encouraged the young to get out and experience our great outback and our heritage, to challenge life in general. For the "not so young", he has endeavoured to show by example that "age is not a barrier, it is merely an excuse and that dreams can become reality if one is prepared to give it a go".

Denis recently retired from Trinity Beach, Cairns in far north Queensland after seven years managing a tourist resort overlooking the beautiful Coral Sea. It was nothing like a desert, being set amidst lush tropical growth and surrounded by the world heritage listed Daintree Rainforest and the Great Barrier Reef. Who could wish for more?

However, at night he dreamed of the desert sands and whispering winds that sigh in desert oaks, of sunsets that set the heavens ablaze and campfires under a star-filled canopy, of empty spaces where one can see forever, of solitude and of adventure.

I guess one day I will see him go again, at least for a time, to reunite his soul with the spirits of the outback – a necessary part of his life's journey. I should know – I am his wife.

Jeanne Bartell

Chapter 1

The Challenge

She clawed her way up the long slope, her little two-stroke motor screaming like a demented demon as the rpm needle headed towards the recommended maximum.

Blue sky momentarily filled the windscreen, then, reaching and dropping over the top, my faithful little Suzuki nose-dived into a deep red sand blow, its rim partly hidden by a covering of cane grass. The depression was filled with dead roly-poly, cane grass and other wind-blown herbage, which scraped down her sides and rolled up and over her bonnet.

Devoured completely, her insides heaved and my gear flew around as she fought for freedom and then ever so slowly managed to extract us from the bunker. We paused momentarily for a breather – me and my little yellow Tonka toy out doing battle in a huge sandy arena, a wilderness of immense proportions. With another dune conquered, we still had over a thousand left to go.

A large mob of feral camels, startled by the sudden appearance and noise of this yellow intruder, wheeled as one and moved off trailed by a defiant and disgruntled old bull. They were feeding on the succulent munyarou plants that were growing in abundance across the face of the next dune, the product of some recent patchy local rains. Further south, crowded over a long section of the lower dune face, lay the most concentrated and beautiful pink wild flower display that I have ever seen.

As I turned the wheel, the shadow cast by a stick tied to my bull bar slowly swung across the bonnet until I stopped it at a pre-determined point on its surface. No need for another compass shot yet. My line of travel now lay straight ahead over the bonnet and I calculated my next climbing angle in a flash. Then we bumped our way down to the valley floor to do it all over again. This next dune, however, developed into one of the steepest I'd so far encountered, forcing our intended path further away from the vertical into a climbing traverse across its pock-marked face.

The decision to abort was made for me as I started to slide sideways down the steep slope. I had hung on too long. At the last moment I swung the front wheels up-dune and the vehicle came to a halt, rocking gently. That was a bad one and I breathed a sigh of relief – that was until the sand gave way and she started to slide once more. I threw myself as flat as I could across the vehicle and hung on, hoping I could keep my legs and arms inside if she rolled. Her soft top would collapse, offering no protection whatsoever.

Seconds crawled past as I clung on desperately, my breathing slow and measured as if not to disturb the precarious balance which had once more been established. I decided to try to escape through the uphill door, thus keeping my weight on the top side. Slowly I unfurled my twisted limbs and started to inch upwards, and as I clicked the latch on the door she groaned as metal distorted and we began to slip again.

This time I got a surge of adrenalin and my mind raced with the gravity of a situation that could so easily leave me trapped or severely injured and unable to summon help. My beautiful wife and kids didn't flash through my mind, so I obviously wasn't fearing death at that precise moment, but I sure as hell was thinking about survival.

Here I was – alone – way out on a trackless section of the Simpson Desert perched precariously on the face of a large dune with a vehicle that was trying to make up its mind if it would like to go for a bit of a roll right back to the bottom.

As best as I could I'd adhered to my notified plan, which meant I should be somewhere on a westerly line starting from Dickerrie waterhole. While this would limit a search pattern – should one become necessary – to a narrow line on a map, no one was really expecting me to report in for at least a week. If I was badly hurt and couldn't get to my HF radio transmitter, then it could be a long wait indeed for help to arrive.

All movement had ceased now for some minutes so I decided to try again. I wanted out! Slowly I reached up and pushed the door, which fell open against the car's body with a loud clunk. So far, so good. Next I pitched out my shovel, which I always carried in the passengers' compartment, then I slowly followed. Nothing moved, which was a bit of an anticlimax really. An inspection soon revealed why: one front wheel had locked itself against the remnants of an old cane grass clump that had stubbornly refused to give way.

I dug holes under the two topside wheels, which allowed my vehicle to sink, with much groaning from stressed metal, into a more stable and secure position. Next I cut two deep curving trenches extending out for a short distance from the rear wheels. Once I started to move, these trenches would quickly guide the vehicle's tyres around so I could safely reverse straight back down the dune.

All went well, and as I'd had enough excitement for one day I decided to make camp a little earlier than normal. Smoke from my fire soon twirled lazily into the sky, and then with a steaming mug of black tea in hand, I made my way back to the top of this difficult dune to sit and immerse myself in my unique surroundings. Scattered clouds to the west soon fired up as the rays of the setting sun reached and caressed them. Overhead an eagle soared gracefully, perhaps seeking one last chance to capture an unwary morsel, while all around hung silence that blew me away with its intensity.

Ahead lay more of the same. A succession of incredibly long parallel dunes, standing like waves of an ocean, rolled away to sundown. Each was topped with patchy clumps of cane grass, and their majestic domes and sawtooth ridges of pure red sand pierced the blue sky. To the north and south these parallel lines slowly converged as they raced away to the ends of the earth. Unscarred by the hands of man, a big, stark, beautiful landscape engulfed me completely and would continue to do so for many days to come.

🦎 🦎 🦎

How did my adventure get started in the first place? It had its beginnings while I was shark fishing out of Eucla on the Great Australian Bight. This is where I first heard of the renowned adventurer Hans Tholstrup. He was on his way around Australia in a small outboard powered boat and I jokingly suggested to my mate that it would be rather neat if I took time off, loaded up my twenty footer with fuel and food, fired up the outboard and departed in the opposite direction so that I could give him a wave as our paths crossed.

At that time, however, I'd had a project to complete and it was not the time to set off on a whim. It's probably a good thing, anyway. Although my dad, Harry, and brother Kevin have salt in their veins, I think I have sand in mine.

But an adventure was tempting. When the door of temptation opened again a few years later I decided to enter it. This time I was home in Adelaide. My farm was under the control of a very good manager and I could take time off.

Hans Tholstrup had completed the first solo crossing of the Australian continent west to east through the middle by vehicle from Steep Point to Cape Byron in a small Daihatsu four-wheel drive. He took 13 days and figured it couldn't be done in much less. I liked the idea of a bit of a challenge, particularly as the route passed through the Gibson Desert where I had worked long ago, and also the Simpson Desert, that I had just started to explore and enjoy. I thought I'd give it a shot to see if I could lower his record. I just couldn't resist the temptation.

As Suzuki was Daihatsu's main rival in the light-weight four-wheel drive market, I approached them to see if they would be prepared to lend me a vehicle for a record attempt, and much to my surprise, they did. Even though theirs was considerably smaller at 540 cc than the model Tholstrup had driven, I still figured that I had a good shot. I promised the South Australian distributor that I would make the first solo crossing of the country from east to west between its widest points, and then on my return journey would try to lower Hans Tholstrup's time for the west to east crossing, from thirteen days to nine.

Because of my bush and general outback experience, I considered the two-way crossing of Australia to be not much more than a long drive, although one not to be taken lightly. Parts of it after all were still very remote, and only a fool would set off inadequately prepared. You needed to be capable of dealing with any emergency, to be completely self-reliant. I also set myself one further goal, which to me was the real jewel in the crown. I wanted to be the first person to cross the Simpson Desert from east to west solo by vehicle, completely cross-country: no roads or tracks.

🦎 🦎 🦎

Though my actual Simpson Desert crossing, if successful, would be a first in terms of the particular challenge I'd set myself, I was following a distinguished South Australian personality, Doctor Reg Sprigg, who had made the first ever vehicular crossing of the Simpson Desert. He ultimately made two crossings, both cross-country, and each from a different direction.

In 1962, Dr Sprigg of Geosurveys of Australia Pty Ltd, with his family, completed the first vehicular crossing of the Simpson Desert from west to east. They had departed from Mount Etingambra on an easterly course and, roughly following the line of the South Australian border, arrived at Poeppel Corner. Here Sprigg found Poeppel's original corner post, which had been erected in 1880, lying on the ground and rotting away. Mr Poeppel had surveyed and marked the junction of the three state borders of Queensland, Northern Territory and South Australia. Sprigg rescued the peg, which is now on display in the Mortlock Library in Adelaide, and continued on to Birdsville to complete his crossing.

In 1964, the Sprigg family was again back in the desert. They departed from near the ruins of Poonarunna outstation on the Warburton, crossed the Kallakoopah, and proceeded northwards roughly following the line of the dunes. He named Lake Griselda after his wife, and a hill located near the middle of the Simpson, Geosurveys Hill. He finally left the desert along the Plenty River floodout and thus completed the first vehicular crossing of the Simpson from south to north.

While Sprigg's journeys clearly demonstrated that this area, which had long seemed impenetrable and hostile, could indeed be crossed by vehicle, an east to west crossing was never contemplated due to the nature of the terrain.

The dunes, which run approximately north-north-west/south-south-east, are long and parallel, and some continue unbroken for hundreds of kilometres. The valley between the dunes, the interdunal flat, varies in width depending on which part of the desert you are in, but it is invariably wider on the eastern side of the desert. When crossing the dunes at right angles to reach the live sand crest, the gentler slope is encountered going eastwards, and the more dramatic, steeper slope if proceeding westwards. This is the reason that it had never been crossed east to west by vehicle: most people considered climbing the steep face of some twelve hundred dunes to be an impossible feat.

🦎 🦎 🦎

I departed Adelaide on 9 July 1977, and after a slow and tiring journey of some 2400 km, reached Cape Byron, Australia's most easterly point, and managed to find my way up the hill in the dark to the lighthouse. I got the lighthouse keeper's son to sign my logbook, and then with Steep

Point a mere 5858 km distant, I was finally on my way.

The drive west towards Birdsville was uneventful, although I certainly realised on the long flat sections that I wasn't driving a high-powered machine. With a headwind blowing we had to be going downhill to top 90 km per hour, but at least the Suzuki was running well, and I wasn't in a hurry anyhow. There was time to enjoy and dream before it all became serious.

For some, the long distances involved in outback travel become monotonous due to the sameness of the landscape for long periods of time. It's never been that way with me. There is always something interesting to catch the eye, another vision to be added to my outback file: a bloodwood tree in full bloom; a flight of corellas; or the magnificent red sandhills that sometimes seem to float magically above the shimmering plains near Windorah, where within the space of a few heartbeats, nature presents masterpieces from its endless collection, one after another. Then beyond to where stark hills stand tormented by another long, hot, dry summer and endless gibber-strewn plains show barely a blade of dead grass. The only green is the thin wavy lines of trees that indicate the paths of rocky waterways.

Sub-Inspector Gilmore and his companions from the Bulloo Mounted Police Barracks, situated near the present day township of Thargomindah, set out in 1871 on a 600 mile ride. They had been instructed to check on rumours circulated by the Aborigines that a long time ago there had been a massacre of a large group of white men, Vinie Vinie, at a place they called Wantata. This is a waterhole on the Diamantina River just to the north of Durrie station. The authorities were anxious to know if this was the final resting place of the famous missing explorer, Ludwig Leichhardt, who had left the Darling Downs in Queensland in 1848 in an attempt to cross Australia to the west through its unknown heart and had never been seen again.

Knowing the outback as I do, I have only to close my eyes and I can picture the scene. Strange, unfamiliar blobs float above a distant ridge: heat-distorted shapes of a line of horsemen approaching. It's 120ºF in the water bag, and the plain is alive as gibbers, too hot to hold, expend their energy. The horsemen hunch up and clutch their hats over their faces as a willy-willy roars through their ranks, blasting them with dust and small debris. The wind is unpleasant, yet welcome in a strange way as it brings a moment of change – and an oath or two from the parched throats of otherwise silent men. Slumped in their saddles, their horses' heads hung low on slack rein, these ragged, gaunt men stumble on over the cruel terrain.

In the desert I have many moments when I pause and marvel at the courage of men like these. I try to imagine what it would have been like to join them in their crossing of this uncharted wilderness – their feelings, their thirst and hunger, their fears that they may never return to civilization, friends and loved ones. Sometimes I wish I was there, regret I can't be. To me, this is the pulse of the outback.

🦎 🦎 🦎

Finally, I arrived at the tiny and remote outpost of Birdsville. Ahead of me now lay the formidable Simpson Desert. I double-checked everything and took on a bit over 200 litres of fuel. With minimum water, spares, food and other items, I departed in what can only be described as a grossly overloaded little vehicle. My destination that day was Dickerrie waterhole on the Eyre Creek, about 55 km north of the South Australian border. I chose this as my jumping-off point as the Eyre Creek was flooded and this was my best place to attempt a crossing.

On the morning of 16 July, I took an exploratory walk across the creek. It was about 100 metres wide and towards the other side, the water was nearly up to my waist – about the top of my vehicle's wheel housing. At least it felt firm and rocky underfoot; I wasn't concerned about bogging the vehicle, more that I didn't drown the motor. To help prevent this, I tied a plastic skirt around the front end, wrapped the coil and distributor in plastic, sprayed the electronics with a water repellent, blocked up the breather hole in the clutch and taped up the doors.

The crossing was thankfully a non-event, and safely on the other side I set my course due west. My line of travel would now take me almost through the middle of the Simpson Desert to a point just to the south of Andado station. Ahead lay 350 km of virtually untouched wilderness, and there was no doubt in my mind that this was going to be one hell of a trip.

I had about 10 km of soggy flood plain to negotiate next. I hadn't long started when I thought I could see a vehicle just slightly south of my course, and angled off to investigate. It turned out to be one of two vehicles that had been abandoned after running out of fuel, their owners' air-lifted to Birdsville just weeks before. It sure served as a reminder of the dangers ahead.

For the next thirty minutes, things went well. My Suzuki was performing admirably and my confidence started to get a bit ahead of our combined abilities, that is until I hit this big dune. While trying to work out my angle of attack during the climb, I misjudged and slithered back into a large clump of trees growing part-way up. I had to axe the whole lot out before I could extract my vehicle and reverse to the bottom for another go. I learned my lesson: you don't wait to select your path, your angle of climb, from the bottom, as with the dune towering above you, you are far too close to assess the best way up; you decide how and where to tackle each dune from the top of the one before. It took me about a day before I reckoned I had it all together and knew what tell-tale signs to look for, and what angle of attack had the greatest chance of success.

There were, however, many spectacular failures, with multiple attempts and frightening situations where the vehicle became stranded sideways way up high, rocking gently on the verge of a rollover. In these situations, I would climb out of the vehicle ever so carefully, shovel holes for the top-side wheels to drop into and trenches to guide the vehicle around, then back down and start again.

It was never far from my mind that a bad accident could easily develop into an absolute disaster. That's part of the deal, however, and must be accepted when you opt for the ultimate thrill of solo travel in remote areas. Solo travel in the arid areas of our beautiful Australian outback brings personal rewards, highs and an intimacy with one's surroundings that can never be obtained in group travel. The downside is obviously the risk of sickness or accident turning into disaster.

Every day was a never-ending battle where each dune had to be fought and conquered. Driving through the dunes of the Simpson Desert is a very different proposition from driving on a track through the desert. There's no real comparison. Similarly, there is no comparison between a desert crossing against the steeper face of the dunes as I was attempting, and one coming from the other direction.

My third day out of Dickerrie, things became even worse. Where previously I had had an easy run down the western side after cresting a dune, now the spinifex became more prevalent and wind- and water-eroded slopes jarred and jolted me mercilessly. My little vehicle sure wasn't made for comfort and it was a physical relief when I could finally settle back in my cosy swag spread under a canopy of brilliant stars. Unless you have viewed the heavens from the clear skies of the outback, you haven't really lived. Most of my city friends prefer five stars. I must be greedy – I like millions.

Most nights there would be a welcome visitor or two who would silently materialise and prowl the extremity of the campfire's flickering light until finally, with a dingo's curiosity satisfied, they would move on. The most I have ever had circling me at any one time was four, which really is a few too many. Makes you think, when in the morning light the prints in the sand show clear evidence of their presence only inches away from your swag and face. Not that I have ever felt endangered – although perhaps sometime in the future, with more human contact, who knows?

Occasionally on a really big dune I would take a break and walk along the ridge to sit atop its highest windswept dome and revel in the commanding view over the surrounding countryside. From my vantage point, the ridges stood like waves of an endless ocean, while to the north and south, interdunal corridors disappeared over the horizons. With a setting sun, lofty domes of sand and sawtooth ridges would glow red until the shadows of night relentlessly extinguished each and every one. It was all so magnificent and awe inspiring; it seemed timeless, endless. The beauty of the desert captivated me totally and at times my whole being felt at peace and at one with this unique area, while at other times the feeling of loneliness, of absolute isolation on this frozen sea, was overwhelming.

As day five progressed, I was starting to become concerned. When I had departed Eyre Creek I knew that I would see absolutely nothing that I could use to determine my position on the map until I crossed the Colson Track, some 240 km distant. I wasn't too worried about my compass work and considered that I could hold a good straight line, but how far I was along that line would be pure conjecture.

We did it the hard way then but it certainly made for a better bushman. Now all you have to do is press a button and your handy Global Positioning System, your pal the GPS, will place you on the map within a few metres of where you are standing. I had allowed what I thought was a reasonable percentage for wheel spin and the extra mileage that would eventuate from numerous failed attempts and detours, but apparently it wasn't enough. By my calculations and speedo reading, I should have reached the Colson Track by this time. With my water and fuel desperately depleted, a graceful exit from the desert was going to be a touch-and-go affair.

Climax then anticlimax became the norm. Every dune I topped brought a surge of excitement as I eagerly searched the interdunal floor below for signs of the elusive Colson Track.

About midday, I stopped for a welcome break on the crest of one of the highest dunes encountered so far that day. Its broad top of scalloped drift was dotted with occasional dense clumps of cane grass, its surface still carrying the tiny footprints of the previous night's activity – endless stories written in the sand, available to those who know how to read them. A couple of butterflies frolicked or courted above while the open door of the vehicle creaked occasionally, ominously, in the almost-breeze and every once in a while I caught myself stupidly straining my ears to position the vehicle's sounds that I knew were not even there. Isolation and quiet does strange things.

That night I repaired a tyre, allowed myself one last drink, and with a solitary dingo patrolling the perimeter of my firelight, settled down to what was to be a sleepless night. What little water remained was now strictly reserved for my vehicle should I blow a hose or damage the radiator. I could carry on for a few days without water – my vehicle couldn't.

Early on day six, I encountered my first sign of man's intrusion into this unique wilderness area since departing Eyre Creek. Nestled under a bush was a small heap of rusty tin cans – just when I was starting to feel I was alone on this planet!

Another couple of sandhills further on, I finally reached the Colson Track, which although it was clearly defined, showed its lack of use by the tree regrowth along its centre. Although I couldn't tell precisely where I hit the track, I was confident that I had maintained a fairly accurate compass course, and if so, my position was confined to a relatively small section along it.

I could now compare the map distance from Eyre Creek to the Colson Track against the actual distance I'd recorded on my speedo. I found that due to multiple attempts to climb the dunes, wheel slip and detours, I was travelling about 18% further than the map distance indicated. With the distance remaining to reach safety, it was evident that my fuel reserves would not be sufficient if I continued along my current line of travel. Therefore I chose to alter direction and took up a new course of 235° which I hoped would bring me into sight of Mt Etingambra. My reasons were twofold. First, if I could locate Dakota Bore, situated near there, I would have my much-needed water, and if not, at least I would be close to the Finke River where I should find a waterhole, or be able to dig a soak. Second, once I got out of the sandhills and reached the hard country, travelling would be much easier and use up a lot less fuel. My destination and safety now lay at Mt Dare station, and with a bit of luck, I might even pick up one of their station tracks along the Finke.

There was the remnant of an old oil exploration track heading roughly in my chosen direction which I followed for just a short distance, until topping a large dune, it disappeared abruptly. I just couldn't believe it! Ahead now lay a vision of absolute desolation, the like of which I had never before witnessed on such a grand scale anywhere in the Simpson, or in Australia for that matter. Spinifex, cane grass and scattered acacia had clothed and softened the desert so far. Now, however, to the south, north and west, there was nothing but barren windswept flats and ridges for as far as the eye could see. Fire had destroyed the lot and it looked more like a scene from the Sahara Desert. It was to remain this way for about 35 km when, again on a high dune, the desert abruptly returned to its more normal state.

I climbed my last dune for the day just on dark, and away in the distance right on course I was sure that I caught a glimpse of what looked like a small dot of blue, which if correct, could only be the top of a hill.

That night I dreamt of water, and when I awoke next morning I was sure it was close at hand. A little bush next to my vehicle was crowded with finches, and they don't travel far from a daily drink. By mid-morning I was continually catching glimpses of a large hill, and finally cut a water course heading in its direction. Well-worn cattle pads, also used by camels and numerous donkeys, led me unerringly to Dakota Bore and my first wash for seven days. Water never tasted so good! Dakota, a free flowing bore, had created a picturesque reed-covered wetland that was home to a variety of birds, and as the range of tracks in the sand indicated, was also used extensively by the numerous and varied wildlife that ranged through this area.

I climbed to the top of Mt Etingambra, which was close at hand, for one last look back over the desert that now lay defeated. I had just escaped by the skin of my teeth and know I'll never forget that journey, that experience, ever. When you think about it, I had driven for nearly seven days towards the setting sun, and of man's existence seen only an abandoned vehicle, a small heap of rusty cans and an overgrown track. How isolated is that? This challenge had been a great adventure creating memories to be taken out, dusted off and relived many times over in the years ahead. At the same time, I wondered how Ted Colson had felt when he, Peter Ains and their five camels, had also stood on this lonely hill back in 1936 looking into the desert they were about to cross. The way ahead must have looked rather daunting. When the two men finally arrived in Birdsville some 21 days later, Ted Colson entered history books as the first white man to cross the Simpson Desert. I didn't know it then, but years later, I would take up the challenge to repeat that trip: heading into the desert from the point where I now stood with an Aboriginal companion and four camels, turning our backs on Etingambra just as Ted and Peter had done, and disappearing into the Simpson Desert.

From my vantage point, I located a track heading in the direction of Mt Dare station and roughly following the line of the Finke, reputedly the oldest river in the world. Around mid-afternoon I spotted the homestead away in the distance, and a large mob of cattle being driven across the flat towards it. At this moment my motor spluttered and died, and it was only from the dregs of several jerry cans that I was able to fire her up again and just make it into the homestead where I was made welcome by the station owners, Rex and June Lowe. They insisted on giving me a huge meal and a bed for the night, and in the morning sold me sufficient fuel to get into Kulgera on the Stuart Highway.

My journey was now through more familiar territory; I had completed the remote and exciting part of my venture. From Ayers Rock and The Olgas onwards, it was all rather civilized with a good, albeit rough, track to follow for most of the way through to my destination, Steep Point. I particularly enjoyed passing Lassiters Cave and then on through the beautiful Petermann and Blackstone Ranges where I relived my first intrusion into this timeless and incredibly beautiful landscape more than twenty years earlier.

At the small Aboriginal community of Warbuton I bought more fuel, then proceeded to cross the lower Gibson Desert along the now-famous Gunbarrel Highway, which was surveyed by Len Beadell. Construction was finished on 15 November 1958 when they reached Carnegie station. From a hill named after him I sat and reflected awhile on the early

European explorers who had first crossed this wilderness area. About 100 km to the north east lay the Alfred and Marie Range that the explorer Ernest Giles had struggled so hard to reach, and surrounding it, a desert that would ultimately take the life of his companion.

🦎 🦎 🦎

Giles, accompanied by Tietkens, Gibson and Jimmy set out in August 1873 from Ross's waterhole on the normally dry Alberga River in an attempt to be the first Europeans to cross the 1200 miles of uncharted wilderness from Alice Springs to the west coast of Australia. They needed to hurry, as two other exploration parties had already departed heading west, led by Major Peter Egerton Warburton and William Christie Gosse respectively. Meanwhile, from Perth, John Forrest was preparing for a departure eastward in a bid to claim the honour for Western Australia. The race was on and a fearsome opponent awaited them all.

Giles, continually harassed by the Aborigines, finally made it to the Rawlinson Ranges and built a fort beside a large body of water that he called Fort McKellar. A sandy barrier like no other encountered so far now lay across his path and would soon prove to be a formidable foe. With dwindling water supplies Giles decided to make an exploratory march westward. He calculated that he should be able to cover some 160 miles, and if he could locate water, then he would be able to move their base camp forward. This was a logical way to penetrate deeper into the unknown with minimal risk.

On 20 April 1874, Giles departed Fort McKellar riding his favourite mare, Fair Maid of Perth. He wanted to take the more reliable Tietkens with him on what he considered would be a most difficult mission, however he was persuaded by Gibson's protests about always being left behind to mind the camp, that this time Gibson should go.

From The Circus, named by Giles and the last known water source on their route, they travelled past a salt lake, which he named Lake Christopher, and then into rolling sand hills covered with spinifex, occasional bloodwood and magnificent stands of the desert oak, my favourite tree. About 60 miles out, Giles hung up two five-gallon kegs of water in a tree plus a little food, and turned the two pack horses loose, believing that they would head back home to their base camp and water. Sandhills now gave way to open, undulating stony country covered with tall, dense spinifex.

On 22 April, they camped about 90 miles from The Circus and about 110 miles from the safety of Fort McKellar. The following day they plodded on, and finally had a glimpse of promising water-bearing ranges some 30 miles to the west. Giles named the ranges the Alfred and Marie Range. They had now pushed their luck to the limit; when Gibson suddenly said that he thought his horse was going to die, Giles realised that they could not risk proceeding any further and started his retreat.

Within a few miles, however, the horse dropped dead, placing them in a very precarious situation indeed. Giles knew how much food they had deposited with the water kegs for the return journey and it was a quite inadequate amount. Gibson had packed the supplies for the complete journey unsupervised and by the time Giles had noticed that the rations that they were carrying were hardly sufficient for one person it had already been too late to return.

With the severity of their situation I am at a loss to understand why Giles didn't butcher at least some of the dead horse to take with them. It would have only taken him minutes to hack off a few slabs of meat.

They took it in turns riding the remaining horse and walking until they reached a point about 40 miles from the kegs of water hung in the tree. Giles knew that they would both die unless he took drastic action, so he decided to send Gibson ahead to fetch help while he continued to walk. Gibson's instructions upon reaching the kegs were to water his horse and leave as much as he could. Giles also emphasised several times the importance of sticking to the tracks laid down by their horses' hooves on their outward journey and not to deviate. Gibson, riding The Fair Maid of Perth, quickly disappeared from sight. Giles staggered on.

To his credit, Giles had chosen to do the hard yards himself and I can understand and relate to that. However, in the situation, and given his complete lack of confidence in Gibson's abilities, this was the wrong decision. In this instance, I believe, the most experienced person should have used the horse to go for help, thus enhancing the remaining person's chances of making it out alive.

Finally, Giles reached the kegs and found that he had been left a little over 2 gallons of water and about 11 ounces of smoked horseflesh. With the 50-pound water keg slung over his back, he pushed on, following the horses' tracks towards The Circus, 60 miles away.

Within about 15 miles, he noticed that Gibson had detoured from their outgoing east-to-west tracks and was now heading east-south-east.

The unbelievable had happened; Giles must have been devastated. The two horses they had turned loose had deviated at this spot, and the inexperienced Gibson was now following their tracks. Giles followed Gibson for a short distance but realised that, in his weakened state, it would be suicide to continue searching further, so returned to his outbound tracks.

We will never know what happened where the tracks split. Did Gibson miss the fork, perhaps while travelling in the half-light? If so, it should have been obvious in the full light of day that where he had once been following a well-defined track laid down by six horses in total – four going out and two going back – suddenly it was down to two. There would also have been no hoof prints pointing towards him – a dead giveaway that he was no longer following their outbound track as directed by Giles. Lack of basic bush skills and attention to detail now set the scene for disaster.

If it had happened about 10 miles further on, he would have been able to see his destination, the Rawlinson Range, just starting to rear above the desert terrain. Gibson's luck had now run out. As the Fair Maid of Perth plodded on gallantly doing her rider's bidding, a terrifying, lonely death lay ahead for both man and beast, in what Giles describes as that 'fearful desert'.

Giles' water had long gone by the time he finally staggered into The Circus. He found a small wallaby, obviously thrown from his mother's pouch, and devoured the dying animal raw – fur, skin and all. What private hell Giles had endured so far can hardly be imagined. As a good bushman, he would have also known in his heart that Gibson didn't have a chance of making it out of his predicament alive.

Irrespective of this, when Giles reached Fort McKellar he set out almost immediately with Tietkens to look for Gibson. They picked up his tracks and followed them for several days. They found where Gibson had departed from the tracks of the two horses he was following and turned even further towards the south. He had burnt a patch of spinifex at this point, possibly to clearly mark the spot. Gibson had, for whatever reason, decided that the horse tracks he was following were heading in the wrong direction.

He may also have been influenced by the compass he was carrying, which had been lent to him by Giles. Giles knew he didn't understand anything about a compass, even though he had tried many times to explain its workings to him. He only lent it to Gibson because he was so anxious to carry it for his return journey.

Finally, in deadly peril themselves, Giles and Tietkens had to abandon their search and turn back. They also realised that it would have been impossible for Gibson or the horse to have survived this long without water.

Giles' agonising walk back to Fort McKellar after Gibson had departed to seek help, was an outstanding feat of survival that merits a distinguished place in the history of Australian exploration. For Gibson there was also a place in history, with a desert now named in his honour.

Warburton won the race to make the first European crossing with his epic dash from Alice Springs to the DeGray River in 1873 and John Forrest came second with his crossing from Geraldton to Peake in 1874.

Giles finally crossed the continent from Beltana to Perth, this time through the Great Victoria Desert in 1875. Giles had realised that horses did not have the stamina for the searing heat of the desert regions, and managed to obtain camels from Sir Thomas Elder, who was breeding them at his Beltana property in the north Flinders Ranges.

As if for an encore, Giles then made a return trip, setting out from Geraldton in Western Australia. On the way, he passed through the range of hills that he had sighted and named the Alfred and Marie Range when he and Gibson had been forced to retreat, and one can only wonder at his thoughts as he again crossed the area of his companion's demise, and the section of desert that had beaten him. He must have relived every painful moment of his walk and then been overwhelmed with grief as he gazed once more to the south where the track split and Gibson had disappeared. From his own experiences Giles knew the agony and terror which would have gripped the thirst-ravaged Gibson in his final hours. In his diary Giles noted: 'The Australian desert is a hell on earth'.

In a sense, the exploits of Warburton, Forrest and Giles brought to a close the magnificent era of early exploration; expeditions had now criss-crossed the vast continent of Australia and it only remained to fill in the gaps. Many more men were to die doing just that. Away to the north-west of Mt Beadell lie the Little Sandy and Great Sandy Deserts and a story of one such tragedy.

Lawrence (Larry) Allen Wells, aged 24, was second in command to Augustus Poeppel when the Queensland–Northern Territory boundary line was surveyed through the Simpson Desert from Poeppel Corner to the Gulf of Carpentaria in 1884–86, a distance of some 650 miles (1040 km). He later joined the Elder Scientific Exploring Expedition 1891–92 as surveyor, under the command of David Lindsay. Their objective was to fill in the gaps left by Giles, Gosse, John Forrest and Mills. It was the largest and best equipped expedition ever organised, consisting of fifteen members, six of whom were scientific officers. While it was a successful journey, they endured times of extreme hardship.

Wells was then appointed leader of the Calvert Scientific Exploring Expedition and on 16 July 1896 he departed Lake Way near Wiluna in Western Australia. This was the last outpost before entering the desert on their journey to the Fitzroy River. On 11 October, at a soak he named Separation Well, he split his party into two groups. Wells would continue northwards with the main party and the second group, consisting of only two men, his cousin Charles Wells and one George Jones, a nephew of explorer David Lindsay, were to head north-west for some 80 miles, then north-east to reconnect with the tracks of the main group.

They didn't arrive at the rendezvous point and Wells, unable to wait due to his own critical position, pushed on to reach the Fitzroy River, arriving on 6 November after a desert crossing of some 1200 miles. Three relief parties were unsuccessful in their attempts to locate the missing explorers, though one, conducted by William Frederick Rudall, spent seven months searching and traversed hundreds of miles of desert terrain, demonstrating remarkable courage and perseverance.

Larry Wells set out once again on 13 May 1897 from Luluigui station. This time, with the unwilling help of the desert Aboriginals, the search reached its sad ending on 27 May. Wells' journal describes the scene. They found his cousin half clothed and dried like a mummy, his features perfect and an open hand outstretched. Wells recalled feeling its strong, hard grip at their parting. George Jones, aged 18, lay nearby partly covered by drift sand, and by his side a notebook with a piece of paper fastened outside it with an elastic band. It was addressed to his father and mother.

I too have sat under the stars at Separation Well, and while there, read his letter to a group of travellers. I don't think that there was a dry eye to be found by the time I'd finished, mine included.

The original is preserved in the State Library of South Australia, Archive Section. It reads:

To My dearest Mother and Father
G.W. & J.R. Jones
Edwin Street
Gilberton
Adelaide.

Do not grieve over me darlings.
How can a man die better
Than facing fearful odds
For the ashes of his fathers

And the country of his God.

Mr. Charles sends his kindest regards he
tells me how good you were to him and
he hopes the Almighty will help you.

My dearest Mother & Father

I am writing this short note, the last one I shall ever
write I expect. We left the main party to return being
away 9 days as we were both far from well. I had
hardly any strength after 5 days spell, we started to
follow the main party, after severe trials some of the
camels died so we have had to walk, we are both very
weak and ill the other two camels are gone and neither
of us have the strength to go after them.

I managed to struggle half a mile the day before
yesterday but returned utterly exhausted, there is no
sign of water near here, and we have nearly finished
our small supply have about two quarts left, so we
cannot last long.

Somehow or other I do not fear death itself, I trust
in the Almighty God. We have been hoping for relief
from the main party, but I am afraid they will be too
late. Any money of mine I think I should like divided

between Eve Laurie and Beatrice. Now my darling parents I will wish you Goodbye, but I trust we will meet in heaven. You both have always been so good to me I should so like to see you again. Mr. Charles has been very good indeed to me, during this trip, he is not to blame that we are in this fix. It is God's will so we should not object. Goodbye to Evie and Beat and all our friends. And now darlings, God give me strength, till our next meeting, God's will be done.

> I remain
> Your loving son
> George Lindsay Jones

What a courageous young man – he did his parents proud. Over the years I have re-read his letter many times and I never fail to become emotional.

The bodies of Charles Frederick Wells, 47, and George Lindsay Jones, 18, were brought to Adelaide, where they were buried side by side in the North Road Cemetery. Larry Wells ended his days at Blackwood in the Adelaide Hills where he was killed by a rail car on 11 May 1938. He was 78 years old.

It is interesting to note by way of comparison that while Larry Wells was conducting his ill-fated journey to Fitzroy River, about 300 kilometres to the east another explorer named David Carnegie was also crossing the desert. He was roughly paralleling Wells as he headed for Halls Creek.

While Carnegie managed a successful desert crossing, just a few days out from his destination disaster also struck his party. Charles Stansmore had gone to shoot a kangaroo so that they could all enjoy a pot of kangaroo tail soup by way of celebration. They heard a shot, but when Charlie hadn't caught them up within a reasonable time, they went back to search for him. They found him dead and the signs were easy to read. He had been carrying his loaded rifle on his shoulder and holding it by the barrel. Descending a steep rocky slope, he fell backwards and the rifle somersaulted and discharged when the hammer struck a rock. The bullet struck him just below the heart and he died instantly.

Carnegie made a successful return journey back to Perth, once again crossing the desert so as to further his exploration knowledge of country never before trampled by white man.

The Australian outback is truly awe inspiring and a place of immense beauty, but unforgiving. It is ever willing to take the life of the unwary, the unprepared or the stupid, and does so with regular monotony even today. I have no doubt it will continue to do so.

ǚ ǚ ǚ

From my vantage point on Mt Beadell, I continued westward along the Gunbarrel Highway towards Carnegie station. Camel pads and human footprints were clearly evident in the sand.

I had first heard reports of Robyn Davidson and her camels from several groups of four-wheel drive tourists who had spoken to her while crossing the Gunbarrel Highway. As I was making a promotional journey for the Suzuki Motor Company which would ultimately pass through that same area, I was looking forward to meeting her. I am all for people who, through personal adventure and challenge, seek to lift their lives above the normal. There should be more of it.

While refuelling at Warburton I had been requested to keep a look out for Davidson as she was, in their opinion, overdue at Carnegie station and they were concerned about her safety. I assumed she wasn't carrying communication, which was the norm back then, and had probably given them a time frame for her journey across the Gunbarrel. They were obviously doing the expected thing by keeping an eye on her progress and here I was, an opportunity not to be missed.

That's how the system operated then. I'd travelled and worked in some very remote areas over the last twenty years, and this was a normal request. It happened all the time. You worked out how long your journey should take under favourable conditions then added a day or so for unforeseen delays. You then informed a responsible person of your plans and timing so that in the event of a 'no show' or no contact, alarm bells would ring somewhere.

We looked after each other and concerns about someone's safety were never taken lightly – not by bush people. You would always go out of your way to help anyone. Let's face it, it could be your turn next. Mateship was still very strong in the outback in that era.

On some tracks, if you were immobilised it could be weeks, if not

20

months or years, before another vehicle came along. Numerous lives were lost in those days and there are many tragic stories of those who had broken the outback's unwritten code. Ultimately forced to leave their vehicles in search of help, they died in agony through lack of water. It is all so needless, although not as frequent now due perhaps to education, better communication, equipment and more people travelling remote areas.

I continued following Robyn Davidson's footprints and camel tracks for the rest of the day, noting her numerous camps, the empty water containers and the discarded notes that had been left for her. Apparently I passed her camp during the night, because when I reached Carnegie station the following morning, management advised me that Davidson had not yet arrived. More importantly, in the next few days the station was to be abandoned for a time due to lack of rain and therefore feed for their stock. They had heard on their radio chatter sessions that she was coming and were surprised and concerned that she hadn't arrived yet.

I advised them that I would be returning in about six days time and if I didn't find evidence of her passing through their boundary gate or any sign of her on the track, then I would alert the authorities.

From Carnegie station I headed to Wiluna, then Beringarra station where I gained rather sketchy information about a relatively new track that had been cut through to the North West Coastal Highway. I found little difficulty navigating my way through the numerous station tracks but realised I would have to be careful on my way back in the dark. With tracks going everywhere it can get very confusing.

Passing through Milly Milly and Byro homesteads, it was then on to a 200 km rough stretch of recently cut track for the rest of the way to the highway. A short drive south along the bitumen and I arrived at the Overlander Roadhouse where I stayed for a couple of days to allow my vehicle to be serviced by the Western Australian Suzuki agent, who had come up from Perth for the occasion.

With only 200 km to go, the leisurely part of my journey was almost over. Now was my last opportunity to make sure everything was in order for the fast run back across the continent, so everything was meticulously double-checked.

I took my time on this final leg, inspecting the Useless Loop salt works and evaporation ponds and feasting on oysters. There's nothing better than oysters opened fresh from the rocks, dipped in the sea and then swallowed. There were a few soft sand dunes to be climbed before finally I parked my vehicle on top overlooking the Indian Ocean. I had reached Steep Point and after 5858 km, I had at last crossed the continent between its widest points.

What a magnificent sight: angry waves, having raced unchecked across a vast ocean, were now being belted into submission by this rugged coastline. The smell and taste of the salty sea spray whipping up and over the rock face with the wind was a pleasant sensation after weeks in the dust and dry air of the outback.

I didn't spend long on this isolated rocky headland, however, despite the fabulous coastal views. After a few mandatory shots of my Suzuki, which I'd parked perilously close to the sheer drop, it was time to depart. An entirely different type of venture now awaited me and enjoying the scenery was not on the agenda.

All I had to do now was repeat the journey back to Cape Byron in nine days to keep the promise made to my sponsors that their little Suzuki would whip the pants off the rival Daihatsu. The route would be identical to that already undertaken, except for the Simpson Desert area, where this time I would use a track which went all the way across and would pass through Poeppel Corner. My logbook was duly signed by the personnel of the nearby salt works and I took off.

Arriving back at Carnegie station after several days of hard driving and about two hours sleep, I found it abandoned as previously advised and immediately checked for camel tracks at the only gateway into the property from the east. There were none, and to make things more difficult the sun was starting to set, which meant I could easily pass her camp in the dark once more without knowing it.

My return journey was about breaking records for my sponsor so I didn't really have time to waste and I certainly didn't need any added pressure. However, having promised to check on her safety, I had no alternative. I also felt obliged to warn Davidson that Carnegie station was now deserted, just in case she was relying on some form of assistance from them.

I was really concerned by now, so it was with some relief that early on in the evening I smelt the smoke of a fire and spotted some camel tracks. Assuming it was her, and not wishing to shine my vehicle's lights on her camp inadvertently, as she was probably in bed, I stopped on the track. Out of courtesy and also so as not to frighten or alarm her, I called out for permission to enter camp. I guess I also didn't want a rifle poked in my face. You never know. To approach an unknown camp at night while traveling through our remote outback is not a really good idea, so I was relieved to hear a female voice inviting me over.

It was freezing cold that night but out of consideration I did not even bother to stoke up her fire to keep warm. In my mind that lessened my intrusion as she had already gone to bed. She had a small yappy dog with her which thankfully quieted once it got back into her swag. While I couldn't see her camels, I could hear them nearby.

We swapped a few yarns and in the thirty-odd minutes of our meeting, Davidson told me as much about her journey as I told her about mine. She certainly was not stuck for words and I enjoyed listening to her story about an Aboriginal companion, what she had learned from him and some of the problems she had encountered so far.

I thought it interesting at the time that Davidson kept teasing her matted hair and apologising for her general appearance. It obviously concerned her that perhaps I would form an incorrect image of her because of the safety pin stuck in her earlobe as she made mention of it. She had apparently lost her earring.

Perhaps she thought she was talking to a city slicker tourist who wouldn't understand what roughing it on a real adventure was all about and would depart with a less than favourable image of her. Whatever, after weeks on a dusty track, sleeping in a dirty swag with her dog, and with limited water available, I would have been really surprised if she hadn't looked scruffy and a bit feral.

Davidson asked me if I was carrying any Stockholm Tar as one of her camels, the young one I think, had cut its foot and she was most concerned. I wasn't and said how much I regretted that I couldn't stay the night and have a look at it for her in the morning. More than that, how I wished I could see how she had outfitted her camels for her particular venture, as I intended to do a camel journey myself one day. I was kicking myself that I hadn't managed to meet up with her in daylight hours.

I mentioned that I had been asked to look out for her on my westerly crossing by the people at Warburton Mission and that, after following her tracks for many kilometres I ultimately missed them and her campsite in the dark. When I worked out how long ago that was, she said she clearly remembered the sound of my vehicle passing on that particular night. At the time she thought it was unusual that someone would be travelling on the track so late. The reason I had missed her was because on that particular night she camped much further away from the track than was her normal practice.

Now that Davidson knew that Carnegie station, which was a couple of days ride away, was deserted and I knew that she wasn't reliant on any form of help from them and I had confirmed her safety, I was rather relieved. I offered her some of my food, but she assured me that she had plenty left. I also mentioned I had passed a windmill not far back where I was sure she would get water before reaching the homestead.

Then, for two people doing two distinctly different types of challenges, one fast, one slow, and each with their own set of rewards, it was time to say goodbye. After wishing her a successful conclusion to her venture I departed, and I must say I was glad to be back in my vehicle out of the cold wind, which by now had chilled me to the bone.

My next rest stop was still hours away, but with a good track I felt sure I could pick up some of my lost time. I had planned to sleep the two hours before sun-up thereby using the sun's rays to wake me. This would be my daily sleep pattern for the rest of the journey.

The only other travellers I would meet on the Gunbarrel Highway section of the crossing turned up very early the following morning. It was two friendly young blokes returning from a trip to Ayers Rock. They said they'd met Davidson while on their way east and informed me that now they knew where she was, they would camp with her again that night. I told them that Carnegie was deserted, thinking that they may have been in need of fuel after their long journey, however they already knew the actual date that the station was to be abandoned, so it was no surprise to them.

In fact, they had apparently timed their return journey so that they would arrive back at Carnegie station after it was evacuated with the express intention of removing a wrecked jeep from the station dump. When I was on the farm, our dump was a necessary repository for all sorts of spare parts and extremely valuable to us. I am sure it would have been for Carnegie also.

My journey back along the Gunbarrel was uneventful. A vast land of spinifex, sand and dense stands of mulga – almost impenetrable in parts – left no doubt as to the hardships endured and the incredible challenges faced by the likes of Carnegie, Giles, Forrest and other early European explorers, when on horseback or camel, they tried to penetrate this amazingly beautiful, untamed wilderness.

Then there is the most magnificent of all trees, the desert oak. To make camp on a soft bed of needles under their canopy and drift off listening to the sigh of the night wind caressing their foliage is unforgettable. Those cute, hairy little fellows dotted around with their long, droopy foliage touching the ground are their offspring. In the moonlight they look to me like clones of Cousin It from the Addams Family. Then again, it could be just a bunch of yetis out on the prowl.

This is Harold Bell Lassetter country. Tales tell of a fabulously rich gold reef that he found and how he died in a later attempt to relocate it. To this day, the existence of his reef has never been confirmed so the myth lives on, occasionally inspiring modern adventurers who seek to solve a mystery most people believe doesn't exist. I stopped for a few moments to visit the cave located just off the track in which he lived for some time before his lonely death in 1931. True or false, it makes a good story and the legend of Lassetter and his golden reef will forever be part of Australia's history.

When the domes of The Olgas appeared, followed closely by that inspiring and world-famous sandstone monolith, Ayers Rock, I knew I had almost reached the half-way mark. I was still going strong, and was about on schedule with my next big refueling stop scheduled for the Kulgera Roadhouse on the Stuart Highway.

This major road, linking Adelaide and Darwin across central Australia, was only a rough, corrugated, dirt track when I first came through in about 1955. It was also around that time that Kulgera gained intense media coverage due to the brutal murder of Thyra Bowman, her daughter Wendy and a family friend, Thomas Whellan on nearby Sundown station. Missing while traveling from Alice Springs to Adelaide, their disappearance sparked the most widespread search ever undertaken in Australia's history at that time. A week passed before the pilot of a Lincoln Bomber spotted their vehicle from the air, where it was hidden under a group of trees. Raymond John Bailey was later arrested in Mt Isa, Queensland, and charged with their murders. He was convicted, and hung in 1958. The Sundown murders, as they became known, changed many peoples' attitude towards isolated bush camping on outback roads.

It was a long night. Finke, New Crown, Abminga and Bloods Creek all passed in a bit of a blur, and it was still dark when I finally arrived at Dalhousie Springs. Although it was nearly time for my two-hour pre-dawn sleep, there was no way I was going to miss out on a glorious soaking in the springs' hot waters.

My journey back across the Simpson was uneventful, but tiring. I had one major problem in the desert centre. My vehicle had been missing badly and then stopped altogether. I found the fault in the distributor where a screw had come loose, dropped through a hole, and destroyed the mechanism. Not a worry when you are carrying a spare – well, that is, until you find that it doesn't seem to fit. It turned out to be for one of Suzuki's other models, but I finally got going by using a piece of wire to extend the offending spark plug lead that, somehow, was way too short.

I topped up with fuel at Birdsville and took off into the night, my destination now easily achievable within my self-imposed time frame – well, that is until a few hours later, when the front wheels sort-of fell off! I was coming around a long sandy bend when the nose dropped violently, spraying stones and dust everywhere, and I came to an abrupt halt. The front of my poor little vehicle was flat in the dirt, its two front wheels at an odd, distorted angle. The torch revealed that the wheels were no longer connected: the axle and its housing had broken in two, and only the spring attachments were keeping them joined to the vehicle. There was nothing I could do, so, absolutely exhausted and with failure staring me in the face, I sank back into the driver's seat and went to sleep.

When day dawned, I jacked her front end up and surveyed the damage. It sure was a mess under there, however not one to be beaten, I thought I could see a way to fix it sufficiently to get me to where I could seek help.

The crisp morning air carried the sound of an approaching vehicle and, long before it appeared over the rise, I knew by the unmistakable exhaust noise exactly what I would see. Sure enough, it was another Suzuki, which I thought was rather fitting. Out jumped Keith and Dinah, who were passing by but ready to lend a hand. For my repairs, I needed a heap of a bushman's best friend – fencing wire – and as luck would have it, they had spotted a large coil a few miles back and went off to retrieve it for me. Now, with the help of the wire and four lengths of steel pipe from my winch kit, I was able to keep the wheels upright by lashing the springs together and winding a heap of wire around the engine to keep the dangly bits in the middle more or less level. A quick test run proved everything was okay and suddenly I was moving again, if only at a snail's pace. I needed help fast.

I made an urgent call to the Suzuki head office in Adelaide, who dispatched a light aircraft with a complete front end which was installed quick smart. Although I had lost over a day, I was still hopeful of making my deadline. You only fail when you stop trying. However it worked out, I was going to give it my best shot. I owed that to my sponsor for their enthusiasm and effort.

It was dark when I again climbed the hill up to the Cape Byron lighthouse. I had crossed the continent both ways between its widest points, and had made the first solo cross-country vehicle crossing of the Simpson Desert east to west. Although I had failed in my personal goal of making a nine-day west-to-east crossing, the two Suzuki representatives from the nearby town of Lismore, who were awaiting my arrival, jubilantly clocked me in at 9 days, 2 hours and 20 minutes: my Suzuki and I had soundly beaten the Daihatsu record of 13 days.

❧ ❧ ❧

I must have really enjoyed that venture, because the following year, 1978, when Suzuki came out with another slightly more powerful model (800 cc), I set off once again to cross the continent. My goal this time for a west to east crossing was five days.

It rained heavily as I departed Steep Point, Wiluna was being closed to traffic as I passed through, the Gunbarrel was washed out, and Ayers Rock was closed to tourists. When I finally reached Mt Dare station, it took me a day longer than normal because of flooding just to enter the western edge of the Simpson.

The damp sand enhanced the desert crossing, but the final run into Birdsville at night was incredible, and incredibly dangerous. Vast sheets of water obliterated any sign of the track for long sections, and in the glow of the headlamps, the whole scene took on a rather eerie appearance. Once I dropped into a huge hole, and the front end of the vehicle went completely under water. Fortunately I had enough momentum to come out the other side, as my motor, with all the water floating around under the bonnet, sounded as though it was going to die at any moment.

Birdsville was isolated, and the police were trying to get urgent supplies through. I passed their food convoy later that night slithering all over the road, and the following day, reached the bitumen. The excitement continued as the police gave me five minutes to get out of town before they closed the bridge ahead – my only exit from the area, which was just starting to go under water. The rest of the journey was a bit of an anticlimax really.

At Cape Byron, I finally extracted my exhausted body from my faithful little Suzuki, my sardine tin on wheels. Considering all things, a time of 6 days, 22 hours and 7 minutes for a baby vehicle under 1000 cc, wasn't all that bad. Given the right conditions, my five-day goal had certainly been achievable. I even considered, but only momentarily, what I could reduce the time down to driving in the spacious, air-conditioned comfort of a larger and more powerful vehicle. But then, that wouldn't be apples for apples, would it? What was really important to me was that I had fulfilled my obligations to my sponsor, Suzuki, and now it was time to move on.

I was 45 years old and fairly secure financially. My wife, Rotha, and I had had many trips overseas and as a family with our children, David, Susan and Richard, had shared some great outback holidays. I thought I had it all together, but it was just an illusion. Something was changing within me, changing my future direction.

The desert – the outback – had ensnared me. Like so many others, I would now find the lure of the outback irresistible, the need to return frequently an unrelenting force that could not be denied. Having reached the top of the hill that I had fought so hard to conquer, having realised my dreams, a different view ahead now unfolded – a succession of even higher, different hills that waited to be climbed.

The temptation was impossible to resist. The adventurous wanderlust spirit of a barefoot kid, long suppressed, was now set free to roam.

Chapter 2

Early Days

I got dressed in my best gear, complete with my Jackie Coogan hat, and busted out. It was only a short walk to the nearest tram stop where I boarded the Bondi express. Unfortunately my adventure was terminated abruptly when the conductor found me, and he just popped me back onto the pavement at the next stop all on my lonesome. I suppose he was upset that I didn't have a ticket. Well, if I couldn't go in style I would just have to walk, and that is how my mother found me: strolling along. I was about two years old, the world was my oyster, and the road ahead looked long and inviting.

Next we spent time living at Hume Park on the Murrumbidgee River upstream of the Burrinjuck dam, about sixteen kilometres from the town of Yass, also in New South Wales. This was my maternal grandfather's tourist park; he rented out motor boats and had the odd cabin to let. He had also built a large dance room with a special floor as part of the main house, and with the pianola in one corner, the ceiling festooned with streamers and Chinese lanterns, it was a favourite dancing and party haunt for the townspeople. Well, for the more adventurous anyhow, as it was a long drive out and back on a dirt road in those days.

My parents had lived there previously during the Depression and like everywhere, times were tough. My father told me that he and a chap named Burt used to take off and spend a week at a time fishing the lower reaches of the river down near the dam. They used gill nets and cross lines, which was illegal, but the money from the sale of those fish kept the family going. I guess when you are desperate it's easy to bend the rules. I think everyone did it, anyhow. They used to take some flour, tea and a few bullets to shoot a rabbit or two, and that is all they lived on. Unlike the city folk, at least they could care for themselves. That's one advantage of living on the land.

Burt was still living there when we arrived, and one day while he was cleaning some fish on the jetty, I completed another 'Houdini' act and went for a stroll to see what he was up to. He apparently didn't hear me coming, just the splash as I hit the water. With his curiosity aroused, he went to inspect the cause, and was just in time to see me disappearing into the murky depths. Without Burt, my adventuring days would have been permanently nipped in the bud.

I went to school there for a short period of time. The schoolhouse was situated on the top of a high windswept hill, and had the most magnificent views over the river and the surrounding countryside. It had the mandatory rusty iron roof and the walls were slabs of timber through which one could see daylight. We were continually poking paper into the cracks to keep out the freezing winter winds. We had a water tank, two toilets, 'long drop' naturally, and nearby was a large gum tree.

It was a mixed class of some 10 to 14 students, and when the lot turned up, we were crammed in like sardines. While there wasn't room to swing a cat, there was certainly enough for the cane to rise and fall. This was a regular happening, occurring with about the same frequency as the screeching that emanated from the girls' outhouse, as they located the sleepy lizards and other creepy crawlies that somehow found their way into their not-so-private domain. Those who were continually late also received 'the cuts' and I had my fair share. The walk up the gully from home to school was nothing short of an exciting adventure, so I hardly ever arrived on time. I used to chase and catch the rams so that I could go for a ride, and there were plenty of logs to look into for bird's nests and perhaps a sleepy lizard looking for a change of scenery.

My father ultimately got a job in Brisbane, the capital of Queensland, and we were on the move once more. We initially lived in what was called a 'typical Queenslander'. This is a house made of timber planks laid horizontally, one on top of the other, to form the outside walls. It had lots of little coloured windows, an iron roof and the whole structure was perched precariously, or so it seemed to me, on top of a heap of timber poles stuck into ground which was invariably sloping. They didn't bother to level the house blocks in those days. Probably it was too expensive. Inside ours the rooms were small, boxy, hot and sparsely furnished, however the thing that I remember the most were the flooring boards. They not only covered the floors, naturally, but then continued vertically up the walls and as if unable to stop, proceeded out across the ceilings as well.

My bedroom had a large mirror, which at night became a small boy's passageway to another world. What with ghost-like people emerging from it to visit, and the incessant creaking of the house as it expanded and contracted with the changes in temperature, it's no wonder I had nightmares. Whenever I see an old Queenslander now, particularly out in the country, derelict and neglected with peeling paint and rusted roof as they often are, I am still overcome with feelings of dread. My wife Jeanne, being born and raised in Queensland, has the same feelings of discomfort and unease. If there is such a thing as a past life, then something dreadful must have happened to both of us in just such a house. I know the southerners rave about the old-fashioned Queenslanders when they visit, but for my money, you can keep them.

The walking 'postie' came twice a day and you knew if you had mail as he would blow his whistle when he arrived at your letterbox. Weekends were heavy with the unforgettable aroma of burning backyard incinerators. Garden leaves were raked by everyone into the street gutter and then set alight. Our house was in a hollow and on a calm day, the smoke haze and smell would linger for hours.

Queensland wouldn't be the same without the magnificent colours of the bougainvillea bush, however their branches hold a deadly array of thick, curved and incredibly sharp thorns. I stood on one which deeply embedded itself in my heel and then broke off flush with the skin. Try as I might to pull it out with a pair of rusty old pliers, it finally disappeared beneath the surface.

I kept complaining for several days, so my parents ultimately took me to the Mater Hospital. The doctor poked and prodded but couldn't see a thing, however due to the insistence of my father, who believed me, they decided to do an exploratory with a knife. This entailed about four nurses immobilising my leg by lying on it as I yelled and screamed while the doctor cut and thrust. In the end he couldn't find a thing and blamed my father for wasting his time.

Now this is precisely why we boys have mothers, and fortunately mine decided to try the old-fashioned way. After saturating a big lump of bread with boiling water, she wrung it out in a cloth and then placed the sticky hot mess over the wound as soon as it was bearable, and wrapped my foot in a towel. The dressing was changed several times a day until — lo and behold — about three days later, out popped this huge thorn, much to everyone's delight. Good on you, Mum!

It was about that time I learnt that dentists and teeth equal real pain. Sitting waiting in his huge, high-backed chair with his drilling apparatus, looking like some modern-day mechanical monster from a construction site looming over you, the dentist was terrifying. He had three operating rooms in a row, with a chair in each and thin walls between; you could track his progress as he came closer by the noise of his drill and the moaning of his patients. I will not even try to tell you what it was like on the one occasion that I needed an extraction! Chloroform, used to knock you out, does something very strange to the mind and makes you as sick as a dog afterwards.

Next we moved to the Brisbane suburb of Moorooka, where we lived on the top of the hill where the tram line finished. Beyond were wide open spaces, numerous creeks, waterlily covered lagoons … up on the nearby hill, the Frogmouth Rocks became my fantasy land.

I went to four schools in Brisbane. The last one was Junction Park State School. The War was on and the schoolyard was ringed with trenches. We had regular practice evacuations and whenever the siren started screeching, we would march to our designated slit in the ground, hop in, insert the wooden clothes peg taken from the appropriately named peg bag into the mouth, and wait for the pretend bombs to fall. I think the pegs were to help with the shock waves created by a real blast, but whatever, it looked rather weird with hundreds of kids sitting in their trenches with pegs sticking out of their faces. There were several compartments in a peg bag, but for the life of me I cannot remember what other pieces of high-tech survival gear we carried.

Except for the very few with affluent parents, most of us didn't wear shoes. That's not to say that we didn't own a pair, but they were for 'best' and mainly worn on a Sunday morning to church. I played soccer, rugby and cricket shoeless, so I usually had bleeding toes with the nails falling off. While I played a good game of all of the above, I really did excel at swimming. After Burt had fished me out of the drink, I had two further attempts at drowning myself before I finally gave it up as a bad joke and learnt to swim. From there on, I was a confirmed water rat.

At about eleven years of age I started my first job. I was up before dawn folding newspapers into a triangular shape, and it was then up to me to pitch them accurately out of a car window as the owner of the business drove around his clients' houses yelling, 'This one! That one!'

With the huge American Army Base nearby, it wasn't long before I became their first newspaper boy. I don't think I shall ever forget that moment when I fronted up to the main gate with my papers slung under my arm. I can still smell the newsprint, and the cooking aromas from their camp kitchens. I was overawed by the magnificence of it all, from the freshly laundered and starched uniforms, their hats and badges, to their vehicles, their foreign voices, the sentries and the sheer energy that pulsed around me. They finally granted me a pass to sell my papers inside and I wandered freely throughout their camp.

Occasionally I was invited to attend a night-time vaudeville show and was forced to accept their never-ending gifts of lollies and chewing gum. I had my first cigarette — it was called a Camel — and I'll never forget it. Struth, was I crook! I thought I was going to die! Their generosity was overwhelming, and from their tips my newly acquired bank savings book started to grow at a very healthy rate. This was truly 'boy heaven'.

Saturday mornings I would get up early and carry my canoe down to the nearby dam to collect the waterlilies floating on its surface. My canoe was a piece of flattened corrugated roofing iron that I had folded and nailed to timber at either end. Clay plugged up the holes and a couple of sticks kept it apart in the middle. I packed the waterlilies between tissue paper in a suitcase, then took off by tram for the city where I would flog my booty for a princely sum. I used to get between five and six shillings for the lot; with a return tram fare of just a few pennies, it was a huge profit margin. When you consider that the award wage at the time for a twenty-one-year-old was about three pounds per week, I wasn't doing too badly for a kid for just a Saturday morning's work. For those too young to remember, there were 20 shillings to one pound.

I remember the tropical thunder storms and lightning displays that shook the house and the incredible noise as huge hailstones pummelled down and ricocheted off our corrugated iron roof. Afterwards, pools of water covered the flats, the creek raced and roared and very soon deep puddles in the grass would be covered in froth containing the seeds of life. Millions of tadpoles, big juicy black things, thrived and matured to become an invasion on a grand scale — a deafening and ultimately irritating bombardment of noise as fornicating frogs everywhere spoke of a system still in balance.

Years later it would be no more. This barefoot kid's wonderland, the big paddocks down the road where the cowboy rode in to graze his milk cows, where billy goat carts roamed and battles were fought with shanghais and bows and arrows, would slowly disappear under the relentless march of time and change. My waterlily-covered dam is now the site of the Moorooka Bowls Club. The creek that I swam in, canoed down when it was a raging torrent, or caught fish, eels and turtles with a bent pin on the end of a cotton thread line, has fallen to urban sprawl — a sea of houses now, where kids in Nikes have vastly different activities and childhood memories. Sadly above all, you can hardly hear a frog call there now.

With my first bike, a real flash-looking unit, I went into the hire business. The son of the corner store owner used to lighten his father's till frequently, and I then helped to lighten his pocket. Charging anything up to five shillings per ride, with his desperation and the duration being the only controlling factors, my bike was soon showing a healthy profit on capital investment.

Generally we spent the Christmas holidays at the seaside town of Burleigh Heads about 80 kilometres away. We camped in an ex-army tent on stretchers, and used a carbide lamp for light. To keep the mozzies away, I collected cow manure, which I ignited and left to smoulder all night at the entrance to the tent. Cannon Rocks was my favourite haunt in the nearby National Park. It was also a peaceful spot to smoke the cigarette butts I'd diligently collected from gutters and re-rolled in tissue paper.

On the way home we passed through swampy land dotted with occasional run-down shacks, and at that time you wouldn't have given tuppence for the lot of it. How things have changed — the area is now known world-wide as Surfers Paradise.

It was always a big thrill to arrive at Yatala near lunchtime and bite into one of their famous pies. I think it was a mandatory ritual for motorists passing by in those days. After all these years, Yatala pies are still being made and sold from the same spot!

Life was full of simple pleasures and worry free — that's if you didn't count teachers, homework and exams. If I knew that I was really going to be in trouble at school, I would simply organise a 'day off' sick and hope they would forget about it. I don't think my mother ever knew that the mess she cleaned up was the result of a finger down the throat.

We had two ways of fighting: boxing or wrestling. When I finally had to front up to the best boxer in the school, I knew I was going to get a thrashing. At the appointed time and place, the kids, informed by the school grapevine, all congregated in the playground for the 'rearrangement of my face' ceremony. I had agreed to box him first and then because of his ego, managed to get him to wrestle me next — that's if I was still alive! The winner would be the best out of two.

Well, I squared up like Tommy Burns the famous boxer, but the event didn't last for long. I allowed just enough time to show that I wasn't chicken before I took a deliberate dive for the dirt, and conceded defeat. It's hard to hit a person lying down and our gentlemanly ways didn't even contemplate kicking someone who'd given in. None of this of course satisfied the spectators, who had wanted to see some blood and guts and teeth, and I could hear the occasional 'get up you squib and fight'.

We fronted up once more and I sure hoped that my wrestling idol, Big Chief Little Wolf, was watching over me. One lost, one to go, I charged like a wounded bull and, catching my opponent by surprise, down we went in the dirt. My left leg lay ready and well-positioned under his back as we fell, then I slammed my right leg across his chest and locked my ankles together. He was in the scissors, and every time he breathed out I increased the pressure like a boa constrictor. Finally, as he was starting to go a funny colour from being unable to move or breathe, I released the pressure just enough for him to gasp to the audience that I had won. As we shook hands, I knew that I would never have to fight him again.

The day hadn't finished, however. We'd been spotted by one of the teachers and were hauled off to the headmaster's office, where he used his long bamboo cane to give us each five cuts on our upturned fingers. It took a lot of courage not to flinch, and to keep your fingers outstretched as the cane came whistling down. Close them, and you could get it across the knuckles, which was a thousand times worse.

I watched Don Bradman play cricket at The Gabba, excelled at marbles, enjoyed being part of the Stephens Scout Group, and had my first girlfriend, Velma. Actually I was in love with Valerie, but she didn't seem to notice me. I don't blame her. Even I hated my skinny little legs and lop-sided smile and with my standard haircut, the monstrous 'short back and sides' (barbers in those days had no imagination), I wasn't going to set the world on fire with movie-star looks.

Saturday afternoon we went to the local picture theatre where we sat in deck chairs down in 'the spits'. That was the cheap section, as up in 'the Gods' was too expensive for us. Velma and I held hands, furtively I might add, as the usher's continual patrols with his torch flashing hither and yon made any form of hanky panky a risky affair.

Sunday was for church and polished shoes and slicked-back hair, and afterwards, if you were lucky, maybe a picnic in the Botanical Gardens or down by the local waterhole. It was okay to run around a bit, or throw a ball provided that you did it quietly, but organised sport was out. Work on Sunday was a definite 'no-no', and you certainly didn't dare to do your washing. That was the biggest sin ever – to hang out your washing on a Sunday! Monday was the 'official' washing day and the rhyme went: 'Tuesday, it was done … Wednesday is my ironing day … Thursday, it is done'.

My favourite challenge, other than how to escape school and make money, was to race the tram home from school. I really did enjoy running, and the fare saved went on lunchtime goodies like chips and lollies, or marbles. I used to wait for the tram to start and then I'd take off. The first section was rather flat and all I had to do was watch out for pedestrians and take care in crossing the numerous side streets. I needed to get in front here as the next leg was a long downhill run where the tram could pick up speed, and also had fewer stops. When we hit the bottom where Ipswich Road forks off to the right, I would be going like a cut cat, but invariably just behind. It was on the last uphill run to the Moorooka shopping corner where it all happened. Occasionally the tram conductor would enter into the spirit of things and urge me on. Sometimes I won, and sometimes I lost, but I never tired of the contest. The distance was some three kilometres.

The first tram that I can remember had seats all the way across and the ticket collector would walk along a platform on the outside of the bucking monster to collect the fare. I think they called the next model the 'drop centre', and lastly came a real flash-looking unit all in silver and fully enclosed. Men doffed their hats to ladies and gave up their seats for them, while kids gave up their seats to adults without thought or question. We respected older people then.

While I owned a rusty old air gun that fired small lead slugs, my favourite weapon was a shanghai, which I could use with deadly accuracy and carried wherever I went, even to school. I lined bottles up on a fence rail for target practice and sometimes targeted birds, the real thing. I can vividly remember my first kill. A well-placed shot with my shanghai and a tiny bundle of feathers fell out of a tree. The lifeless body of a small

Silver Eye didn't even fill my child's hand.

Once, I even used my shanghai against other kids. There were three of us playing up on the big hill at the back of Moorooka in the vicinity of our beloved Frogmouth Rocks when we were attacked by about five youths throwing a barrage of stones. We beat them off but they promised to return in force and kill us.

We dug in on the edge of a jumbled mass of rocks and laid in a good supply of pebbles for our shanghais and heaps of large stones for Saunders, who was a big lad and could hurl a missile with deadly accuracy. It wasn't long before the yelling in the scrub left us in no doubt that they had made good their promise to return and then suddenly about 15 of them burst into the clearing, raining rocks upon us. By crikey, I thought we were done for and were going to get a hell of a beating. However we had chosen our possie well, and although we couldn't retreat, having a sheer drop behind us, they had to cross clear ground to get at us. Rocks flew everywhere and the shanghais ran hot, but it was Saunders who carried the day. He was yelling like a banshee and hurling his giant rocks until finally they broke ranks and took off with us after them — well to be truthful, two of us probably ran after Saunders who ran after them!

We had a small, conventional house complete with icebox, flash radio and a not-so-flash outside toilet, referred to as 'the dunny'. This was the era of the night-cart man and weekly he would arrive, remove the bucket from under the seat of the outhouse through a rear door, and replace it with an empty one. Over his shoulder he wore a leather pad for protection and he would balance the bucket on this, steadying it with one hand while he walked back to his cart. What a job! And you might reckon your job stinks!

One morning, he kicked my mother's Pekinese dog and she wasn't too impressed. He had to exit the property on the lower side of the house, which placed him below my bedroom window level and rather vulnerable to anyone intent on revenge. When he arrived next, I knew he would be in trouble if the dog so much as whimpered. My mother saw him coming and came into my room where she reached under the bed and extracted my full night potty, then carefully balancing her missile, she stood by the window waiting for her dog to get another kick in the ribs. Damn it, there wasn't even a peep out of the bloody dog, so what was shaping up to be an exciting event in my day just fizzled out. The dunny-cart man went on his merry way never knowing what had lurked above him.

One day we had a very important visitor to our house to check on my mum, who was expecting. It was Dr Cilento, whose daughter Diane later married Sean Connery of James Bond fame. I was doing the ironing at the time and she patted me on the head and said what a good little boy I was. When I informed her that I also darned the holes in my socks, patched up my shorts and could bake an apple pie, she was most impressed.

My mother never ratted that I continually drove her up the wall worrying over some of the things I used to get up to. To reduce her stress levels she would invariably 'have a nice cuppa and take a powder' which seemed to be normal practice for the ladies in those days. Vincent's APC or Bex — you had a choice. Each dose came in a little piece of folded paper and you just sprinkled the contents onto your tongue.

Our ice was delivered in block form by the ice truck, milk came in bulk and was put into its own container, which we left with the money on the front steps. The bread was delivered by horse and cart and the aroma of freshly baked bread emanating from that cart was something you couldn't forget in a lifetime. They were the good old days, and really in the scheme of things, it was not that long ago.

If I could repeat this part of my life, I wouldn't change a thing, other than to put more time into my school studies. For someone who had entrepreneurial tendencies and a desire to succeed, how come I was so dumb as to not recognise the extra advantages that would come from gaining a higher educational standard?

🦎 🦎 🦎

The war finished in May 1945, and not long afterwards we moved back south to Hume Park, near Yass, for a short time. The river was full to the brim, the fish were plentiful and I will never forget my encounter with the largest Murray Cod that I had ever seen.

I heard my grandfather yelling directions to the dog, which was never a good sign. It generally meant that my turn was coming, and next thing Biddy appeared at my side wagging her tail and carrying a rolled-up piece of notepaper in her jaws: I was being summoned. He wanted me up at the house quick smart and, since I'd thought I was in trouble again, it came as a pleasant surprise when he said, 'Denis, I want you to load up one of the motor boats with these supplies and deliver them to that group of fishermen who came in from West Wyalong last week. You remember where we left them on that bend in the river just past the island, don't you?'

I assured him that I did and lickety-split loaded up and departed before he could change his mind. I couldn't believe my luck, as he had never allowed me to take such a long journey in one of the motor boats before.

It was a cold, damp day, so the fishermen were squatting around a roaring campfire when I arrived. As I pegged my boat to the shore, a tall, bearded man smoking a large pipe, which was clenched firmly between his few remaining stained and broken teeth, strolled down to greet me.

'Hi young fella. My name's Bill and I'm sure glad you arrived today We're running a bit short of tucker.' I moved to unload the boat. 'No, don't worry about that now. Come on up and meet my mates and have a cup of tea and a nice chunk of damper with treacle, or if you prefer I think we can do dripping and pepper. You must be hungry and cold after your long journey.'

I chose the treacle, and with a huge chipped pannikin of black tea, sat on a log near the fire to warm up a bit. Around me was displayed an incredible sight. Long, heavy-gauge wires were strung in rows between the trees and suspended from them on wire hooks were dozens of fish of all sizes. Several lines carried only Murray Cod and I guessed most were in the 15–30 lb range.

Off to the side and partly obscured by a makeshift canvas fly which served as a shelter for the men hung a single line of real monsters that made all the others look like tiddlers. They were huge! I couldn't even begin to guess their weight. In later years I would look back on this moment and realise how privileged I had been to witness a sight that in a few short years would never be repeated on such a grand scale. These were normal fishing catches of that era, both in quantity and size, and any photo taken at that time would be drooled over with envy by today's river fishermen, who were not yet born.

Soon it was time to depart and Bill, thoughtfully looking at the lines carrying the 'tiddlers' said, 'Well young fella, for all your trouble you can have any one of the fish we've caught as a present. All you have to do is to be able to carry it by yourself as far as the boat.'

I thanked him for his offer and headed around his shelter to where the big ones hung. Up close, these Murray Cod were real monsters. Slowly I moved among them until I finally stood next to the biggest of them all. Its huge eye seemed to stare challengingly at me and when I pulled its mouth open, it could just about have swallowed me whole.

'Are you sure, lad, that this is the one you want?' he said, as if reading my mind. 'It's going to be damned heavy for a young bloke you know, and remember, you don't get a second chance.'

I didn't take too long in making up my mind. This fish was going to come home with me.

'Yes sir, I'd like to give this one a go if that is okay with you,' I replied.

They cut a slit in its lower jaw to insert a good-sized rope as my hand grip, then two of them lifted it off its wire hook and slowly lowered it onto my shoulder. My skinny legs nearly buckled beneath me as I took the full weight, however being a determined little bugger, with all the strength I could muster, I slowly staggered towards the boat with the tail of this giant fish dragging in the dirt behind me. Well I made it, and with congratulations all round, they helped me place it in the bottom of the boat between several wet hessian bags for the journey home. How much did it weigh? My grandfather put it on the large platform scales and the balance indicated 98 lb. That's a big fish!

Then the inevitable happened: the river started to dry up as they released more water from the dam for irrigation projects and drought-affected areas downstream. Ultimately it reached the lowest level that I had ever seen it and teemed with little red fish. In parts it was so narrow you could jump across it, although a few deep holes remained for swimming. Finally the drought broke, the rain set in and it wasn't long before we received word from upstream that the river was in full flood and the headwaters should hit us that evening.

My grandfather had about twenty motor boats sitting way down near the water's edge. Thankfully they were out of reach of the frontal surge, but as the water started to rise, we were kept busy inching them up the slope one at a time. The only light we had was a Tilley lamp, and with the noise of crashing logs being swept down by the racing torrent, it was all rather eerie. The water kept rising — way above our expectations. Finally it crept around behind us and marooned us on a rapidly shrinking island. My grandfather brought the car down to use as an anchor, and then ran a rope out to me where I tied it to a peg. Each time I could float a boat free, I would swim it over to him along the lifeline and then go back for another. That was quite a night, but we saved them all.

Morning light showed a wide, swirling river. I couldn't help but think again of the explorers, Hume and Hovell, who my grandfather said were believed to have made a river crossing at this very spot, and from what I could understand, under similar conditions. This is why his tourist venture was named Hume Park.

※ ※ ※

In 1824, Hume and Hovell had departed from Hume's station on Lake George, in an endeavour to cross the uncharted lands that existed between there and Port Phillip. When they reached this point, the river was flooded, but not to be deterred, they removed the wheels from the cart and wrapped a tarpaulin around it to create a punt. By swimming the river they attached a rope to the other side and then floated their punt backwards and forwards to transport their supplies. They then crossed the mighty Murray River in similar fashion before finally reaching the southern coast after a harrowing two-month journey. What should have been a great memory of how they had triumphed over adversity together, was soured at the time because one newspaper credited Hume as the leader, and another Hovell.

The real blow-up, however, came about thirty years later, and developed into a mud-slinging match, each making accusations about the inadequacy of the other in a string of letters and published statements. Sadly, they died bitter enemies. However their feat will always hold a special place in the journals of Australian exploration, and irrespective of how they, in the end, may have wished otherwise, their names will be forever entwined.

※ ※ ※

Hume and Hovell were the first explorers that I can remember feeling some affinity with, and time would prove that they wouldn't be the last. In my boyhood dreaming, I could see them coming over the opposite hills and down to the water's edge. I wanted so much to be an explorer just like them and set out to conquer the unknown.

As a growing boy I really loved living on the banks of the Murrumbidgee River; there was such a variety of things to do. I was now thirteen and had been given my very own Lithgow 22 single-shot rifle, so hunting rabbits was one of my favourite pastimes. One day my grandfather allowed me to take his 12-gauge shotgun up the hill to pot a few and, believe me, it had a kick like a mule. I didn't dare tell him, however, of the incident that occurred on that occasion on the steep rocky section of the hill at the back of the house.

I had cocked the gun and was just about ready to pull the trigger when the rabbit moved behind a rock. To get his head back into view, I had intended to move just a couple of steps sideways, remaining, however, ready to take him on the run should he bolt for better cover. Well, my foot rolled on a loose stone and as I crashed to the ground, the gun spun out of my hands. I froze in horror. Lying there, I was looking straight down the barrel of a loaded and cocked shotgun, which could so easily have blown my head off.

We killed rabbits not only because they were classed as vermin and we were legally required to remove them from the property, but also because they formed a regular part of our diet. Referred to as 'underground mutton', we had them roasted (my favourite) or as a stew.

I could remove and stretch the neck of a rabbit caught in one of my steel traps within seconds, although the thick neck of a big buck occasionally tested my strength. A few slits with a knife, and in a flash, off would come his skin to be stretched over a wire bow to dry, ready with the fox and possum skins, for sale when the fur merchant called.

Occasionally I would take a motor boat and the shotgun upstream where I hunted a variety of wild duck for the table. They were extremely plentiful and I always returned with a bag full. When I cleaned them I saved their down, which was used as pillow stuffing or to make an eiderdown for the bed.

Snakes were plentiful and occasionally found inside the house; when the cry went up, we grabbed the shotgun or the always handy stick, which had attached to it a length of heavy-gauge wire, and the intruder was dispatched quick smart. The only good snake near your house was a dead one.

My chores included chopping the firewood, helping to build, repair and paint the boating fleet, milking cows and separating the milk to make cream and butter.

One job I particularly enjoyed was in my capacity as 'chief dunny officer'. There were several long-drop dunnies dotted around the park for use by the public. First I had to make the toilet paper. This consisted of newspaper cut into six-inch squares, which I attached with a nail to a post within easy reach of the dunny seat. On the floor was a large, open-top four-gallon ex-kerosene tin and this I had to keep topped up with ash carted from our kitchen stove. When you finished your business, the procedure was to use the small tin, also provided, to tip some ash down the hole and over the 'you know what'.

Then came the exciting bit for me — I emptied the contents of a small tin of petrol down the hole and into the pit below, and then dropped in a match. This was to burn off all sorts of nasties, and in particular, to decimate the venomous redback spider population who loved to live around the toilet seat in great numbers and inspired a song to that effect. As a kid it was always a worry letting one's dangly bits drop down through the hole.

My usual dunny petrol-measuring tin, which I had been told to use by my grandfather, was missing, so I acquired another which was considerably larger and filled it to the brim. The redbacks were going to be in for a shock this time! I tossed the contents down the hole and followed it with a wax match. Well, the whole joint more or less exploded! The flimsy dunny structure shook violently, the floor glowed red between the cracks, and fingers of fire licked around my bare feet, while through the dunny seat, a mighty sheet of flame roared skywards just like the afterburner of a modern-day jet. It frightened the heck out of me and thereafter I was never so liberal with the petrol.

Under the huge peppercorn tree was a concrete cylinder that was used to smoke fish. Nearby was a large, blood-spattered log where I chopped the heads off the chooks and ducks and I nearly removed my big toe with the axe too. It was also where I prepared an endless supply of wood for the kitchen stove, the fireplaces, the huge copper used for boiling the clothes on washing days and also for filling the tin bathtub on bath night, a once-a-week affair.

My mother used a washing stick to stir the clothes in the copper and to lift them out of the boiling water to rinse in cold water before putting them through the wringer. This was a set of hand-operated rollers used to squeeze out the water. It was a contraption to be wary of, as little fingers which strayed into its jaws ended up somewhat flattened. The clothes were hung on wire lines which were then propped up in the middle by a forked stick called a 'clothes prop'. Years later the backyard scene was changed forever with the introduction of the rotary clothes line. The Hills Hoist was a wow for kids as they suddenly had a merry-go-round to swing on. A blue bag was dunked into the boiling water to get the clothes whiter than white (they hoped) along with shaved bar soap as the washing medium. The blue bag could also be put on a bee sting to give relief while the bar soap had its own useful purpose other than washing.

There were two drastic ways to unblock one's bowels that I remember. The dreaded water treatment, the enema – when you saw that contraption coming, it was your worst nightmare – or a sliver of carefully sculptured bar soap which was pushed unceremoniously into the backside. Frequent doses of castor oil (yuck) were given to help prevent resorting to either of the above and for a quick flush of the system, a drink of Epson Salts in warm water moved things along rather rapidly.

The wood stove remained alight all day, and around its edge stood an array of flat irons ready to be heated, should anything need ironing. We had 12-volt lighting for occasional use, but mainly used hurricane or Tilley lamps, or candles for bedtime. We had lunch at precisely the same time every day and you didn't dare speak, for it was then that Blue Hills reigned supreme on the radio, and I don't think that any country person would miss an episode.

My grandfather used to command the dog to fetch, and me to run, and a lot of my day was spent running backwards and forwards at his bidding. While we lived only about 16 km from the township of Yass, you needed a special reason to undertake the 'long' journey. Shopping was a once-a-week affair and was really a big deal. One had to dress up too!

My grandfather was going to Sydney by train and intended leaving his car in town until he returned. I said I would ride my bike up to the top of the hill near the old, now disused, schoolhouse and wait for him at the gate. When he didn't arrive after a reasonable time, I sort-of just kept pedalling, and when Yass became closer than home, I decided that I may as well wave him goodbye from the station. I'll never forget his anger when he finally arrived. I was told in no uncertain terms to get going before he belted the daylights out of me. You know, I believe that what really sent him around the twist was that this scruffy-looking kid in patched shorts and no shoes would be an embarrassment if any of his friends happened to be on the platform. Or maybe it was that I'd made the 'big trip' into town seem insignificant.

I don't remember my mother's mother, as she died when I was very young, but apparently she was a real lady. As it was her wish to be buried in Adelaide, my grandfather had her put into a sealed coffin, meaning, I suppose, lead-lined, popped her on the back seat of his car and drove her over himself for the funeral. A thousand-odd kilometres over bad roads in an old vehicle must have been some trip back then and I guess it would have taken him several days at least.

My grandfather was a different kettle of fish. A big, powerful man with giant hands, he was a scheming, manipulative, lying, cheating bully and as cunning as a rat. While he had friends in high office in Canberra and Sydney, he sure had some local enemies, although to be fair, I am not convinced he was entirely to blame. In later life I came to the conclusion that the area had been full of hillbillies anyhow. One night he went out by boat to check another boat sneaking quietly around his area and amongst his equipment. A neighbourly fracas ensued with some boat jousting and flailing oars and he finally returned home with a bullet hole in his hat.

Life was never dull, that's for sure, and it occasionally reached the high grounds of intrigue. The wife of a neighbour had gone missing under what the local cops considered to be suspicious circumstances. Months later they brought in the detectives, and as part of their investigation they came out to Hume Park to question my grandfather. They wanted to know if he had ever noticed anything suspicious. Well as it turned out, he remembered coming home late from Yass one night and spotting car headlights disappearing over the hill in the distance, then returning some time later to his neighbour's homestead. As this was definitely not normal, he had clearly remembered it and mentioned the fact.

Based on this information the cops put 'stake outs' in the hills, armed with binoculars. It wasn't long before they realised that a lone horseman rode out frequently from the homestead to the area pointed out by my grandfather. On each occasion, the horseman followed an identical route through part of the main area under surveillance. Finally, a thorough search unearthed his wife stuffed down a rabbit hole. Guilt and fear that someone may have found her — and his continual checking of the rabbit warren to make sure they hadn't — had been his downfall.

When my grandfather took over the lease of Hume Park in about 1929 there was really nothing there except a rough tin shack with the inside walls papered over with newsprint. To his credit he built, for that time, a very substantial house and surrounds with determination and damned hard physical work. Hume Park would become well-known far and wide, particularly to those who loved fishing.

When his lease was about to run out some thirty years later, he sought a new lease to enable him to have something to sell. This was refused, so apparently he bought a whole heap of explosives and hid them around the property. The ultimatum: either they gave him a lease so that he could gain some benefit from the years of hard work and expenditure or else he would blow the lot up and return it to them in the condition of original purchase. Knowing my grandfather, it could have been the ultimate bluff — however I suspect that he would have carried out his threat. Let's face it, he had nothing to lose. He got a new lease.

My grandfather never changed or mellowed with age and when he ultimately died, at 93, there were only three people present to put him down. I only went to make sure he didn't sneak back out again.

Finally my family left Hume Park; we went by steam train to Adelaide to start a new life in the city of my birth. On that journey I seem to remember we had to change trains at Albury and Melbourne, and then again at Serviceton, due to the different state rail gauges. They weren't very bright were they? I don't remember much of the journey, although one thing does stick in my mind. It was dawn as we puffed our way through the hills after leaving Murray Bridge and I was really thrilled. They had rabbits down here too — they were everywhere.

My father bought a block of land at Cumberland Park, and again we were on the outskirts of the city, which suited me. There were restrictions on the size of house that you could erect, and difficulty in obtaining materials. We were still getting over the effects of the war. While we waited to build, we lived in two caravans parked amongst the sandhills near Brighton, a small seaside suburb. I don't think that we had any formal permission, but just squatted. With the beach across the road, we were on prime real estate I can tell you.

What happened next dramatically changed my direction and thinking in life, and I will be forever grateful to my parents for the financial sacrifice that they made to allow it to occur. They sent me to Kings College to complete my education and enrolled me as a boarder. Those were wonderful years of discipline, direction, challenge and pride.

The boarding house was in part of what was once a grand residence. Originally a one-storey dwelling built in the 1870s, with a top floor added in the 1890s, it was bought in 1923 and converted for school use. Kings College was officially opened in 1924 by the wealthy Lancashire soap manufacturer, Lord Lever Hulme, who gave the world 'sunlight soap'. He accredited his success in life to having ardently followed the old doctrines of thrift, hard work and self-denial. Most of the boarders were from the country areas of South Australia, and my greatest joy was to be invited back to their respective properties during school vacations. I am indebted to all those who shared their homes with me. There is no place like the bush.

I have often thought back over those last three years of my schooling. They were without doubt the most influential of my life, and the changes they wrought in me would stand me in good stead for my forthcoming entry into adulthood. The school and what it stood for, and all the people associated with it, left me in no doubt that you don't have to be ordinary. Create the dream, set the goals, think like a winner, get off your backside, and if you give it your best shot, anything is possible.

Chapter 3

Making a Quid

My first job was at Cooper Engineering. They installed shearing plants and milking machines, and I saw this as a way to maintain my links with the bush. Even my dreams were not that grand then that I could see myself owning a farm one day, so this was the next best thing. While I enjoyed working in overalls in the factory, I was really looking forward to the day when I would join the installation team and head out bush. Whenever they returned, I listened in awe to their stories of the vast sheep stations and the towns that they had visited.

The Government, however, had other plans, and I was conscripted on the 6 August 1952 into the Army to do a mandatory three months National Service training. This would be the fate of all 18-year-olds who did not have sufficient reason to justify non-compliance. We were sent to the Woodside Army camp in the Adelaide Hills, without doubt one of the coldest places in South Australia. It sure didn't help that our first month was spent in tents. I actually enjoyed the whole experience and feel that it should have been for a longer period. I also consider that we should make it mandatory for all young people to undergo this form of training now. Not only do I think that they would emerge better disciplined and more equipped to tackle life, but our country would be infinitely better prepared to cope with any outside threat to our lifestyle and our freedom. I don't believe as a nation we should play the bully by openly waving a big stick, but we sure as hell should be prepared by carrying one behind our back.

Having said that, there are obviously exceptions and top of the list would have been a classmate of mine who was called up after me to serve his mandatory time. This kid had the brains of a genius and his school marks, always around the 100%, made him top of the class. His body however left a lot to be desired and could easily be described as an uncoordinated mess. Unfortunately, he suffered constant verbal teasing whenever we had to do anything physical like sport or gymnastics.

I was shocked to hear years later that he had hung himself from the rafters in the army camp shower block and can only conclude that he couldn't cope with the raw edge of army life.

Some of the initiation rites carried out and accepted in those days were, in hindsight, degrading. One was to forcibly strip you, blacken your private parts with boot polish and then turn you loose outside naked. Most blokes easily handled it and accepted it as part of the deal. But here was a sensitive, gentle person, and if carried out on him — as I suspect may have happened — then I can easily imagine how it could have freaked him out sufficiently to drive him over the edge. He hadn't a snowball's chance in hell of fitting into army life.

There were about eight hundred of us, and we were all driven out to the rifle range to participate in a shooting competition. It was a cold, wet, miserable day and we all wore great coats to keep warm. We were given two clips of five bullets each, and I put mine in my pocket to keep dry. We lined up and fired our first five rounds, then marched forward and fired off the remainder.

Some weeks later, a group of us were invited to Adelaide to witness the winner receiving his prize and the presentation was held at West's Theatre in Hindley Street. It was called the Winchester Cup and was named after a movie that was featuring at that time. I can still see the cup to this day. It was huge. The winner was a lad from Port Lincoln and he had beaten me by one point. There were no prizes for second.

Now I don't say that I could have won anyhow, but when we had finished our shoot-out and were marching back to the trucks to return to camp, I found one bullet, which had obviously slipped out of the clip, remaining in my pocket. I had only fired nine rounds instead of ten. Maybe I would have missed completely, but if I hadn't, I had the potential to score anything from one to five, and I only needed two to win. My carelessness and lack of attention to detail had cost me any chance that I may have had, and I have never forgotten that lesson. I often think of that big cup.

When I returned to work on the completion of duty, I found that someone younger and less experienced than me had been promoted above me due to my absence. I decided I wasn't going to sit around and wait for the next chance, which appeared to me to be some way off.

I wanted to be a salesman and sell farm machinery, so I applied to join Elder Smith & Company Limited. I dressed meticulously, complete with my school tie, and fronted up for an interview. The building was impressive, the office was huge, the desk was mammoth, and the man standing behind it matched the surrounds. He offered me a job in the accounts department as he thought that was the best place to start. What came out of my mouth then surprised even me.

'Sir, how far down in this company can one start?'

When he asked me what I meant by my comment, I said, 'Sir, I would like to start at the bottom, for if I am to become a top salesman, to be the best, I need to know what I am selling inside out.'

I wasn't sure, but I think there was a tendency towards a slight smile, and he advised that I could start immediately at the very bottom down on the factory floor, which was at their Mile End premises. I thanked him and said, 'Sir, I'll let you know when I'm ready to come back up'.

I repaired engines, assembled giant harvesting and bailing machinery, and at lunch time munched my peanut butter sandwiches sitting on a box while I listened enthralled to the words of wisdom uttered by my 'elderly' work mates as they shared their life experiences with each other. There seemed to be an awful lot to learn about women.

Finally I started installing windmills and pumping equipment and was tutored by one of the best in the business. Ultimately I took over and enjoyed a few wonderful years erecting windmills all over the country.

I have fond memories of the 'wild west' town of Wentworth and the grand station homesteads along the Darling River. These were the days of huge, profitable sheep runs and their wealthy owners' names were mentioned like royalty, particularly in South Australia. Wentworth is situated at the junction of two of our mightiest rivers, the Murray and the Darling.

It was while I was working along the Murray River downstream of Wentworth that I saw my first paddle steamer. It called in to drop off some mail, and I couldn't help but wonder what it must have been like in the days when dozens of them plied the river, bringing up much-needed supplies, and returning with barges laden with wool and other produce. While motor transport and rail finally brought this magnificent era to a close, a few paddle steamers did remain, and one well-known one was the Avoca. It was moored at Mildura, and every Sunday night there was a cruise and a dance on board. I managed to go once and there met the most beautiful girl in the world. She was a woodcutter's daughter from way out of town, down Karween way I think, and although I tried to find her sometime later, I wasn't successful.

I found the farmers on the west coast of South Australia were some of the nicest and most genuine people that you could ever wish to meet. I was amazed at how many of the older ones had never visited their State's capital city, Adelaide, their greatest adventure being a shopping trip to Port Lincoln, and even that was a rare event.

I had to install a new windmill for a couple of characters who lived up near Streaky Bay and that encounter left me with a memory that lingers to this day. This was one of the largest windmills available and it needed three deep holes to concrete the monster to Mother Earth. The only trouble was that I couldn't punch the holes through several feet of solid sheet limestone with my crowbar. 'Not a worry,' according to the two brothers, who were 'experts'. Well that's what they told me, having had plenty of practice blowing holes for fence posts all over their property. What's more, they had plenty of jelly.

We prepared the three holes, inserted a good-sized chunk of explosive into each, complete with fuses and got ready with the matches. The plan was to light the fuses, jump into our vehicles and depart the scene lickity split. The signal was given. I lit up and hopped into my vehicle and roared off. At what I considered to be a safe distance, I did a broadside so I could watch the action. I couldn't believe my eyes. They were still sitting in their truck only a few yards away from the holes, obviously trying to start the bloody thing. I don't know who was doing the countdown or watching the shortening fuses, but suddenly the doors burst open and these two farmers took off across the donga like Olympian sprinters with Old Nick himself after them.

There was a hell of a bang — three actually — I counted, because I wasn't going back unless there were. Rocks flew high into the air and forming a huge arc, rained down in a circle around the site. Unbelievably their vehicle was unscathed except for a little dust. Our Olympians, well, they weren't saying an awful lot, but I bet that is the best bush workout they had had for a long time. I like the west coast and its people.

Lives of the country folk in the main revolved around their work, their town, the pub, football, machinery field days, the sale yards and the occasional dance at the local hall.

Those were the days of the big companies like Elder Smith (fondly known as Uncle Elder), Dalgety and Goldsbrough Mort, and they played a dominant part in the day-to-day life of most country towns. Other prominent businesses were the banks and their managers, who rated second only to God, and generally took over the role of social head for their area.

Every town had the mandatory pub or several. The front bar was the meeting place of the farmers, where they could discuss business, socialise or toss the bull while they sank a schooner or a pint or two. There was never a lady present in this most sacred area: it was illegal. This place was for was blokes only. The ladies were in the parlour or the lounge, where they could sip a soft drink with their husbands, or perhaps have a shandy, a mix of lemonade and beer. Unadulterated beer was considered a little strong for the gentler sex.

The pubs also provided the only accommodation available, which was mainly used by travelling salesmen. Generally the rooms were fairly basic, consisting of not much more than a couple of single beds, perhaps a cupboard, and maybe a wash stand with a jug of water. Down the hall was the bathroom. In a few of the pubs in isolated areas, when the publican went to bed, he would leave a list on the front door nominating all the rooms that had vacant beds in them. Many nights I have been woken by someone slipping into the other bed, and occasionally a drunk would stagger in, which wasn't very pleasant to say the least. You tended to sleep the rest of the night with one eye open.

The beds were atrocious: usually a saggy wire base and a thick, dusty, lumpy flock or mattress. I think the mattresses were stuffed with kapok – unless you've experienced sleeping on one, you haven't really lived! I vividly remember staying the night at a little country pub, the Watervale Hotel, where my room was located in the area now used as a front bar. That was the greatest bed that I had ever slept in, and I was so impressed that I stripped it down to find out who had manufactured it. The innerspring mattress had arrived, but it still took a long time, particularly in remote areas, to replace the old.

The going rate for dinner, bed and breakfast was about 17 shillings and sixpence, although at a good pub, I paid up to 21 shillings. I remember having to stay at Whyalla for one night and the only accommodation available was at a brand new hotel, without doubt the most modern that I had ever stayed at. They charged me 30 shillings, which I thought was exorbitant. I didn't feel I could charge my company this extravagant amount, so I billed them for 20 shillings on my expense sheet and paid the balance myself. I was earning about 10 pounds per week.

It was 1954 and the Royal Adelaide Show, an annual event, was on again. As I was in Adelaide at the time, it was my job to check the windmill and pumping display and to make sure that all the stationary engines, milking machine, and other farm equipment were serviced and operational, ready for the sales staff to demonstrate. I could have sat around in my overalls when I finished, but instead I changed into a coat and tie — not that I was going to impress anyone, I was after all only one of the workers from the factory — it was more a pride thing I suppose, and perhaps a statement that my mentality was flexible, and that I didn't intend to sit at the bottom forever.

There was a manufacturer over from Western Australia demonstrating his product on our stand, as he was trying to get our company to take on the distributorship for South Australia. The basis of the unit was a portable air compressor and it had about ten functions, including a shearing hand piece, sheep jetting unit, spray gun and drilling unit. When he set his plant going it created a hell of a noise, and as the crowds gathered around, he went into a well-rehearsed spiel that lasted for about three quarters of an hour. Over a period of a few days and nights listening to him, I suddenly realised that I knew his speech verbatim. As he was demonstrating, I was reciting his words just ahead of him and knew his every mannerism. Just like an actor, I found myself playing his part.

It was the day before the show finished, and he had just completed another demonstration playing to a packed audience. I heard him mention that he had business over the other side of the showground and would be away awhile. What possessed me to do what I did next, I have no idea, as it really was out of character, but looking back it's quite clear that one of life's many doors had suddenly opened, and I could pass through if I was game. I waited until he disappeared from sight, filled up his machine with petrol, pulled the starter cord, and with a roar it burst into life. I squeezed the trigger of the hand drill, the noisiest piece of equipment, on and off, and the intermittent racket slowly drew in a huge audience. Like a true professional, I played the crowd for all I was worth and never missed a beat. I was word perfect. I drew them ever closer to me as I endeavoured to conjure up images in their minds of what life would be like, if only they possessed one of my magic machines.

I was about three quarters of the way through my spiel when I turned around to select another item for demonstration, and nearly fell over. Standing right behind me was the manufacturer, who thankfully had the biggest smile ever on his face, as he mouthed a few words of encouragement. That wasn't the end of it because as I turned back, I just happened to glance off to the side of the crowd, and there standing on the steps of our building, were all the top managers of our company, including the big chief himself.

Well, I didn't have to let my boss know when I was ready to come back up — not in words anyhow. A couple of weeks later I was requested to present myself to head office, and was informed that they would like me to become one of their sales staff. My 'overall' days in that company had finished.

I did a stint at head office before being sent to the south east as a merchandise representative based out of Keith and Bordertown. It was boom time, as research had solved many of the problems associated with farming this poor soil area, and amongst others, the AMP Society, a major Australian insurance and investment firm, was opening up huge tracts of land. The orders for fencing materials, implement and shearing sheds, equipment and fertilisers seemed never-ending.

I gave up my job after about eighteen months to help a friend develop his property, and this was one of the most rewarding periods of my life. Bert Pexton was the true Aussie battler, and more than anything, I think that this is what drew me to him in the first place. Even though Bert, at 48, was a lot older than me, we were good mates.

To make ends meet, we milked cows, grew pigs, ran sheep and did some cropping. Most of the property was still scrub, and the little money that we earned was spent in clearing land. First we pushed the scrub over with a wooden roller, and when it was dry, we burnt it. If you got a good burn there was nothing left — well, on top of the ground anyhow. When it was ploughed, up came thousands of roots, and because we didn't have a machine to pick these up, we cleared them by hand. It was back-breaking work. Wealthy people threw them into heaps and burnt them, but because we needed every penny that we could lay our hands on, we loaded them on to our truck and took them to the local siding, where we filled enormous railway trucks, to be sold to the wood merchants in Adelaide. Mallee roots, as they were called, were in strong demand because of their superior burning qualities. With the money we received we bought more fuel, then ploughed more land, and so the cycle continued.

Our truck, fondly called Lizzie, was archaic. It had a wooden cab, no doors, holes in the floor and not all the wheels were of the same size. To help protect the tyres from punctures, we would cut the sides out of larger tyres, deflate those on the truck, slip on the prepared rubber, and reinflate, thus increasing the tread thickness enormously.

While Lizzie was unregistered, had half a windscreen, no horn, no lights and no brakes, she sure had heaps of character and the heart of a lion — although to the inexperienced eye, she possibly looked like a derelict heap of junk. On a damp, cold morning start, you would light a fire first, then remove the perished spark plug leads and heat them over the flame to dry them out. This generally did the trick, but occasionally you would have to tap the carburetor three times with a spanner. In lieu of a starter motor, mainly because we didn't have one, we used to turn a crank handle to start the old girl.

We had to cross the main Dukes Highway to the rail siding to unload our truckload of stumps, and we would sneak slowly up to the corner, then if all was clear, we would go like hell to cross the asphalt as quickly as we could. This day I gave the 'all clear' and away we went, but before we could cross the highway, up roared a police prowl car and slowly followed us down the dirt track towards the siding. If they had stopped us, they would have had a field day, but I suspect they took pity on a couple of battlers and let us be with a silent warning not to get caught again.

We cut and split our own fence posts, dug the holes by hand and if we wanted a water trough, we would fell a large tree and hollow it out with the axe. A lot of our building iron was acquired from the highway dumps. We would collect the old 44 gallon tar drums, cut out the top and bottom, split them down the side and then hammer them out flat. We made sheds and pig pens using these sheets of steel, and while they didn't look too flash, they were economical. Everything we had was old and worn out, from the horizontal stationary engines that powered the milking plant and 12-volt generator, to the tractor, the ploughs, and our harvester, which I would say would have been classed more as a relic. Even the poor old horse that we used to ride around the property to save on fuel was stuffed, and should have been sent to the knackery years ago. Things were always breaking down, and our ingenuity was continually tested to the limit, to work out how to affect repairs.

During my time on the farm, we accomplished a lot, and many acres of land were cleared. Unfortunately, however, it would be years before one would see any real benefit from the fruits of our labour, and even then, due mainly to the small size of the property, the returns would not justify two good incomes. My wages were 10 shillings per week — that's all we could afford — so I wasn't saving a thing, and it became obvious that if we were both to survive, it was time for me to move on. I had given up a good job, good wages and a promising career, but I rate that period down on the farm as the most rewarding ever spent in my life. I well and truly learnt the art of how to 'make do'. While it would seem to many that I had gone backwards, in fact I had been preparing myself to go forwards.

I decided to experience the big smoke, Sydney, and got a job in a towel manufacturing company. Dozens of huge weaving machines thumped away on the factory floor, each with its female attendant, and when I was taken into the sewing room, sixty pairs of female eyes swivelled to take in the new recruit. With no more than a handful of males in the entire building, it was rather daunting.

This is where I came face to face with the 'bundy' clock for the first time. For those not familiar with this piece of equipment, it is simply a device that stamps your work arrival and departure times on a personal record card that you insert. With hundreds employed, I guess it was necessary to keep track of everyone, although fresh from the farm where we worked from daylight to after dark, it was rather a shock to see how the lives of some were organised to the minute.

At 3.55 pm the whistle went and the machines stopped almost in unison, as if controlled by a master switch. The air was now electric with anticipation as people fiddled with unimportant jobs until, at 3.59 pm, another whistle sounded and the race was on to get to the bundy clock and then depart. I used to watch in amazement and the exodus reminded me of rats deserting a sinking ship.

After about three weeks the Manager confronted me and said, 'Denis, I've been studying your bundy card and have noticed that you are one to two minutes late every day. If you're not on time in future, I'll have to dock your pay, or worse'.

I looked him straight in the eye and said, 'Sir, I've been watching you, and you are not only a good manager, but a fair one. I know that you would have also noticed that when the mad rush started to punch the bundy clock at knock-off, I continued working and constantly gave you ten to fifteen minutes of my time free, while I tidied up my day's work ready for a clean start tomorrow.' I thought, hell, I've done it this time, so his reply came as a bit of a shock: 'Denis, would you like to do a management course at our expense?'

While I gave every job I tackled my best shot, this really wasn't my scene so I didn't take up his offer and left soon after.

Next I spent a year in New Zealand, where I had a variety of jobs. I was a barman in Wellington, a porter at the Chateau Tongariro, a furniture removal man in Christchurch, worked at a caravan park, and finally on a multi-storey building site, erecting all the steel work.

When I returned to Adelaide, I got a job looking for minerals out on the edge of the Gibson Desert. Len Beadell, now well-known for his surveying and road creation, had just cut his first track through the area and we used it for access.

It was the start of winter, and was it cold! A dish of water left out overnight would freeze into a solid block of ice. We slept in tents, cooked over an open fire, and our food was basic tinned junk, supplemented occasionally with some fresh meat and vegetables. We certainly didn't live in the lap of luxury as modern day exploration crews do. However, I loved every minute of it all, and with the princely sum of 20 pounds per week being paid into my bank account, and the nearest shop over 800 kilometres away, I was sure going to save a bundle.

The summer heat was incredible, and with it came the flies. You started out with the usual hand waving, the great Aussie salute, the slapping, the killing, the brushing, the cursing until finally, unless you wished to go mad, you came to accept the miserable little devils as part of the deal. You soon became an expert at the art of blowing them out of each eye alternately, and the rest you just simply forgot about. With your shirt off, they quickly formed a black crawling carpet over your back. I have never at any other stage of my life experienced flies in such numbers.

During the year that I spent in this remote and scenic area it rained only once, although towering storm cells frequently marched across the sky, generating brilliant lightning displays that were awe-inspiring.

In those days it was still possible to find nomadic Aboriginal people living life in a manner unchanged for thousands of years. Smoke from their hunting fires always graced the skies, and occasionally you would come across a group of women and children collecting grass and other seeds, or digging for lizards and snakes. Their humpies or wiltjas, which provided accommodation and shelter, were a simple timber structure covered with spinifex. Mostly, however, they just erected a windbreak of boughs in front of which they scooped out a line of trenches to lie in with just enough room for their dogs. Between each trench, a fire was lit to help keep warm.

I was fortunate on leaving the desert to be able to visit Ayers Rock, or Uluru, as it is now known. There was nothing there then: no footprints, no guiding chain up the rock and no buildings. How different now with a huge resort, air strip and bitumen road access catering for thousands of visitors, both local and overseas. Over the years I have visited this awe-inspiring, timeless area on numerous occasions, have climbed the monolith about ten times, and have witnessed the area's steady growth into a premium tourist destination.

I feel rather sad these days when I return to some of the places that I visited so long ago. Where I once roamed freely enjoying every nook and cranny — a welcome dip in a rock pool, the solitude — it has now all changed so much. There are rangers and fees, rules, permits and regulations, signs and fences, and designated paths and tracks that you don't dare deviate from. Unfortunately, however, it cannot be any other way. With the magnitude of vehicles and sheer numbers of people visiting these areas, without controls they would soon be destroyed, and the pressure can only increase. Not much is remote any more, and I consider myself privileged that I was able to experience our great outback when I did.

$$\text{\raisebox{0pt}{🦎 🦎 🦎}}$$

Tall, willowy and attractive, she waltzed by. It would have been impossible to miss her. I was at a wedding in Adelaide at the time, and was standing close enough to hear her partner whispering things in her ear that I figured a young lady wouldn't or shouldn't need to hear. With a tap on his shoulder and a 'Do you mind if I cut in?' which was standard procedure in those days, I removed this lecherous individual with his tight embrace from the object of his desires. Naturally, I hoped that this would be acceptable to his partner. There followed a sleepless night, and before the sun had risen on another day I departed once more for the outback. This time, however, I felt a distinct lack of enthusiasm for my forthcoming venture. It didn't take me long to realise my problem: I had left my heart in Adelaide.

I finally married my princess, Rotha Tait, at a fairy-tale wedding at a magnificent old church in the township of Gawler, about 32 kilometres north of Adelaide. We spent our first few years on a mixed farm (cattle, sheep, pigs, cropping), one of the many agricultural and sheep station properties that belonged to her grandfather, Tom McKay, then moved to our own small acreage on the outskirts of Gawler. Here we raised three wonderful children, David, Susan and Richard, and developed a large egg-producing farm.

Before starting this venture, I had researched many poultry farms and found one in particular that was considered to be an extremely well-run and highly profitable unit, so I based my operations on his procedure. He was running 2000 laying hens and considered it was a full-time job for one person.

I had only just started to build my sheds modelled on his operation, when by a stroke of luck, a friend also in the poultry business imported from Sydney a new type of housing where the birds were controlled in cages. Blind Freddie could see that if you didn't make use of this system, you wouldn't be in the race, so I switched quick smart. To give some idea of my advantage over the farm running 2000 hens, within a couple of years, I had built my sheds up to accommodate 9000 birds and was just able to manage these by myself.

Within a short space of time we were able to accommodate 18,000 birds, and, although not big by today's standards, it was then one of the larger farms in South Australia. Finally, with an excellent manager on my farm, we moved to the city and I became involved in many companies from processing to manufacturing to mining.

One venture I really did enjoy was when I went to Eucla, out on the Nullarbor, to check on the possibility of setting up a shark fishing operation. The road over from Ceduna was dirt, and Eucla consisted of a roadhouse, its staff and Harvey Gurney and family who lived on the opposite hill.

Once one of the busiest communications centres outside the capital cities, the ruins of the old Eucla telegraph station, operating between

1877 and 1927, are located down on the flat near the ocean. Only the station's stone walls remain visible, the rest of the town is now covered by shifting sands. From the now derelict jetty, they used to ship out the produce of the area, which was mainly kangaroo hides and sandalwood.

I'd towed over a 20 foot boat, and the few months that I spent netting for shark along this magnificent, remote coastline are truly memorable.

There were many characters, workers from the outlying sheep stations, the rabbiters and the railway workers living at the sidings on the Trans Continental railway line about 100 kilometres to the north. All frequented Eucla for a beer and an occasional night out. One young bloke who used to wander in, generally barefooted, and carrying a snake or a lizard in his pocket, which he would produce at the bar to frighten the daylights out of the female tourists passing through. He is now known Australia-wide as the Maverick from Kalgoorlie — Independent politician, Graham Campbell.

Scottie was a kangaroo and fox shooter and a damn good one, so I'd heard. I was in my usual position at the bar right next to the pie warmer and had sunk a few quiet schooners before Scottie finally decided to slide along the counter to introduce himself. A few hours and beers later, we were well and truly into a 'deep and meaningful', mainly one-sided discussion on his profession and prowess with a rifle.

'Would you like to come out one night, mate, and I'll show you what roo shooting is all about,' he slurred. 'Not many city slickers get the opportunity to see what life's really like in the bush. As a matter of fact, you can even have a go if you want to.'

What Scottie thought he saw and what he would ultimately see would be like chalk and cheese. While my city side shone through like a beacon to a moth, beneath that facade a ghastly plot was forming. 'That'd be great Scottie. I'd like to give it a go, but I don't think I'd be very good at it and you can bet your last dollar that I won't hit anything. I reckon, mate, you could safely put money on that.'

'Don't worry. I'll show you how to use a rifle, mate,' he said. And then as if for extra encouragement, he added, 'and I'll give you ten dollars for every roo that you manage to shoot'.

Bingo, the trap was set. I thanked him for his most generous offer and hoped he wouldn't be disappointed with me as a pupil.

When the big night arrived, he showed me how to load and reload his rifle, how to sight it on the target, and what to pull to make it go bang. We then took off into the night. Roos were plentiful and we soon spotted a mob of about eight, which were still a considerable distance away when he stopped the vehicle. Was he really testing me with such a long shot, or was he just taking out some insurance against luck? I slapped the rifle to my shoulder and, lightning fast, I had three down dead in about as many seconds. I would have had more if he had been quick enough to get the spotlight on the remainder, which had bounded a short distance away and propped momentarily before taking full flight.

Obviously being an enthusiastic student, it was natural that I should ask him how I was going for a city bloke, and did he have any other pointers for me. Also, I asked if he could please move a little faster with the light, as I could have got at least another two. He just sat there for a time with this sickly, stunned look on his face … I put it down to him being in a state of financial shock. Unfortunately for Scottie, things didn't get any better, and by the end of the night he had lost a lot of money. I don't know when the penny finally dropped that he had been conned, however, one day over an ale I told a rather subdued Scottie the story of that damned big Winchester Cup and how as a boy I had roamed the hills potting rabbits with my old 22 calibre single shot.

Another character was Alan, who would become a crack shot and dedicated bird stalker. He spent years waging war on the starling menace trying to migrate from the Eastern states across the Nullarbor into Western Australia.

And who could forget Big Ted, who was built like a tank, and – although I never witnessed the feat – was supposedly able to lift a 44 gallon drum of fuel off the ground onto the back of a truck?

Ted was the rabbit king of the Nullarbor. He owned numerous rabbit chillers dispersed throughout the area, and each one was serviced by a group of shooters. During his day he must have removed millions of rabbits from this area. The first time I met him, it was business related. I needed a chiller to freeze my shark catch, and as he had one for sale, we arranged to meet to see if we could conclude a deal. I departed Eucla, he left Forrest up on the Trans Continental, and we met in the middle of nowhere. I could see his vehicle lights across the treeless plain for at least an hour before he finally drew up alongside. We haggled, I wrote out a cheque, and within 10 minutes we had gone our separate ways.

This was the land of the world-famed Nullarbor Nymph, who

was hunted relentlessly by the world media. To my knowledge, only one slightly blurred photo of her was ever taken, as she was caught momentarily off guard frolicking with the kangaroos. With her long hair streaming out behind, her naked breasts heaving, and her lower half suitably wrapped in a kangaroo skin, she sped off barefooted through the thick scrub, easily eluding the press photographer who, suitably plied with the local amber, and with the aid of several of the resident wags cum-bushmen and renowned trackers, had relentlessly pursued and finally located her. It is hard to tell, the photo being so blurred, but I could swear that I had seen her and her wrap-around kangaroo skin somewhere before. Her sexy attire looked very much like the one that was used as floor mat in a caravan that at one time had been parked next to mine at the Eucla caravan park.

Sadly, my time on the Nullarbor came to an end. While I had enjoyed my shark fishing adventure, it wasn't what I would call a great financial success. Even though I had sent away tons of good quality shark to the eastern markets and received top prices, my boat was too small. I could see the potential for a much larger, refrigerated, ocean-going vessel with the ability to stay at sea and roam at will along this enormous, almost uninhabited coastline. The shark were there in numbers, I had proven that, but a small boat carrying limited nets contending daily with difficult unprotected ocean beach landings and needing a four-wheel drive just to get the catch up and through the sandhills back to the freezer wasn't the way to go.

Before departure I made a final journey north to the rail sidings of Reid and Forrest. These lonely outposts of civilization are situated on the longest straight section of rail track in the world and are part of the rail network linking the eastern and western seaboards of Australia. They also sit out in the middle of the Nullarbor Plains. Nullarbor was derived from the Latin 'nullis' and 'arbor' meaning 'no trees'. When camped out next to the line, the 360° view is of a flat treeless plain that stretches to the horizon. It is truly one of life's unforgettable sights.

At night, lying in your swag beneath a cloud-free and moonless sky, the heavens offer you their treasures with a clarity unavailable to the urban dweller. A star-filled sky of immense magnitude and beauty cocoons you under a jeweled dome that stretches from flat horizon to flat horizon. Away in the distance a small man-made glow suddenly intrudes, then many hours later you are woken from a deep sleep by blinding lights as the Trans-Continental, its belly full of sleeping passengers, finally roars past you on its ribbons of steel.

I had wanted to inspect some of the small blowholes in the vicinity, which either suck or blow air depending on the atmospheric conditions. They erupt from a huge system of underground caves that stretch across the Nullarbor Plains and lie just beneath its surface. I remember the story of a tourist guide, whose party trick at the blowholes was to throw his hat over the hole, letting it shoot high into the air to the amazement of all. This particular day, however, he didn't realise it was in suck mode, and his hat was consigned forever to the caverns below.

On my return to Eucla, I took time to climb down the side of the collapsed roof of Wee Bubby Cave for a welcome last dip in its large lake, some 100 metres below the surface. When swimming along its subterranean tunnel, my torchlight illuminated a colony of tiny bats clinging to the ceiling, while the view beneath my feet showed, through crystal-clear water, a bottom at least 30 metres below.

I spent my final day roaming the immense, magnificent sand hills that lie at the foot of the Eucla escarpment and stretch away to the east until finally contained by Wilson Bluff. When the old Eucla telegraph repeater station and township was in full swing back in the 1880's, cricket was played on the flat between it and the jetty. Now little remains as the sand continues it relentless march westward, covering history in its path.

I drove along the beach, then up and over the frontal dune to stop at a hollow on the other side. Digging down through the sand base for about a metre I drank from the seepage of fresh water that quickly filled my hole. Knowing where to look for soak holes such as this can mean the difference between life and death in the bush. Indeed it saved the lives of a very determined white man and his Aboriginal companion a long time ago …

🦎 🦎 🦎

In 1840, explorer Edward John Eyre set forth from the fledgling city of Adelaide in South Australia to go where no white man had been. His mission was to survey the country to the north, in the hope of finding new grazing lands for the colony. He intended also to reach the Tropic of Capricorn, the very heart of Australia, and plant the British Flag.

The arid wastelands around a huge salt lake, which was later named

Lake Eyre in his honour, proved insurmountable and he was forced to retreat. Rather than return to Adelaide a failure, he struck off for Streaky Bay. Re-provisioned, he then departed westward on an ambitious journey to cross the unknown, waterless wastes of the Great Australian Bight. With him were John Baxter and three Aboriginals. It soon developed into a horror trip, as days without water slowly decimated their stock. Two of the Aboriginals rebelled; stealing the shotgun, they killed John Baxter, stole a quantity of food and departed. Eyre pushed on with Wylie, the remaining Aboriginal, who stayed faithful to him.

Eyre and Wylie dug for fresh water in the sand dunes behind the beach, just as I had done, and killed and ate their horses as they staggered on over 1000 kilometers. Fortunately, conditions then improved, with surface water and food available for them and their remaining animals. The two tattered and emaciated men stumbled upon a whaling ship anchored in an inlet and spent several weeks on board recuperating. The captain supplied them with food and they set off once again. Finally, in mid-1841 they arrived at the township of Albany, in Western Australia.

It had been an incredible feat of endurance and survival — a 1600 km journey through hell. Eyre was acclaimed a hero and his remarkable accomplishment would live on in history as one of the great adventures of the early European exploration of Australia. To those who consider the norm mundane, it would be more than just a story. It would be an inspiration.

I returned home to Adelaide and tried to settle down, to become involved once more with city life, but found it extremely difficult. I missed the outback, the colours, the vast open spaces and, I suppose, the freedom to roam.

I remember walking through the city during lunch hour one day. There were all these people hurrying everywhere with no time to stop or smile as they jockeyed for a position on overcrowded pavements, while others played Russian roulette with an endless flow of stinking, noisy traffic. The ones in suits, particularly those in grey, reminded me of rats trapped in a never-ending cycle, as they scurried through draughty concrete canyons where the sun's rays paid only a momentary visit each day. Life seemed to me to be too short to settle for confinement, and the words of a song continually rang in my ears: 'Don't fence me in … just turn me loose …'

Life teases and tests as we walk along our chosen path. Many doors open, some perhaps only once in a lifetime. All offer new directions, new challenges, new hope. They admit the brave and those who have prepared themselves to take advantage of opportunities when presented. They are there for the dreamers and the achievers, those who believe that one little step up is far better than no steps at all.

Dreams can come true if you work at it.

Chapter 4

The Day of the Gecko

It was early 1979 when I picked up the phone. It was the editor of *The Overlander* magazine on the other end.

'Hi Denis, remember me? Michael Richardson. I did a story on your solo east-west vehicle crossing of the Simpson Desert back in 1977. Just wondering if you would be interested in another desert venture? I'd like to re-enact CT Madigan's journey for the magazine and was wondering if you would consider taking me over?'

'Give me a few days mate and I'll get back to you,' was my enthusiastic reply.

In fact, wild horses couldn't have held me back, but before making a commitment it seemed prudent to get my maps out, acquire some information on Madigan's trip and study his route. I knew of Madigan and his desert association, but nothing in detail of his 1939 camel crossing.

Although I hadn't travelled in the northern Simpson, I didn't consider that I would encounter anything more severe than that already conquered in other parts. I think I was more interested in what little miracles I might be asked to perform as I endeavoured to follow Madigan's route over that trackless wasteland.

I acquired a copy of Madigan's book Crossing the Dead Heart and studied it in detail. Nothing too difficult there, although I knew immediately that I could not locate his campsites, as I was unable to use a sextant (too lazy to learn), relying solely on a compass and bush experience. Finding a small dot in featureless country after days of running a compass shot while climbing and descending rows of seemingly endless sand ridges in a bucking vehicle is near impossible. I needed bigger dots! A lot bigger than, say, the wooden signpost that Madigan erected at his Camp 8, even assuming that after forty-one years it would still be standing.

Dr CT Madigan was born in Renmark, South Australia, went to Prince Alfred College in Adelaide and studied geology at Oxford University, as a Rhodes Scholar. As a meteorologist, he worked with Douglas Mawson in the Antarctic and was awarded the Kings Polar Medal for his contribution to exploration. After serving overseas in World War I, he returned to Australia to take up a teaching post. While conducting geological research in the MacDonnell Ranges he became interested in the Arunta Desert, which lay away to the east.

He states, 'There is still one patch of Australia where the white man's foot has never trodden, and that is the sand ridge desert in the south eastern corner of the Northern Territory north of Lake Eyre.'

With the financial help of Alfred Allen Simpson, President of the Royal Geographical Society of Australasia (SA Branch), Madigan was able to organise an aerial reconnaissance of the dry lakes of South Australia and the unknown desert regions to the north of them.

In 1929, with the assistance of the Royal Australian Air Force, Madigan conducted three flights over the desert and proved beyond doubt that there were no hidden mountain ranges, no fertile pastures – just an endless vision of parallel sand ridges. He states that, 'from the air, the earth appeared a flat pink disk, ribbed from horizon to horizon with red sand hills'. Madigan named this inhospitable desert region the Simpson Desert after his sponsor.

Madigan spent the next few years becoming familiar with the desert's perimeter, then in 1938 he delivered a lecture on 'The Simpson Desert and its Borders', in which he said that although its broader features were known, it still had not been crossed on the ground. He likened it to Mt Everest, whose summit had been seen and photographed so that it seemed there could be nothing more to be discovered, yet man must still set his foot on the topmost point. Madigan said: 'The Simpson Desert should be crossed on foot from west to east across its centre ... the distance across the difficult central parts is only about 300 miles'.

Explorer Captain Charles Sturt, in 1845, had been the first white man to take on the Simpson Desert, endeavouring to force a path from its eastern boundary, near Kudarree waterhole, to the centre of Australia. However, the desert had proved to be insurmountable and Sturt had been forced to retreat.

Mr Simpson wanted his desert to be further explored, this time on the ground, so he agreed to finance a scientific expedition to be led by

Madigan. Departure was planned for the winter of 1939, using camels for transportation.

Madigan had achieved much in his life, but I think having worked for so long in the shadow of the eminent Douglas Mawson, he saw in the desert a chance to make his own mark in history. I think he must have been dismayed not to be the first white man to cross the Simpson Desert. He writes: 'David Lindsay in 1886 managed to get across the southern end of the desert as far as the Queensland border ... Colson in 1936 made a very successful complete southern crossing and returned by a more southerly route. Colson later planned to cross the middle of the desert, the route that I had selected for my journey, but he had failed in his attempt'.

Madigan had already mentioned, in reference to the desert, its centre and the difficult central parts and now the middle. It's obvious to me that he considered the desert hadn't really been crossed because no one had actually passed through its centre, its heart. Did Madigan's selected route pass through its centre, thus enabling him to claim its first true crossing?

Well-respected Adelaide bushwalker and trekker, C Warren Bonython, who with his companion, Charles McCubbin, had made the first crossing of the Simpson from north to south by foot, calculated that its geographic centre lay at 25°22'S–137°05'E. If we use this point as an approximate centre for the desert, then we find that Colson's journey was almost as far south of the magical centre as Madigan's was north. The only people that I know of to have passed within a few miles of Bonython's centre point were D Von Sanden in 1962, Reg Sprigg in 1964 and myself in 1977, all by vehicle.

There's only one other fact to consider. Was the northern Simpson so vastly different to the rest, was it so inhospitable, the terrain so difficult, that it set itself apart to such an extent that one could only claim a true first crossing by passing through it?

I had already crossed the Simpson through its geographical centre, and along the approximate route taken by Colson, as well travelling extensively in the areas further south. Do I consider that, had Colson crossed through the centre, it would have rated higher in effort and achievement than his more southerly route? The answer has got to be, 'No'. Did I consider that the northern section was going to differ so vastly from the centre section? Well I didn't believe so, but I was about to find out.

I advised Michael that it was a 'go-er' and started preparing vehicles, equipment, supplies and mapping out the course. Cornell Suzuki in Adelaide, South Australia agreed to supply me with a traytop LJ81 and I would use my own Suzuki LJ80 hardtop. They also donated enough spare parts to carry out extensive repairs.

The vehicles were stock standard and nothing much was changed, as this was also to be a test by the magazine of the vehicles in standard form as supplied to Suzuki customers and not tricked up. The exhaust system, however, was re-routed out the side of the bonnet and over the cabin roof so as to keep it clear of the thick spinifex that I knew we would encounter. A build up of tinder-dry vegetation around a hot exhaust is a recipe for disaster; it must be cleared away regularly, and it can build up so quickly. Occasionally the vehicle can become hung up on a huge, sand-filled spinifex clump with all its wheels off the ground. When you get that first whiff of burning, it's panic stations. Also, to help protect the radiators from becoming blocked by seeds, particularly spinifex, screens were made to fit in front of each.

The preparation and build-up prior to departure is always the most worrying period for me. Have I calculated enough spare parts, fuel, water and the numerous other factors that have to be taken into consideration to ensure survival and success? Once I am on my way, I generally relax, sure in the knowledge that I have prepared meticulously and confident in my ability to overcome any obstacle. Success should be assured before you set out. Really, shouldn't that apply to any journey in life?

Within a few weeks, two well-prepared Suzuki four-wheel drive vehicles were ready to roll. Michael flew into Adelaide, and we departed as soon as we were loaded with all the necessities to sustain our vehicles and the two of us for an arduous journey. Our destination was Mt Dare station, which we reached after some exploratory detours three days later.

On the way we had stopped at the township of Finke to leave our details with a friendly, obliging young policeman, Max Pope, who greeted us in shorts and bare feet. We marked his maps with our planned route and advised him that, should we need help, our rescue would be funded by Suzuki Cornell.

On our arrival at Mt Dare station, I was once again made welcome by Rex and June Lowe, who invited us both into their house for dinner that night. Rex ran about 5000 head of cattle and had been in the area on and off for some forty-odd years. With the help of a liberal dose of Bundy Rum, we yarned past midnight and increased our knowledge of the area and its characters considerably.

Rex told us about the legendary Fred Sharpe from Andado station, who, incidentally, met Madigan and his party at the Abminga rail siding, while he was in collecting his mail and supplies. Fred had a camel-drawn old Ford car, minus the engine, with his spare parts – three other camels – tied on behind. It was great for crossing the sand dunes up near Andado, and he could make the 80 mile journey from there to Adbminga in a non-stop day. Fred used to occasionally get a five gallon keg of plonk delivered up on the railway, pop it on the back of his car, and then crawl underneath with a siphon hose, staying there until the keg was drained. According to Rex, Fred reckoned this was as good as a three-week holiday.

We said goodbye to Rex and June the following day and headed for the Abminga rail siding, but needed to take a small detour on the way. Rex was worried about a young bloke named Rod Gooch who intended to cross the Simpson along the French Track by camel. Rex was concerned that he wasn't carrying enough water. We finally located Rod just past the crumbling ruins of Ted Colson's old home at Bloods Creek, and delivered some extra drums for him to carry. He didn't have a compass, carried only minimal maps, and really had no idea what lay ahead of him. We hoped he made it.

After a welcome swim in a dam along the way, we finally rolled in to Abminga, a rather desolate, badly neglected looking rail siding. Other than the addition of a few extra buildings, it probably stood much the same as it had when Madigan unloaded his truck and supplies from here on 27 May 1939. What little life and pride existed here now would soon be snuffed out, however. The new standard gauge railway some 85 miles to the west was nearing completion and the fettlers, Abminga's only inhabitants, would move on, leaving another part of our history to decay into the dust.

We departed Abminga and now followed Madigan's route as he and his party made their way over the Gibber Plains to Charlotte Waters. When he had arrived, the old telegraph relay station, once a busy centre, was closed and deserted, although its well-made stone buildings were still standing. Built much like a fort, there were loop holes in the walls and main door, no doubt put in to repel any attack by the local Aboriginals.

Charlotte Waters, in its dying days a police station, had over the years played host and created a safe sanctuary for many travellers. Explorers such as Giles, stockmen and drovers and camel trains passed through on their long journey from Marree to Alice Springs. It had gained its name from the telegraph construction crew who had found water in shallow holes in the nearby creek, now called the Coglin. Fred Sharpe had found its last inhabitant just a few days before Madigan's party arrived, when he located the decaying body of an old man in one of the rooms, and with police help, had removed the remains on a sheet of tin and buried him nearby. Madigan recalled that the stench made it impossible to linger in the house.

It was here that Madigan met up with his team of camels, which had been walked all the way up from Marree, taking some three weeks for the journey. The animals had been individually selected by that grand old Afghan camel man, Bejah Dervish, who had made many journeys into the remote areas of the outback. He had been camel handler for most of explorer Larry Wells' desert journeys, and had accompanied him on his ill-fated Calvert expedition in 1896–97 from Wiluna across the Great Sandy Desert to Fitzroy Crossing. Bejah, much to his regret, was too old to accompany Madigan, so he sent his son Jack to manage the camels for the expedition.

Madigan assembled his team, double-checked the loading of supplies and equipment, and then, with the scientific staff on board the truck, drove on to Andado station where they would spend the next three days on research while they waited for the camels to catch up.

On the fortieth anniversary of Madigan's crossing, we too rolled into Charlotte Waters, only to find that the buildings were now reduced to nothing more than rubble. They sat atop a slight rise overlooking a flat gibber plain shimmering with mirages.

I wanted to re-enact Madigan's crossing as closely as possible, so I decided to follow his route down the Coglin, even though the track he had used had long disappeared. The Coglin finally ran into the floodout country of the Finke River, which was heavily treed, resembling an oasis of green after the recent rains. We didn't strike a large main channel as I had expected, but numerous small waterways meandering through a wide flood plain about 3 kilometres across.

We located McDill's well and bore without much trouble. The windmill was well maintained, and so too the nearby track heading northwards, the way I wanted to go. The well was named after Bob McDill, who had opened up Andado station as a cattle property capable of running some 7000 head.

Once we reached Mayfield Bore the track lay between sandhills until Peebles Creek, where they terminated. Ahead lay pools of water, giving the immense flat plain a tundra-like appearance.

We camped at the new Andado homestead that night, and were made welcome around the family dinner table by Molly Clark, the owner. Molly's husband had had a heart attack in 1978 while he was flying home. He had crash-landed somewhere out in the desert sandhills on the last leg of his journey.

When I'd arrived in Kulgera on my west to east crossing of the continent, the service station owner had asked me to remain in radio contact in case I was needed. I guess he figured that as I'd proved my vehicle's capability in the desert, they may need my assistance in searching for him. But Mac Clark had trimmed his aircraft ready for landing when he suffered his attack, and crashed in the sandhills only four minutes from the homestead. He was located from the air by Rex Lowe, who had flown in to assist, and that night Mac had guided his rescuers to him by flicking his cigarette lighter on and off. Unfortunately, he had suffered a second heart attack and died a few days later.

The following morning we topped up our water containers and gave our vehicles a very thorough check. This was our last outpost before Birdsville and I couldn't afford to take any chances. Like Molly, who over dinner had stated, 'Michael, this is not a country that lets you make mistakes', I knew and understood only too well the dangers that lay ahead.

We bade farewell to our friendly host and went on to the original Andado homestead, some 17 kilometres away, on the other side of several very large sandhills. It was because of the difficulty in negotiating the sandhills' ridges that, in 1954, a new house was built out on the flat.

Old Andado looks much today as when Madigan arrived, a typical cattle station homestead. A white-washed corrugated iron house was surrounded by a meat shed, saddlery, windmill and a well-built stock yard set amongst a sprinkling of gum trees. The whole lot sat between two extremely high, windswept red sand ridges that stretched as far as the eye could see.

The house's framework was built from waddy timber, which is so hard that it cannot be nailed together and must be tied with wire. The wood, Acacia peuce, can only be found in two locations throughout the world and they are both here in Australia. All that separates them is the Simpson Desert. One site is just out of Birdsville, and the other about 30 kilometres north of Old Andado.

When Madigan departed Andado he mentioned that, 'Everyone got into his desert dress'. When they had left Adelaide by train, they were dressed in suits, ties and hats, and a photo taken at the Abminga rail siding shows them similarly dressed. I assume that they arrived at Andado in the same gear after a ride on the back of a truck! It made me think back some 26 years to my very own train and mail-truck journey: I went to fix up a windmill on a remote sheep station, and I too wore a suit. We sure had strange ways back then.

We stopped off to visit a large and impressive stand of waddy trees that had been fenced off to protect their young seedlings from the cattle. The trees resemble she-oaks but have a different seed — pods rather than cones. The area is called the Mac Clark Conservation Reserve.

From there, we pushed on past nearby North Bore to East Bore and then turned northwards for Poodinitterra Hill and the junction of the Todd and Hale Rivers. After about 9 kilometres of open country, we entered low sand dunes until finally, in relatively easy going, we were running alongside the western edge of a low tableland.

Near Poodinitterra Hill we glimpsed another vehicle and I detoured slightly to intersect its route. It turned out to be two rangers from the National Parks, who had been fencing around more waddy trees. They told us that they had been trying to reach the Hale River and follow it to reach Alice Springs via Numery station, but had been beaten back by the thick re-growth in the river bed. They were now heading home via Andado and New Crown station. It sounded as though our first real challenge lay just ahead, because that was the way we needed to go to reach Fletchers Hill, which I intended to make our jumping-off point into the desert.

It was mid-afternoon by the time we reached The Twins, which consisted of two very low hills; Madigan had erected a cairn on the most northerly one. We found not one, but two cairns, and a brass plaque explained the mystery. The second cairn had been erected by Reg Sprigg in 1962 to commemorate Madigan's crossing. From this vantage point we

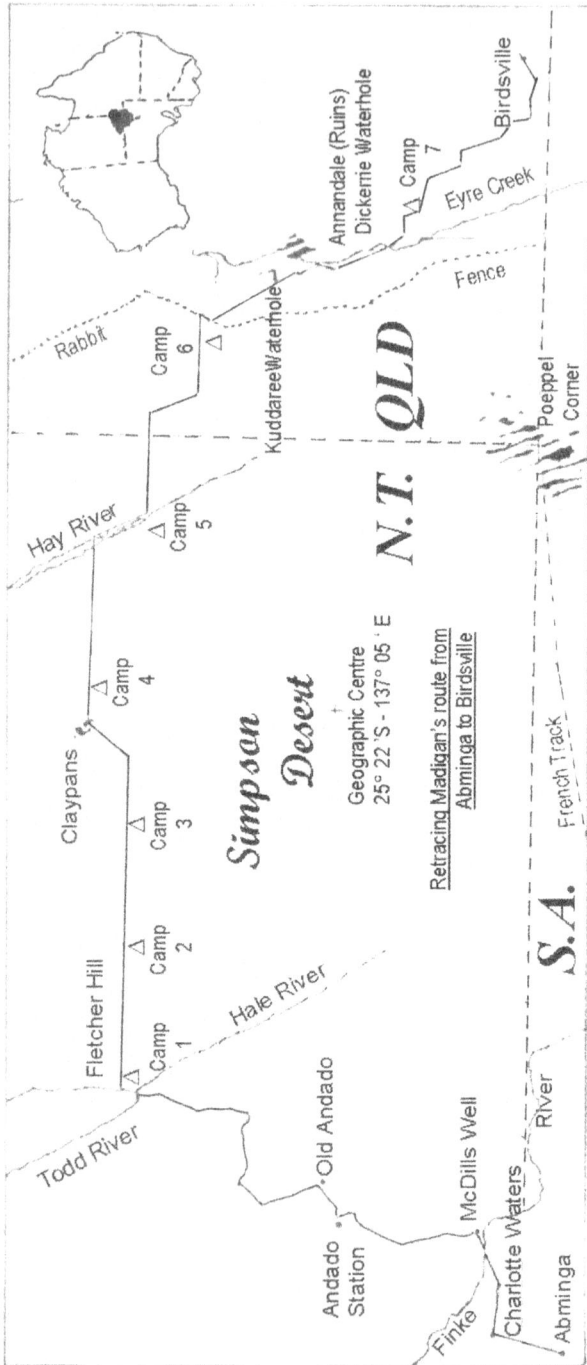

could now see Fletchers Hill, a low tableland some 10 kilometres away, and the area between, a combination of sand ridges and the floodout country surrounding the junction of the Todd and Hale Rivers.

The thick re-growth that the rangers had encountered certainly slowed us down, but by using a combination of compass and shadow, I was easily able to maintain direction. We arrived at Fletchers Hill just on sundown where we made a pleasant camp amongst the gum trees and acacias.

Madigan's well-equipped party, consisting of nine men, 19 camels and a dog also camped near here. Next day they continued upstream for about 8 miles to dig a soak in the river bed and give their camels one last drink and a final camp up before Madigan turned and committed his party to the desert. I would start out from our present position, and slowly converge onto his course

It was a chilly night, but we had ample wood for a good fire and sat around yarning. I could see that Michael was rather agitated with pre-departure jitters, enhanced no doubt by the comments made to him by the ringers back at Andado station. They had said that although our vehicles were well equipped and more than suitable for sandhill travel, our standard bar-tread tyres were definitely inadequate and we weren't going to get too far.

'Den, what do you reckon?' he finally asked, his concern quite evident in voice and expression. 'With all the experience these station people have had mustering cattle in the sandhills out here, do you really think we have any chance of making it across with these skinny tyres?'

'I wouldn't have agreed to leave them as standard just to please the Suzuki motor company if I'd believed them to be unsuitable,' I explained. 'You know mate, experience is a great teacher and I have had a fair bit of it in my time. Remember, I have used these tyres to good effect in similar conditions to those we are going to encounter over the next week. They may not be the best, but we will get there, trust me'. I hope I didn't sound like a used car salesman when I said it.

I could understand Michael's apprehension. However I let my mind wander to the very first time that I had confronted this desert. Even then, with years of bush experience already under my belt, which Michael didn't have, I couldn't help but feel intimidated by the vast, unfamiliar area that lay ahead. Although I wasn't intimidated now, I certainly hadn't become complacent. Over time comes knowledge, but only the fool allows complacency, as familiarity tries to initiate contempt.

Many a death in the outback can be directly contributed to apathy, ignorance, arrogance or stupidity. You plan to fail by failing to plan, and I'd planned to win.

We awoke early, carefully checked over our vehicles, and climbed to the top of the hill. Ahead, the landmarks disappeared and we gazed into a sea of sand and spinifex with rolling, wave-like dunes, each crowding closely on the one before it. No tracks to follow and just the needle of a compass to guide the way; this was how I liked it. Real adventure, real challenge. The only thing topping it would be setting out to do it alone.

On 1 October 1979, I took my first compass shot of 84 degrees, which represented the line marked on my map to follow for the next few days, and we set about our venture.

'Okay Michael, this is it mate. Time to do battle.'

The grin on his face and his enthusiastic reply, 'Let's do it Den!' left me in no doubt that he now had last night's fears well under control.

My first objective was to locate a series of large claypans about 130 km away that I believed Madigan had spotted on his aerial reconnaissance, and intended to visit, but missed on his actual journey.

After 20 km of relatively easy going, we reached the Colson Track. It was no longer covered in re-growth as it had been when I struck it on my solo east/west vehicle crossing two years ago. There must have been oil exploration activity down south, for the track had been re-graded and showed signs of heavy traffic.

We were making good time, and in three and a half hours had covered 25 kilometres. The dunes had not been very difficult and there were occasional large grass-covered flats. Lunch was at 35 km beneath a gum tree inhabited by a crow and her family; the mother circled continually overhead, protesting our intrusion into her domain.

Since leaving Adelaide, the weather had been pleasant, but the temperature had been climbing slowly, and that afternoon reached 35 degrees Celsius. The dunes now started to close ranks and increase their size, and spinifex was becoming more predominant. Some of the taller dunes needed a run-up to get over their big, fiery crests, and the drop down the other side became steeper and steeper.

I shot up to the crest of one big dune and ended up precariously perched on the edge of a large wind-blown hole that had been concealed by overhanging cane grass. I needed Michael's help and weight to prevent a roll-over. While he hung on to the side, I extracted myself and the shovel and dug the top tyres down to level her up a bit before driving out.

Our camp that night was amongst wattles and grevilleas at the base of a large dune whose sawtoothed edge towered some 25 metres above us. By the light of a good fire we repaired a flat tyre, fuelled and checked our vehicles thoroughly, and cleaned the radiators that, despite their protective screens, were starting to clog up with spinifex seeds and dust. We had covered about 45 km for the day and our radio call to our Adelaide contact reported that Five Sierra Bravo Xray was A-OK and enjoying a cheery fire under a cloudless, star-spangled sky.

For navigation I was using the same method that had served me well for my trackless desert crossing in 1977. When I had finished that journey, I was able to calculate that, at the most, I had only been about 4 kilometres off course in over 350 kilometres, so it works if you're meticulous.

In this featureless terrain where one's vision is limited to only a few dunes ahead, endless, time-consuming compass shots would be necessary to maintain an accurate course. Instead, I'd walk in front of the vehicle and with the compass, sight my heading on a nearby bush or tree. Back in the vehicle, I would turn it to centre on my marker, and then look for a recognisable shadow on the bonnet or dash, and note its position. It could be from the stick that I had tied to the left-hand side of my bull bar, my exhaust, or in the afternoon, the aerial mounted in the centre of my roof. Then for about the next twenty minutes, every time I reached the top of a dune, I would swing the vehicle until the shadow returned to its noted position. Dead ahead was approximately where I should be. However, if I could only climb over the next dune some distance left or right of that point, then I would add or subtract that estimated distance next time around.

Day two in the desert, and the relatively easy going ceased. Spinifex now crowded all but the very tops of the dunes, and the sand trapped in their bodies, together with the wash-aways in between, created humps and bumps that tossed us around mercilessly as the ridges became more difficult to cross.

Finally, we reached the floodout of the Illogwa Creek, which was dotted with gum trees. Strangely, Madigan made no mention of crossing this well-defined floodout. I was now able to calculate that we were losing about 6 per cent for wheel slip and detours. In other words, for every 100 km as measured from my map, I would need to travel 106 km on my odometer. This was about 1 per cent less than I had anticipated based on past experience.

By mid-morning we were in a furnace. The temperature had reached 44 degrees Celsius, or 110 degrees in the old Fahrenheit scale, and to make matters worse, we had a tail wind. This restricted the flow of air into our dust-clogged radiators, and our motors were overheating, necessitating frequent cooling stops to blow out the core with our air-bed pump. Every few hours we would do a more thorough clean by removing the outer screens, the grilles and then the inner screens. My vehicle's radiator was probably the worst affected by seeds and dust. It took the full force of the tall spinifex, but left a broken, cleaner path which was to Michael's advantage.

That day was terribly slow, tiring and bloody hot, and to make up distance, I had pushed on for one hour's night driving. We made camp near the top of a dune out of reach of the spinifex. Of this area Madigan had written: 'This was the very height of desolation'. His camp 8 had been about 10 kilometres further on, and as he'd settled down for the evening, it had started to rain, not stopping for the next couple of days. Water had not been a problem for Madigan.

Because of the heat, we were starting to use more water than I had planned, so it was now limited strictly to drinking, cooking and topping up the radiators. We still had a long way to go, and I wasn't going to wait until it was too late to apply restrictions. I'd rather be dirty and alive, than clean and dead. As I explained to Michael, 'In the desert, you must learn to live like the gecko, conserving everything you have. One day, your life may depend on it'.

Day three dawned clear, and we departed camp under the watchful gaze of a young dingo, rather earlier than normal, as I wanted to get in a few extra hours of driving before the heat of the day once more engulfed us. The sandhills were now some of the largest, but as the spinifex didn't encroach as far up the slope as it did on the smaller, more tightly clustered dunes, the driving was a little easier.

Madigan, however, while travelling through this area had been doing it tough. On one day they managed only 20 km, as the party struggled over 44 giant sandhills as big as any they had seen. The camels had begun to falter, and it was food, not water, that was their main concern. The summer rains over the desert had been patchy and where they were was absolutely barren.

We startled a huge feral cat, damn near the size of a kelpie, and it wasn't sticking around for a bowl of milk or the lump of lead that I had in mind. Cats are stripping whole areas of their small mammals and reptiles; when you consider the harshness and remoteness of our present location, then you see that no area is really safe from these efficient killers.

By lunch time we had covered some 37 km, which was one kilometre more than we had managed for the whole of the previous day. I calculated our position to now be 11 kilometres away from the claypans that I was seeking, and altered course to the north-east to try to intersect them. There were now better vegetated valleys, and grevillea and wattle had started to again appear in numbers. When I stopped at the 11 km mark we were in a wide interdunal corridor with only a few small claypans evident – certainly nothing like I was looking for. The first gidgee we had seen since entering the desert dotted the landscape. I was rather dejected but it had, after all, been a big ask to hit the tail end of a small dot over such a large distance.

Next stop was the Plenty River. I turned back onto my original bearing of 84 degrees and we climbed to the top of a nearby dune. Dejection turned to elation, for just to the north of our position and smack on my previous course, I could now see a large claypan some 4 km long. In 130 km, I had been less than one kilometre out.

At the bottom of the claypan, there were a group of small, noteworthy knolls, each about 8 metres high, while a ridge about 15 metres high marked the south-eastern boundary. This was the feature that Madigan had been seeking, not the few small claypans that he had encountered. At 200-odd metres wide they weren't big enough. In no way does this belittle Madigan's achievements, however, for it must be remembered that he had sighted and plotted this obvious feature from his aircraft reconnaissance some ten years earlier. Furthermore, the pilot only had to be slightly off course to alter Madigan's calculations considerably. We had the benefit of modern, more accurate maps.

Michael was excited that we had reached our target.

'Do you know Den,' he said, 'there wouldn't have been too many white fellas, if any, who have stood where we are now standing. Whadaya reckon?'

We had climbed one of the small knolls and I was soaking up the raw beauty of our surroundings and enjoying a welcome break from being continually thrown around the vehicle as we bumped our way across this magnificent landscape.

'You could be right, Michael. One thing is for sure, you now have joined a select few who have been anywhere in the northern Simpson, let alone on this spot.'

Back on course, we were now heading for the Hay River some 62 km away. We made camp after dark 17 km further on which gave us a total for the day of 66 km, at a mind-boggling average speed of 5.5 kilometres per hour. Before we turned in, we attended to the never-ending task of cleaning the radiators, then checked and readied the vehicles for the following day. I also made a radio transmission advising that we were okay. Although they finally got our message, there was obviously something inside the set intermittently shorting out our transmission. That was a bit of a worry, particularly if it failed completely and we needed help.

Day four was another early start, and for the next 10 km it was easy going through rolling low dunes punctuated by claypans and clumps of gidgee. As the day wore on the temperature climbed, and by midday it was a real scorcher. In the last few kilometres I was rather sloppy in my navigation, tending to cross the dunes more at a right angle. The continual lurching from spinifex clump to spinifex clump, plus the heat, was finally getting to me, and I figured that it didn't really matter if I hit the Hay River a few kilometres off course.

It burst upon us without warning: a wide valley massed with gum trees, though after crossing what turned out to be an outer branch, we found the main channel over the next sandhill. Here, we stopped for lunch and a billy under the welcome shade of a large box tree before setting off south along the river to try to locate Madigan's blazed tree. Around us, scattered stone chips indicated that the Aborigines foraged down this far in good seasons.

Just before dark we located Madigan's tree, and although the blaze was partly overgrown, it was still legible. That night we opened up a bottle of red wine that Michael had ferreted away just for this occasion, and drank a toast to Dr CT Madigan and crew. Not that Madigan had been doing it tough when he set up his camp here either. They had had ample water, and feed for the camels had been plentiful in this area. Madigan had stated that although they were not quite out of the woods, they could whistle with confidence. Crocker had shot a wild turkey and Marshall had produced a bottle of whisky, so they too had had themselves a party.

From here Madigan rode due east for 18-odd miles to the Queensland border and then turned south east-to cut a bend in the old, abandoned rabbit-proof fence. As I didn't have a sextant to determine our exact position, I decided to take a slightly different route and try to cut the fence to the north of the bend, then follow it down before turning east for the final run into Kuddaree waterhole.

Day five and the going was easier. Although the dunes were bigger, they were spaced further apart. By 11 am we had covered 30 km and were in the sunny state of Queensland. The temperature had reached 38°C and kept on climbing, and so did our water consumption, with Michael quite worried that we didn't have enough. About 10 km further on, I turned down-dune for 18 km and then turned eastwards once more, heading for the old rabbit-proof fence.

The temperature reached 44°C and we had to continually blow out our radiators. At 4 pm, the temperature had fallen back to 38°C (100°F), the lowest in six hours but then it began to warm up again; the air lashed us with its fiery breath, and the sand on top of the dunes became softer and more difficult to negotiate.

When we reached the point where I calculated the fence should be, there was nothing to be seen. We paused on the slope of a high dune to survey our surrounds, and to give our vehicles, which had boiled frequently, another drink.

Michael again mentioned the meagre amount of water remaining and his concern. 'Are you sure we're okay Den? We really didn't take enough to start with, did we?'

Unfortunately what you would like to have and what you can carry are two different things. Many a vehicle has broken down due to gross overloading, springs mainly, as they're only built to take so much, particularly in this rough terrain. It's always a juggling act and sensibly you prune to the absolute minimum then add a bit in case of emergency. I wasn't really worried at this point, but we sure had taken a battering with the unexpected high temperatures.

This is where bush knowledge comes in handy. 'Michael, sometimes we think we need far more than we have, and sometimes we have far more than we think.' I bent down and wrenched out the huge munyeroo plant growing at my feet, then, like wringing out the washing, I twisted it until its copious supply of life-giving moisture ran through my fingers and fell like huge rain drops to saturate the parched sand at my feet.

'You know, Michael, we are both fit, we have two vehicles in excellent condition, and I could almost get us out of here overnight. That's how close we are to safety, so don't let's panic yet. Munyeroo,' I said as I munched into a sprig of its succulent leaves 'is edible, and you can use it as a vegetable. The Aboriginals also ground their seeds into a paste for cooking. That was part of their diet'.

I pulled out about a dozen of the largest plants and removed their tap root, which is quite sizeable, about the thickness of a finger. I would cook them tonight for a few moments in the white ash of the fire so Michael could try a bit of desert tucker.

About 8 km further on, we made camp with still no sign of the old fence line. Perhaps we had crossed a section of it that had been buried by the drifting sand, but whatever, that was for tomorrow. I'd had enough for the day.

While eating our meal that night we heard a strange sound, and investigating with the torch, found a bull camel patrolling our campsite. He even allowed Michael to photograph him with his flash light, and was still circling our camp when we turned in at midnight.

Day six and I headed up the nearby dune at daybreak with the binoculars. I was peering through them intently when I was startled by a noise close at hand. I spun around and there was our friend (I hoped) from the night before just a short distance away. He had followed me up the dune just like a faithful old dog, and when we departed camp that morning, he gazed at us with such doleful eyes that we felt that he was about to burst into tears.

Within a few kilometres we finally cut the now-tattered remains of the old rabbit-proof fence, and a nearby sharp bend in its direction enabled me to get a positive position fix on my map. The run into Kuddaree waterhole was now down wide grass- and saltbush-covered flats, where cattle grazed and a small flock of brolgas danced in the heat haze.

Kuddaree carried a large body of water some 500 metres long by 100 metres wide, and with the temperature again in the forties, it didn't take us very long to strip and immerse ourselves in its cool embrace. Hundreds of corellas and cockatoos voiced their disapproval at our presence, while pelicans, along with a few dead cows, shared the water with us. As we feasted on fresh water mussels and biscuits washed down with Michael's special brew, Kuddaree tea, we congratulated ourselves that we had finally crossed a desert and left behind a worthy adversary.

Michael was quick with the camera to record the event.

From Kuddaree I dropped us down into the dry bed of the Eyre Creek, which offered smoother, faster driving than the surrounding country, and after about 30 km we reached the ruins of Annandale station.

When Madigan had arrived in 1939, they found the homestead deserted and rapidly falling into ruin. The harness and store rooms still had their iron roofs intact – the house itself was roofless, but to their amazement, the furniture was still in it. When we arrived, in 1979, it was definitely a ruin, and drift sand was slowly covering it over. Nearby lay a beautiful old boiler and steam engine. The property once belonged to Sir Sidney Kidman — the Cattle King — but had been abandoned in the 1920s.

We dropped back into the creek bed to continue our journey south towards Dickerrie waterhole. It was pitch black when my lights picked up a gum tree that looked familiar. The first and only time that I had been in this vicinity was three years earlier, when I had to swim my vehicle over the flooded Eyre Creek before beginning my east to west solo cross-country vehicle crossing of the Simpson Desert. This looked like the gum that I had passed on my way over and had planned to use as an anchor point if I needed to winch myself back out. When I located the remains of a windmill a few hundred yards upstream, I knew precisely where I was: this was Dickerie Crossing, and a reasonable station track would now take us into Birdsville.

Michael was worn out, and continually requesting over the CB our estimated time of arrival for Birdsville. I'd promised him a beer and a hot shower if he could hang on. I'd also lied outrageously, leading him to believe that Birdsville was a lot closer than it really was, in terms of time.

I knew from past experience that Taffy would still be manning the front bar provided that he had at least one customer still vertical. I was really looking forward to renewing an old acquaintance and to a cold beer, which I knew would be forthcoming provided we could get there early — say by two am!

Based on my memory, I had left the track and headed across the gibber-strewn plain to cut a corner and save a little time, when I received the most plaintive of all calls on the CB, and I knew that time had run out. 'Den, I keep nodding off. How much further do we have to go?' Bugger, that beer was so damn close!

I stopped my vehicle and made camp on the rocks. I don't think there was one grain of sand or dirt showing, just rock, rock and more rock! Nobbly and bloody hard! I was asleep before Michael managed to peg his tent down. On the several occasions that I awoke during the night, I could hear him continuing to do battle with the rocks, the pegs and a mighty wind, which now threatened to blow him and his tent off the face of the earth.

Daybreak. The only sound to shatter the calm came from where Michael snored beneath a jumble of cloth and protruding poles that bore little resemblance to its designer's dream.

'Wakey, wakey, Michael. It's time to go.' Nothing stirred.

My second request received no more that a mournful sound, something between a grunt and a groan to be followed by a plaintive declaration: 'Denis, I think I might just have a little bit of a sleep-in'.

Well I had news for him. I packed, fired up the engine and was on my way. In my side mirror, the jumbled mass that I'd left behind suddenly exploded in a frenzy of activity. Hell, I'm mean. When I reached the top of a nearby sand dune, I had one last glimpse of Michael frantically packing his vehicle before I descended down the other side to a large pool of claypan water for a morning wash.

After what seemed an eternity, Michael blasted to the top of the dune and paused momentarily. I was soon to find out what was going through his mind. My parentage was brought into question, plus a few choice words, which were in no way complimentary. I think Michael will forever believe that I deliberately stopped on the gibbers, knowing full well that nearby was a large sandhill to break the wind, soft ground to camp on and to top it all off, a beautiful big puddle of water to mess with. I honestly didn't know about the puddle!!

Well, we finally made it to Birdsville and that elusive beer. Our adventure had been successful and near flawless. I'd had a good companion with me, so who could ask for more. Michael's first trip across the Simpson was, I am sure, educational and motivational. It would leave him with memories to last a lifetime, and I'd wager my last dollar that one day the lure of the desert will see him return.

When Madigan's expedition had arrived in Birdsville, he'd stated 'This bare and wretched little town, the most remote in Australia, was a beautiful sight'. The townspeople had turned out in force to greet him, and they had even planned a reception ball, while the transmitter ran hot with news of his success to the outside world, and congratulatory messages flooded in. Madigan's highly financed, well-equipped expedition, through his meticulous planning and the help of a good crew, had successfully completed their mission. Theirs was the first major scientific foray into this unique area and it provided significant data on the climate, soil, dune formation, geology, fauna and flora.

Madigan followed his trip with a series of lectures, and wrote many reports for the Royal Geographical Society. He will be forever remembered as a man who dramatically advanced our knowledge of the Simpson Desert.

🦎 🦎 🦎

Ted Colson, however, who had arrived unannounced in Birdsville some three years earlier than Madigan, had been greeted more with disbelief than fanfare. After the mandatory signing of his log book, he and his Aboriginal mate, Peter Ains, departed and once again crossed the desert to return to his home and his wife Alice, who no doubt was anxiously awaiting his return. Colson's two-man, unfinanced expedition had successfully crossed one of Australia's last frontiers, and he ended his diary with these words: 'Though I have nothing very spectacular to offer, I think I can say, something accomplished, something done'.

Colson wrote to the South Australian Director of Lands offering to come to Adelaide and give a full account of his crossing if they could give him some modest financial support for the journey. Their reply stated that they would be pleased to receive his notes on the journey from which all information of value to the department could be extracted without the expense of his coming to Adelaide. Weren't they cheapskates!

There was little glory for Ted Colson from the bureaucrats or the establishment. I guess he was considered to be of no great importance. After all, he was only a self-educated man who had difficulty in writing and spelling, and lived in a bit of a tin shack out in the middle of nowhere. However, the modest little Aussie battler and rough-hewn bushman was the first European to cross the Simpson Desert, and a plaque was finally erected in his honour outside the Birdsville Hotel in 1973. It commemorates his achievements and those of his Aboriginal mate, Peter Ains.

So, was the northern Simpson so vastly different from the rest? After considering all factors — distance, terrain, vegetation — I came to the conclusion that the difficulties facing a camel journey traversing any of the routes were so minor as to preclude any further discussion on southern or middle crossings. Both Madigan's and Colson's crossings were great journeys through difficult terrain and they could both feel justifiably proud of their achievements.

As we rolled out of Birdsville on the completion of our Madigan re-enactment, I knew that it would only be a matter of time before I returned, once again, to the land of the parallel dunes.

Chapter 5

In the Footsteps of Lindsay

It was May 1980 and I once again found myself heading northwards for the Simpson Desert. This time my 12-year-old son, Richard, occupied the passenger seat of my brand new diesel Toyota. Although he had visited many parts of the outback already, this would be a totally different experience for him.

I was on a mission that had started a few months earlier, with a call from a contact in the National Parks SA. He was seeking information on my 1977 east-west journey through the Simpson Desert. One thing led to another, and he mentioned a series of lost native wells. In 1886, explorer David Lindsay had used these wells to survive when he penetrated the Simpson Desert. A Government expedition had set out to locate them in 1975, but had failed in their attempt. My questioning must have sounded rather enthusiastic, because next I was being offered Lindsay's journal, but only on the understanding that I would take up the challenge to find the wells. He didn't have to ask twice.

David Lindsay was born at Goolwa in South Australia on 20 June 1856 to John and Catherine Lindsay. His father was a Scottish sea captain who had migrated to South Australia from Dundee. At 17 years of age, Lindsay started as a cadet surveyor, and five years later he moved to Port Darwin where he began a long association with the Northern Territory. As a surveyor, he traversed the north, central and western areas of the Australian continent, and in 1885–6, he carried out what he called The Great Central Exploration Expedition from Adelaide to Port Darwin. It was on this journey that he entered the Simpson Desert for the first time.

In 1891, he led the Elder Scientific Expedition from Warrina in South Australia across the Great Victoria Desert to near Kalgoorlie in Western Australia. Lindsay had interests in mining, was a share broker, and had accumulated considerable wealth in his heyday. His main financial interests were in Queensland and Western Australia, with a family base in Adelaide, until he moved to Sydney in 1912 and more or less lapsed into obscurity in his declining years. He was in the Northern Territory, selecting suitable cotton-growing land for a large syndicate, when in 1922 he died of a heart attack and was buried in the Gardens Road Cemetery, Darwin. The World War II bombing raids on the city destroyed the cemetery and his headstone, but his gravesite was finally relocated by his son Donald. Today a new headstone marks the resting place of this excellent bushman.

After studying Lindsay's journal in detail, I concluded that I really didn't have a snowball's chance in hell of locating any of the wells that he had used, but I was sure going to give it my best shot. I had only one known feature out in the middle of my Simpson Desert map that I could positively identify from Lindsay's journal, so that became my starting point. I re-calculated all his compass bearings and plotted his course on my maps as best I could. All his distances between turning points and well locations were measured in camel time (about 3 miles, or 4.8 kilometres, per hour), but with the difficult terrain that he was travelling through, one could only guess at his accuracy over such a long distance.

Before departing Adelaide, I had contacted Dr Luise Hercus of the Australian National University, who had been on the failed Government expedition in 1975. I was informed that a Mick McLean, one of the last survivors of the desert Wangkangurru people, had accompanied them in their search. Dr Hercus had a detailed picture of the culture and mythology of the desert dwellers gained over a period of some twenty years from Mick, his sister Topsy McLean and part-cousin Maudie Naylon.

Even though they had departed the desert at an early age, they still had an immense store of knowledge, and gave Dr Hercus significant information on the well sites, the songs, and how life was conducted on a day-to-day basis. Dr Hercus had everything but the well sites, and if I could locate these and ultimately arrange for an archaeological study, then the picture of Aboriginal occupation in the southern Simpson would be complete. I also learnt from her that the last of the Wangkangurru people had departed the desert in 1899/1900, so with 80 years of erosion and sand drift, there wasn't going to be much evidence left, if any, of where they dug for water.

Oodnadatta was our last fuel stop before Birdsville, some 1200 km away, and then Richard and I headed northwards for Dalhousie, which now stands as an imposing but crumbling station ruin surrounded by lush green date palms. This was once a watering place for the Afghan camel drivers and their large teams of animals as they made their way north with long-awaited supplies for a growing outback population. It was also a breeding ground for superb horses destined for the Indian Army.

The Dalhousie/Spring Creek area is surrounded by hundreds of square kilometres of arid country. In this oasis, many forms of life live untroubled by the frequent droughts which can last for years. These permanent spring-fed pools vary from cold to hot and teem with life — gobies, catfish, spangled grunters — all swimming in tea-tree shaded overflows lined with reeds.

With the thermometer reading 110ºF in the shade, David Lindsay departed Dalhousie on 4 January 1886 to begin his desert crossing. With him were Mr C Bagot and an Aboriginal named Paddy, from the Murraburt area. They had with them three weeks' provisions and carried enough containers to hold fifteen gallons of water on their riding camels.

Richard and I spent some time exploring the numerous springs that make up the fascinating Dalhousie area and enjoying a welcome swim in a reed-fringed pool before departing to rejoin Lindsay at his first campsite at Oolarinna waterhole.

The drive down the mighty floodout of the Spring Creek Delta is always impressive, and this time it afforded us fast travel over its relatively smooth, flat surface. This type of soil, however, can easily become impassable once it rains. A big mob of horses converged with our route, paralleled us for a while at full gallop, then cut across our course and disappeared northwards, trailing a plume of dust and leaving us with an unforgettable image of power and grace. Near the floodout's termination the open plain is dotted with trees and massed in lignum, which is really a tall woody grass. Here we spotted several camels, a large mob of donkeys and an inquisitive plains turkey.

We finally arrived and made camp at Oolarinna waterhole, which is curved around a sand-covered point of a rocky headland. From the top of the headland the view to the east is of lines of rolling dunes unmarked by any protruding feature.

Lindsay's path now lay past the nearby cone of Old Man Hill, and on to Etilkertinna waterhole, some 12 miles (20 km) distant. When he arrived, he found it to be dry and covered by some 4 feet of sand drift. Lindsay now took up a bearing of 122 degrees and was immediately swallowed up by the desert. For the next 59 miles to the native well, Murraburt, Lindsay altered course some seventeen times. He was being guided by Paddy, who had grown up at Murraburt and knew the area like the back of his hand.

The numerous changes to direction probably came about every time Paddy recognised, from the top of a ridge, a clump of bushes or the features of a dune formation, and altered his course accordingly. Lindsay recorded every stop, the time travelled, the time lost, and every new heading. By using 3 mph, the estimated walking speed of his camels, he calculated the distance travelled. When they finally arrived at the well, they were disappointed, as they had expected to find a large supply of water.

Lindsay writes in his journal: 'The well is first twelve feet deep perpendicular, and then eight feet slope, so small at the entrance that I had to take off my clothes before I was able to go to the water'.

Even though the water was very dirty, they didn't miss the opportunity to fill up their water containers and give their camels a bucketful each. Six more changes to direction, and some 14 miles later, they finally arrived at the next well site, called Beelpa. Here they found that the well had fallen in, and had to remove about 3 feet of earth before they could reach the limited supply of fresh water. The well was 8 feet deep.

It was at Beelpa that I hoped to rejoin Lindsay's track once again. The reason that I had chosen this well as the first to search for was simply because I had a few more clues from Lindsay's journal as to its surrounds than I had for Murraburt. Every time Lindsay had altered course, if his estimated distance travelled was incorrect or varied, each error would compound significantly on the other. Over seventeen compass shots, I didn't fancy my chances. I didn't as yet know Lindsay's worth. I had to give myself the best chance possible, and if I could locate Beelpa, I would return and run the shorter back bearing to Murraburt at another time. After all, I really didn't know what I was looking for, and even if I was fortunate to stumble on top of a well, would it still be recognisable as such after all this time? I was absolutely certain that any holes dug by the Aboriginals would be now well and truly filled up and covered over by the sand.

I intended to use a series of connecting tracks to take me well into the desert and position me as close as possible to Beelpa. The tracks I would follow were cut by the oil exploration companies, and allowed quick access into the desert. Very few of them are maintained, and a lot that were cut have since faded almost beyond recognition. Most are dead ends.

From our camp at Oolarinna waterhole, I detoured to show Richard an Aboriginal rock placement site on the top of a small hill. Rock placements are arrangements of rocks to form a pattern or series of patterns on the ground. This ceremonial area was quite extensive and intricate in design. I explained to Richard as best I could its significance to the Aboriginals who once lived in this area and he was intrigued. The site was perched on the leading edge of a line of stark, incredibly beautiful, disjointed hills with ridges and flat tops running north and south. They stood in my mind like a protective barrier repelling the rolling thrust of the sand invader coming in from the east.

As Richard wandered, immersed in thought, along pathways that had carried the feet of past beings over thousands of years on their journeys through life, I sat on a large upturned rock, which possibly represented someone's birth stone. I tried to let my feelings become one with the shadowy figures my mind had created to perform their ritual in front of me. With the mighty Simpson Desert hung like a backdrop to their ceremonial stage, it didn't take much imagination to understand how this setting could generate deep spiritual feelings.

Next we recrossed the Spring Creek floodout, finally arriving at the very first sandhill of the Simpson Desert. We made a quick stop – not because it is impressive, mind you, it is only a few metres high. It's a bit of a ritual I have: sort of like saying 'Okay desert, I'm back again. Now let's not get carried away and make things too difficult — agreed?'

That night we camped at Purni Bore, the last permanent water supply before Birdsville, and enjoyed a bath in the reed-encircled hot water pool. Richard had started wheezing badly, which I thought must have been due to dust or pollen. The hot water seemed to ease his symptoms, although he remained very restless throughout the night.

Purni bore was put down by the French Petroleum Company in 1963. They were looking for oil, but instead got lots of water, which flowed at about 2.5 million litres per day with a temperature in excess of 80 degrees centigrade at the bore head. Despite the warning sign clearly displayed, I know of two people who had burnt themselves badly walking on the crust near the outlet. One was air-lifted out and the other wore his socks, which were stuck to his skin, all the way across the desert to Birdsville!

This free-flowing bore had created a wetland habitat for a variety of plants, birds, and animals. Other than the lack of firewood, it was a great spot to camp and spend time in observation, particularly early morning when the birds wheeled in just above dune height for their first drink of the day. We enjoyed it, but didn't linger; we topped up our water containers and were away early. For the next few hours we would have comfortable driving following a series of tracks to the east.

It would be easy to call the desert tamed, as you trundle across it in your four-wheel drive with the mechanical arrogance of our age, secure in the knowledge of good preparation, excellent maps, radio and a thousand comforts. But it can bite.

The parallel sand ridges of the Simpson Desert run in almost unbroken lines, forking as they thrust southwards. On the western edge of the desert, the dunes are closer together, smaller, and have a liberal sprinkling of wattles, grevilleas and other stunted growth. Eastward, the interdunal flats are wider and the dunes can grow to massive proportions. Spinifex, the curse of all early explorers, abounds, with cane grass high up on the ridges holding the dunes together. In the south-east portion, associated with the great salt lakes, are the large grass plains where Aboriginal people used to collect seeds. These are dotted with occasional dense stands of gidgee and corkwood. The Todd, Hale, Illogwa, Plenty and Hay Rivers to the north – normally dry, but sometimes raging torrents – slash into the desert, fighting their way southwards to finally die in the sands.

To the south is Lake Eyre, a vast, usually dry salt lake, remnant of a wetter period of Australia's geological history. Periodically though, the big rivers rage — the Cooper, Diamantina, Eyre Creek, Macumba, and the Neals – and they fill this basin, which becomes a haven for birds who flock here in their thousands to breed.

The average rainfall is 100 mm and the temperature can range from freezing at night to a mind-bending high during the day that saps the body of strength and drains it of fluids in a matter of hours. In a big wet it is a garden land bursting with energy, the time-locked seeds madly racing to grow, mature and propagate. Rabbits will again intrude and multiply on the rich abundance of feed, only to fade to near extinction when the vegetation dies.

Finally, Richard and I swung down a long interdunal corridor where

I hoped to intersect Lindsay's track on the last stages of his journey into Beelpa. I had wanted to get myself on course this day, but the fading light beat me and we were forced to make camp.

Firewood was scarce again, and the night was chilled by a southern wind. We soon had company: several dingoes patrolled the perimeter of our campsite, and the biggest spider that I had ever seen wandered in for a look. I took Richard for a walk along the dune top to watch the night life – an astonishing range of creatures all busily engaged in their pursuit of survival – and the torchlight soon picked up a beautiful little gecko. We didn't stay out long, however, as Richard's attack of asthma, allergy or whatever, which had persisted throughout the day, now increased in intensity, perhaps due to the cold night air. Listening to his laboured breathing I was becoming concerned. This was not a good experience to be having in the middle of the Simpson Desert.

Before we left Adelaide, his mother, who had enthusiastically encouraged this trip, said to me: 'Just make sure you take good care of our son and don't let him get into any trouble or lose him! You haven't spent a lot of time with Richard over the years, so this is a good opportunity to make up and do a bit of quality bonding. It will also do you the world of good.' Hell, I wished Rotha was here to take over as always when any of us were sick. This bonding is scary stuff when you feel so under-qualified.

Richard finally dozed off and I sat around the fire for a while pondering our chances of finding any sign of the native wells David Lindsay had used. I had done the best I could in the interpretation of his journal. I was extremely confident in my bush experience, but realistically, it was such a long time ago. What could possibly have survived some 80 years in the shifting desert sands?

The dingoes moved to the furthest reach of the fire's glow and then settled down to watch and wait. Once I went to bed they would come in and silently pad through our campsite looking for food scraps or just a chewable smelly boot. These wild dogs will come incredibly close to your face – only inches away – while you sleep in your swag. If some travellers realised this they would be terrified. I know, for out of habit I always check my campsite in the morning for night tracks in the sand; I am often amazed at their nerve.

At dawn, while Richard broke camp, I walked to the top of a high sandhill, and from my vantage point I soon had what I considered to be an accurate fix on my position. I was sure we had come too far south. We finished our packing and then I drove a short distance to enable me to position the vehicle on the dotted line that I had marked on my map. Lindsay's visual description of the area seemed to fit.

David Lindsay recorded in his journal:

> This well is in a depression with limestone and acacia bushes — very salty looking country — eight feet deep — the sand had fallen in and after taking out three feet of earth came to fresh water, but the salt water was running in too fast for us to cope with so after lunch, we went on towards Balcoora which our boy assured us was a good well — good country — no spinifex — good flats — fine bushes — low ridges.

I ran Lindsay's compass bearing of 120 degrees for 1.6 km, which brought us to the southern end of several small sand dunes, around which were clearly visible the signs of past Aboriginal habitation, mainly in the form of stone chips. After a short run of 0.6 km on 140 degrees, I then stopped the vehicle. This should be it.

About forty metres away was a small depression, and on close inspection, I noticed that the ground in the middle had subsided slightly. It was the sort of feature that one would normally drive on past without a second glance, but I was looking for something unusual, and it seemed to fit the bill. With what little I had to go on, plus my own observations, I was fairly confident that we had located the native well, Beelpa. Just in case, we searched on foot an extremely large area in a circle around our position, but nothing else even remotely resembling a well site was found.

Richard and I departed Beelpa and with the salt pan, Norpa, bearing to the south we headed cross-country towards the next native well, Balcoora. From now on I would be trying to stick religiously to the course followed by David Lindsay. We hadn't travelled far before I decided I'd have an early lunch and take a break as Richard, who had helped enthusiastically during our search, was now wheezing badly.

'Are you alright, son?' I asked, although I knew what he would say.

'I'm fine Dad. Don't worry about me. I'll be okay,' he gasped.

Richard was one of those great kids that any father would be proud to have as a son. He was never one to complain, but listening to him,

I knew he was far from okay. My dilemma was what to do about it. I estimated that we could finish our search and reach Birdsville in about four to five days. Should I push on, or get out now and perhaps never come back? I made the decision to wait one more day, then, if there was no improvement in Richard's breathing, I would make a hasty exit. Birdsville was less than one day away if I put my foot to the floor.

Now I didn't know anything about asthma, if that's what it was, but I thought I could remember Rotha saying something about how attacks could be triggered by emotional issues or stress, particularly in adolescents, and this got me thinking. Looking back over the past few days, some of Richard's questions now led me to think that he might be concerned about our whereabouts and safety, particularly now, when we were only just into the first major cross-country stage of our journey.

'Dad, you know where we are, don't you? We won't get lost, will we?'

The way ahead was represented only by a thin pencil line on my map marking our intended route over a sea of parallel sand dunes, which must have appeared never-ending to Richard. I tried to put myself in his shoes and came to the conclusion that my worst fear would be if my father died. How would I cope out in the middle of nowhere by myself? I figured it would be pretty frightening so I decided to start immediately with some training that might boost his confidence.

'Okay son, I could do with your help, mate, so I think the time has come to teach you how to navigate and communicate.'

I pulled out the maps and showed him the dot that represented the previous night's campsite. I then worked out its position in latitude and longitude and wrote that down beside it. This, along with tripping the mileage to zero, would be my job every night and would represent Richard's starting point for the next day. His job from now on was to be in charge of the maps, which were all marked with the route we intended following to each native well, and also the distances between Lindsay's numerous turning points. The compass bearings that we would use on each leg were also highlighted. Each time we reached a turning point, Richard was to note the time on the map, the distance travelled and then advise me the bearing to take and how far to the next point.

My next move was to get Richard to master the HF radio. He unpacked the transceiver, set up the aerial, lifted the vehicle's bonnet and coupled the power leads to the spare battery. Then he switched on the set and tuned it to the Alice Springs Flying Doctor Service from the series of instructions I compiled.

After writing down the position of last night's camp and listing in order all our changes of direction and distance travelled so far for the day, he made his first pretend call.

'VJD Alice Springs, this is Five Sierra Bravo X-Ray. Do you copy?'

I took over the Flying Doctor role: 'Five Sierra Bravo X-Ray, this is VJD. Go ahead'.

Richard responded, 'This is Five Sierra Bravo X-Ray. My name is Richard Bartell and I'm out in the middle of the Simpson Desert. I am 12 years old. My father is very sick and I need help.'

Richard then relayed all the information he had written down, which would be more than sufficient for an aircraft to easily locate our vehicle. He finally wheezed his way through the whole exercise and after another practice run, I gave him one hundred per cent.

We spent the rest of the day traversing magnificent plains, which were used by the Aborigines long ago for the collection of seed, and climbing moderately high sand hills. Occasionally we caught glimpses of the large white salt lakes which abound to the south of this area.

At the completion of Lindsay's last bearing into Balcoora, we could find nothing in the near vicinity. Lindsay wrote: 'The well is 20 ft deep and sloping — some large native mia-mias are here — after leaving Balcoora we met a tree which grows about 10/12 ft high — nine inches in diameter with a very rough thick cork-like bark'. Lindsay filled their water containers, and gave the camels three gallons each.

I re-checked my maps, and also Lindsay's bearings to make sure that I hadn't made a mistake. Everything seemed in order, and it wasn't until I re-read his journal that I could see the possibility for an error on Lindsay's part. He had met five of the local natives who then travelled with them. They said that the water was only a little way away and I think that, believing that they were nearly there, Lindsay may have become slightly sloppy in his recordings. Either that or I was off course.

Lindsay didn't make it that night, and he had one further correction to course before they arrived early the following morning. I drew a large square on my map, and then proceeded meticulously to comb the area. Several hours later, I considered that I had finally located Balcoora. Signs of Aboriginal habitation lay scattered around, and nearby, the corkwood trees mentioned by Lindsay were evident, one of which I blazed as a future marker.

Continuing from Balcoora, I detoured slightly to show Richard a large eagle's nest, when I spotted two ears outlined above its rim: it was a large feral cat, which I dispatched forthwith. This day we also saw a large mob of camels – a magnificent sight as they plodded in single file along the top of a dune.

Lindsay wrote:

> 'The well, Beelaka, is 10 chains south of a clump of dark corkwood trees which are visible for miles'. From my vantage point on the high dune, I glimpsed a dark clump of corkwood in the distance, and on running his last compass shot for 3 kilometres, I arrived right on target. There was now, with the experience I had so far gained, no doubt in my mind that I had located Beelaka native well and the birthplace of Mick McLean, the last survivor of the Wangkangurru tribe. For added confirmation, many skeletons lay exposed on the shifting sands of a nearby dune.

Again, as a future marker, I blazed a nearby corkwood tree. I hadn't thought of carrying steel pegs and tags to mark any sites found, however, this was a more unobtrusive, natural, and environmentally friendly way. At that time I didn't visualize the extensive involvement I would ultimately have with the Simpson Desert, and thinking that I might never return, my marked trees would ultimately act as confirmation if I ever tried to direct others to the sites I had located.

From a particular, unmistakable feature that had been given to me by a member of the 1975 Government Expedition, I now knew that they had also camped near here during their search, without knowing how close they were. Mick McLean was no more than 800 metres from his birthplace, but had said nothing to them. Although he was sick and had failing eyesight, I have a strange feeling that he knew precisely where he was. Irrespective, Mick had indeed returned, knowingly or unknowingly, for one last look at his birthplace, and had reconnected with his desert spirit. Beelaka was a major habitation site with a good supply of water, which Lindsay records as 12 ft deep, and after they had cleaned it out, they took 27 gallons.

We had expended a lot of physical effort walking around this site, and by the time we had finished, I noticed Richard's breathing was almost as measured and normal as mine. There was very little sign of wheezing so it was with confidence now, and tremendous relief, that I headed for Wolporican, and hopefully my first real link with Lindsay, who had written:

> The well is under a sandhill on west side of
> the plain, and there are some prickly cork trees
> near, on one of which, 10 chains west of the
> well, I cut my initials DL and nailed up a tin
> plate on which is stamped D. Lindsay 1886.

We found the site easily enough, and while I searched around the well area, I sent Richard off to the west to look for the tree. I located a bit of rusted metal from some type of container, but I couldn't say if it belonged to David Lindsay. It could easily have been traded into the area by the Aboriginals. Anyhow, there was no way of knowing for sure. While I was examining this, Richard's excited yelling left me in no doubt of his success.

'Dad, Dad! I've got it! I've found Lindsay's marked tree. Come quickly!'

I hurried over to him. There it was, just as Lindsay described, a big old corkwood with the blaze standing out quite clearly. Not only was I excited about finding this direct link to Lindsay, but it confirmed beyond all doubt that the other sites we'd visited so far were genuine. I ran my metal detector over the surface of the tree and it indicated the presence of metal just above the top of the blaze. The tin plate nailed up by Lindsay had disappeared, but the rust from the nail was evidently still embedded in the wood. I had no need to blaze a tree at this site: we had Lindsay's blaze!

Reaching my next target, Boolaburtinna, was very slow. On course, I passed Lake Warrabulla, and then the area where Lindsay records, 'The blacks came down from the north, and here slaughtered a great number of the local natives. This was a long time ago'. Reaching Boolaburtinna, once 17 feet deep, it showed the usual signs of past Aboriginal occupation, and after photographing, recording and then marking a tree, Richard and I continued to Perlanna, where I was able to confirm by compass its exact location.

Lindsay's journal reads:

> Perlanna Red Point sandhill west side of plain
> bears 305 degrees about one mile. White Point
> sandhill east side 345 degrees. Well 22 ft deep.
> The cleanest cut well we have seen; splendid water.
> Marked a gidgee tree and nailed up a tin plate.

A search of the area soon produced a fine old gidgee blazed 'DL'. The tin plate was again missing, but this time, there was no evidence of nails remaining in the trunk.

Around the area, there were numerous signs of past Aboriginal occupation, and we found the structures of several *mia-mias* (shelters) still standing. Just to the north, on a blown-out area, lay scattered many artifacts, including a greenstone axe head, stone chips, shell pieces and animal and human bones. Lindsay's journal only mentions blazing two trees, and I found myself persistently dwelling on the reason why – probably through disappointment that there were no more to search for. I had been enjoying the chase.

While standing next to his tree I wondered if perhaps he had lost his chisel, or the Aborigines had nicked it. For the rest of the afternoon these questions rattled around in my brain, almost as though they were begging an answer. But how could there be one?

Perlanna was a major Aboriginal site set in a broad valley massed with gidgee. That night the sky was overcast, and the gidgee, which emits a strong, distinctive odour whenever rain threatens, performed to perfection. We had a great camp in this beautiful spot, and thankfully Richard showed no sign of distress. His breathing was even and he was thoroughly enjoying the adventure.

In the midst of some very rough country lies Kilpatha, the last of the native wells visited by Lindsay. Augustus Poeppel and Larry Wells had also taken water from this site when, in 1884, they had surveyed the western boundary of Queensland north of Poeppel Corner. Kilpatha, along with Yelkerrie and Mudloo wells, had provided much-needed water for camels and men as they pushed northwards through the desert, marking the Queensland–Northern Territory border with mile pegs. I was disappointed to find that it had been found and opened up with a bulldozer by an oil exploration company, destroying it.

When Lindsay reached Kilpatha in 1886, he was met by some forty natives who were rather astonished to see him coming in from the west. He records the well as 'twenty feet deep with a good supply and numerous mia-mias'.

Lindsay had then intended travelling on to Yelkerrie native well on the other side of the Queensland border. Yelkerrie is named after a plant which grows in the interdunal flats, the bulbs of which were harvested, roasted and then eaten by the Aboriginals. Lindsay's interest in the area, though, was that he believed there were white men there. When he was informed that this was not the case, he continued only to the Province boundary which he states is 'well pegged and very clearly defined'. Lindsay then turned, and more or less retraced his steps back to Dalhousie, but it wasn't a pleasant journey. Mr Bagot had taken ill, and by the time they reached the Finke River, they only had half a gallon of water left between them, and had not eaten for some three days. When they arrived at Etilkertinna waterhole only a few miles away, they obtained a good drink and were glad to eat some of the cooked rats that were offered by the natives camped there.

Now that I knew Lindsay's worth, I would have been happy to have had him as a companion on any desert journey.

After one final, abortive attempt to again penetrate the Simpson Desert, Lindsay went northwards, ultimately reaching the Gulf of Carpentaria near Borroloola and completing some 6500 km of exploration. Had Lindsay continued from the Queensland border for about three more days, he would have become the first white man to cross the Simpson Desert, some fifty years before Ted Colson. I think he felt, however, that the land east of the border was known country, having been crossed by Poeppel and Wells, and therefore didn't consider it worthwhile to proceed any further.

Richard and I left Kilpatha and worked our way down to Poeppel Corner. From there we turned eastward along the old French Track, and when it terminated, we continued along an ill-defined two-wheel track to reach the Eyre Creek and finally Birdsville. It was the end of a most rewarding desert crossing, and would certainly leave Richard and me with many memories. We had relocated, some 80 years after they had been abandoned, a total of six Aboriginal well sites, or *mikiri*, and had found and photographed the two trees that had been blazed by Lindsay in 1886.

Before I set off east of Birdsville to search the sandhills near Wantata waterhole for any sign of the lost explorer, Ludwig Leichhardt (1847), I managed to organise a flight to Adelaide for Richard. Trust him: as they taxied past, there was my best mate, as perky as can be, sitting up front in the co-pilot's seat. With Richard now back to full form I knew that the pilot was in for an interesting time. I felt sure that by journey's end he would know more about the Simpson Desert than he would have ever thought possible. He would also have been asked to explain every item in the cockpit and it wouldn't have surprised me if Richard got involved in the navigation. Richard's departure was an emotional moment for me. We sure as hell had bonded and I was thrilled to hear later that he had told his mother, 'I got to know my dad'.

When I finally returned to Adelaide, I contacted the National Parks with a view to seeing how the sites and trees could be best protected, and to try to work out if we could arrange for an archaeological assessment of the native wells. The lady to whom I was directed was quite happy to take all my notes and maps, thank you very much, but I had a sneaking feeling that if I handed them over, that would be the last I'd hear of it, and certainly the last of my involvement. While I was deliberating, she asked me if I could point out on the map which lay open on the desk, the site of Lindsay's tree at Wolporican. I drew a circle on the map with my finger which probably covered an area of some ten kilometres in diameter, to which she responded 'Oh well, that will be easy to find'.

I thought, 'You don't really have any idea what you are talking about, and if it is that easy, then you can go out and find it yourself'. With that, I picked up my papers and walked out without another word.

🦎 🦎 🦎

The following year, 1981, I decided to cross the desert once more while on my way to the Kimberley region to go gold fossicking. First I revisited Perlanna, where once again, standing next to Lindsay's tree, I felt a strong curiosity about his chisel, and found myself repeating the questions that I had asked before: had he lost his chisel, or had the Aborigines nicked it? It became like a monotonous chant that was hard to get out of my mind.

I had really only come back to the desert to re-photograph Lindsay's other blazed tree at Wolporican, because the photo that I had previously taken was of such poor quality. When I arrived at the site, I drove straight to where I remembered the tree to be, but it had disappeared. Some limbs and part of a tree trunk protruding out of the sand caught my attention, and when I dug the sand away I could feel the blaze underneath. We had nearly lost this connection with Lindsay.

I immediately contacted National Parks by radio to see if they would like the tree removed so that it could be preserved as part of history, and ended up wasting a full day while I waited for their reply. They considered that relics should remain on site. I cut the limbs off, dragged the heavy trunk to a nearby corkwood tree which I then blazed as a marker, cleared the area of all rubbish and tied a message to Lindsay's tree stating its importance. Its life now was limited to say the least – rot or fire would see to that. Great thinking National Parks! I renamed the site Stupidity Well!

When I reached Beelaka native well, I used some aluminium drilling rods specially acquired for this occasion to drill a hole where I thought the well site would have been. At just over 3.5 m, or 12 ft – in line with Lindsay's records – I struck water, and drew up a small quantity to sample using a bailer on a string. It was all rather exciting. In my opinion, based on the material extracted, the water probably lies on a depression of impermeable clay, which, over thousands of years, has been covered by sand. If I am correct, then the supply, while adequate for the needs of a small group of people on an indefinite basis, would soon be exhausted by modern pumping methods.

After another great desert trip, I arrived in Alice Springs, where I phoned Miss Ruth Lindsay, one of David Lindsay's descendents, and told her what had happened regarding the tree that he had blazed and how I had had to leave it in the desert to rot.

Some months later, now with a pocket full of gold, I arrived back in Alice Springs to find a letter from the Director General, Department of Environment and Planning, waiting for me. It read, in part:

> 'I wish to advise that approval has been given for you to remove David Lindsay's tree from the Simpson Desert and bring it to Adelaide. This approval is subject to your placing the tree in a Museum which meets the approval of the History Trust of South Australia, and that no Government funding will be made available for the venture. I have provided Miss R. Lindsay with a copy of this letter'.

Rather interesting, as I had never asked for financial help from anyone.

When I rang Adelaide, my wife told me that Ruth Lindsay had apparently driven everyone mad, from the State Premier down, with her persistent requests to save the tree. I understand that it was with the help of the Ombudsman that she finally won the day. Knowing Ruth, I don't think that I would have wanted to be in her line of fire once she got her dander up. She was a real terror. This was rapidly becoming a very expensive lump of wood. I drove home via the Simpson Desert, collecting Lindsay's tree on the way, and delivered it to the Art Gallery of South Australia, where it was to be fumigated and then stored for the History Trust.

I had previously advised Dr Hercus of my success in locating six of the well sites, and that I considered I could find a further two without much trouble. Dr Hercus urgently wanted to visit the native wells to enable her to round off her extensive study of the Wangkangurru people, and was excited at the prospect of visiting them if I could arrange it.

For myself, I wanted to see the sites assessed by an archaeologist before others, particularly four-wheel drive clubs or tourist groups, found them and destroyed or removed anything from these pristine locations. Having located them, I now felt a sense of responsibility to the desert's past inhabitants to see that the story of their life was fully told.

I could finance myself and supply my own vehicle, but I really needed a fuel sponsor and several more four-wheel drives to carry personnel. It didn't take me very long to organise. With the inducement of an exclusive story (native well site locations to be suitably disguised), I found a magazine willing to supply two vehicles and fuel. Dr Hercus arranged for an archaeologist to accompany us, and in May 1983 I found myself once again back in the Simpson Desert.

We visited all the sites and I drilled and obtained water from several. With the knowledge that I had acquired previously, it was relatively easy for me to locate for the expedition the two extra wells that had also been used by Lindsay: Murraburt and Pudlowinna. This made a total of eight sites, not including Kilpatha, which as previously stated, had already been found and destroyed by an oil company.

When we arrived at Perlanna native well, we all parked next to the gidgee tree that Lindsay had blazed. I remarked to the group that it didn't look as healthy to me as it did when I had first located it some three years earlier. While staring at this monument to the past, I was suddenly overwhelmed by a feeling of intense sadness. It was like it was saying to me, 'Denis, I am very old and I have waited a long time for you to arrive. Now that you've found me, it is time for me to move on. My job is done'. This damned tree seems to affect me every time I come near it.

I sent the team off to explore an extensive wind-eroded section to the north which was full of numerous artifacts, including exposed bone fragments, human and otherwise. I knew there was enough material there to keep them busy for some time and as always, I eagerly awaited their expert interpretation and summary to add to my expanding knowledge of Aboriginal desert inhabitation.

No sooner had they departed than the familiar, monotonous internal sing-song popped into my head once more: had he (Lindsay) lost his chisel, or had the Aborigines nicked it? My brain kept repeating it over and over like a stuck record. It was more forceful than at any other time.

For something to do, I unpacked my metal detector, deciding that I could fill in time while they were away, and in any case I needed a bit of practice for my next gold fossicking venture. With my head down, I took off walking more or less in a straight line without any pre-conceived point of direction, swinging and tuning my detector as I went. At about 100 paces, I looked up, and slightly to the left of my line of travel, I spotted some sticks poking out of the ground, which appeared to be the remnants of an Aboriginal *mia-mia* or *wiltja* (shelter).

I altered course and headed in that direction and, just as I thought, it was the framework of an old wiltja that had stood uninhabited for some 80 years. Just in front of the wiltja my detector indicated metal. I scraped the sand away with my boot, and uncovered charcoal, the remains of a fire. Passing the detector head over the charcoal, it again indicated metal, but this time my boot rolled an elongated object out of the ashes. To my utter amazement, it was a rusty old chisel.

Of all the places in the desert that I could have played with my detector, and even the direction I chose to walk from my vehicle, why here at this site and near this very tree that seemed to continually prompt questions of me that one would think could never be answered?

Now I don't say for one minute that what I had found was David Lindsay's chisel, because I don't even know if he indeed lost a chisel. The one I found could easily have been traded into the area from a long way away — but why a chisel, and not some other product of white civilisation? Why the same chant in my head over many years every time

I was in this vicinity? Why me? There are many things in life that we don't understand, and to me, an incident like this encourages one to keep an open mind.

Of one thing I am sure — the last person to hold that chisel was an Aboriginal. I had located it near the very top of the ashes, and wood that had formed part of the handle had not been entirely burnt away. This chisel was thrown into the last fire ever in front of that wiltja and I would bet it occurred the day they abandoned their home and walked out of the desert never to return. That rusty old chisel now has pride of place in my home.

I had accepted the challenge handed to me and found eight of the native wells that David Lindsay had used. There was one other that he had mentioned, giving only a rough bearing as to its location, but which he never visited. Lindsay records it as Burraburrinna (*Parra-parranaha*) which means 'the long one', and it was one of the deepest wells. It was a 'men's only' site — no women allowed — and of major significance. I finally located this site in 1984 and to mark the spot, blazed a tree. This time however, I never mentioned my find and its location to anyone, deciding that this special area should rest in peace forever.

In 1986, Mr Colin Harris from the South Australian Department of Environment and Planning contacted me to see if I would be interested in leading a Government expedition over the Simpson Desert to visit all the well sites I had found. Due to mining exploration activity and the increase in tourist numbers in the desert, they wanted to see first-hand how best to protect these sites and the area in general. We had an interesting journey. One of the highlights for us all was when I drilled and located water at several of the sites. At their request, I had acquired from my farm three steel fence droppers, which they ceremoniously positioned over the actual site where David Lindsay's blazed tree at Wolporican had once stood.

When Lindsay blazed his two trees in 1886, they would already have been sizeable and of some vintage; when I found them both some 94 years later they were near the end of their lives. The corkwood at Wolporican would be dead and lying on the ground half-buried in the sand within a year. Three years later, the gidgee at Perlanna was distinctly 'off-colour' and when I visited again in the early nineties, it was leafless and, I believe, dead. I find it strange that two different types of trees that obviously enjoyed a long life decided to turn up their toes within a few years of my finding them.

Looking back on my initial journey of discovery in 1980, I feel that it was so easy for me, it was almost as though I was guided. I suppose I believe in some way that I had been chosen to unravel the mystery of the sites so that the wells, and the artifacts in their vicinity, would enable the professionals to gain a deeper understanding of the desert Aboriginal culture. I had played my part, and mythology and well sites were now unified.

***

It is not my intention to cover in detail the archaeological findings of these expeditions or the Aboriginal mythology, as Dr Hercus has adequately documented these in her many publications since then. But in summary, the Wangkangurru people moved freely through the southern Simpson Desert, their water supply guaranteed by a series of *mikiri* or native wells, which stretched almost from one side to the other. They had a diverse supply of food available, including rat-kangaroos, hare-wallabies, bilbies, mice, dingoes, snakes, lizards, birds and grass and munyeroo seed. Unlike the areas surrounding the desert where white man's intrusion drastically altered, and even wiped out, whole sections of Aboriginal life as pastoralists took over their tribal lands, here in this inhospitable wasteland of rolling dunes, the Wangkangurru were safe and secure.

They were not forcibly driven from the desert. They left in about the year 1900 of their own volition, never to return. In so doing, they abandoned forever their spiritual connections, their heritage and their homeland. Imatuwa, Mick McLean's uncle, gathered together and led the last of his people from a region that their ancestors had possibly occupied for thousands of years. Was it the lure of an easy food and water supply from the stations and missions that tempted them? We will never know. However, one thing is for sure, the Wangkangurru people were finally on the march away from a stone age civilization, just as my ancestors had done, and into a new and unfamiliar way of life that would be full of challenges.

A culture had vanished like so many others before them, but then hasn't that been the way since the dawn of time?

Chapter 6

Bushmen and Heroes

Leichhardt vanishing without a trace, Burke and Wills plodding on to a lingering death on Cooper Creek — these are our heroes. Their names will remain forever etched on Australia's roll of honour, and be taught to and admired by continuing generations of school children. Yet many successful explorers of the same era are virtually forgotten, ironically, perhaps because they lived to tell their tales. Lindsay, Barclay, Wells, Howitt, Carnegie, Forrest and Landsborough are among the many explorers who opened up the inland, but who today are only dimly remembered, if at all. They survived because of their superior leadership qualities and down-to-earth abilities, learnt the hard way. They were our bushmen. Amongst their ranks was John McKinlay, whose name surely should be close to the top of the honours list.

When word was received in Melbourne that Burke and Wills were missing on their dash from Cooper Creek to the Gulf of Carpentaria, four relief parties were organised. Frederick Walker and William Landsborough set out to cover the Queensland end, while Alfred Howitt led a group north from Melbourne. The South Australian Government also organised a search party, under McKinlay, with the subsidiary objective of exploring the country between Eyre Creek and Central Mount Stuart.

I set out, over a century later, to retrace the desert section of McKinlay's route, north of the Strzelecki Track. I was driving a Toyota BJ40, well-equipped with spares, water, fuel, food, maps — and high hopes of finding some relic of McKinlay's expedition.

McKinlay's camels were unloaded from railway trucks at Kapunda, 80 km from Adelaide, on 17 August 1861, and placed in the stables of the Sir John Franklin Hotel. On 13 May 1981, some 120 years later, I visited the hotel and found the stables still standing. McKinlay's expedition had then spent several days at the nearby homestead, Anlaby, waiting for repairs to their cart, before heading north to McBaker's station, Blanchewater, which they reached on 22 September. They checked and rechecked supplies and equipment, and at midday on 24 September 1861, the eleven-strong expedition left Blanchewater. The caravan consisted of 4 camels, 24 horses, 12 bullocks, 100 sheep, a dog and a light cart. Accompanying the expedition as far as Lake Hope were Mr Elder, Mr Giles and Mr Stuckey, the owner of Manuwalkaninna station.

Today Blanchewater has been absorbed by Murnpeowie station. The ruins of the old homestead, about 160 km up the Strzelecki Track from Lyndhurst, nestle beside a (usually dry) creek bed. Such tales the walls could tell, if only they could speak!

Several kilometres downstream I searched for and found a truly magnificent waterhole, sparkling and crystal clear. Legend has it that a stockman once drowned in a mighty flood, and his body was recovered from the fork of a tree at this waterhole. His ghost is said to prowl the shores at night and although it was near camp-up time, I decided that I had urgent business elsewhere! I departed for Murnpeowie station (controlled by the Beltana Pastoral Co), where I was made welcome by the new manager and his wife.

Next morning, I surveyed the magnificent buildings, a loft packed with ancient saddlery, and a cellar of beautifully written, leather-bound records dating back well over 100 years. In early times, around 110,000 sheep per year were put through the shearing shed. The sheep have now gone, replaced by some 8000 head of cattle – a move necessitated by the continued havoc wrought by dingoes.

From Mumpy, I travelled northward by station track for 50-odd kilometres to Doveholes dam, and then drove due north cross-country hoping to locate the ruins of Manuwalkaninna homestead, and again link up with McKinlay.

It was late afternoon before I found the remains of the old dog fence. Not without effort due to the dense regrowth, I managed to cross the creek on my left, and almost immediately located the remains of the station and outbuildings. This came as a surprise, as the station manager had told me that he believed that there were no ruins in the area. Remnants of the post-and-rail yards McKinlay used to hold his horses still remain, and I could imagine him carrying out minor repairs in the nearby blacksmith's shop before departing this last outpost.

Just to the north now lay the narrow connecting channel between Lake Gregory and Lake Blanche, and I made haste in the remaining light to see if a crossing were possible. Failure to find one would involve a detour of about 100 kilometres to bring me back on course. I located the channel, and to my disappointment, found it too sloppy to cross. I decided to try further west, but the combination of poor visibility into the setting sun and too much haste soon saw me stuck down to the floorboards. After several hours' hard work, I managed to platform my way out, and, spattered with mud, retired in disgrace to higher ground. When McKinlay had inspected this area, he had reported 'the prospect for the next few days' march to be no ways encouraging'.

With the first rays of morning light splitting the darkness, I was on the move. I had spotted what appeared to be a small sandhill to the east, running right up to the channel. I reasoned that the blowing sand might have partly filled the watercourse, reducing the amount of water and sludge to be crossed. This proved to be correct and I hit the 2 metres or so of questionable muck at a speed that left no doubt as to the outcome. Safe on the other side, I climbed a large sandhill and took a back bearing on the Manuwalkaninna ruins to locate my position.

I set forth for Point McKinlay, which is on the southern shore of Lake Hope, or Pando, 45 kilometres away on the other side of continuous sandhill country with a strike running approximately 20° west of north.

🦎 🦎 🦎

Hodgkinson, the expedition's second in command, went ahead of the main party on camels, leaving McKinlay to follow with the bullocks and cart. In his diary, Hodgkinson reports of this area:

> At 11.5 miles from 'Manuwalkaninna' a dry
> salt lake is passed lying half a mile west. The
> remaining distance affords nothing worthy of
> comment. Rolling sandhills in which one sinks
> ankle deep at every step, and denuded flats, the
> very picture of desolation, combining together to
> present a most disheartening piece of country.

Hodgkinson arrived at the lake after a wretched trip. Realising that the bullocks bringing up the rear would be unable to traverse the whole of the arid track between Manuwalkaninna and Lake Hope with the small quantity of water he was able to leave for them en route, he returned southward, taking every vessel capable of carrying water. Having deposited all the water, save a part-filled canteen for themselves, Hodgkinson and his companions began to retrace their steps back to the lake. A moment's lack of concentration, and they strayed from their tracks, becoming quite simply lost.

Hodgkinson had left his compass at the lake: the stage was set for disaster. For the rest of the day, they travelled in what they considered to be the right direction, and it was not until they had covered more kilometres than should have been necessary to reach the lake, that they began to backtrack.

The next day Hodgkinson recorded: 'The hot wind still fiercely swept around us, clouds of drifting sand gave a fiery gloomy appearance to the horizon, and a glare from the burning sands beneath us almost took away the power of vision'. By midday they were completely exhausted and unable to walk or see their outbound tracks, so they took refuge beneath a miserable parched acacia that scarcely sheltered them from the sun.

By nightfall they were barely able to stand, and in desperation bound themselves to their saddles and turned the camels loose. The animals wandered into the night, stopping only once to rest. Then, just before daylight they reached the summit of a lofty sandhill, and there, some 8 km distant, was the silvery gleam of a large body of water. The wonderful instinct of the camels had been the men's salvation. They had arrived at a large lake some 11 km to the west of Lake Hope.

McKinlay, bringing up the bullocks, had also had his share of troubles. One of his men was tossed by a bullock several times into the air, and was lucky to be alive.

🦎 🦎 🦎

If only Hodgkinson had occupied my spare seat! I would have carried him through a garden land bursting with energy. The sand was firm, and wildflowers of various types were massed as far as the eye could see, giving a kaleidoscope of colour. There were sleek dingoes, mobs of emus, and plentiful bird life, with brumbies nearer to Lake Hope. With my rifle, I dispatched a feral cat, which had been enjoying the sun in the fork of a tree. Finally, from the top of a high sand ridge, I gained my first look at Lake Hope. What a splendid sight — some 14 km long and 4 km wide, it was filled with water, and even from that distance I could see it teemed with bird life.

I descended to the lake level through a patch of large gums and broke out on to a magnificent sandy white beach. While taking a much-needed wash, I caught a flash of light at the northern end of the lake. The binoculars confirmed I was not alone. There were two vehicles, which turned out to be a party of avid bird watchers from Port Augusta and Oodnadatta. They had turned off the Birdsville track just north of Etadunna station, and followed a station track up the Cooper to Lake Appardare, then down to Lake Hope. The first question they asked was, 'How did you get here? We didn't cut any fresh tracks'. They were surprised that I had managed to penetrate the sandhill country from the south.

Formalities over, I returned to the southern side of the lake to search for signs of McKinlay. A set of eight bearings recorded by Hodgkinson enabled me to site myself within a few hundred metres of their campsite, which had been in a treed section at the southern end of a small inlet. A drawing depicts this area and shows a large blazed tree on its western edge. I couldn't find one there, however, on the eastern side a marked tree was a distinct possibility although the rotting away of the hardwood now made it impossible to tell with complete certainty. As I re-examined the drawing, I noticed it was marked 'Vincent Brooks Lith'. I suddenly realised that this meant lithograph, which produces a mirrored image of the original. Suddenly the tree is on the eastern side!

I camped for the night on the sandy beach, a cheery fire to keep me warm, and a beam of light pencilled clearly across the still water from the other camp to remind me that I wasn't alone.

Morning light revealed a mangy dingo eyeing me off from a discreet distance, and a lake alive with birds. I took time off to photograph some avocets feeding near the shore, and then shared a welcome cup of tea with the bird-watchers. They estimated there were at least 5000 pelicans in one big mob just in front of their campsite. The bird-watchers were making for Wankatanna waterhole to further their research, and so was I. It was McKinlay's second camp after leaving Lake Hope.

We travelled up the inlet from Lake Hope to its junction with the Cooper Creek. The flat was lined on either side by sand ridges. The timber was box and acacia, and there was a good sprinkling of Old Man Saltbush. As we approached Lake Appardare — McKinlay's Lake Camel — samphire flats and dead box became predominant. This would be a messy area for vehicles if it rained. Finally the track entered the sandhills to the west of Winthekarrina waterhole, then gradually arced around to Wankatanna. We soon cast lines into this magnificent, tree-lined waterhole, and in no time the flapping on the bank indicated that the main course tonight would be fresh yellowbelly.

Next morning I took my leave, departing on compass for Lake Perigundi, some 40 km distant. At first I negotiated the sandhills with ease, then gradually the going deteriorated due to water erosion and rabbit holes; the many samphire flats lent an air of desolation to the area. From occasional high sandhills, I caught glimpses of the densely timbered Cooper Creek away to the east. A set of bearings, recorded by Hodgkinson, enabled me to position myself in the area of their camp, but again I found nothing positive to indicate their passing. McKinlay called this campsite Siva Lake after his camel, which became bogged there. He also mentioned that several hundred Aborigines were leading an apparently 'well pleased existence by the aid of its fish and countless fowl, and their many humpies or wiltjas were constructed by arched sticks coated with clay'.

I pushed on to McKinlay's main base camp at Lake Coogiecooginna (Lake Buchanan in McKinlay's day), passing his campsite at Cooroomunchena waterhole on the way. The going became very difficult in part. I had to cross flats covered with dense lignum taller than the vehicle, and my speed was reduced to a crawl as I bumped my way over flats covered with deep depressions and wide cracks. These are formed as the earth dries out, and you could easily have poked a stick a metre long down into some of the crevices. I call them crabhole flats.

In the fading light I nearly lost my vehicle down a wash-away on the top of a sand dune, and was lucky to arrive at Lake Buchanan in one piece. This was a long narrow dry lake, but it had been full of water when McKinlay arrived. It was here, at the southern end, that he made a base camp, while he made a run to Lake Mundooroounie (Hodgkinson's Lake Kadni Bieri) to confirm reports by the Aborigines of the massacre of white men and a camel in that vicinity. I located a tree possibly blazed by McKinlay and marked a nearby one for future reference. From the northern end of Lake Coogiecooginna, I set a course for the middle of

Lake McKinlay. Cooyeeninna waterhole was full.

I had arranged a radio schedule with Mike Steel of the Innamincka Trading Post, and at the appointed time he came on loud and clear. We were endeavouring to arrange a meeting on the western side of Tirrawarra Swamp, then to visit Lake Mundooroounie together. We agreed that he would remain on standby at Innamincka until I reached Lake McKinlay, at which time I would have a clear idea if I could make it to our meeting place before dark.

Cooper Creek presented no problems: I found a crossing place only a few hundred metres off course. I reached Lake McKinlay at 2 pm and radioed Mike that I believed I could make Tirrawarra Swamp before dark. From the southern end of Lake McKinlay, I ran direct to Lake Moolionburrinna, a nearly circular lake about 2 km in diameter, and on the way disturbed a big mob of brumbies, which gave me an exciting run for several kilometres. From Lake Moolionburrinna I set a course for the western edge of Lake Amagooranie. Mike confirmed that he had left Innamincka, and I was forced to reduce speed due to rough terrain. Some of the dunes are more difficult to negotiate than those in the Simpson Desert due to water erosion and rabbit holes.

Lake Amagooranie was dry, and its grassy, plain-like appearance promised fast travel. Obviously Lake MacNamara would be the same, so I set a course due east, which would take me through the centre of both lakes. I needed to make good time now, as the sun had started to set. To the south was a forest of gums, as far as the eye could see. Both lakes turned out to be the worst crabhole-riddled flats I have ever encountered, reducing my speed to a crawl. Finally I crossed Lake MacNamara in the dark, still holding my easterly course, and climbed to the top of an extremely high dune. By my reckoning, I should now be overlooking Tirrawarra Swamp.

I made radio contact with Mike, who was now waiting patiently for my arrival, stuck in a creek bed on the eastern edge of the swamp. Actually he had very little alternative, with one half of his yellow four-wheel drive F100 on dry land, and the other half unwilling to join it. No, he could not see my lights, but if I was correct in my position, I should strike a track soon after descent, which would circle around the northern end of the swamp to his enforced campsite. He was right and in no time I reached their welcome fire and received a warm greeting from Mike, his business partner Andrew Gassner, and Jack Herrin from the Moomba gas fields. We rescued his vehicle from the drink.

Departing camp early the next morning, we proceeded around the northern end of Tirrawarra Swamp, which was thickly massed with lignum. As Hodgkinson had recorded, there were many bean trees evident.

Finally we reached the dry bed of Lake Mundooroounie, which is bounded on all sides by high sandhills, except for the northern end, where its feeder creek enters. About 2.5 km from the lake, on the western side of the creek, McKinlay had found a grave containing the skeletal remains of a European. Near the bank of the creek, some 200 yards to the east, he found traces of a European camp, and nearby a quantity of horse and camel dung, which Hodgkinson states, 'Indisputably identifies the party as Burke's'. From this, and information supplied by the Aboriginals, McKinlay concluded that he had found the remains of a member of the Burke and Wills party, killed by Aboriginals. Nowadays this area is referred to as Lake Massacre.

❧ ❧ ❧

McKinlay's party had a brief skirmish with the Aboriginals of this area. Hodgkinson wrote:

> At four or a little after, a dark mass, feebly shown
> by fire sticks, was within half a mile of the camp,
> and quickly a large group of blacks led by Keri Keri
> advanced towards us. When Bulingani [McKinlay's
> Aboriginal guide], speaking to them, told them to
> keep back or they would be killed, they burst into
> frightful yells of 'White fellow, white fellow', and
> boldly ran at us. We would have been surrounded
> had not McKinlay given orders to fire, upon which
> our two rifles and doubled-barrelled gun came
> into play, and successfully forced their retreat.

McKinlay returned to his base camp at Lake Buchanan and sent a party south with the news. Several weeks later the party returned with the news that the Victorian relief party, under Howitt, had found the bodies of Burke and Wills and that King was the only survivor. King had mentioned that they had buried Charlie Grey near a small lake.

McKinlay therefore assumed that the body he had found was Grey's.

Later reports confused the issue. Herbert Kenny, a bookkeeper for Innamincka station, suggested that Charlie Grey was buried some distance north-east of Lake Massacre. He had obtained this information from an Aboriginal who remembered the incident, and concluded that the body found by McKinlay was a member of the Leichhardt party. Findings at the time discounted this theory. Burke's party was completely spent by the time it reached this area on its return journey, and I cannot see them taking another route in their dash for base camp. They would have returned by their known track, which took them near Lake Massacre. The possible site of the grave is today indicated by a steel marker post.

McKinlay visited the scene of Burke and Wills' death and found trees blazed by Howitt marking the locations of the bodies when found. McKinlay returned to his base camp and then pushed on northwards. I would rejoin his tracks at Lake Talinnie.

🦎 🦎 🦎

Mike and his party re-crossed the channel at Tirrawarra Swamp, this time without incident. As they disappeared towards Innamincka, I turned north on a good seismic track and followed it to the west side of the overflow at Coongie Lake, where I camped just past an old yard.

The seismic line terminated on the southern side of Lake Talinnie. From there, I followed a track around the lake's western shore and then turned due north for about 4 km to cross an overflow. On the other side I linked up with a track running westward, which ultimately joins up with the Birdsville track near Koonchera sandhill. Following the track westward, I arrived at Lake Karangie, now dry, which McKinlay named 'Jeannie' after a Miss Pile of Gawler, when he camped on its western edge. I could find no positive trace of his presence, just one tree as a possibility.

The shore and lake bed were littered with the shells of freshwater mussels, indicating the abundance of food available to the Aborigines who roamed these shores in McKinlay's time. Occasional midden heaps indicated their feasting areas. I retraced my steps about 10 km, then turned northward to Lake Apanburra.

McKinlay had four campsites in this area over a period of about six weeks as he explored to the east and north. Although he described his camp locations adequately, and blazed several trees, I found nothing to indicate his presence. Where the creek joins the eastern shore of Lake Apanburra, McKinlay mentioned that the natives used to pass his campsite with their nets to drag the creek and would come back 'laden with its denizens'. Lake Apanburra — McKinlay named it Lake Hodgkinson — is some 10 km long, and ringed with a beach of white sand. It was dry, and its smooth, hardened surface was a pleasure to travel over after many days of slogging it out over rough terrain. I drove around its northern end then down the western side past a very large tree standing isolated near the shoreline. I think McKinlay's last camp in this area was near this spot. I then hopped over a few dunes to Lake Strangways, and made for its northwest edge. From there I set course to cut the Birdsville track near Bobbiemoonga waterhole.

Difficulty in climbing some of the dunes made navigation a rather haphazard affair. Actually, *dune* seems an inadequate term to describe some of the sand ridges in this area. To me, viewing them shimmering in the haze, they looked more like mountains. It wasn't until I had climbed a high sandhill, and could see opening up to the northwest a vast stony plain, that I could fix my position. I took a series of compass shots of the southern extremities of the massive dunes to the north, and drew these bearings on tracing paper. Sliding this over my 1:250,000 map, I soon located my exact position.

I joined the Birdsville track just south of Geakes Hill, and took time off to visit Birdsville for some refreshment. Things had changed somewhat since my last visit to its camping ground, and I was glad to be able to sleep in. On my previous visit, a vehicle had emerged out of the gloom before the crows had uttered their first squawk of the day, and with engine running, stopped only a metre or so away from my swag, its driver waiting to collect the camping fee. Now you could pay at a respectable hour.

Using station tracks, it was an easy exercise for me to visit McKinlay's campsites on the Diamantina, south of Birdsville.

As McKinlay's party pushed up the western side of the Diamantina, they had found the remains of Burke's horse and saddle, and noticed camel dung in the area. From his camp near Lake Woowaranie, McKinlay and his party had managed to travel only 8 km for the day, due to oppressive heat. McKinlay was also suffering an acute attack of dysentery, which delayed them for several days. Out of curiosity, McKinlay weighed himself and found that he had lost 6 kg in three days, and 24 kg since leaving Adelaide. The excessive heat, and the dreadful nature of the country forced McKinlay to abandon his cart, and some supplies.

It was in this area that I came nearest to feeling at one with McKinlay and his party. As I travelled this 8 km section, I could understand why he would want to get rid of the cart; the terrain was extremely difficult.

Once recovered, McKinley then pushed on through about 2 km of box-covered and flooded land, finally breaking out on to a bare mud plain destitute of any vegetation. As I sat at the end of a sand spur 120 years later and gazed over this vast, barren, shimmering plain, a wave of admiration for those gallant men swept over me. They had reached Sturt's furthest, the country ahead having been crossed only by Burke and Wills. Then they pushed on into the unknown.

Driving from Birdsville to Betoota, the modern traveller would cut McKinlay's path several times. Approximately 15.5 km from Birdsville there is a sand ridge on the right. About 6 km along this dune is a stony hill forming part of the dune, with several trees growing on top. It was here that McKinlay blazed a tree on 23 February 1862, and I suspect that the large rotting trunk lying on the ground was the remnants of that tree.

On 24 February 1861 Hodgkinson tendered his resignation as second-in-command, following a pattern familiar to many of our early exploration parties. Hodgkinson's diary terminates with these words. 'Resigned my appointment as Second Officer and Draftsman from the impossibility of co-operating with McKinlay in the discharge of my duties.'

Further on towards Betoota, the current road crosses three concrete causeways in quick succession, and almost immediately after arrives at an old turnoff to the left, which leads to Durrie station. From there, McKinlay's Camp 10 lies next to the creek on the right. The trees with the beautiful red curly bark are called Red Mulga or Mineritchie.

Away to the north, about 20 km distant, occasional glimpses of large sandhills are visible over a vast lignum-covered plain, and where the Diamantina thrusts its way through this sand barrier lies Wantata waterhole. This I believe to be the resting place of Ludwig Leichhardt and his party, who in 1848 had departed the Darling Downs in an attempt to cross the continent.

Gordon Frederick Connell in his book, *The Mystery of Ludwig Leichhardt*, which was the result of some 8 years research, puts forward a compelling argument that Leichhardt and his party were massacred by the Aboriginals in Western Queensland at a place called Wantata. It is situated in an almost endless lignum swamp riddled with crabhole flats. The big sandhill mentioned by Connell abuts the waterhole and there are some small sandy spurs immediately to the north, where, in 1871, Sub-Inspector Gilmour found the remains of four skeletons.

Gilmour commanded the Bulloo Native Mounted Police, whose barracks were located at the present site of Thargomindah, some 500 km south-east of Wantata waterhole. He had been instructed to search for a white man who was reported to be living with the Aboriginals in the vicinity of Cooper Creek, and who may have been one of the Leichhardt party. Questioning of various tribes convinced him that a massacre of white men had occurred, and finally he was led by a native of the nearest tribe to Wantata, where he found the skeletons. The remains were sent to Melbourne and were considered to be those of white men.

McKinlay had passed through the area only nine years earlier, and Gilmour was also taken to where he had made his camp and marked a tree. McKinlay, on returning to this camp after reconnoitring the area, had recorded that he had found in a native hut, parts of a European great coat lined with red flannel and a native head ornament that he considered was made of goat hair. Had McKinlay found the first traces of Leichhardt?

Apart from this, time and the occasional mighty floods of the Diamantina have, I believe, removed all evidence of Leichhardt's last journey. Was this the place of Leichhardt's final camp? I believe so, but I doubt now that we will ever have clear proof. It is too long ago.

Tribal legends from away to the west and the south all include a tale of the massacre of seven people at a lake called Wantata. Legend also has it that 'Vinie Vinie' — their name for a white man — sits down at Wantata and 'sometimes that fella comes out and walks around with foot like emu'. One night while I was collecting wood for the fire, with the big sandhill of Wantata bathed by the soft light of the moon, a shiver ran down my spine — imagination born of desire, or had Old Emu Foot just passed by?

A few kilometres past McKinlay's Camp 10, I passed through the Wills Range and soon noticed a cone-shaped hill protruding above the sandhills on my left. McKinlay named this Elliotts Knob.

On this journey, I only followed McKinlay's tracks as far as Dippery waterhole — about 20 km west of Betoota, and then drove home to Adelaide via the Strzelecki Track.

McKinlay had carried on to finally cross the continent, but like Burke and Wills, was unable to penetrate the mangrove swamps to reach the sea. Desperately short of food, he turned eastward on a mad dash to the nearest homestead, over 1000 km away. After killing their horses and finally their last camel, Siva, for food, the party just made it back to civilization. It was almost 12 months since they had departed Adelaide.

McKinlay was back into exploration a few years later. He had made a base camp at the mouth of the Adelaide River and set out, at Government request, to seek a site for a new settlement. Torrential rains turned his journey into a nightmare, and one of his party went mad. They were locked in for weeks at a time by crocodile-infested floodwaters, and were continually on the defensive, fighting numerous battles with hostile Aboriginals. Stuck on an island in the Alligator River, with their supplies so desperately low that they now had to start killing their horses for food, McKinlay was forced to retreat.

He decided to build a raft to float down the river and into the sea in an attempt to reach his base camp. They made the framework of the raft from timber lashed together, and then, killing their remaining horses, stretched their hides over this frame to fabricate their boat. From their tents they fashioned a sail, and with some crude paddles, pushed off. The stinking hides attracted the crocodiles and when they reached the sea, it was the turn of the sharks and swordfish to harass them. Despite their boat literally rotting and falling apart beneath them, they finally made it to safety.

McKinlay then explored the area around the Daly River, reporting it suitable for settlement, before returning home to his pastoralist activities. This was his last major journey. McKinlay had crossed the continent, as had Burke and Wills, but he had lived to tell the tale. He had carried out exploration work that would rate him with the other greats of Australian exploration. He was a good bushman.

My objective on this trip had been to find some mark left by McKinlay, and while I could find most of his campsites through his descriptions, absolute proof of the trees he blazed eluded me. I had found blazed dead trees in the correct positions that he could have marked, but as the hardwood peels away over time it carries with it any identifying marks — so I can claim nothing that's conclusive. I had, however, followed a great explorer, camp by camp, and through his journals and Hodgkinson's, I was able to relive their dreams, their fears, and their hardships. I could see this country, which was largely unchanged, through dead men's eyes – and in so doing, carved on my heritage tree another notch of understanding.

I had followed a bushman and a hero.

Chapter 7

Murray River Solo Marathon

I first met Martin Reynolds in 1977, after I'd completed my vehicle journey across Australia in the little yellow Suzuki. He worked in publicity and had been engaged to do a story on my crossing. At the time, he had expressed the desire to escape city living and experience some of our great outback scenery. It was mid-1981, and as I needed some help to bring my next adventure to fruition I immediately thought of him.

'Hi Martin, it's Denis here. Just wondering if you'd be interested in a break from the office? I'm thinking of going for a little boat ride and need a helper.'

Knowing me as he did, he replied 'Nothing you do is little, Denis! So what are you up to now?'

'Well Martin, a group of West Australians boated the Murray River from the Hume Weir to Goolwa in little 10 foot tinnies carrying two people each to share the driving.'

'Yes,' he interrupted, 'so what?'

'Well, they took eight and a half days and I reckon that I could do it in about half the time, solo. Would you be interested in driving the back-up vehicle? All up it should take less than a couple of weeks from start to finish. What do you reckon mate?'

I wanted to enjoy a different kind of adventure! My mad scheme to shoot the great grey-green greasy waters of the Murray River and create a new record for the 2350 km trip needed some extra help. Although it was to be a solo trip, it wouldn't be a solo effort, and Martin was not backward in coming forward.

'You're on Den. I'll drive the 4WD vehicle and be your support crew, refueller, progress reporter and cook.'

'Thanks Martin, you're a sport. I'll keep in touch.' It would be Martin's job to follow the river as closely as possible and set up pit stops where I could grab fuel, food and encouragement.

With my farm under good management and an understanding wife keeping my back, I could devote my time totally to the venture ahead. Being the wife of an adventurer cannot always be easy! It means being both unselfish and capable of managing the family and household alone for long periods of time.

I remember meeting a young guy who came to see me to get some advice in preparation for an outback venture; he was single-minded to the point of ignoring anyone else around him, including his wife and two young daughters, whilst in the pursuit of his own dreams. He had a regular nine-to-five job and used his leave to indulge his passion for adventure. It seemed to me that his family took a back seat. Though I didn't see it at the time, when I think about it, I was probably just the same. My wife, Rotha, understood my need for exploration and adventure and capably managed our home affairs in my absence. Rightly or wrongly, she indulged me.

I spent the next few months acquiring maps, sourcing a boat and motor and planning meticulously. I was fortunate in my endeavours to meet Bob Voysey of Leyland Power Systems. He agreed to lend me two 6.5 horsepower outboards (one as a spare), and other necessary boating paraphernalia. Phil Hansen of Dolphin Boats at Berri came up with a rugged-looking flat-bottomed 10 foot (3 m) aluminium punt. It was just the sort of craft that I had visualised for the record run, although a little on the heavy side. Ben Beck of Beck Outboard Services lent his expert engineering skills in setting up the boat and motor.

I had to plan around my back problems: I didn't think that I could steer the outboard for hours on end sitting sideways in the conventional manner, so a front-mounted steering wheel was installed. I had damaged my back through sport, heavy lifting on the farm and a few tumbles from the back of a horse. One day it had given out completely, and for about six months I suffered the most incredible sciatic pain down my left leg – many times it brought tears to my eyes. Ultimately I could bear it no longer and got a laminectomy on my lower spine, which was risky, but successful. My back, however, remains a concern and I should treat it with caution, something I frequently forget.

Initial testing showed a very worthy little boat capable of just under

32 kph with a fairly full load, which was not bad considering I was using the smaller 6.5 hp Tohatsu outboard. The Western Australian teams had claimed speeds in excess of 40 kph using 7.5 hp Mercury outboards during their run, so I was behind the eight ball before I started. I would have to try even harder.

On board I would carry fuel, courtesy of BP, the spare motor, emergency rations, all-weather clothing, and a 12 volt battery to power the front-mounted spotlight. A large bean bag became the perfectly moulded seat, and also kept my weight down low to the water. This was a touch of genius. Everything came together, and when Martin arrived in Adelaide we loaded the boat, now adorned with the sponsors' logos, on to the trailer and headed for our starting point.

We followed the river upstream, establishing check points, fuel supplies and suitable access to the river in the remote areas. We confirmed that all locks would be open, as the mighty Murray was now in full flood, just as it had been when the Westralians had made their record run. This meant that there would be no waiting for locks to be opened officially, or time-wasting portage after hours. The only obstruction would be Yarrawonga Weir.

On Monday 12 October 1981, we arrived at the Hume Weir Caravan Park, a very pretty spot just downstream of the weir. This was to be our last night of comparative sanity. We would both be under intense pressure in the days ahead if we were to take the record away from the Westralians. We could expect little sleep, and I would need to navigate through the nights in a swirling, flooded waterway. We spent the evening checking, stowing and rechecking the gear. Everything had to be right. Finally we were able to relax by our glowing campfire under a full moon and allow a little time for last thoughts. I worked out that if I were to achieve my goal of a four-and-a-half-day run over the 2350 km course, then at 32 kph (questionable with a full load), I would be driving for some 16.3 hours per day. Take into account refuelling, food, any repairs, portage around the Yarawonga Weir, reduced speed and difficult navigation after dark, etc., and it was obvious that there would be very little time for play. Maybe I should consider five days?

At 8 am the next morning (the 13th) after my log book had been officially signed, I vaulted into my boat and disappeared around the bend upstream, much to Martin's astonishment. I had to touch the wall of the Hume Weir before I could begin my journey, didn't I? Then, at full planing speed, I zoomed past my one-man back-up crew, and as I headed downstream, Martin leapt into the Land Rover and set off in pursuit.

The run to Albury was narrow, winding, and in parts, tree-choked. There were also gravel beds, which occasionally chewed chunks out of my propeller. However, from Albury onward, the river was more defined, deeper, and gravel or rock ceased to be a problem. When I finally met up with Martin again at Howlong, I was rather excited. The little motor was running like a dream, the weather was only marginally imperfect, the river was like a millpond and Martin had decided that I could have Heinz baked beans for lunch.

My next stop was Yarrawonga, where we would meet at about 4.30 pm, next to the weir. We would then load the boat onto the vehicle, truck it around the weir and drop it back into the river on the other side. However, it didn't end up going quite to schedule. My only navigational error for the whole journey occurred amongst the mass of dead trees in Lake Mulwala, the man-made lake behind the Yarrawonga Weir. The main channel seemed to be going around in a giant circle and after I was positive that I had seen the same dead tree for the third time, I slowly boated to the nearest shore to seek help. Here I was met by a lovely lady with a knowing smile who had been watching my antics. She jumped into her boat and guided me into the correct channel. It was a bloody maze in there, and I saw enough dead trees to last a lifetime! The locals would recognise that I had been on the merry-go-round known as Five Ways.

I was 90 minutes late to our rendezvous point, and although we worked quickly, it wasn't until the sun was just setting that I took off from below the weir for my first segment of night travel. Sunlight slowly gave way to a full moon, which created a silver highway just as I had planned.

At about 1 am the following morning, I arrived at the little river town of Tocumwal. I shocked the driver of an interstate semi parked near the river, when I emerged from the river bank – out of nowhere – to ask if he would mind signing my log book.

'You must be bloody mad,' he said, when he found out what I was doing. But when he mentioned that he was driving his rig clear across the country to Brisbane before dawn, I wondered which of us was the sane one; he already looked spaced-out to me.

The moon was providing good light and the river banks were well defined, so I decided to press on to Echuca and forget about my planned rest period. My bow spotlight was aimed ahead to pick up floating tree trunks, and more importantly, the tell-tale pressure ripples of submerged snags.

My memories of that first night are of wildly racing flood waters. I could have sworn that I was actually travelling downhill – that I could see the river was tilted – particularly as I rocketed around the tight bends. It may have been an illusion partly brought on by tiredness and a narrowing river. Whatever … it was weird. There were severe whirlpools clearly visible on the surface, which grabbed and shook my outboard leg like a terrier would a rat. Linking it all together were the unforgettable tall gums of the Barmah State forest as they flashed by, ghostly in the glow cast by my weaving spotlight as it momentarily opened and then closed visual passages into its darkly mysterious heart. The river, which had had been steadily rising, finally overflowed its banks creating an eerie scene. The trees, instead of lining the banks of my river, were now in it with me and we were all sloshing around together as my wash dissipated somewhere in their midst. As my eyes were very sore, I pulled over and had half an hour's rest curled up in my bean bag.

The morning light showed swamp land stretching away to the left and what appeared to be a large lake, which was massed with a variety of bird life. The river was shrinking dramatically in width. Suddenly a collection of river shacks appeared on my right and I was forced to stop and drag my boat through the boughs of a huge river gum that had fallen across the river and was completely blocking my path. Finally, I swept past the entry of the Goulburn River and, 24 hours and 507 kilometres into my journey, I pulled into the Echuca ramp for a welcome break and hopefully, a hot drink. Even though I had put on all my warm clothing under my spray jacket, with my life jacket over the lot, it still wasn't enough to stop the icy wind from penetrating. I was freezing.

Nearby was the old Echuca Wharf, and tied to it was a collection of magnificent old paddle steamers and river boats. What a scene this would have been in its heyday with dozens of paddle steamers and barges, each with its own legendary river captains, jostling to load or unload their goods at the bustling port terminal.

Martin finally arrived, after having been told by one of the locals that they had seen me waiting on the ramp.

'Sorry I'm late,' he said 'I didn't expect to see you so soon. You must have travelled almost non-stop. You're sure making good time.'

'Yep, I'm going great. Martin,' I replied. 'And what's more, we are not far behind schedule, although I must admit I started to worry that you'd had an accident when you weren't here.'

As if reading my mind he unscrewed the thermos cap and poured me a steaming mug of coffee. 'Here, get this into you mate. You look a bit buggered. Do you reckon you can last the distance at this pace?'

'I don't know Martin, but one thing's for sure, we can't stand around yakking. Let's top up the fuel and I'll eat when we get to Torrumbarry Weir — perhaps a real meal?' I ventured hesitantly, not wishing to upset the cook. 'What do you reckon?'

He even gave me the options ... 'What do you think you'd fancy?' he asked, with a twinkle in his eye.

'Well, mate ... cornflakes with cold milk — must be poured down the side of course ... lashings of bacon and eggs sunny side up and big mobs of toast on the side with marmalade. Then coffee — black with one — would be great'.

'Not a problem Den. Too easy.'

However, the smile on his face suggested I might just be in for another dose of Heinz. Of course I could get lucky and have spaghetti instead of baked beans; he might even heat it up for me for a change.

I brightened up as the morning progressed, and the 80 km to the weir was comparatively easy. The outboard was buzzing away without missing a beat, and with the boat now an extension of me, I could devote time to enjoying the beauty and serenity of the Murray — and to thinking. Here I was careering down the sixth largest river system in the world in something not a lot larger than a shoe box, with no one to help me if anything went wrong. I figured that I was now about three hours behind time. The slower night travel would continue to pull me back and my four-and-a-half-day goal was starting to look a little unrealistic. I calculated that I was only getting a top speed somewhere near 29 kph with the load that I was carrying. Further down, where Martin would have more vehicle access to the river, I might be able to lighten my load and lift my speed marginally.

The owner of the Torrumbarry Weir Caravan Park proved to be typical of all river people. He just couldn't do enough to help and even lent us the key to the executive loo! And I got my bacon and eggs. Maybe Martin couldn't find the can opener.

I had a good run for the rest of the day on a deserted river and took on fuel at Barnham, with another stop planned for early in the evening. I anticipated reaching Swan Hill late that night where we had planned a stop-over for a few hours' sleep. Martin was to meet me on the river bank just downstream from the caravan park and directly opposite the rotunda in the council park.

When I hadn't arrived by 2 am, Martin panicked, thinking that maybe he was supposed to meet me at the caravan park, so he moved camp and took up a waiting position by the water's edge. He couldn't see more than a few metres as a thick fog blanketed everything. Not long after a boat without lights appeared out of the mist – me. I slowly came to rest and held a mainly one-sided conversation in which I soundly cursed Martin for not being at the correct meeting place. How I finally located him in those conditions I do not know.

I'd been hours without a light due to a flat battery, and then, when the fog set in, I had to grope my way along the edge of the river for miles, which really slowed me up. I wasn't in a good mood by the time I found Martin, and after my outburst, I thought I had probably guaranteed myself Heinz for the rest of the journey. Three hours later, we'd rolled up our swags, eaten and pushed off into the mist. Lord knows what the nearby caravaners made of the proceedings.

My next major stop, at Boundary Bend, was a little happier. I had recovered my equanimity after the two hours' sleep, Martin had topped up my battery using the Kawasaki 12 volt generator, and we were able to have a hot shower courtesy of the local BP service station and caravan park owner. But it was Thursday afternoon and we were still less than half way; there was no time to lose. Fuel and food stops at Robinvale, Euston Lock and Wemen took us through to early Friday morning. It was all just a blur. We were slipping behind, and it looked as though my dream of completing the trip in four and a half days was just that — a dream.

By the time I arrived at Mildura it was 8 am on Friday morning. I was all in, and needed a steadying hand to exit my boat. Total time 72 hours. Total sleep about 5 hours. We were over the half-way mark. Martin had arranged a hot shower and a quick breakfast for me, then we did some radio and TV interviews and got back to business.

'Take care, Martin. Drive slowly,' I said. To which he gave his usual retort: 'Take care, Denis, and drive quickly, you bastard'. The adventure was on again.

The 320 km stretch of the Murray between Mildura and Renmark is one of the most isolated sections along the river, and afforded little access for Martin's vehicle. I would see him on Lake Cullulleraine for a lunch stop and then again when I reached Renmark. If I had an accident or mechanical breakdown, the record attempt would be over, as Martin would be unable to get to me. I was averaging about 32 km per gallon, so with 13 gallons of fuel onboard, I had ample to complete this stage

I didn't encounter any problems until just after dusk, when I came across a strange phenomenon. Ahead of me, illuminated by the spotlight, I could see a huge cloud floating just above the river. It looked like some sort of weird fog and it wasn't until I entered it that I suddenly realised what it was. Midges! Millions of them! It was like being sand-blasted. I slowed down, but the little devils got in everywhere — in my mouth, up my nose, in my ears! Not only was it a most unpleasant sensation, but they tasted terrible.

The night was pitch black and the river was wide. I had to swing the boat occasionally from side to side to spotlight the river banks, which then enabled me to maintain a rough line down the middle. I could see the cliff ahead and as I prepared to swing to the right, there in front of me was another patch of white, low down. More insects I thought, but when the boat began to tremble, I yanked the throttle off. Too late! I hit the foam-covered whirlpool and bounced over three huge logs in quick succession which thumped the hell out of the boat and motor leg and threw me into the air. Fortunately there was no damage that I could see, but it was quite an experience. I realised later that I'd just navigated the notorious 'whirlpool bend'.

We had partially solved the flat battery problem by rotating the Land Rover battery with the boat battery. However, on long night runs without access to Martin and his vehicle, I would switch the light off whenever possible, making do with starlight or the glow of the moon, to conserve power.

Upon arrival at Renmark, I was met by the ABC radio journalist 'Johnny Gurr' — real name Yvonne. She had been in love with the river since the age of four, and is a confirmed river rat, with her own houseboat and riverside home. When she insisted that we stayed the rest of the night on her houseboat, I reviewed my plans for the remainder of the trip. If I kept going I would complete the trip in well under five days, but it would mean virtually no sleep for the second night running.

Alternatively, if I had four to five hours sleep, I could still make it to Goolwa by 8 am Sunday morning, which would then be exactly five days. As I didn't wish to blow it on the home stretch through extreme tiredness, I changed my goal: I would shoot for a five-day run.

We slipped out before daybreak on Saturday morning and were into it again. It was a delightful morning and the few hours' sleep had certainly rejuvenated me. Our next stop was Berri, one of the prettiest towns on the Murray. Loxton, Kingston and Waikerie all passed without incident, although near Waikerie there were heaps of large gum trees floating down in the strong current, and I hoped that I wouldn't collide with any during the long night's run ahead. This was the worst concentration of debris that I had encountered so far.

A quick bite to eat (Heinz of course) and then it was on to Morgan. Here the river bends to take up a predominantly southerly direction and it should have been a straightforward stretch, but instead it was straight into a strong southerly wind, which whipped up the waves. The spray was flying over the boat and I was forced to reduce speed because of the pounding I was taking. Flat-bottomed boats are not made to handle these types of conditions comfortably. I was also very cold. We were within striking distance of Goolwa, and close enough – if I could keep going – to come in well under the five days. While mentally and physically this journey had at times pushed me to the limit, I was confident that I had enough emergency reserves of energy and willpower to carry me through, provided that nothing unforseen happened.

At dusk, I pulled over for a quick stop at Swan Reach. Except for the occasional relief afforded by sheltered bends in the river, I had been battered all the way and it was finally starting to take its toll. Darkness was now upon me, the wind had not abated, and the moon would not be up for hours. I decided that I would proceed direct to Murray Bridge, so I took on extra fuel and the very heavy Land Rover battery. I hoped it would last me through the moonless period, but I wasn't really concerned as I'd had a lot of experience now running with just starlight. We had Heinz again, and then as Martin's lights slipped away, I took off once more into the corrugations. I was suffering already from the evening chill and still had a long night ahead of me.

Walker's Flat, Purnong and Bow Hill remain a distorted memory only, and it wasn't until near Teal Flat that the moon rose, the wind dropped and I again rode my silver highway. Waves of tiredness came and went but I was extremely confident — everything was on target. I would make it. Surely nothing could stop me now.

When I left Mannum after topping up the fuel tank from my reserves, I was heading into known terrain, having water-skied up and down the section to Murray Bridge many times. However, I'd only gone a few kilometres when the first wispy threads of fog appeared, and then gradually thickened and descended to cocoon me. I was forced to bring my speed right back, as I couldn't see more than a few boat lengths ahead. As I remembered it, willow trees lined the banks for most of the way ahead, so by following them, I should've been able to continue slowly. We weren't beaten yet, but I really didn't need this in the state I was in. It might sound easy, but it wasn't. The willows also line the swamps, and when suddenly the propeller is hooked up in the wires of a fence, not only are you way off course and probably in someone's flooded cow paddock, but how the hell do you find your way back to the main river?

The hours slipped by as I fought for every kilometre. I stopped to study my highly detailed map, and concluded that I should probably now be in a long straight section of the river. I set up a course with my compass and, as I could now see the glow of the moon above, used its position relative to my boat to steer by.

A small sandy bank and a jetty came into view, jogging my memory from water-skiing days, so I changed direction to angle across the river. When I saw the huge river gum, and nestled beneath it a friend's weekend shack, I knew exactly where I was on my map. By staying on this side of the river, I had an almost unbroken line of willows which would take me to my rendezvous point with Martin. I couldn't increase my speed much but at least I knew where I was.

Despite creeping along, I nearly ploughed into the side of a houseboat tied up amongst the willows. As I gunned the motor to avoid a collision, I realised that I must have frightened the living daylights out of its occupants. I guess there were many people that night, tucked up in their warm beds, who wondered what the hell was going on out on the river.

I finally located the little park upstream of Murray Bridge where I had arranged to meet Martin; I could just see the outline of his vehicle in the pea-souper. Hours of bone-shaking corrugations and then extreme fatigue had left me weak and groggy: so much so that while trying to climb out of my boat onto dry land, my legs didn't want to work and I slipped and ended up knee deep in the freezing water. I found Martin sound asleep in the driver's seat, his head resting on the steering wheel. When I woke him, his first words were, 'How in the bloody hell did you manage to get here? It's impossible'. He had been so absolutely convinced that I would never find him, let alone make any progress in the fog, that he hadn't even left his warning lights on to help guide me.

We searched for wood to make a fire to thaw me out, but could only locate a few twigs. We burnt what paper we had, but were really just wasting time. My legs still felt like blocks of ice. It was about 3 am and I knew the fog wasn't going to lift until sunup, however if I could find my way to Wellington by 6 am, then I figured that I would have just enough time to get across Lake Alexandrina and into Goolwa by 8 am and achieve my five-day goal. The odds were really against me now, but I didn't intend to move the goalposts again just to slacken the pressure.

The other reason I needed to be on the lake very early was to make a crossing before the wind came up. Lake Alexandrina, some 35 kilometres long and 10 kilometres wide, is notorious for its ability to change quickly and has claimed many lives over the years. For this reason, Ben Beck and his cameraman should be waiting for me at Wellington. They would follow me across the lake as back-up in their big boat and I wanted them ready to depart when and if I arrived. Martin's job now was to locate their camp and have them on standby.

My legs were so frozen I couldn't really feel them and I shivered uncontrollably as the icy slipstream cut through my clothing. I managed well with my maps and the moon, and finally, with the fog just starting to lift and thin, I spotted their camp just upstream of the Wellington Ferry. It had taken me nearly three hours to cover about 38 km. They were still in bed. Martin had been advised by the nearby all-night ferry operator as to their whereabouts, but before he got to their camp, had decided that he could go no further, and went to sleep by the side of the road. I woke the camp, had a cup of coffee, and while they finished packing and loading up their twenty foot cabin cruiser, I departed. With their faster speed, they would catch me by the time I reached the entrance to the lake.

The wind was slowly increasing, and as I entered the lake it was starting to chop up. Ben had now arrived alongside, and on a compass course, I headed for an invisible shore and my re-entry point back into the river for the final run.

By the time I reached the middle of the lake, it was obvious that I was in for a hard time. The land had all but disappeared and the strengthening wind now whipped the tops off the waves, which had grown at a frightening speed to a good two metres high.

This is one of the most dangerous lakes in Australia. Suddenly I took a big wave over the side that drenched me and poured gallons of water into my tiny, flat-bottomed craft. I was numb with fatigue but the shock of the freezing cold water snapped me out of my lethargy as I fought now for dominance over the elements. I'd come too far, struggled too hard, to be beaten so near to my destination.

Because of the narrow trough between the waves, I couldn't find a rhythmical way to ride over them. To make matters worse, the waves were going approximately the same way that I wanted to, creating an almost impossible situation for me.

Another big wave caught me from behind and thrusting me forward, threatened to force the bow of the boat under the wave in front. I threw on full power and just managed to keep the bow up. I tried to run side-on to the waves but took a breaker over the boat. This was definitely not the place for a ten foot flat-bottomed tinnie!

Ben tried everything he could to shepherd me with his larger boat, but to no avail. He was caught and thrown high, and I only just managed to escape from beneath his crashing bow. Ben backed off, his thoughts easy to read — it would only be a matter of time before he plucked me from the freezing water. I was completely on my own. With my exit just starting to appear on the horizon, I fought every wave as I moved ever so slowly towards my destination. Win or lose now rested on my ability. I removed the bung at the rear of the boat, so the water that poured in could slowly drain away. Ben kept his distance, but occasionally I heard a cheer as I fought and conquered an exceptionally big wave.

Martin by now had arrived at Goolwa to find the media and a large crowd of well-wishers awaiting my arrival at 8 am. They had a long wait ahead. Eight o'clock came and went, and so did nine and ten! At 10.30 the Channel 9 helicopter, which had previously searched the river section, took off to search the lake, everyone believing that an accident must have occurred.

I finally burst through the worst of it, and although still taking a pounding, had just about reached the safety of the river entrance. I was staggered when I looked at my watch, and realised that I had spent hours fighting to stay afloat on a lake crossing that should have taken less than one hour. Funny how time flies when you are having fun!

This was where the helicopter found me, and they followed awhile, filming my departure from an experience that I hoped I would never have to repeat. I could now understand how this lake has claimed so many lives. Just before noon I spotted the township of Goolwa, and then, 5 days, 4 hours and 2350 kilometres since departing the Hume Weir, I eased my boat up onto the beach of the ski club.

From the press I gained the title 'King of the Murray', and from my wife and friends, a celebratory beer – or was it a scotch and soda? I really cannot remember. Having completed our mission, I only had one thought left: how quickly could we get back to Adelaide and my nice, warm, dry, comfortable bed? I needed to sleep for a long, long time.

Martin and I slipped away from the crowd of well-wishers and the press to spend a few moments of reflection beside the majestic river we both loved.

Martin finally broke the silence, 'You know Den, it was a great journey,' he said. 'Although I didn't get to ride it as you did, I thoroughly enjoyed the part I played.'

I didn't say a thing, allowing him to relive his experience and share with me whatever he wanted to of his memories.

'I remember those nights in lonely places sitting by the bank of a river for hours and desperately hoping that you'd arrive safely. And what about those bloody fogs where I couldn't see a thing and yet you just somehow magically appeared as if out of nowhere. Mate, I saw so much of the Mighty Murray that I would never have seen otherwise.'

That's the thing with the Murray. Most people get a disjointed experience of it, as they only cross little bits at a time, generally on interstate journeys. They don't get to piece enough of it together in one fell swoop to grasp the enormity of this, the sixth largest river in the world. As I said to a local boatie who pulled in to welcome us and asked how far I'd come: 'Mate, you could take your boat 2350 km upstream from here right now and only need to pull it from the water once to navigate a weir'. The expression on his face said it all.

Martin handed me a small package. 'Yeah, it was great Den — something I wouldn't have missed for quids. This is a gift to remember me by. You'll probably wake up one night with the cravings and won't be able to get back to sleep until you get a fix, so keep it handy.'

I burst out laughing when a can of baked beans emerged from the wrapping. Well, what could I say other than 'Martin, thanks for everything. I couldn't have done it without you — and by the way, you're the best damned Heinz cook, hot or cold, I've ever met!'

For me, well I'd enjoyed the challenge — we had given it our best shot. If only my boat had been capable of that extra 8 kilometres per hour that the West Australians had, I would have bolted in under four and a half days — and without the fogs and the drama of the winds on Lake Alexandrina, it would have been an easy five days. However, we had completed our journey to the best of our ability, in the circumstances we found, and that was all that really mattered. Despite the hardships, we had always remained focused.

I try not to lose sight of the dream when faced with adversity. If I have to move the goalposts, that's fine, provided I put them straight back in again. What the hell: it's my dream, my life, and I choose my own goals.

Claypan water from a recent rain
provided a welcome desert wash.

Just one of numerous compass shots.

Due to excessive temperature, continually blocked radiators and a tail wind, we regularly overheated our engines forcing us to stop.

The remains of an old boiler near the ruins of Annandale Station.

Michael enjoying a cuppa at the end of another long day.

Curly bark of the Red Mulga or Mineritchie. The tree grows in stony water courses on the western edge of the Simpson Desert.

Harmless Woma Python. Good Tucker!

Below: Ruins at Dalhouse Springs.

WARNING VERY HOT WATER.
SALT CRUST MAY NOT BE SOLID.
YOU MAY BE SEVERELY SCALDED.

Purni Bore-
An oasis on
the edge of
the Simpson
Desert.

Aerial Purni Bore -
A welcome rest spot
for wildlife and
travellers alike.

Wild donkeys roam
the fringes of the
western desert.

Human skeleton uncovered by the desert winds

David Lindsay's blazed tree at the native well Wolporican (1886).

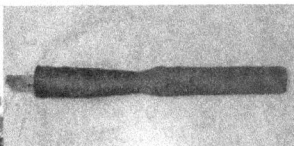

Chisel found in the ashes of the fireplace at the entrance to this Wiltja.

Above: Remains of an aboriginal Wiltja or hut abandoned over eighty years ago.

Right: Large mobs of feral comels roam the Simpson Desert.

Poeppel Corner: Concrete post marks the junction of three states: Queensland, South Australia and The Northern Territory.

Beautiful old buildings of Murnpeowie Station (Mumpy).

Steam engine at Murnpeowie Station.

Ruins of Manuwalkaninna Staion.

John McKinlay stayed here in 1861 on his way
to search for the explorers, Burke and Wills.

Birdsville, my destination, lies 400kms away on the other side of some 1200 parallel sand dunes which block my path.

My cart carries everything necessary for a complete crossing, other than sufficient water.

Note: Aluminium drilling rods form part of the cart's structure. Dissembled, they will be used to drill and find water at about the halfway mark.

Crossing my first salt lake brings welcome relief from the exhausting struggle of dragging my cart up and down the soft sand of the dunes.

Footsteps left on the salt crust can remain visible for many years.

To lighten my backpack by 23lbs, I advised the RFDS Base in Alice Springs Five Sierra Bravo Xray-all okay" and confirmed my arrival date into Birdsville. I then abandoned my HF radio, battery and solar panel in the tallest tree.

My water is now assured. From a depth of twelve feet I draw up my first tube of water then fill all of my containers.

Walking into Birdsville having completed my solo unaided crossing of the Simpson Desert.

Left: Departing Burketown on the Gulf of Carpentaria, I set out across the Plains of Promise. My destination is Glenelg on the Gulf St Vincent about 2500kms away.

Right: After a five day forced stay resting my injured knee, I load up my cart with four weeks provisions and depart Camooweal. My next town is Maree, 1300kms away. As a local in the pub remarked "That's a long way to go between beers, even if you're flying".

Left: Last cattle station before entering the Simpson Desert.

Right: I receive a check up from the Royal Flying Doctor nurse who is visiting Atula on clinic duties.

The children of Atula Station take a break from their radio session with the School of the Air and hitch a lift to their front gate. Ahead of me now lies the formidable Simpson Desert and my next station homestead, Cowarie, is about 600km away.

Into the desert.

Left: In a few days I abandon my cart to the station owner of Atula and the media who have flown in for a visit. It will be returned to me at Cowarie Station. To get there I will have to walk cross country about 500kms carrying my back pack.

Right: With the press waiting below to greet me, I cross my last sand dune of the Simpson Desert. Note the light colour of the sand compared to the older red sands of the northern desert.

Left: My welcoming committee as I exit the desert.

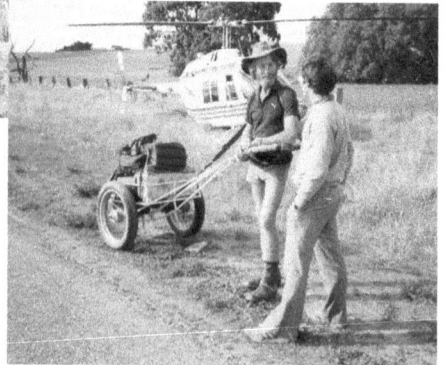

Right: Dick Smith, the founder of the Australian Geographic Magazine in his airborne four wheel drive drops in for a chat.

Walking into the city of Adelaide.

'Miss Glenelg 1985' escorts me into the crowded Mosely Square.

My reception into Glenelg was hosted by the Lord Mayor. Receiving congratulations from the Premier of South Australia, Mr. John Bannon.

Glenelg Jetty. I pour the water bottled in the Gulf of Carpentaria into the Gulf St. Vincent.

The Royal Flying Doctor Service advised that my walk has raised over $70,000 in donations to their worthy cause.

Chapter 8

Darling River Solo Marathon

Wednesday, 12 October 1983 started out as just another ordinary Adelaide day. The only thing looming on the horizon was a few scattered clouds rolling in from the west. For something to do, I decided to check on the Murray River water levels from Yarrawonga to Lock 1 during October 1981. I had never recorded the river levels in my log book for my record-busting solo boat journey down the Murray River.

In March 1982 the West Australian group whose 8.5-day record I'd successfully overturned had gone on to establish another river record when they completed the longest journey ever made on an Australian river. They had departed from the Mole River Bridge near the south-east Queensland border, and, again using two people per boat to enable relief driving, had travelled down the Mole River, then the Dumaresq, MacIntyre, Barwon, Darling and into the Murray River, finally terminating their journey at the Murray Mouth. Their time for the distance of about 3500 km was 12 days, 23 hours, 17 minutes. I guess it was a logical extension of thought that had me enquiring also on the present river levels for the Darling, just to see how they compared now with when they undertook their trip.

One thing led to another. My first phone call to Bourke on the Darling River indicated ample, but falling water downstream towards Menindee Lakes, and good water well upstream. Several phone calls later I located Les Raymond at the Queensland Water Resources Commission, Goondiwindi. Les is a typical Queenslander: slow voice, full of hospitality — and due to his work, he knows the top end river section backwards. I explained that I was seeking river levels at the time the Westralians had made their descent. He mentioned that he had seen them depart and the river levels there were about the same as now, but falling. However there were high flood waters from Goondiwindi to Mungindi. His exact words were 'up in the top of the trees'. My next question on how long the upper reaches around Texas would remain suitable for boating brought a calculated response, 'I reckon about two weeks, no longer.'

'See you in fourteen days, Les,' I said. It all happened as fast as that. The day was now anything but ordinary – my next challenge had arrived. Suddenly I had a river to conquer and no time to waste.

Just how this would all come together in my self-imposed time frame, I didn't have a clue. I needed a boat, motor, trailer and safety gear. I had absolutely nothing. I also needed detailed maps of the complete river system, and most important of all a back-up vehicle and driver. The first map that I could lay my hands upon was a tattered old Ampol road map. It wasn't much, but it was enough to show the enormity of the project. It was big. It was very, very big.

Next I phoned Martin Reynolds, my back-up man for the Murray River run. He didn't hesitate. When I suggested another river record attempt, he shot back 'You can count on me mate. Where to this time and when do we start?'

I could hear the excitement in his voice. 'In precisely two weeks, Martin, we will slide a boat, which I haven't yet acquired, into the Mole River.'

'Where in the hell is the Mole River? I've never heard of it.'

'It's on the Queensland border upstream from the town of Texas and about two days drive from Adelaide,' I replied. 'I boat 3500 km down to the Murray River mouth in ten days max. What do you think about that, eh?' His jaw must have dropped, for he took a while to come back. 'You still there, Martin?' I asked.

'Struth,' he finally blurted, 'that's a bloody long way, but then you've never been one to think small, have you? You obviously reckon we can beat those pesky West Australians again.'

'Sure, mate, but only if we keep focused and give it all we've got. See you soon and thanks.'

I hunted Adelaide for a suitable boat, to no avail. I could get one in Perth, but they couldn't transport it to me in time. In desperation I rang the owner of the boat I had used for my Murray record. Sorry but he had sold it to a chap in Renmark named Paul Dempsey, who had painted it up and was pretty proud of it. He doubted if he would lend it to me, although he did give me his phone number. Five days later I had an offer of a motor and all safety gear, but still no boat. Maybe the pretty paint job had faded, and if he knew that I had already created a record in his boat, he may want to go for a second one ... what could I lose? Time was running out.

I picked up the phone and crossed my fingers. I dispensed with the formalities fairly rapidly and got down to the business of selling my project. Things seemed to be going well until he asked me what make of motor I would be using.

'It's a Tohatsu, Paul, brand spanking new, just like the one I had on your boat when I captured the Murray River record.'

'That should get him', I thought. 'Who wouldn't want to be the proud owner of a boat with a grand story to tell, and another even bigger one ready to happen if he'd just say yes?' I didn't expect his reply.

'Sorry mate, but I really couldn't allow that brand of motor on my boat'.

'Bugger', I thought. 'What a pathetic reason for not lending me his boat.' Then as if reading my mind, which hopefully he hadn't, he came straight back

'Denis, don't be disappointed. Would you consider using another brand of motor?'

Would a drowning man clutch at a straw? I wasn't about to play favourites.

'I sure would, mate. What did you have in mind?'

'Denis, I'm the Renmark agent for Yamaha outboard motors. Let me see what I can do and I'll get back to you in a couple of hours with my answer.'

It seemed like an eternity, but true to his word, he called back. 'Denis, Yamaha Pitman's of Adelaide will supply an 8 hp motor, and all safety gear if you are prepared to use their brand.' He didn't have to ask twice.

Nine days into the countdown I arrived in Renmark to prepare the boat. Martin would use his own vehicle for back-up, and $160 worth of maps were on their way from Sydney. Ampol confirmed that they would supply the necessary fuel. It was all systems go. Eleven days into countdown saw the boat fitted out with forward steering, lights, radio, etc., then it was on to the 'Florence Anne', Martin's paddleboat moored at Mildura, for the final preparation and my first look at the maps. Well, almost — two were missing. I derived a measure of consolation from Les Raymond's words – 'Anything thrown into the Mole River ultimately comes out at the Murray Mouth, some three months later' — so who needs maps anyhow?

Our two-day drive to Goondiwindi was uneventful, with the four-wheel drive Nissan Patrol running well. We had been forced to detour via Broken Hill as the Pooncarie Menindee Road was cut by flood waters. This could be a problem on our return. Wherever possible we had a look at the river and weirs, and both of us agreed that the major problem would be vehicle access to the river, particularly if it rained in the black soil country.

Our early arrival at Goondiwindi gave us a much-needed pause to conclude the final preparations. The river looked good, but I was concerned about the section between Goondiwindi and Mungindi, as the Westralians had mentioned having map-reading difficulties in this area.

I rang Boronga homestead, downstream of Goondiwindi, and was told there was no shortage of water in their area. They said that the river was up in the tree tops and would make boating extremely difficult. That was something I didn't want to hear, so I decided to forget their comments. It didn't work; that night I had one of the best nightmares I had had for a long time.

A daybreak start on day fourteen got us to the Mole River bridge around mid-morning. My only concern was whether this was the exact place that the Westralian group had started from. A friendly local rode up on his motor bike and informed us that we were indeed at the correct location as he had seen them depart. I don't think he rated our puny little two-man effort as a potential threat to the record. I had planned departure for 12.28 pm, the exact time the record holders had taken the plunge, and on the dot I was away into the racing flood waters.

The river at the start was about 15 m wide – boulder-strewn and flowing swiftly as it twisted its way through the trees ahead. This made it hard to control my direction, and I was concerned about damaging the outboard motor leg as I continually bounced over numerous rocks. However, the river soon stopped teasing me and spat me out into the Dumaresq for some real action.

A vastly different river now confronted me. The Dumaresq was wide, full of trees, logs and fast-moving water. My adrenalin flow immediately shot up another notch. There was no time for sight-seeing as I fought rapids, dodged rocks and struggled through the tangled maze of trees which in parts almost blocked the river.

I miscalculated and crashed to a grinding halt jammed amongst the rocks. With one leg over the side, pushing and heaving, I finally managed to dislodge my boat and immediately went into a long, steep run of racing white water. At breakneck speed I hurtled around a large clump of trees that had blocked my forward vision and confronted a most daunting sight: immediately ahead lay my worst nightmare – a series of huge pressure waves, all ready to end this adventure quick smart.

I had just enough time to reach forward and drag the two heavy fuel containers towards me to lighten the front end before going down the big drop. The first wave now towered above me. To my surprise I rose up and over it effortlessly, still balanced and in control. The second and third, however, were not so well formed: and for a while I thought I may be upended as their conflicting currents tossed me around violently. After what seemed an eternity, I finally crashed over the top and down the other side, straight into the final one, which thankfully I conquered with ease.

This proved to be the last of the big rapids; as I moved further away from the hills they disappeared altogether. There were long reaches of clear water now with only the occasional tree blockage, but I had to lift the boat over several partly submerged bridges.

My first day on the previous Murray River run had also been the most difficult. Not only was the river itself pretty wild, but I had not been in a boat for two years. The only damage was a broken propeller tip, which I continued to use, as rocky sections were still prevalent.

Due to the length of the journey, I had decided my strategy would be to get ahead of the record holders in the first day or so, then match their pace if possible until down near Poncarrie, where I could again put on the pressure. My goal was 10 days, which, if achieved, would better their record by about three days.

I passed their first night's camp late in the afternoon, and pushed on into the night. There was only one major problem left for the day's run that we knew of — the Cunningham Weir. Here, my back-up man was to warn me of its approach by flashing a torch. There was no ripply line to indicate its presence, just a nice smooth 3 m drop into a foaming, turbulent swirl. What happened next was the closest I came to complete disaster.

Martin had stopped me well upstream of the weir as arranged, and we waded the boat along the shoreline to the rock embankment. After quite a struggle, slipping and sliding, we managed to heave the boat up and over the boulders and back down into a small, relatively unobstructed section of the river bank about 5 m from the base of the waterfall, where we could reload my gear. The noise was deafening and the feeble light from our torches cast an eerie glow over the tumbling mass, which boiled and frothed the water around us.

I hopped in and started the motor but couldn't put it into gear immediately as a large quantity of wire littered the area, which could have entangled my propeller. Martin yelled 'Take care', threw over the nose rope and then pushed me off down stream with some gusto. I had expected to move ahead, away from danger, but instead was almost immediately sucked backwards towards the waterfall. Off balance now, I finally managed, after what seemed an eternity, to locate the lever and slam the motor into gear. The resulting jolt nearly tossed me over the rear as the boat surged forward. Another metre or so and it could have easily been all over, permanently. Tons of water would have engulfed me, pushing down hard. If I was really unlucky, the water could have held me pinned to the rocky floor of the river bed. It sure made my heart race, and gave us something to talk about when I finally caught up with Martin at our next stop. We made camp for the night beside the Keetah Bridge, the top of which was only inches above the racing flood waters.

After an early start and a rather sedate run into Goondiwindi, I refuelled and was on my way by 8.30 am. I had now opened up a clear lead of one day. River conditions were good and I suspected that they would remain that way for several hours at least.

Up to now, the river had been defined by two lines on the map, and I wondered why the map makers had not continued to mark up the map in the same manner rather than a single line for the approaching section. I was soon to find out.

The long, open reaches slowly started to disappear and finally the swollen river deteriorated into a meandering maze choked with ti-tree. Now, instead of following a defined river and boating beneath the overhanging boughs of the trees lining its banks, I was up in the tree tops, which, floating together, restricted my path. The flood waters spilled out on either side over the low-lying countryside, creating a multitude of islands and waterways. The branches trapped floating logs and debris, and the shuddering, then screaming of the motor as the propeller bit deep into timber, became an all-too-familiar sound. Great rafts of debris held the discarded products of our age – bottles, tins, and all manner of rubbish. Seeing so much junk on top of the water, I could not help wondering what the river bottom must look like.

Navigation became a somewhat haphazard affair, and it wasn't until I came to the first of the foot swing bridges that I was happy, as I now knew where I was. The bridge was in the water, but it was possible to slide under it near the bank.

Boronga homestead finally swept into view, and standing on the bank was a welcoming committee — a big mob of yapping dogs, and two of the nicest people you could meet waiting patiently for me to arrive. Someone further upstream had heard my boat pass their property and had given them the timing, so they knew roughly when to expect me. Mike and Shirley Carrington run about 3000 head of sheep on their property, and were certainly going to have a good year when the flood waters subsided from their paddocks.

'Denis, could you stay the night?' Shirley asked enthusiastically. 'We have a spare room and I've been baking just for you. We don't get many visitors drop in by boat.'

Mike interrupted: 'Shirley, we don't get visitors by whatever means, and if any of our friends attempted what Denis has just done, we would probably never see them again.'

I secured my boat and as we strolled up to the house, they informed me that I was their first visitor for three months, their property having been isolated by flood waters for that period. A shopping spree for them to the nearest town, Boomi, meant a boat ride for several miles, and then continuing by tractor across the swamp lands to get to their vehicle. Well, I couldn't stay the night, although it was tempting, however the hour I lost on the river was well spent over tea, sandwiches and freshly baked cake while gaining information on their particular section of the Macintyre River. Mike and Shirley were deeply concerned about pollution from the large cotton farming properties now using their waterway. The once-pristine river was slowly being destroyed and I got the feeling that despite their great love for their property and way of life, they would move on rather than see it ruined before their eyes.

In my view, it's a pity that Government jealousy and the 'I'm alright Jack' politicians and local Government bodies did not share their concern for this part of Australia's mightiest waterway and life blood. Indeed a concerted effort by all will be needed to save the entire Murray River system from becoming just a gutter.

Mike and Shirley waved me goodbye and I promised I would return one day. It was still difficult going, however I finally made it to Boonangar Bridge just on dark and found Martin leaning over the railing waiting anxiously, torch in hand. The road had been flooded in several places but he had managed to set up camp about one kilometre back on the track in a dry area. Getting there was simple — I just boated up the gutter alongside the road. It was a worrying camp, however, as that night we heard by radio that rain was falling near Bourke and heading our way. Rain on the surrounding black soil country could spell disaster as it would cut Martin's access to the river and leave me without a back-up vehicle.

I made a daybreak start, and travelled on a reasonably well-defined river for several hours, until it again broke down into long tree-blocked sections. Map reading went by the board, and I concentrated on letting the river tell me where it was. The length of the pressure ripple created by obstructions became my guide. The flood waters made straight lines out of bends, as they raced across connecting land. Sometimes it was possible to tell by the type of trees that I had missed the main channel, but it really didn't matter. As long as I followed the speed, the main thrust of the river, I was headed in the right direction.

It was understandable but annoying that I couldn't maintain an accurate position fix on my map. Keeping my speed up as I fought for a fast passage through the trees required my full attention. In the occasional sections of open water, I endeavoured to solve the problem of map reading. It turned out to be a simple exercise. I estimated the length of the reach in front of me and drew a representing line on a piece of paper, with a corresponding line to the sun's position. With my base line established, bends and reaches thereafter were treated in the same manner, their estimated distance and direction, as drawn, always relating to the sun. After a half dozen or so reaches, a neat map started to form, and although not the same scale as my purchased maps, gave a positive position fix every time. It was dead easy.

Looking back, this flooded top section was the most exciting of the whole trip. There was the ever-present challenge of maintaining speed through an obstacle course, without ending up 'up a wattle' in a literal sense. The wildlife continually attracted my attention — big mobs of kangaroos swimming, or bounding drenched through the swamp lands, and wild pigs by the score. They squealed like hell as I flashed past, close enough to give some of them a pat on the rear. Spring had been in the air for several weeks now, and young birds were flapping in their nests as I passed only feet away. And the ever-present smell of the ti-tree flower lingered heavily in the still air.

This section also demonstrated one of the plus features of the Yamaha outboard: the lack of shear pins. I used the motor continually to force my way through blocked sections, regardless of the thumping the propeller received from the logs. I would have been forever replacing shear pins in some other motors.

I was approaching Mogil Mogil, the site of our third nights' camp. Darkness had fallen and the numerous well-defined billabongs made navigation difficult. I lost about an hour trying to find my way back through the maze to the main channel. Martin's cheery fire was a welcome beacon, perched high on a cliff. Martin's a great cook. We had Heinz baked beans — shades of our time on the Murray.

This proved to be the last of the difficult sections that I would encounter as I was now entering the Barwon River stage of my journey. Rising banks combined with falling water levels would now rob me of my view of the surrounding countryside, as I sank ever lower into a defined channel.

The next day's run to Collewaroy station, camp four, proved uneventful. The towns of Collarenebri and Walgett were behind us. It was a good river now: wide, with little to worry about except perhaps what would be on the menu for dinner. The rain had held off, and the back-up vehicle was running well.

It was while on this section that I noticed some long necks protruding from the water. I knew they weren't swans, so I angled over to investigate. To my amazement, two large emus emerged from the water and scrambled up the slippery bank. Obviously they can swim!

I arrived at our pre-determined campsite late that night. I certainly could not have missed it. The vehicle was positioned on a prominent high point, its hazard lights flashing, but when I landed, no one came to greet me, which was unusual. With my torch, I managed to find a way up the steep cliff to reach Martin, all the while hoping that he hadn't had an accident. Instead I found him lying on his sleeping bag, nestling a blaring radio and clutching a lighted torch, no doubt to show me where to land. He was dead to the world. I didn't have the heart to wake him. I ate Heinz, straight from the can.

The run to Bourke was pleasant, although emerging rock banks and bars caused some concern. In places, the unusual heaps of rock indicated the presence of Aboriginal rock fish traps. Homesteads, some obviously derelict, became more frequent, and so too the rubbish spilling down the banks — out of sight, out of mind to all but the river traveller.

The outhouses or 'dunnies', those little rectangular boxes of necessity, always seemed to occupy a prominent position with a commanding view. Perched high on the bank, their doors facing the peaceful river, they offered their users the ultimate in tranquillity, perhaps a restful place to contemplate the size of the next wool cheque.

The Bourke Weir proved to be no problem; we used the old lock chamber, which gave safe passage to the mighty Darling River, then headed for the next weir to make camp five. Darkness fell and I switched on my lights, still maintaining full power.

It wasn't long before I smelt smoke, and then noticed flames coming from beneath my left elbow, near the radio. I cut the motor and leaned over, intending to gather water in my cupped hands to douse the flame. I assumed I must have dropped a cigarette butt at my last stop. Then it suddenly hit me that the fire was electrical. I came out of my bean bag seat fast, and spun around. Arcing was now occurring all over the boat as wires melted, sparks flew everywhere and I knew I was a goner if the fuel went up. I grabbed a collection of wires entering the battery, averted my face to protect my eyes, and pulled hard, ripping them free. There was no big bang, just pitch dark and deadly silence.

I had this big knot in my stomach knowing what could have happened. By torchlight, I surveyed the damage. My motor was fine, as it wasn't connected to the battery however the wires from the battery around the boat to the bow spotlight and my radio were a burnt-out mess. I managed to salvage several undamaged lengths of cable and used these to re-wire my spotlight and power my radio. I then advised Martin that Five Sierra Bravo Xray would be late for dinner.

It didn't take much effort on my part to figure out what had happened. When I got my electrical harness wired up at Renmark, they had obviously failed to install a safety fuse in the line, and I stupidly hadn't made a thorough check of their work.

The first weir next day was portaged with ease. Martin, with the inducement of stubbies all round, had managed to stay the departure of a fishing party until I arrived, and their help was appreciated. With good vehicle access to the river now, we lightened the boat as much as possible to give me extra speed.

Around midday, the bridge at Louth loomed up, with Martin waiting on the bank. I didn't take on extra fuel, as the next stop was to be the weir, a short distance downstream. Martin assured me that the road to Wilcannia was okay, wet but passable, and that was the last I saw of him until late the following afternoon.

I arrived at the weir and was surprised to find Martin missing, so pushed on intending to make contact with him at our next radio sked. This proved unsuccessful as his radio had died, due, as he later realised, to a flat battery.

A phone call to Louth from Bellsgrove station, and I was advised that the river road was impassable due to rain. Martin would have to detour via Cobar, and then try to reach me at Tilba. I managed to borrow some fuel and pushed on in pouring rain, but without my wet-weather gear I was soon drenched and freezing cold. The township of Tilba came up just before dark, where the locals told me that the road into Cobar was also impassable — I had no alternative but to push on.

Late that night the rain finally stopped. I pulled into a sandy beach, lit a fire and dried out my saturated clothes, then curled up on my bean bag for a few hours sleep. This was camp six. I awoke with what I thought at first was the smoke of my fire hanging over the river. It wasn't, and I took off in thick fog. Numerous large fallen tree branches and submerged logs close to the river bank meant it wasn't really an option to use the river's edge to guide my progress. When I moved out towards the clear water in the middle of the river to escape these hazards and pick up extra speed, I could no longer see or use either bank for guidance. The river wasn't very wide so I solved my navigation problems by using my hand-held spotlight to illuminate, wherever possible, the tops of the tall river gums growing on either side. This enabled me to steer a rather erratic course down the middle of the river, mostly keeping away from danger and increasing my speed considerably. There were many times, however, when gaps appeared in the trees, or they were obscured by the fog for short periods, and when this occurred, particularly on a bend, I would suddenly find that I was heading straight for the bank.

I acquired more fuel from various station homesteads nestled along the river bank, and reached Wilcannia around midday. Martin was not at the appointed meeting place. The local baker organised money, fuel and some food, my first since the previous morning. I now resigned myself to doing the rest of the trip without back-up, and was just getting ready to push off when Martin showed up. He had finally made it to Tilba that morning after abandoning the trailer in the mud, only to be told that I had departed the night before. He hadn't got bogged - it was just a long, slow, slippery trip. We now had ourselves a convoy — almost! Martin was bogged in the caravan park on the other side of the river and needed help, which the local police force supplied willingly.

Despite our problems, I had now gained time and was ahead of schedule. Camp seven was at Billila station, and the run from there to the Menindee Lakes was uneventful.

I had expected Lake Weatherall to be a vast body of water — instead I found a lake choked with trees, except for the well-defined river channel lined with dead gums. Portage was necessary around Menindee Weir, and we made our next stop the town weir, where I took on extra fuel for the long, non-stop night run to Pooncarrie.

As the river road along the next section was also flooded, Martin had obtained a mud map which hopefully would detour him through the station country west of the river and then back to our next rendezvous point. He departed and I set off on the long leg to Pooncarrie, hoping to arrive around midnight. The extra weight of the fuel, however, was too much: the boat couldn't get onto the plane, forcing me to dispose of about four gallons to lighten the load. I hoped I still had enough fuel left to complete the section.

Leaf-strewn, sluggish water now created frequent cavitation around the propeller, resulting in a scream from the motor and loss of speed. To fix it, I had to stop, reverse to clear the leaves around the propeller, then power away. It made for a slow trip!

I was several hours late into Pooncarrie, where I met my anxious back-up man. He'd been in the local hotel bar, where the locals gave me little hope of arriving that night, reckoning that the risk of losing my head to one of the many thin phone lines crossing the river was too great. These, of course, were normally out of harm's way, but the height of the flood waters brought them close to the water, necessitating constant vigilance on my part. The lack of decent lighting certainly didn't help. To protect myself, I had broken a straight limb off a tree and held it in front of me with one hand, hoping that if I missed seeing a wire, it would be diverted over my head.

But there I was. And after a quick TV interview and two hours' sleep, I was away. The next stop was Wentworth, though the run was slower than expected due to spark plug trouble. A helpful station owner robbed his own outboard engine of plugs to help me out.

Finally, the moment I had been looking forward to for days arrived as I swept out of the Darling River at Wentworth and into the mighty Murray. It was midday Thursday and I was falling behind time. However, there would be no more navigation problems, snags or leaves; just a few locks and then the Murray Mouth, the finish, only 827 kilometres away.

I should have arrived at Lock 9 just before dark to meet Martin and refuel, but I was forced to hole up in a creek for several hours to escape a fierce storm. I pushed on as soon as possible but the pounding I had received opened up several holes in the bottom of the boat as welds tore and fractured. There was a hole in the middle which squirted a jet of water skywards, so I plonked my foot over it. The drain hole out the back of the boat with the bung in it was still the larger, so I figured there was no real cause for concern, although I didn't like the way the side was flexing.

Martin had his fair share of difficulties too, arriving at Lock 9 around midnight after a mechanical breakdown. We only had a few hours' sleep and apparently I was delusional – Martin woke to find me sitting up paddling my swag and yelling 'Don't worry Martin, I'll make it somehow'.

My original plan had called for a departure from Lock 9 at midday on Thursday, which would have allowed two nights with ample sleep, and had me arriving at Wellington to begin crossing Lake Alexandrina at daybreak. Arrival at the Murray Mouth would then have been several hours under my ten-day deadline. However, I didn't leave Lock 9 until just before daybreak Friday, which meant I would now have to run almost non-stop to achieve my goal of arriving Saturday morning.

The boat was welded up at Renmark. New plugs and a propeller were fitted, and a new wiring harness connected so that I now had full use of my lights. In addition, we took all the surplus gear out of the boat and I carried minimal fuel, as we had good bitumen road access to the river for the back-up vehicle for the rest of the way. All locks were open except Lock 1, which I reached about 1 am Saturday and had to portage my way around. From there until daybreak, my memory of events is just a blur as I was overcome by extreme fatigue. I had to buy fuel at Mannum, as due to a misunderstanding, Martin was waiting downstream at Murray Bridge.

The wind was now stirring the tops of the willow trees as I raced towards Wellington and the entrance to the lake. The last time I had made this crossing I had had to contend with 2 m breaking waves, and I was not looking forward to a repeat dose. Once was enough. I was lucky this time, and had a fast crossing on a moderate chop. Lake Alexandrina is so wide, that from the middle looking backwards on your track, the land has disappeared over the horizon.

After a quick interview with the media, who had helicoptered in to see me, all that remained was a bone-shattering run down the river past the township of Goolwa to the river mouth. The wind was increasing in strength all the time. A quick trip through the lock at the Goolwa barrage and a few more minutes travel, then, 10 days, 2 hours, 7 minutes after departing the Mole River bridge 3500 kilometres away, there it was — a slot gouged in an otherwise unbroken line of sand dunes.

Here at the Murray Mouth, this majestic river disgorges its water, discoloured by the mud collected from over a million square kilometres. Into it drain a thousand streams, hundreds of creeks, and dozens of rivers. In one mighty unification, it then thrusts its contents into the rolling breaker line, re-colouring the otherwise blue southern ocean for miles out to sea.

This journey left me with an appreciation of the vastness of a river system and its importance to this, the driest continent in the world, which can never be fully experienced other than by travelling upon it. I feel privileged to have had the opportunity to witness an ever-changing river, its scenery, its moods and the wildlife it sustains on its long journey from the mountains of Queensland to the ocean shores of South Australia. It was also a privilege to enjoy the hospitality of the river people, and to top it all off, I had the thrill of another challenge.

Chapter 9

Solo West–East Simpson Desert Crossing

I stood in the middle of a small gibber-dotted claypan, hemmed in on either side by high parallel ridges of sand. The steep ridge face to the west rose like the frontal view of a breaking wave, while to the east the ground curved more gently to a crest of live sand along the top of each dune. To the north, or south, the ridges ran like railway lines, terminating somewhere beyond the range of sight.

I was about to take the first hesitant step of a journey that would take me 390 km east, on foot, across what has been called some of the most hostile country in Australia. Ahead, a thousand-odd dunes blocked my path, each to be climbed and conquered, alone. I was not the first; however, others had led the way.

The early explorers had penetrated the fringes of the desert, but it was David Lindsay in 1886 who made the first major assault on its hidden interior. Lindsay and his two companions, all mounted on camels, passed within a few kilometres of where I was standing, as they headed in a sweeping route for a position about 40 km due north of Poeppel Corner, the corner marker joining the three states of Queensland, South Australia and the Northern Territory. Although Lindsay could have carried on, and in about three days completely crossed the desert, he turned around and retraced his footsteps – having reached the Queensland border line, he had achieved what he had set out to do. The first crossing of this desert was finally achieved fifty years later by Ted Colson and companion, also riding camels, who completed a journey from west to east in 1936.

Before the explorers, and after them too, there were those who walked this desert, as I intended to do — one foot after the other. The original inhabitants, the Aborigines, roamed this unique area, perhaps for thousands of years. They carried their own burdens, their worldly goods, as they moved from water to water, using the string of established wells even in the driest of seasons, seeking the best hunting and food gathering areas.

In May 1984, I stepped inside the foam-padded steel ring of my cart, lifted it, and then adjusted the shoulder straps.

Why was I doing this trip? People always asked me this: baffled as to what might motivate me. Sometimes their questions were intended to elicit an answer that would make a good newspaper headline, like 'Honour, Glory or Gain'. But I had yet to see honour or glory emanate from any adventure I had undertaken and it was certainly not for the money. There's very little of that in adventuring.

Generally my reasons varied from challenge to challenge, and occasionally a venture would start out for one reason and end up being entirely different. This solo, unaided walk across the Simpson Desert was one such adventure. I had initially conceived it about four years earlier as a straightforward physical challenge. I wanted to be the first white person to cross this hostile area completely unaided, on foot, using no animals, vehicles or back-up crews. I would walk and survive alone, carrying the necessities of life on my back.

I felt that doing it this way I would come closer to understanding the mental and physical challenges faced by the early explorers. However, I recognised that my knowledge of this vast continent, its physical features, the problems to be encountered, and the help at hand – all unknown and unavailable to the early explorers – would prevent me from ever being completely at one with them. Although I could re-enact their adventures in great detail, the complete experience, their experience, is now unattainable. I guess I was born too late. Or have I come back for a second go? Well, that's how this dream started out ... a straight physical challenge to defeat a desert. I wasn't to know then that it would turn out to be the challenge of life — my life.

🦎 🦎 🦎

I remember the morning that Len died all too well. It's as clear now as when it happened back in 1982. I had met Leonard on the gold fields around Kalgoorlie in Western Australia and we had teamed up for a month or so gold prospecting throughout the area. It wasn't a profitable time for Len, as he only found a few small pieces, whereas I had 8 ounces, worth about $4000.00, stashed in my vehicle. When we parted I gave him a beautiful one ounce nugget as a gift.

The following year I decided to try the old gold mining areas around the town of Halls Creek, in the remote northern regions of Western Australia. I managed to locate Len, who was now living in Queensland, and we agreed to team up once more. This time, however, we agreed to share all the gold we found. It makes it easier, and most times averages out anyway. It's also called trust.

We arranged to meet at a caravan park in Alice Springs, which was about the half-way mark for both of us. When I arrived there he was waiting to greet me at the entrance, his shirt wide open so as to display on his hairy chest my gift, which now hung around his neck on a heavy gold chain. He was so proud of that nugget, and also excited at the prospect of our forthcoming venture. We took a day's rest to fix a puncture, double-check our vehicles and top up our provisions, then left the magnificent McDonald Ranges to head out along the dusty Tanami Track. Our destination, Halls Creek, was about 1100 km away and there was very little in the way of civilization in between.

Slowly the stands of dense mulga gave way to more open, flat country covered in spinifex and dotted with ant hills. The thunder storms that had looked so threatening treated us to no more than a few drops of rain, which pitted our dust-covered vehicles, before marching away, taking with them their incredible noise and light displays. To witness these towering monsters at night while camped on a vast featureless plain in the outback is truly awe-inspiring. At times it can be rather dangerous, as lightning strikes, nature's way of rejuvenating the landscape, torch tinder-dry vegetation to form scattered fire fronts.

We arrived at Rabbit Flat in time to refuel and have a few beers with Bruce Farrands, the proprietor of this isolated outpost. I had recently read an interesting article on him and his wife and how they started their enterprise on this remote track. The article said that the store was well fortified, which it was, but not as I had mistakenly visualised – with numerous goods on display to cater for the needs of the traveller. It had an entirely different meaning.

Bruce served petrol with a pistol stuck in his pocket; the store was designed to be virtually impenetrable, and when he closed the bar at night, he made sure he wasn't silhouetted in the doorway as an invitation to cop a spear or a bullet. A high fence surrounded his house, his family and their vicious dogs and he told me, 'Denis, I have enough fire power inside to wipe out a small army attempting to gain entry over the perimeter fence and I'd sure use it if I had to'. I had no reason to think he was kidding.

Bruce Farrands was a person who was damned if he did, and damned if he didn't. He told me that when he first opened his store he served alcohol to all and sundry travelling by until he finally gave in to those who were continually crucifying him for contributing to the declining health and well-being of the Aboriginals who frequented his premises. So he resisted for some time the temptation to take the bundles of notes thrust under his nose to buy grog, until finally the other side got stuck into him for discrimination and he knew he couldn't win either way, so he took their money.

The track deteriorated badly and didn't improve significantly until we were well into Western Australia. We detoured for a short run into the Wolfe Creek Meteorite Crater Reserve and climbed its almost-perfect circular rim, which rises about 25 metres above the surrounding countryside. What an incredible sight awaited us. A huge depression some 850 metres in diameter, its floor 50 metres below the rim, had been blasted into the surface of the earth over one million years ago. It was well worth the visit.

Finally we reached Halls Creek, got out of tourist mode, and for the next four weeks worked from daylight until dark, six days a week. We sure were keen. Finally, however I was forced to confront my mate:

'You know Len, we're not doing very well are we?' And not waiting for his answer, I continued 'In the last month I have found about 70 pieces of gold and you have only found two. What's the problem, mate?'

He looked rather stressed; it had obviously been playing on his mind also. 'Den, I am sure my luck will change shortly,' he replied.

I felt that lady luck had been given more than enough opportunity and came to the conclusion that Len was either suffering from deafness, which he denied, or lack of attention, which seemed strange as I had watched him work hard enough. Whether he was concentrating or not was, I suppose, another matter. He had mentioned to me some time ago about the wife he had but didn't want and the lady who lived with them that he loved and wanted, but couldn't have. What complicated lives we lead! Maybe personal problems were distracting him. Whatever. We couldn't go on like we were, so having found all the gold, I made an executive decision, much to Len's horror, to spend most of our profit on a brand new Garrett Groundhog detector to replace his cherished old unit. Logically, it seemed to me that this could be the only other reason he was under-performing. At the moment we were running a very lopsided partnership which couldn't survive much longer, so at least this was a starting point of elimination.

We went into town for supplies and at the same time, I ordered a brand new Garrett to be sent up from Perth pronto. The following week Len showed no improvement, so it was with some relief that we headed back to town to do our weekly shopping and found that Len's package had arrived.

Back to the bush that night, Len opened his present by the light of the campfire. As the contents spilled out, he was like a kid in a toy shop – I had never seen him so happy or excited. I helped him rig up and test his machine. It worked perfectly.

'Den,' he said 'I can't wait to get into it tomorrow and you'll be so proud of me. Just you wait and see. Are you sure you don't want to go out tonight for a few hours with the torch?' It was a real buzz to see him so elated and I felt that his contribution from now on was going to add significantly to our depleted gold reserves.

I rolled out of my swag at daybreak, our usual practice, to find Len already up and about and the fire lit, which was normally my job. As he ambled towards me with the billy in his hand, I gave him a cheery greeting 'Hi Len, today's the big day, mate! You look a bit hungover. Are you alright?'

He paused at the front of his vehicle and seemed to stare straight through me before answering. 'Not really, Den. I had a bloody awful night and hardly slept. I just wish this pain in my chest would go away'. He leant over to siphon water out of the jerry can fixed to the vehicle bumper bar to fill the billy and looked up at me once more, his expression strangely vacant. His mouth opened as if to talk and then he fell over backwards.

I thought at first that he was having some form of fit and used the folded end of his soft hat to stop him biting his tongue. Then I realised that he appeared to have stopped breathing. I couldn't find a pulse. I started resuscitation, but to no avail. When I finally gave in, I rigged up my HF radio and managed to get a call through to the Flying Doctor Base some 800 km away in Darwin. They were wonderful to me. I guess they realised by my voice that they were talking to a very distressed person. I think now that Len was dead before he hit the ground, although then it took me a long time to accept the fact that I could not make him come back to life.

Len died of a massive heart attack at the age of 52. I was advised that, even if he had been in town and near a hospital, they wouldn't have been able to save him. His death that day was ultimately to change my life dramatically. I was to have only one more year of being the old me. At 49 years of age, I still thought of myself as a young man. Physically I was fit, and mentally, death was as remote a thought as it was during my youth, or so I believed.

The following year, 1983, I was back in the Simpson Desert experimenting with water-making equipment and trying to work out how I could cross the area on foot and unaided. I had devised a system and a plan, but a lot would depend on the desert having a good season. With rain the desert blooms and so too the plants from which I could extract water. If the numerous salt lakes out in the middle were carrying sludge, I would also have the necessary equipment to condense this into water.

I remember sitting by my campfire and thinking that if only I were 21, my physical strength and recuperative powers would have enabled me to attempt a crossing with half the effort and only a remote chance of failure. That's the first time that I can recall ever querying whether I was as good as a 21-year-old, although equally perhaps it could have been my first admission that I was getting older.

It wasn't the danger. I was prepared and experienced for most things, but as a perfectionist, the prospect of failure did concern me. To attempt such a feat and fail would have been difficult for me to deal with then.

Having completed my experiments, I left the desert and went on to Halls Creek in Western Australia, to spend a few days renewing old acquaintances before going on to the Marble Bar and Nullagine gold prospecting areas.

As I signed into the Halls Creek motel, the memories flooded back, as I suddenly realised that I had returned to the area where Len had passed away, and that in two days it would be the first anniversary of that unforgettable day.

Where Lennie died I had marked a tree with his name and a large cross. The following day I drove out to the site to pay my respects to his memory. Although I hadn't known him for very long – months only – he was a true bush mate.

That night I ordered dinner in the motel restaurant, but before it arrived at the table, I had departed on a mad dash to the local hospital. I had experienced chest pains and was convinced that I was about to die. A thorough checkup with an electrocardiogram showed no indication of a heart attack.

For the next few weeks as I worked my way south through the old gold-mining towns of Western Australia, I knew that something was wrong. Even finding gold had lost its appeal. Lonely nights under star-filled skies normally filled me with the pleasurable peace of isolation, and flickering camp fires became windows to dreams. Now, however, demons stalked the night, leaving an imprint of fear that, try as I might, I couldn't erase. I cut short my trip and headed home, and it was during this long drive that I suffered my next bout of absolute panic.

It started in a rather strange way. I'd stopped for fuel and food at a place called Norseman. From there it was all eastward across the mighty Nullabor Plain to my home in Adelaide 2000 km away. I was enjoying the drive and feeling great when, for no particular reason, I started thinking about Scottie, the roo shooter I had met in Eucla years ago — wondering where he was and what he was doing. I couldn't get him out of my head. It was like one of those silly songs or sayings that you find yourself repeating in your mind like a broken record, sometimes for days at a time. After a couple of hours I was starting to get really sick of it, and then it happened: as an approaching vehicle passed, there was Scottie. I couldn't believe my bloody eyes.

How this sort of thing has happened, not once but many times to me, I cannot explain. Is it coincidence, or freaky intervention from another place? I chased and caught him and we spent a short while reminiscing on our days in Eucla. I couldn't help reminding him of the time he taught me how to use his rifle!

I took off, settled back and things looked good until I opened a carton of banana-flavoured milk. I had only just finished it when, before I could even stop the vehicle, I was forced to vomit out of the window. I felt as though I had been poisoned and was really sick. This, I believe, triggered my next panic attack, which forced me to stay overnight at

Madura in the safety of a motel and near people.

The next day I battled occasional waves of fear until finally, when I arrived at Nullabor homestead, I made a desperate phone call to the Ceduna Hospital advising them that I believed that I might be suffering symptoms of a heart attack, and would they please have help available the moment I arrived. That two-and-a-half-hour dash was just a blur, and I was trembling violently by the time I reached their sanctuary. Again a medical check indicated nothing was wrong with my heart, and the doctor suggested I book into a motel and get some rest. A handful of pills and a good night's sleep had me fit and well by next morning, although feeling rather stupid with my whole performance. Only 800 km – a day's drive – and I would be home.

With fifty kilometres to go, I found myself standing in a phone box, desperate and frightened. Tears were streaming down my face. I could not read the phone book and the name of my doctor was beyond recall. I was convinced that I was going to die of a heart attack.

Why was I feeling like this? After all the challenges I had encountered, the battles I had fought, the control I had exercised over mind and body, where had all my strength gone? I had faced and overcome so many difficulties before; what was different this time? There was no visible threat from any direction, only an anguished, desperate feeling occupying all my senses and consciousness.

I cannot remember how I managed it, but ultimately I ended up arriving at a medical centre rather late in the day. Tests proved again that there was nothing wrong with my heart, but during our discussions I started talking about Len and his death, and we came to the conclusion that my trauma was nothing more than fear related to dying. Finally I reached the safety of my home and Rotha's caring arms, but the feeling of security didn't last for long.

In the early stages, when the uncontrollable attacks came, I would race to the phone and ring my doctor for assurance. They were moments of absolute panic that I can't begin to describe. Slowly I learnt to ride the waves myself – recycling my breath in a paper bag during an attack seemed to help enormously. I couldn't even go for a walk without my wife holding my hand to control my fear, and I will be forever grateful to her for nursing me through a period that must have been extremely frightening and difficult to come to terms with. I believe she was told that I probably wouldn't get better.

The best way I can find to describe how I was feeling was to liken my fear and trauma to a nightmare. I was walking down a long, isolated road. Bearing down on me from behind was a massive truck which I could not hear approaching, but I knew it was coming — sometime. If I could not hear it, how then would I know when to turn and face it, to fight for my life? It could annihilate me the way it did Len. Somehow I had to confront the situation. I took pills that I don't ever wish to take again, made a few visits to a psychiatrist, and in time, the gaps between normality and panic grew slightly further apart. Outside of an attack I was as normal as I have ever been in my life, but once they started, it was as though the wiring in my brain had been rearranged and I had absolutely no control over my thoughts. There was a short circuit in there somewhere.

After one difficult bout, my doctor visited me at home and suggested that perhaps I should spend some time in a hospital. They were the best words that I could have heard; although the doctor didn't mention where, or perhaps even intend it, I immediately thought of a psychiatric ward, and that was all I needed to get me up and running. That was the precise moment that I began the fight to regain control of my life in earnest.

The problem was that I was growing older. My physical life was changing — I was no longer 21. The end was now closer than the beginning and I had so much left that I wished to accomplish. Simply put, I didn't want to grow old. I was having a mid-life crisis. I feared that my heart was going to stop prematurely, just like Len's. The memory of his death, the first that I had ever had to contend with, and the way he died in my arms continued to haunt me. Even though I had been checked many times and assured that there was nothing wrong with my heart, and that heredity was on my side, it didn't help. Knowing with the mind was one thing — convincing my inner self was something entirely different.

My solution, I decided, lay in the desert. That would be my battle ground: the place where I would turn and fight the bloody great truck on my ground and my terms. The reason I chose the desert was simple. I would put my heart to the ultimate test. I would tackle a solo desert crossing and either stay there, or walk out a different person — a person more able to cope with whatever my destiny had in store for me. I would push myself to the limit — this was win or lose. There was no way I was going to remain as I was. I was 51 when I departed from Adelaide and headed for Alice Springs to attempt a solo unaided crossing on foot of the Simpson Desert from west to east.

My concept was to backpack all the way. Water would be the major problem. I knew that I could not carry sufficient water for the entire journey and therefore planned to use a desert plant called munyeroo, to supplement my supply. Its fleshy leaves are laden with moisture and the roots, when cooked, are edible.

Driving up to Alice Springs along the western edge of the Simpson Desert, I encountered my first major problem. I knew that rain had fallen in the late summer and I had expected to see the area green and alive. What I didn't realise was that the area had then suffered a prolonged period of extreme heat. This had scorched off the new growth and returned the land to its more normal, barren, dry state. The few green munyeroo plants that I could find were in an advanced stage of decay, the rest already reduced to dry stalks.

One thing you learn in the outback is not to judge the overall area by one small sample. Rains, when they come, are generally patchy thunderstorms. One location may receive several inches of rain, while another, only a few miles away, gets nothing. Therefore, what was out in the desert waiting for me was unknown. What I had seen however, over a vast area of the western desert edge suggested that I would receive very little help, if any, from the munyeroo plant.

By the time I had reached Alice Springs, I must admit I was starting to believe the journey would be beyond me. When I had first conceived the idea a few years ago, my wife was very much against the idea. Now when I phoned home, I received her encouragement. I hate to think what would have happened to me if I had given up at that point. I knew, however, that the anxiety I was experiencing was only a surface feeling, a game to be played prior to departure. Deep down I was still very much committed. My salvation lay in the desert and I would allow myself no alternative but to try. A friend in Alice made the comment that, surely with my knowledge of the desert, there must be a way. There was. I had forgotten.

Explorer David Lindsay's 1886 journey out into the Simpson Desert was my answer. For his survival, Lindsay had used a chain of native wells to supply water for him and his camels. These wells, which stretch across the desert, were abandoned by the Aborigines in the year 1900, when they walked out of their harsh environment and discarded that heritage forever. Eighty years of time, wind and erosion have completely filled in these wells, so that the casual observer, even standing on top of one, would not suspect the existence of good water only metres beneath his feet.

I was fortunate to have located all these wells and even the two trees blazed by David Lindsay with his initials. One of these wells could now play an important part in enabling me to cross the desert. It would supply water, hopefully, at roughly the halfway point. The well was 'Beelaka' and as Lindsay records, 'It is 12 ft deep and a good supply of good water'. He took 27 gallons from it.

I had some aluminium drilling rods with me in the vehicle, but to carry these, along with everything else I would need on my back, would be too much weight. I decided therefore to build a small two-wheeled cart to carry the load well out into the desert, where I would then abandon it. Obviously, dragging a cart would extend the time that I would be in the desert and my progress would be at a snail's pace, compared to back-packing. I could, however, carry the provisions necessary to cover the extended time.

I borrowed motorbike wheels, not the most suitable but readily available, from the local bike shop. I accepted the fact that the tread was not the same on each and that the axle sizes were different. Beggars can't be choosers. The only high tensile bolts available to be used as axles were too small, but I figured that I could pack them out with brass shims to make them fit.

Scrap steel for the cart came from the backyard of a friend's home and, hey presto, within a day, the frame of my shiralee, my burden, emerged! It was not high technology, but it would do the job. Years of necessity on the farm had taught me the art of making do from scrap. I had nothing against aluminium, which would have been lighter, but I would have had difficulty in acquiring a suitable product at such short notice. More importantly, I suppose, I knew how to weld steel and put my trust in the known. I spent the next few days in continued walking with a pack and an occasional stroll at night with the cart.

I wrapped my food carefully into one-day packs and sealed them in plastic. Maps of my route, with details of my radio call sign, frequencies available, and ground signals to be used in case of emergency, had to be prepared and supplied to the Police in Alice Springs. They were requested to advise the Birdsville Police on my behalf that I was coming and that they had complete details of my crossing. This is an important courtesy: everyone travelling in a remote area should inform some responsible person of their intentions.

I had no desire to use public money, or police time, in my search and rescue, should it become necessary. To cover myself, I made a deal with a pilot and news cameraman that would allow him to film the start of the walk, when I drilled for water, and then collect me from Birdsville. In return for the film rights, he would fund any rescue attempt. If he hadn't, I would have paid for it myself.

He told me that as a reporter for the local newspaper, he had covered an attempted solo walk across the Simpson Desert during the previous year. This was news to me, but then emotionally I'd been in another place around that time.

Paul Sharp had departed Alice Springs and headed out into the Simpson Desert but was ultimately forced to call for help. Rescued by the police, he said that he had abandoned any idea of further attempts. However, a short time later he was again reported missing in the desert, this time out near Birdsville and the local police were called in to investigate.

Sharp finally arrived in Birdsville and claimed to the now eager press that he had made the first solo, unaided walk across the Simpson Desert. But the police who had carried out the desert search disputed his claim. They had found one of his food supply dumps which held empty water containers. Sharp admitted that supplies had been left for him, but said he had only opened the water to taste it to see if it was still okay, then tipped it all out. Unfortunately this ruined his credibility with a lot of people, including the reporter. Did he or didn't he? Only Paul Sharp truly knows the answer to that.

While it appeared that my original reason for attempting this crossing was possibly unachievable now, I was seeking a much more rewarding goal. I was out to do battle with the desert and hopefully defeat my demons. First or last didn't seem to matter much anymore.

We flew out of Alice Springs at first light and headed for Alka Seltzer air strip, on the western edge of the desert. How we managed to load three people, the cart, cameras and numerous other items into such a small space I do not know. We certainly deserve a Storeman and Packer's ticket.

From my aerial platform the desert loomed ominously, its parallel waves of sand dunes rolling like a frozen sea, terminating over the horizon to the east.

I had originally intended to go completely cross-country by the shortest possible route. Now, due to my late decision to drag a cart, I chose to use some of the seismic lines which thrust out into the desert. The French Track was the shortest route, but unfortunately, would take me well to the north of my native well. I therefore chose a more southerly track, which would terminate at about the place I wished to abandon the cart and would take me near to the well. I would next have a cross-country dash to reach Poeppel Corner and then direct to Birdsville.

At Alka Seltzer I assembled the cart and double-checked my equipment. My obligations to other people finished when the camera stopped rolling mid-afternoon. A few minor adjustments to the harness on the cart, a wave to the aircraft as it headed homewards, then forward I lunged, taking that first step. This one-man wagon train was on its way — the journey of a lifetime lay before me.

🦎 🦎 🦎

I maintained a brisk pace over the first few wide, hard interdunal flats. My destination for the night would be Purni Bore, only 8 km away. Purni is the last permanent water available until Birdsville, some 390 km distant, unless you know where to find the reserves hidden beneath the sands.

It was dark when I arrived, and as I wasn't carrying artificial light I had to burn some spinifex clumps to gain enough vision to collect firewood to cook the evening meal. This caused some consternation to a group of travellers camped near the water only a few hundred metres away. They had not seen or heard a vehicle arrive and wondered what the hell was going on. However, they managed to contain their curiosity for about an hour, before making the first of several sorties to establish who, how and why. After a chat around their breakfast fire the following morning and then topping up my water containers, it was time for a wash. That splash was to last me for over three weeks. Pinned to my hat was their Lions Club badge, which I promised to carry across the desert.

Within the hour I experienced the first of many misgivings. If only I could have afforded the time to get wider tyres freighted up from Adelaide. The track was excellent for vehicles. Progress for me, however, was pitifully slow, as the too-narrow tyres bit deep into the soft sand.

I now established a daily pattern, which I would maintain until just a few days before abandoning the cart. I prepared breakfast in the dark and then moved out as the first rays of light appeared in the eastern sky. Around midday, I took lunch and several hours' rest; later I made sure to choose the evening campsite before nightfall. Collecting wood to cook the evening meal was the first job. However, I also required the firelight, as I was not carrying artificial light.

One early problem I experienced thankfully only lasted for several days, then almost disappeared — millions of flies! The black horde milled like parched cattle around an almost-dry waterhole, as they fought dementedly to suck the moisture from my eyes. I only partially solved the problem by bending my sunglasses to form windows for my eyes.

It was also during those first few days that I faced my greatest temptation. I was slogging away when this grader crew came upon me. They were heading out into the southern Simpson region to prepare tracks for oil exploration activity to begin soon. I mentioned the difficulty I had in judging distance and wished that I had installed some form of meter to the wheel. They departed, and later I saw their vehicle parked for a while on top of a very high sandhill away in the distance. When I finally approached their stopping point, I anticipated finding a note with the distance I had travelled since our meeting. Instead, sitting smack in the middle of the track was a large bottle of beer. I guess they felt I'd earned it, but for a person trying to do an unaided crossing, their gift was a problem. The task I had set myself was an unaided crossing, which meant no help. I worried that the grader crew could say to their mates that they had helped me in my crossing. I threw the bottle on top of my load, not knowing what to do with it. Fortunately, the following morning one of the crew returned to grade the old but reasonably firm track. Although when he'd finished it looked smooth and inviting, his work with a grader blade had made its surface very soft and more difficult for me to pull the cart through. As we sat cross-legged in the sand I handed him his gift back and watched while he demolished its contents in quick time. Problem solved. My beer would have to wait until I reached Birdsville.

Fortunately, I only had a few miles to go before his graded track turned southward and I could continue on an old, disused traverse not cut up by vehicle or blade. By no means a highway, it did save me the necessity of navigation, as I knew its termination point. Also, in the event that rescue should be required, my position could be relayed more easily. It did not help me in climbing the dunes, as I tended to use the much firmer undisturbed sand off to either side of the track.

If it hadn't been for the life around me, the next five days to where I would drill for water could easily have been just a mindless slog. As it was, my slow pace enabled me to see and be intimate with desert life - nothing large, except an occasional mob of camels or a solitary dingo sniffing out my tracks. I saw mainly birds and insects — the sort of things you miss when travelling by vehicle, moving fast, trapped in your noise machine. I never made camp feeling that I was a stranger to that particular area. How could I be? I moved at the pace of the desert, at one with the desert, as content and familiar as I would be in my own home.

Dragging the cart up the sandhills began to sap my strength. I would guess the number of stops required. It became a game. Rest and calculate. Would I be able to take four more steps? Perhaps I could make it six before my next panting stop? Coming down the face of the dune was easy. The only problem was how to keep in front of the cart.

The days were cloudless, and although not unduly hot, I perspired freely due to exertion. The stunted desert trees afforded only scant shade for the most part. I was forced to ration my already meagre intake of water.

I remember stopping and resting after one particularly difficult climb and becoming lost in thought wondering if I would ever make it the rest of the way. I seemed to be getting slower and slower. My left hand had been doodling in the sand and when I looked down, I was amazed to see that I had drawn a perfect cross. I am not a churchgoer but that symbol has been rather special to me ever since.

The Kulgera Police must have been monitoring my radio transmissions on the few occasions that I gave a position report to my back-up man in Alice Springs. They came on the air one day and wanted to know where the native well was that I intended to get my water from. I told them that I was keeping it secret as I didn't wish the site to become common knowledge and possibly vandalised. They then advised that they had spoken to the local Aborigines in their area and were informed that they knew of no wells out in the desert. There weren't any. I agreed with him that they wouldn't know of any. How could they? The last Aboriginal from this area had walked out of the Simpson Desert some eighty-four years ago. I couldn't do anything about it and still protect the sites that I had found, but suspected that he and the thousands of others around Australia who were listening in on our broadcast probably believed that the only water that I would find out in the desert was coming by air. I would just have to wear it.

By radio appointment the camera crew, which included a French reporter, flew over me at the nominated time. My signal mirror flash clearly pinpointed my position. They winged off to a rough landing strip located near where I was to attempt to find water and I arrived many hours later, suffering from heat exhaustion and possible early signs of heat stroke. My hands vibrated like tuning forks and even my old fear returned momentarily, but I resisted blowing into a plastic bag as I had done so many times back home. My canteen contained only a few mouthfuls of water. I had pushed my luck to the limit.

Finally I reached the well site and assembled my drilling rods, which had formed part of the structural strength of my cart. I was carrying enough rod to penetrate 16 ft, just under 5 m, which should be more than sufficient, as Lindsay's diary records, 'The well here is 12 ft deep'.

The crew could have easily brought in sufficient water for the rest of my trip, but that wasn't what I wanted – it would have defeated the purpose of the whole exercise. It was all or nothing, and as I started to drill, I silently prayed that I wouldn't be flying back to Alice Springs with them, as had been previously arranged if I was unsuccessful. I had got water here before … maybe I was lucky then … maybe it had now dried up.

Moisture started to appear at about 8 foot and spot on at 12 foot, water! I cleaned the hole out a little further and then lowered a small tube on a string. My bailer came up full of liquid. It was muddy but drinkable, and after the first container had been filled, the water started to clear. I took about thirty litres. This would now have to carry me to my destination, Birdsville.

My only other possibility for collecting water lay in the vast salt lakes that I would soon be crossing. If they contained mud, I had the necessary equipment to heat the salt sludge and condense the moisture.

With the water filming sequences over, I took time to survey the evidence of past habitation in the area. Stone flakes used for cutting and remnants of seed grinding rock slabs were scattered around, and so too human remains, their burial sites uncovered by the shifting sands. I think the French journalist was rather impressed with the whole deal. There sure wouldn't have been anything like this back where she came from.

Finally the film crew departed, having extracted a promise from me that I would camp and rest for several days. I didn't even stay one night there, but moved out before dark. I had no intention of spending time with the spirits of those original inhabitants dotting the nearby sandhills! Also, my food was now hardly sufficient for the remainder of the journey, which meant that I had to move fast. I didn't have time to dawdle.

The track finished and it was now by compass that I made my way east to pick up a large salt lake. By following it northwards, I would reach the French Track and then I'd be about 27 km from Poeppel Corner, which marks the corner of the three States, South Australia, Northern Territory and Queensland.

The only sign of recent human activity was a relatively fresh set of vehicle tracks heading northwards, which I crossed. They probably belonged to a seismic group working in the area.

Soft sand for the last few kilometres to the lake was sheer hell and I was absolutely exhausted by the time I dropped down on to its western edge. I knew that I wouldn't have the energy to drag my cart much further. It was hotter now, and I spent the rest of the afternoon wrapped around the butt of a low bush to enjoy its patchy shade. The lake forked to the south and the easterly leg, about three kilometres wide, disappeared shimmering beyond sight. The two towering sandhills which rose from either shore of the main lake ran unbroken northwards, the lake gradually narrowing.

My journey up the edge of this massive salt lake was not as easy as I had hoped. The surface was a little too soft to enable the cart wheels to roll easily, however it was certainly preferable to weaving in and out of the spinifex clumps and climbing numerous sandhills.

The moon was almost full, and in a few more days it would be rising as the sun set. My timing was perfect. I needed full moonlight when I abandoned the cart for my dash out of the desert. To make the necessary daily mileage, I would have to walk at night. This would also allow me to rest during the heat of the day and so conserve water.

The second night on the lake, I cut a set of vehicle tracks crossing the lake. With my fingertips I felt out the tread pattern. It was the same vehicle whose path I had crossed some four days earlier. They were now swinging eastward. It was also the night I realised how weak I was becoming. My diet was not sufficient for the effort I was expending. The next morning I would reach a point about 4 km south of the French Track and it was there that I intended to abandon the cart. I was nearly out of food, except for a 6-day pack of dehydrated goodies to last me for the 200 remaining kilometres. That night I just lay on my bed of salt, too exhausted to care about normal comforts.

On reaching my destination the following morning, I pulled the cart to the top of the sandhill to the east. That last climb required three portages of gear to make it to the live crest. This is where the two-wheeled monster would stay. It had served its purpose and to be burdened by it any longer would jeopardize my mission. It was now 17 days since I had set out.

Around midday, I directed a light aircraft to my position by flashing my signal mirror. The press from Adelaide had arrived for an eagles eye view. I had been advised by radio that they were coming. What they didn't tell me was that my wife and a friend were with them. This encounter brought home to me most forcibly my isolation in this vast hostile area — and the difficulty should I need to be rescued. Having guided them in by mirror, they saw me standing on my lofty perch, waving madly. After a circuit, then another run over my position, they had difficulty relocating me. Admittedly they were not experienced in aerial spotting. If they had taken note of my position, relative to the natural features around me, it would have been much easier. I guess they were also excited at seeing me. I was only a fly speck amongst a million such dots in that landscape. The aircraft spent about half and hour overflying the area before heading to Birdsville to refuel for the long trip back to Adelaide. My job now was to sort out what I needed to carry for the last leg of my journey.

It didn't take me long to select and then transfer the gear required from my cart into my backpack, and I was eager to depart. Birdsville was still a long way away. As I bent and tried unsuccessfully to swing my pack onto my shoulders, I quickly realised that I had a severe weight problem. I went through my gear again, making more sacrifices. The 5 lb rifle had to go. I cut the bottom from the tent, reduced the number of bandaids, etc. This time, after a struggle, I succeeded in getting the pack on, then stood upright. Well, sort of. I guess I was at about the same angle as the Leaning Tower of Pisa, though not as steady. There was no way I wanted to lift this weight after every rest! Fortunately, for that reason I made a wise decision. I selected a metre length of light aluminium tube from my drilling rods, not as a walking stick, but as a prop. Whenever I wanted to rest I would lean further forward, stick the tube under my pack, then stand upright. It took the weight off my shoulders, as I stood three-legged with the rod carrying the load. I wouldn't say that I cut a dashing figure as I set off, but at least I was mobile.

I crossed the next lake to the east just before dark, then waited for the full moon to climb into the star-scattered sky. It was then easy to see and to maintain a good compass course — the moonlight was more than sufficient. However, one false step with that load – a foot down a hole, for example – and I could be in real trouble. Occasionally, a cloud marching across the sky would switch off my light, forcing me to prop on my tripod legs.

I awoke next morning stiff and sore, not having covered the distance I had expected. I would have to lighten the load further before I either hurt myself or ran out of time. At this pace I would be out of water before Birdsville. The big problem was what to discard. The only item of any weight that I could neither eat nor drink was my radio and battery, which weighed about 23 lbs, or 10.5 kg all up. I decided to hang on to it until late in the afternoon and then reassess my position.

Occasionally I came upon a small patch of green: the odd crotalaria, a few flowering plants and the hardy caltrop, its spiky fruit now drying off. Perhaps it was their position on the sandhill, or a later shower that had enabled them to cling tenaciously to life. I'd had one nasty experience with the caltrop previously while I was pulling the cart. I was bent low to the ground, straining uphill in the harness, when I slipped, driving the spikes of several seeds deep into my knee and making it look like a pin cushion.

At 5 o'clock I made my last radio call to the Royal Flying Doctor Base at Alice Springs. It was a Friday and they would be closed over the weekend. I advised them that I was abandoning the radio and that my anticipated arrival time in Birdsville would be Wednesday, around midday.

Now, 10.5 kg does not sound much by itself, however, on top of the rest of the load, it was the straw that was breaking this camel's back. I wrapped the radio, battery and solar panel in plastic and hung them in the tallest tree that I could find. I was now easily able to swing my pack to my shoulders, and at long last could walk upright. I could have hung on and perhaps jeopardised the trip, sacrificing the weeks of hard slog, but I was not prepared to do this. Success was now only days away, and I meant to walk unaided to my destination. I alone knew my ability and situation. I was not gambling on the known, only the unknown — an accident.

I reached Lake Poeppel late in the evening and was surprised to see several lights on the far shore. It turned out to be two vehicles and three people from Queensland, who, without direction, had managed to find their way to the border peg. When they showed me their log of how they had managed to get here, I was most impressed. Distances and change of bearings were all noted meticulously — a professional effort.

However, the useless searching and backtracking they did as they endeavoured to locate the right tracks leading here could have been avoided. Their trip could so easily have been made more enjoyable, and more importantly, safer, with very little effort. They told me that they had approached the authorities in Birdsville seeking information as to the best tracks to use but received no help whatsoever — they just weren't interested. To me, that was disturbing to hear, especially when I'd been promoting, in my articles and talks, the need for people travelling in remote areas to notify the authorities or some responsible person of their movements.

Unfortunately, theirs was not an isolated case. Just a few weeks before I had left Adelaide, two different groups phoned me for directions and information on crossing the Simpson Desert. I advised both groups to contact the authorities in Birdsville; both said they already had and that they had wasted their time and money. They weren't interested. The travellers were going regardless, and my help hopefully made their journey a little safer. I have never struck this anywhere else in Australia. Perhaps normally accepted rules are not valid for that particular town.

I took my leave of the travellers early next morning and headed east to cross the last two salt lakes. The next major feature on the map was the Eyre Creek, about 100 km distant. The sandhills were becoming higher, but as if to compensate, the interdunal flats were increasing in width, which enabled me to make good time.

I was now into my last container of water, the one that I had taken first from the well. As I drew the cleaner water from the top, the remainder grew more turgid. When this was added to a packet of normally white macaroni and cheese, it took on a dark brown colour, full of grit and foreign bodies. If only the manufacturer could see his product now! I steamed off the water, using my specially prepared billy and a tube of plastic as the condensing surface. When this was finished, all that remained in my container was a baked blob of mud, sand and sundry other particles.

With three days to go my feet decided that they had had enough and blistered badly. Several blisters burst, which explained the moist, slippery feeling in my boots. Each toe was now wrapped in a case of Elastoplast. The next time I would view the damage would be at Birdsville.

Even though the days were warm and pleasant, I was feeling cold, and at night I froze. It was then that I realised how much weight I had lost. All my fat, my insulation, had disappeared. My bowel movements were dry, hard berries, my urine dark. My body was compensating for the lack of food and moisture by stripping my reserves and making sure nothing went to waste. I was slowly consuming myself.

I had reached a fairly defined two-wheel track and was right on course when a light aircraft flew over and circled me. A message was dropped asking me to signal if I was okay. It was the Birdsville Police. Strange, I thought, as I certainly wasn't overdue on my advised arrival time and hadn't requested at any stage any form of assistance from them. I couldn't understand how or why they needed to get into the act.

I crossed the dry, cracked bed of the Eyre Creek as the sun was setting, and with a full moon to light my way, made a further 18 km before camping on top of a large sandhill.

My water consumption, which was pitifully inadequate for my efforts, had been around 3.25 litres per day, but now, one and a half days from my destination, I had less than 3 litres remaining.

On Tuesday afternoon I crossed the last major sandhill of the desert, which I had previously named 'Big Red', and passed down onto the gibber plains. Here, I hoped that a station dam in the vicinity was carrying water. It was. When I look back, it seems strange that I didn't take a wash. Perhaps after three-odd weeks and with only one night to go, I savoured the anticipation of a luxurious hot shower. Or maybe it just didn't matter any more.

That evening I marched through a sea of grass, eerie in the moon's glow. A dingo ghosted along close by, stopping when I stopped, moving when I did. We shared the stars — we owned the night. Somewhere in the vagueness of it all, I do remember posing the question: 'If I were to die now, would you eat me while I'm still warm or wait until I'd cooled off a little?' I missed his company when he departed in answer to a call from a distant place.

About 9 am I rounded the southern end of a sandhill and spotted the lights of Birdsville. Another 16 km and my journey would come to its end. It was now twenty-three days since my departure. The wind had sprung up again and I managed only a few more kilometres before the cold forced me to seek the shelter of a small clump of trees skylined on a ridge some distance off to the side. I built a bough windbreak and settled in between it and my fire. That day I had covered about 44 km.

It was not until early morning that I managed to drop off to sleep, and I therefore woke up late, around 9.30 am. How strange it was to be lying back, not a care in the world, watching the sun climb into the sky! Normally I would have done about three hours walking by this time. I consumed the remaining food for breakfast, packed in a leisurely way, then set off. The pain of my blistered feet took the usual half hour to disappear into numbness. It would be interesting to see what they looked like when I pulled the plaster off.

Soon I could see the radio masts of Birdsville protruding above the sandhills. To one side, the tall river gums and the flights of birds clearly marked the path of the Diamantina River.

I rounded the last sandhill and there it was, my destination. The town of Birdsville lay before me. I cannot remember my feelings — over the past few days I had become a machine running on willpower, forcing myself on. Physically, I knew I was very sick; things were definitely not right within my body. Queer sensations pulsed and radiated over me in waves. I trembled internally. Mentally, however, I was strong, and my burning desire to reach Birdsville would have had me die on my feet rather than give in. While I lived, nothing could have stopped me from reaching my goal and the miracle that I expected, perhaps almost demanded, was going to happen.

The film crew from Alice Springs should have met me a day earlier by vehicle, but hadn't turned up. Obviously, something had gone wrong with their plans. As I drew closer, the dark blobs dotting the roadway turned out to be people. There were the press and TV from Adelaide and a large group of tourists. When my wife Rotha appeared from amongst their ranks, that's when I became human again, and appreciated the warmth of greeting displayed by those present.

Immediately, the shapeless things stuck in my boots started to complain, reducing my walk to a painful shuffle. I had now stopped pumping adrenalin; the journey was over.

In retrospect I could have made the crossing faster and therefore less painful physically and mentally. I should have abandoned the cart about ten days after departure; pulling it the extra distance had only sapped my strength. Also, I should have given more thought to the type of foods I used. Obviously, what I had taken was not nutritionally balanced for a long, sustained effort.

Someone suggested that I should have had a back-up vehicle to make the journey safer and easier. It sure would have, but it would have changed the very nature of the walk. I would have lost the solitude which had made my journey so enjoyable. I had chosen the most difficult, and therefore to me the most rewarding way to cross a desert. I had pulled or carried the necessities of life on my back, and been sufficient unto myself. Without being spurred on by spectators, my adrenalin had come from within. I had enjoyed the complete experience.

Well, that was until the press and my wife had departed, and I went to report in and thank the police for keeping an eagle eye on me, even though I didn't need it. For my trouble, I was ticked off for not advising them of my journey before I had set out. I explained that the police at Alice Springs held complete details of my crossing and that I had requested this information to be sent to the Birdsville police the day I departed. I was told that they hadn't received a thing until about two weeks after I had set out and in any case, they didn't have anything to do with the Northern Territory police. Interesting.

Being so sick and physically drained – which, knowing my normal temperament was probably just as well for all concerned – I became extremely distressed and confused that my meticulous plans had somehow gone astray. The queer sensations and internal trembling that had plagued me now for days returned with a vengeance. Radiating from deep within my core, it felt to me as though my body was fighting for its very survival, which it probably was given the way I had treated it.

Something was way off base here but I didn't have the mental capacity to sort it out. I couldn't come to grips with what was happening to me. Everything had been done, as they say, 'by the book'. My crossing was as planned. I had achieved my goal. I had won my battle with the desert and, I felt sure, with my mind, yet now someone was trying to belittle and destroy my credibility.

My aircraft finally arrived to carry me back across the land of the parallel dunes. When we arrived at Alice Springs, I went immediately to the police station to find out why they hadn't carried out my written request which, complete with maps, I had paid to have delivered to them by courier the night before I departed for the desert. I was annoyed, to say the least, as they had obviously let me down.

They went back through their files, sat me down and told me to say nothing, then picked up the phone and rang the Birdsville police. Yes, Birdsville confirmed that they had been notified on the Monday, the day of my departure, just as I had requested and then they asked if I was going to make trouble, to which my bloke replied, 'He's not like that'.

The only thing that I can put it down to, other than some form of power play over an obviously distraught person, is that I hadn't notified Birdsville directly by phone or posted them their very own set of plans before I departed. However, had I done so, would it really have made any difference? When you consider the treatment so many others had advised me they received when endeavouring to notify Birdsville of their intentions for a desert crossing or had sought information and help, I tend to think not. I believe I would have been damned if I did and damned if I didn't. Perhaps my crime was that I actually managed to walk across the desert, solo, on time and unaided.

There will always be parts of this country that will remain hostile to the fool, the ill-prepared, or just the unlucky, however, these areas are shrinking. The Birdsvilles of Australia are no longer the same as they were only a few years ago, irrespective of how the locals wish to maintain their image. Roads, vehicles, communications and knowledge have changed all that. Much more is accessible to the ordinary individual. The desert, the remote areas, are no longer the domain of the rugged outback dweller.

I believe that to experience the bush and our great outback is a necessary enrichment of a city dweller's life and should be encouraged. I am also for the individuals who dare to challenge themselves – our strength as a nation can only be enhanced by them. All that anyone has the right to ask is that, in venturing outside frequented areas and away from established tracks, you make contingency plans for your own rescue.

In a world of rapid technological advancement and pace of life, I think we have moved ahead of our evolutionary time scale and the body is finding it hard to adjust. To come back to nature, to meander at a slow pace through wilderness areas, to simply sit by a shady stream seeing life away from a concrete jungle of noise and pollution can only enrich the soul and the mind.

To a person striving to achieve a personal goal, failure can be bitter. However, success can also hurt if you let it — there are plenty of knockers out there. Like the night I arrived in Birdsville and a drunken yobbo, asked by the camera crew what he thought of my walk, said, 'So what. It's already been done by Burke and Wills, the explorers'. The great Australian knocker is alive and well.

But then there are people like Taffy Nicholls, merchant seaman, drover, boundary rider, publican, poet, painter and a true bushman. A long-time Birdsville identity, he had asked me years ago, 'Denis, where is this Big Red sandhill you write about? I've got tourists coming into the pub all the time after reading your article wanting to go out and visit it'. When I told him, he instantly recognised it as the Nappanerica Dune. His comment on my walk? 'Well, mate, I take my hat off to him, that's for sure. Yeah, he did a good job'. Thanks, Taffy!

Was I the first white man to walk the Simpson Desert solo and unaided? I'm not claiming it. And I wouldn't want to detract from anyone else's achievements. I'm just claiming that I did it. Others can draw their own conclusions.

The sudden death of my friend Len, who died in my arms in that remote creek bed, triggered my first panic attack a year later. No longer in complete control of my mind, I came crashing to my knees — a humbling experience. I thank Len for starting me down the path towards the most incredible journey I have ever undertaken: a challenge of mind and body beyond my wildest dreams. I am proud that I had the guts to ultimately tackle my problem head on. The moment I took that first step into the desert, two words hammered in my brain: death or freedom.

The desert crossing, my salvation, now lay behind me. While it took months to feel physically well again, my mind had been rewired. I had not only crossed a desert, but I'd used it to resolve a personal problem. My reward for my effort was my freedom. I had regained control of my life. The conflict between my inner mind and my conscious mind was resolved and the balance restored. I did it my way. I fought my mental battle alone in a desert arena without drugs and I won.

I had defeated fear.

Chapter 10

Desert Walker — Gulf to Gulf

It was January 1985. I had almost recovered from the physical trauma I'd inflicted upon my system the previous year, during my solo, unaided walk across the Simpson Desert from West to East. Rotha had nursed me back to health and I hadn't suffered any further panic attacks. My children, David, Susan and Richard, were all well and my business interests were doing fine. However, something was missing.

Already I could sense that this was going to be another restless year. To satisfy the powerful driving forces within, I needed to chase another dream, to challenge myself once more. My soul was searching. Time would reveal the purpose of it all.

It finally came to me in the form of a vision. When I awoke, I knew precisely what I had to do. The desert had called again and was offering me perhaps its last remaining challenge. A north to south solo walk. I just couldn't refuse.

While I was training in the Adelaide Hills for this latest adventure, my gaze was drawn over the ordered expanse of this beautiful city to the tall Norfolk Island Pines like guiding beacons lining the foreshore of the seaside suburb of Glenelg. I was thinking about the Royal Flying Doctor Service at the time and suddenly it all tumbled together in my excited mind. Why just settle for the Simpson Desert when I could knock that off on the way? Why not cross Australia? Why not walk for the RFDS? Why not walk into Glenelg? Why not?

And so was born Gulf to Gulf: a solo walk across the continent from Burketown on the Gulf of Carpentaria to Glenelg on the Gulf St Vincent via the centre of the Simpson Desert.

I had been aware for some time that the Royal Flying Doctor Service urgently needed funds to update its ageing fleet of aircraft, and considered that perhaps I could help in some small way by dedicating my walk as a fund-raiser for them. While I had never used their facilities for an emergency while on an adventure, access to help had always been available through my radio if needed.

The walk would also pay tribute to the early Aboriginal inhabitants of the Simpson Desert, the Wangkangurru people, to the explorers who made it into our history books (some by their abject failure), as well as those who didn't but should have, and to all the pioneers and their marvellous women who opened up this vast beautiful country of ours.

The remoteness of my planned walk meant that if donations were to be generated they would have to be forwarded, not collected by me en route. It obviously needed a well-planned publicity promotion and to this end I approached TV and the press for their support, offering an exclusive on my journey.

I asked the Piper aircraft organisation at Parafield Airport in Adelaide to supply an aircraft to get me and my equipment to Burketown, my starting point. Instead of the one plane I asked for, they supplied two so that a television crew could film my departure. I couldn't believe their enthusiasm and generosity.

It was all systems go now with a departure time scheduled in May. Once set in motion, this operation had to be faultless. There was no option if I was to receive the support of the media and particularly the citizens of Australia, who I hoped would rally to the cause.

The ensuing months were taken up with training, planning the route in detail and sorting out the food I'd need. In my solo crossing the previous year I had suffered through lack of water and poor diet, and while sections of this journey would place the same limitations of weight and carrying capacity on me, things could certainly be improved for this journey.

I sought the advice of a nutritional expert and finally settled on the type of diet that he thought would sustain me throughout the long duration of my walk.

He drew up a complete menu for 24 hours formulated by product type and weight, and then said, 'Okay Denis, that's day one,' as he handed the sheet to me for comment. 'All we have to do now is make up a series of different menus so that you can have plenty of variety'.

'Don't worry mate,' I said. 'It looks good to me, so don't let's waste time eh? All I have to do is multiply these ingredients by five and a half months. Simple.' His expression of horror was worth seeing.

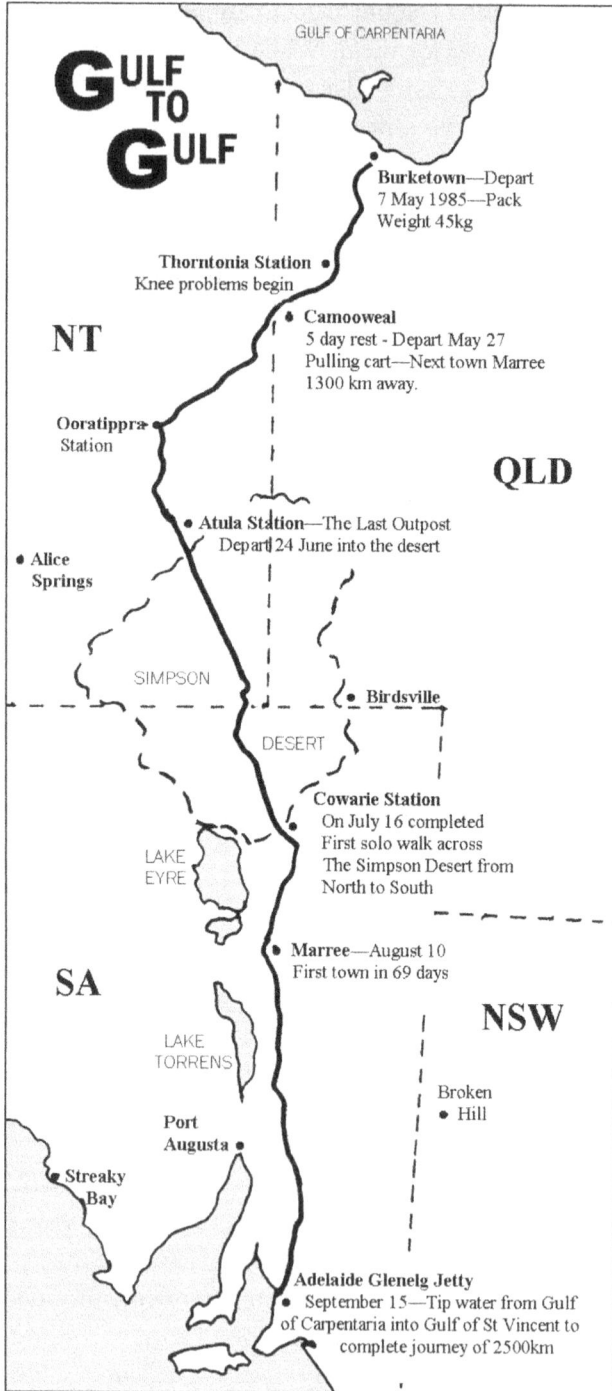

Gulf to Gulf

GULF OF CARPENTARIA

Burketown—Depart
7 May 1985—Pack
Weight 45kg

Thorntonia Station
Knee problems begin

Camooweal
5 day rest - Depart May 27
Pulling cart—Next town Marree
1300 km away.

NT

Ooratippra
Station

QLD

Atula Station—The Last Outpost
Depart 24 June into the desert

Alice
Springs

SIMPSON

Birdsville

DESERT

Cowarie Station
On July 16 completed
First solo walk across
The Simpson Desert from
North to South

LAKE
EYRE

Marree—August 10
First town in 69 days

SA

NSW

LAKE
TORRENS

Broken
Hill

Port
Augusta

Streaky
Bay

Adelaide Glenelg Jetty
September 15—Tip water from Gulf
of Carpentaria into Gulf of St Vincent to
complete journey of 2500km

Seriously though, I believe that if you can stand the sameness of it all, it's the way to go. When you have to either lug it all in a cart or in your back pack, space and weight can be more easily calculated. Enjoyment has nothing to do with it. My body needed fuel and that is exactly what it would get.

I built the cart myself. It was simple and based on the one I'd used on my last walk, although I did acquire slightly wider tyres. The cart width was set initially to handle the bush tracks, but then the axles could be hacksawed free to expose two other axles, reducing its width to more easily negotiate and manoeuvre in the rough terrain of the actual desert section.

I always find that the build up and preparation to any venture is the most stressful period. There is no room for error, particularly for a perfectionist like myself, even more for this journey, as it would be conducted over such a vast distance of hostile terrain. Without back-up vehicles, everything had to be meticulously planned, every aspect carefully considered and nothing left to chance. Once I set out, I am generally fine and quickly settle into a routine of enjoyment, freedom and thrill of the challenge — foolishness or accident are the only bogeys.

However, it didn't take long to realise that I had added a new and very powerful dimension: a monster that could easily devour me. On my previous adventures, if anything major had gone wrong I could always back off, retreat, and no one would be the wiser – not that I'd ever had to. Now, with the dedication and commitment, financial and otherwise, that I had inspired in all involved with my planned walk, fear of failure loomed large. What if I let them down? Moreover the media, so necessary if I were to make it a financial success for the Royal Flying Doctor, would have a field day. There would be nowhere to hide. On this journey I would carry more than the pack on my back, and no matter how hard I tried to control my thoughts, the fear of failure was ever-present in my mind. I still had some lessons to learn.

Once more I said farewell to a family I wouldn't see for five months or more and, with gear stowed aboard, two very laden aircraft finally climbed sluggishly into a cloudless sky — destination Burketown on the Gulf of Carpentaria.

As we skimmed the beautiful Flinders Ranges I couldn't help but think, 'Enjoy this trip, Denis — your return will be nowhere near as pleasant or as fast'.

We passed over the semi-circle of dry salt lakes that had defeated explorer Edward John Eyre, when in 1840 he tried in vain to plant the British Flag on the Tropic of Capricorn in the very centre of our continent. On our port side was Lake Eyre, a death bed for the contents of occasional mighty rivers and creeks that channel flood waters and drain a huge area of central Australia. Its enormous white, salt-encrusted surface some 130 km long and 80 km wide dominated my vision and contrasted magnificently with the vibrant desert colours of its surroundings.

Continuing northward, the journey remained smooth and uneventful, and with perfect visibility, the sight of the Simpson Desert now unfolding beneath our wings was at once inspiring, beautiful and awesome. It is the largest parallel sand dune desert in the world.

Spotted, irregular burnt patches torched by lightning lent a mosaic effect to vast areas as they ran like red stains across a mottled green carpet — forking, twisting, driven by the wind until finally their grasping fingers were unable to find enough suitable vegetation to sustain life.

During the hours that I gazed down on this majestic terrain with its parallel dunes terminating over the horizon, I thought many times of the enormity of my project. I knew the desert well – its size, its loneliness, its hidden dangers – but now with my eagle's eye view, it seemed immense: more desolate and forbidding than I had previously imagined. This was awe-inspiring scenery on a grand scale.

In 1929 Dr Cecil Thomas Madigan, flying in a Westland Wapiti Aircraft, made the first airborne reconnaissance of the then loosely named Arunta Desert, renaming it the Simpson Desert in honour of Alfred Allen Simpson, President of the Royal Geographical Society of Australasia, SA Branch. Madigan commented at the time, 'There is still one patch of Australia where white man's foot has never trodden'. Madigan later crossed the desert in 1939, and I'd retraced his steps in 1979.

At Atula station, on the northern extremity of the desert, we landed and left a package of supplies for my return journey. At Camooweal I deposited my cart and more food, and finally we reached Escott Lodge, on the outskirts of Burketown, to begin the final countdown to my walk.

I was all psyched up ready to go, however my commitments to the media meant that several days would be spent filming. Not that I minded, as I was able to renew my acquaintance with horses again after some twenty-odd years, as we rounded up the cattle for the TV camera.

After a quick race flat-out across the plains with the ringers, who didn't give me any leeway — and I certainly didn't give them any quarter

— it was into a chopper for my first ride ever. Mad Max was at the controls and I was assured by all and sundry that he was the best.

Max was a mustering pilot. It was his job to locate, then round up the cattle scattered throughout the dense, in parts almost impenetrable, scrubby areas of the property. He would then slowly guide the mob towards open ground where the ringers, directed into position by his radio, would be waiting in their vehicles to take over for the final push to the nearest stockyard. It's an exciting way to earn a living, and a dangerous one, as many badly scarred or dead helicopter pilots have found out.

On my ride we went searching an area for solitary bulls that had escaped the main muster. Soon we spotted one concealed in the thick scrub – what followed was a white-knuckled ride for me! Finally we landed near the ringers' vehicles just as they were preparing to winch our foam-flecked rogue bull up the ramp and onto the back of their truck. He didn't look all that happy.

My short mustering flight with Max had stirred my imagination: I could see it now from another perspective.

> The bull stood motionless on the bank of the
> dried-up waterhole. The first rays of morning
> light had switched off the stars, and soon the
> sun would climb into a cloudless arena.
>
> He would continue his search for water in the cool
> of the evening. The only energy he intended to
> expend now was to find a leafy canopy and rest.
>
> The years had been kind to him, although the scars
> criss-crossing his huge frame bore testimony to the
> battles he had fought and won. Sure, he had lost
> occasionally, but mainly during his maturing years
> while he learnt the technique of battle, the art of
> survival. Nothing could touch him now. He walked
> with wisdom and strength — king of a vast domain.
>
> Unchallenged and unchallenging, he no
> longer had a need to prove to anyone,
> let alone himself, his superiority.

This time he heard it clearly, and with ears pricked
and eyes dilated, strained to identify the direction.
There was no mistaking the sound and no forgetting
the last encounter. He had it positioned now,
coming upwind with the rising sun behind.

Quickly he moved to a nearby dense section
of scrub and stood motionless, knowing
his only defence lay in not being seen.

How well he remembered that last time. His
great strength had been pushed to the limit,
dodging and weaving for miles, and all the
time unable to shake the screeching, flapping
tormentor who pursued him so relentlessly.

Then suddenly it had all been over in a crescendo
of noise and flame as the demon fell to earth,
becoming a charred remnant of its former self.
Nothing then had moved save the thin spiral of
black smoke climbing into the sky and his heaving
flanks as he realised the danger had passed.

The noise was overhead now. The wind moved the
canopy violently and dust rose to blanket and choke
him. Then came the shattering piercing scream of the
siren. Trembling, he forced himself to stand motionless
while every muscle in his body demanded flight.

There was a sharp crack, then the fire of pain
as the shotgun pellets bit deep into his rump.
Galvanised into action, he broke cover and bolted.

Carefully his enemy manoeuvred him to an
almost treeless plain. No cover now — all
he could do was run — run for his life.

They pushed him for over five miles

before the first signs of tiredness set in,
flecking his coat with white foam.

Overhead a radio crackled, guiding the
ground vehicle onto a converging course.

He saw them coming, their plume of dust stretching
out behind. No mistaking the enemy — nothing
he had ever fought moved at such speed.

Soon they were next to him, unfamiliar shapes
pushing, bumping, trying to knock him
to the ground. Whichever way he turned,
he could not elude them. Their speed was
superior to his and he was tiring rapidly.

Finally flesh and steel met in a sickening
thud and his legs buckled beneath him.

Through the thick, swirling dust he could see
rearing above him, pinning him to the ground,
the four-wheeled conqueror, while in the sky the
winged monster departed in search of more prey.

Because of production costs, distance from Adelaide and limited time, I was driven the 320 kilometres southwest to Camooweal, where we filmed an enactment of my departure with the cart. The local residents were co-opted as extras and the owner of the roadhouse, his wife and their lovely young son in arms, bade me farewell. Then as the sky fired to a brilliant sunset, I walked back into town carrying only my backpack. What a weird feeling as I watched myself that night on replay, arriving and departing Camooweal – and I hadn't yet left Burketown! Driving back to Burketown, we detoured to take some footage of the Riversleigh fossil area, which I found most interesting.

My walk began in earnest on 7 May 1985 as I departed Burketown. The Lord Mayor had organised a send-off and the whole town turned out — even the school kids were marched out to participate. With an official Burketown pass entitling me to a free meal of fish and chips anywhere in their shire, I thanked all for their support and donations to my cause, hoisted my heavy backpack onto my back and walked out of town. I carried a small bottle of Gulf water, securely packed, which I intended to pour into the sea at journey's end. With a mighty roar and a wing wave, the television crew flew low overhead and suddenly I was all alone — destination Adelaide, some 2500 km away.

It was a very hot, muggy day with not a breath of wind as I marched along across a shimmering, flat, almost treeless plain. The fierce sun beat down mercilessly on my old army hat, its sweat band soon saturated, while beads of perspiration ran in droplets down my face, at times obscuring my vision. I wasn't accustomed to this oppressive humidity so I knew it would take a little while to adjust and settle in.

I must admit there were moments that first day when I wondered what the hell I was doing. Was the project beyond my physical capabilities? But I wouldn't give up. The TV producer had made a comment the day before that both disheartened me and strengthened my will. He had spoken to the Royal Flying Doctor's publicity chief in Adelaide and with a 'Don't know whether I should tell you this', advised me that they had no confidence whatsoever in my completing the mission. That hurt. Well they didn't know me very well, as I was now fully committed: I knew I would get there one day even if I had to crawl all the way on my hands and knees.

As far as walking was concerned it was easy going across soft, flat country and I settled in to a comfortable pace averaging about 32 km per day. This meant that I would cover the 117 km to the Gregory Downs Hotel in a little under four days. The bird life was prolific and pretty face wallabies were continually bounding across my path.

I was on the Plains of Promise. Discovery of this area was well documented by William Landsborough, who kept a detailed diary of his journey of exploration. He had been commissioned by The Royal Society of Victoria to look for the missing explorers, Burke and Wills, and had been directed to begin his search at the mouth of the Albert River and proceed towards Central Mount Stuart.

Landsborough's party departed from Moreton Bay aboard the MV Firefly. They survived shipwreck on the Great Barrier Reef and having their goods looted by drunken sailors. Finally, under tow from their escort vessel, they landed at the Albert River near present-day Burketown. In November 1861 Landsborough set out and, journeying southwards, camped beside a magnificent stream of crystal clear running water shaded by drooping tea trees. There were large Leichhardt trees, tall cabbage palms and pandanus and he commented that it was the finest and greenest river that he had seen anywhere in Australia. He called it the Gregory River.

Landsborough named the Barkly Tableland and during their 100-day march south, they located magnificent pastoral country never before seen by white men. Finally they reached a station on the Warrego River where they were informed that the mystery of the Burke and Wills expedition had been solved. Landsborough continued, crossing the continent back to Melbourne.

Gregory Downs was settled in 1865, abandoned in 1868 and resettled by the Watson brothers in 1876. They had come up from the Murray River where their father owned several stations. Burketown had been abandoned for some 12 years due to an outbreak of fever and because of the difficulty of getting supplies; the Watson brothers hired a schooner to freight in goods from Townsville. Ultimately they built a general store to cater for outlying stations and in so doing, breathed life back into Burketown. In 1877, they established a pub and store at Gregory itself in its present position.

🐦 🐦 🐦

I walked into the Gregory Downs Hotel right on schedule and with the inducement of a free bed in the motel, I decided to stay over. That night in the bar crowded with outback characters was memorable. A roving band of musicians, suitably plied with the necessary beverages, sat on the floor and entertained us with a variety of instruments. A small altercation had one musician demolish his guitar on the head of another musician, but the ensuing ruckus was only a minor inconvenience to the serious drinker.

The following day I bade farewell to my generous host and his ever-present performing parrot and pushed on for about 30 km, then turned off the track to make camp beside the Gregory River. Here was a magnificent section of fast flowing clear cool water and after the heat and exertion of the day, I enjoyed a swim. No wonder Landsborough was so impressed when he located and named the Gregory in 1861! I decided that one day I would return to camp for an extended period of time.

Soon I started to climb up to the Riversleigh Plateau, passing the turnoff to the scientific dig site that the film crew and I had visited just over a week earlier. The fossil-bearing area of the Riversleigh Plateau is in a rocky and inhospitable landscape, though where I had waded across the river to reach the research operation's base camp was idyllic. Situated amongst tall palms on the edge of this beautiful waterway, the camp had all the visual impact of that Hollywood series, 'Gilligans Island'. If Gilligan had walked out from under the canvas awning shading the cooking trestles, I would not have been surprised.

Dr Michael Archer, Associate Professor of Zoology, University of NSW, with his team of professional and amateur helpers, used this beautiful setting as their headquarters while they reworked previously located fossil areas and searched for new and exciting finds. In earlier field trips to this area, Dr Archer and his team had doubled existing knowledge of prehistoric Australian mammals. Now, they had not only doubled that accumulated knowledge, but located significant new fossils.

Of this Riversleigh area, Dr Archer states: 'There is nowhere else in Australia where you have in one place the ability to peer into the evolutionary development of Australian mammals over such a lengthy time span — some 50,000 to 15,000,000 years'.

In 1984, Dr Archer's team had found the teeth of a 'Thingodonta' — not a scientific name, just a fill-in until they can work out what it is, and give it a proper name. Dr Archer described the Thingodonta to me as a 'phenomenally weird animal. To give you some idea of its weirdness, it would be like finding the first whale, or the first bat, or the first monkey if they had never been found before. It's a new order of mammal never seen anywhere else in the world. All we know is that it's about the size of a rabbit with the strangest teeth'.

Several tons of rock had been selected for further laboratory testing and breakdown, and one can only hope that Dr Archer will find, nestled within, a complete Thingodonta skeleton. The Thingodonta was formally described in 1988, and given a new genus name: Yalkaparidon.

I didn't detour to the Riversleigh dig site this time. I was limping and my right knee was swelling. I put this down to the rocky surface of the road and hoped it would settle down.

At Undilla station, where I spent the night with a truly delightful family, I heard the tragic news that the son of the Camooweal roadhouse owner had died. Apparently his father had moved a large refrigerator back from the wall to effect repairs, when, unnoticed, his son had crawled in and inserted a screwdriver into the works. The family we had captured on film only a few weeks ago had suffered the cruelest blow any parent could imagine.

I wanted to walk into Camooweal just on dark as per our enactment, and with time up my sleeve, spent several hours resting under a shady tree to escape the heat of the afternoon. Flat on my back with one leg resting on my knee, I felt a slight scratching. Opening my eyes, I saw a Willy Wagtail using me as a resting place in between dashes to collect the flies which congregated around me. I would see a Willy Wagtail nearly every day for the rest of my journey, even through the remote heart of the Simpson Desert. They were the most widely dispersed species I noted.

I entered Camooweal at sundown on the day planned and immediately contacted the TV producer in Adelaide to advise him of my arrival, and that, unbelievably, that I had a magic sunset similar to the one we had filmed.

'Denis, I'm glad you made it on time' he said. 'We have just finished showing your arrival on the news.' I hope they didn't expect the same perfection in timing for the rest of the journey.

The local doctor checked out my knee and suggested a few days' rest to reduce the swelling. He wasn't hopeful for the rest of the journey, particularly the desert section where I would be carrying the maximum load on my back.

I hadn't been to church for years, but at the request of the grieving family I attended their local church meeting. While saddened at the cruel blow dealt them, I felt uplifted in the knowledge that with their faith and the support of their community, they would survive with increased strength from this tragedy.

I departed Camooweal on 27 May after a five-day break. Ice packs had reduced the swelling, and I was raring to go. No pubs, no takeaways, no icecream. My next town was Marree, a massive 1400-odd kilometres away — too far to dwell on. In between I would pass by twelve cattle station homesteads and conquer a 450 km trackless section of the Simpson Desert.

My backpack was now stowed securely on top of my two-wheeled cart and once in the harness, I was pulling well in excess of 125 kg. I had enough food to reach my next depot, Atula station, some three to four weeks away. I also had water for about two weeks, with top-ups planned at several stations and whenever the opportunity presented itself.

After a day's walk west along Highway No. 1, I turned southwards once more and, now on station tracks, passed Austral Downs homestead. Cattle grazed on well-grassed black soil plains, which seemed endless.

Dark clouds were marching across the sky – a deluge was imminent. The last thing I needed was to be caught in black soil country in the rain: nothing moves. Ahead I could see a change of country indicative of sand, and hurried to make it before the rain. I didn't. Finally, a drowned rat now standing about seven feet tall and towing a cart whose wheels had grown enormously with clinging mud, staggered on to a sandy base. I was now into desert country.

That night was the most miserable for the entire trip, sleep wise. It rained continually and my 'el-cheapo' tent leaked like a sieve; I was forced to cut holes in its base to let the water out. But my sleeping bag was excellent: I slept naked and stayed warm all night, even though it was absolutely saturated and had to be wrung out in the morning.

I turned westward again along the Sandover Highway (a dirt track) heading for Ooratippra station some 200 km or about six days away and settled into a comfortable 32 km per day routine, my pace so constant that I could accurately forecast my progress by my watch.

On this section I encountered only two vehicles. The first zig-zagged down the track in an erratic cloud of dust, belching smoke and clattering noise, until finally it spluttered and died about a hundred metres away. It was jammed full of Aboriginals, their duffel coats turned up around their ears — stockmen by their appearance. They just sat and stared at me, perhaps not believing their eyes. Finally, unable to contain themselves or miss an opportunity, they wound down a window as I drew level and one uttered the all-too familiar phase, the only variable, the request:

'You wouldn't have any petrol mate?'

Quick as a flash I came back: 'What would you like, super or standard!?'

Several days later, the second vehicle came around a bend and braked hard to stop just behind me.

I turned to say hello, only to be greeted with, 'Well you have certainly buggered up my day'.

Hell, I thought, this is all I need — to strike a real live nut in the middle of nowhere, or worse still, someone who believed I was.

'Just finished telling the missus and the kids', he continued, 'This is it. We're so remote and isolated from help that if anything happens to us or the vehicle now, we can be in serious trouble — perhaps even die. They were rapt with my importance as leader until we came around the bend and spotted you. You sure destroyed the moment,' he said with a smile. 'Anyhow, we were just going to have smoko. Would you care to join us?'

Tea and biscuits later, I used their HF radio to call Alice Springs with my progress report. On hearing my call sign, 5SBX, he leafed through an old scrap book, and there it was. We had spoken to each other on radio some seven to eight years ago. As I waved them goodbye, I couldn't help but think it's a small world.

I was glad to finally get off those monotonous straight stretches, and after a night's stopover at Ooratippra station, I said farewell to my generous hosts and turned southwards again along a winding two-wheel station track through pleasant country. The weather was cooler now and I had left the humidity behind, not that I wasn't perspiring freely hauling my heavy load through soft sand.

At Lucy Creek station I was invited to stay the night and accepted a dinner invitation. The meal consisted of the largest steak I have ever seen, which overlapped the plate on all sides. A solitary small potato hiding in the corner kept it company. This was a cattleman's meal, and boy did I suffer that night. For the last six weeks, my diet had consisted mainly of easily digestible small portions of food, and consequently my stomach had shrunk. I was in agony.

I fronted up for breakfast as invited.

'It's ready in the kitchen mate. Help yourself'.

I couldn't believe my eyes. There sat its twin, a gruesome reminder of last night, less the potato naturally. It was, after all, breakfast! I mumbled something about perhaps sticking to my diet. Nothing was wasted however, as my host demolished my portion for seconds! It's a big country — everything's big out here.

Passing through the Jervois Mine camp, which was in caretaker mode, I reached the Plenty Highway, a good dirt track, and camped the night. An aircraft overhead the following morning seemed to be searching the area, and by the time I reached the entrance to Jervois station homestead,

I found out why. The press had arrived in a station vehicle to meet me. We walked, talked, filmed and re-enacted until finally, exhausted, I marked my position on the track and, loading up my gear onto their vehicle, we drove the 30 km into Atula station.

Over the next few days, they filmed everything they could until – finally satisfied – they departed. The station owner then drove me up the track to where I had previously marked my position, and I walked back to the homestead. I didn't want any section of my journey across Australia devoid of my footprints.

I departed Atula on 24 June down the Plenty River on a two-wheel track that soon sapped my strength, as the wheels bit deep into the soft sand. Just off the track I visited the remains of a blue streak rocket that had been launched from the Woomera Rocket Range in 1966. Originally ninety feet long and weighing 100 tons it had travelled 700 km in six minutes before crashing beside the Plenty River. Although badly mangled, it was still an impressive sight and a reminder of Australia's involvement in the Space Race. Finally, I reached a fence at the end of the track, and the start of my cross-country section over the desert, which I hoped to exit at Kalamurina station some 450 km away.

I now had four days of hard work dragging the cart through soft sand and rough terrain. I soon realised the tyres should have been much wider. The floodout country of the Plenty River shrunk and died and the interdunal flats narrowed as the sandhills closed ranks as if to repel an invader.

A huge feral cat, the scourge of small reptiles and birds, lay concealed as I passed within about 4 m of his position. Spotting him, I slowly reached for my survival rifle. He didn't wait around. I believe that the destruction they cause warrants urgent research into some form of biological control of all non-domestic cats in Australia, and stricter management of their domestic equivalent.

The press had enlisted the help of the station owner at Atula to track me down so that they could capture some more footage. Advised by radio of their coming, I camped at the base of a large sandhill, prepared a signal fire and awaited their arrival. They were nearly a day late, having had several punctures, and difficulty following my wheel tracks. My signal fire and mirror eventually guided them to my position.

Finally they were satisfied with their filming, and loading my cart onto their vehicle, they departed. The rest of the journey across the desert would now be done with a backpack, allowing me to cover more distance per day than the pitiful amount I'd achieved towing the cart these last few days.

I was glad of the media people's company, even though they destroyed my solitude and my totally focused concentration, which I really needed to complete the job at hand. Probably part of me wished to escape back to comfort with them, if the truth was known. After every visit I noticed that it would take me several days to readjust.

I had planned to carry about twelve days' water on my back, sufficient to enable me to reach the native well, Beelaka, where I would top up for the final dash out of the desert. By drilling down about 3.5 m with my aluminium drilling rods, I would be able to draw the water to the surface with a small bailer on the end of a string.

My pack weighed over 55 kg, and as I struggled to swing it onto my back, I knew I had a problem with its weight. The battery, solar panel and HF radio weighed about 11 kg. I couldn't eat it, drink it or leave it, although I was tempted. I would have been crucified by the media if I'd got into trouble and didn't have it. I re-checked my pack, but there was really nothing I could discard. The only clothes I'd kept were what I stood up in, plus a jumper, light waterproof jacket and hat. My load consisted of a sleeping bag, ultra-light bivvy bag that I had deposited at Atula station on the way up, small air mattress, water, food, billy, spoon, sheath knife, matches, small medical kit, maps, compass, pencil, signal mirror, aluminium drilling rods and bailer, equipment to distil water from mud or salt sludge, radio, battery, aerial and walking stick. My only luxury was some toilet paper, and half a comb for vanity. I had no artificial light, and had even discarded my reading glasses. It was impossible to travel any lighter.

I had discarded the cart and picked up my pack on 4 July; by that afternoon I was well and truly in trouble. My right knee had swollen enormously and my spine, which had been operated on some years ago, was under severe pressure. I limped badly and was resting about every one hundred metres. I made it into a game: 'Let's try for another hundred steps'. Then I would stop, place my walking stick under my pack to let it carry the load, and stand upright. Finally it got down to fifty steps. That night, tucked in my swag, was probably the worst in my life. I wept in anger and frustration. I didn't sleep. I had failed myself and all those who had faith in me. My body could no longer support my mental strength

— my dreams. I wasn't going to make it — not this way anyhow. I tried again for a few hours the following morning — a last desperate attempt I suppose, but it was pointless. I could no longer carry the necessary load to complete my mission.

My midday radio message read in part:

'Either battle on and risk severe physical injury requiring lift out, and therefore jeopardising the complete Gulf to Gulf walk, the fundraising for the Royal Flying Doctor, or as an example to others, I now show a responsible attitude while I am still well. In consideration of all factors, and not wishing to inconvenience or put at risk the lives of others, I am prepared to concede defeat in my unaided attempt. However, if it is possible to arrange an air drop of food and water in about six days time, I will continue on with a reduced load. Sorry. Denis Bartell.'

Almost immediately, the radio crackled back 'Five Sierra Bravo Xray. All okay and understood. Airdrop can be arranged. Good luck. See you in six days.'

With the time and details confirmed, I set about my venture with renewed vigour. I reduced my load of food and water, the only expendables, to sufficient for six days. Based on previous experience, I knew I could survive on three litres per day, at least for that duration, though it is grossly under the recommended level. I repacked eighteen litres, had a huge drink and pushed off. Suddenly I could stand upright, and although still limping badly, I was now capable of making a mile.

The interdunal valleys were rough and matted with spinifex. While I was able to dodge most of the spiky clumps, wherever possible I would ascend to the dune tops. Here, long sections of relatively smooth open sand patches dotted with cane grass allowed faster progress. Although the sand was softer, I was able to swing my leg rather than bend it, and did not suffer the painful jarring that occurred in the rougher terrain below. Occasionally I would climb to lofty domes of windswept fiery red sand and stand enthralled at the magnificent views afforded as they towered above their surrounds. How I enjoyed the isolation, the endlessness of it all, the feeling of being at one with this unique landscape as I moved in harmony with it and its inhabitants!

I left nothing behind to remind of my passing save a faint trail of footprints in the shifting sands. Other footprints laid down overnight told their story — a map of life, variety, intrigue and survival. The footprints of a tiny beetle made a dash out across open ground towards the sanctuary of a nearby cane grass clump only to disappear abruptly as those of a large lizard crossed its path. One carried on, his belly full as he awaited his turn to be devoured by a larger or more ferocious prey in the never-ending cycle of life.

A speck in the distance caught my eye and I knew immediately by its colour that the desert was about to change. Scrappy, isolated acacias had so far clothed my way, but that night I camped on a small clay pan encircled by a lone stand of gidgee. How I enjoyed the warmth given by the best firewood in the desert.

Next day I crossed at right angles the first track I had seen since departing the floodout some twelve days earlier. It was an old seismic line cut for oil exploration and I advised the Royal Flying Doctor of my location by radio, as it would give the only clue to my whereabouts should I be off course. A message from the pilot indicated that he knew of the track, and that I had made 65 miles from the Lone Gum.

Heading for a prominent sand ridge just to the south which would afford uninterrupted views in all directions, I made camp in a small dune-locked, gidgee-covered valley at its base to await my airdrop.

I stripped, slipped into my sleeping bag, and zipped up my portable home. Of my meagre possessions, the bivvy bag was my favoured piece of equipment. A few seconds to roll it out, push in four aluminium pegs, slip in the fibreglass hoop to keep the material off the face, and presto, four star accommodation! The material was Gore-tex, which keeps out the rain, but allows body condensation to pass through it. In other words, it breathes. Some might consider being encased like a mummy claustrophobic, but I did not find this to be so. Unless it was likely to rain, I only zipped up the mesh in front of my face, so that I could see the stars and watch the fingers of flame from my camp fire. When you are preparing for the land of nod, this has got to be the only way to go. It beats the heck out of a room with a black ceiling and holes in the wall.

As I didn't wish to rough it, or perhaps out of consideration for ageing bones, I carried a self-inflating three-quarter length Thermarest mattress. For very little extra weight, this adds some comfort to the all-important insulation layer between you and the earth. Boots, with my clothes on top, formed my pillow.

The next day was the big day, and I hoped for perfect weather. I needed clear skies, particularly to the north, and very little wind. I believed my track, or heading, was good, and provided this was so, the aircraft would approach my position from the north.

It had been arranged that the pilot would fly from Alice Springs to intersect the Plenty River some 250 km distant. Its floodout is clearly defined by the dense tree growth, a feature of all inland rivers. He would then turn southward, follow the floodout to its termination and my camp, The Lone Gum, then fly my track of 154° true or 148° compass.

We'd selected early morning for the drop, with the sun high enough in the sky to enable me to use my signal mirror to attract the pilot's attention. Calmer wind conditions are also more likely at that time of day. I needed calm so that, should the aircraft or I be to the left or right of my intended track, if I could not see their approach, I would at least hear them. It would then be a simple matter to contact the aircraft by radio and guide them into the drop zone. Well, that was the plan, but it didn't quite work out that way.

I was up before daybreak, as usual, and prepared breakfast from my few remaining supplies. I had one good drink, and then deposited the water container in my pack, out of sight, out of mind. The last mouthful I had left would have to get me to the native well, Kilpatha, should anything go wrong with the airdrop. Although Kilpatha had been destroyed as a pristine Aboriginal well site by a bulldozer looking for a good supply of water, at the base of this huge, deep hole, it is still possible to tunnel in and get enough seepage water to survive in an emergency.

Kilpatha is situated in the Northern Territory, 343° true and thirty-three kilometres from Poeppel Corner, which now has a concrete post marking the junction of the three states. Poeppel's original timber corner peg had been removed a few years earlier, and is now preserved in Adelaide. While I knew the exact location of Kilpatha native well on the map, I didn't know my own exact location. I had no doubt that I could eventually find the well, provided I didn't dehydrate first. Anyhow, I would start to worry about that small problem only if the aircraft failed to arrive today.

The sun rose on an almost cloudless sky, and conditions were calm. Lady luck was smiling down upon me. I packed all my gear and hung my backpack high in a tree so that prowling dingos would not rip it apart. With my radio, battery, solar panel, compass, maps and signal mirror, I then climbed to the top of the adjacent sandhill, and to the site I had chosen for the airdrop. My first job was to set up the radio and couple up the solar panel, then mark out the line of the drop run. Next I prepared a number of signal fires using cane grass and spinifex.

I made contact with the Royal Flying Doctor Base in Alice Springs when they began their morning transmission, and determined that the aircraft had just departed and its estimated time of arrival was about 9.00 am. At about 8.45 am I lined up their incoming course with my compass and then began to flash with my mirror a rectangular section of sky of sufficient size should either of us be off course. I wanted to give as much warning as possible of my position.

By 9.30 am, having neither seen nor heard any aircraft, I was really concerned. As a pilot myself, I knew that to be thirty minutes late, something had to be astray. Even if the wind strength and direction supplied by the meteorological office and used for flight planning were wrong, it wouldn't be to the tune of thirty minutes. It seemed more likely that something had happened to the aircraft, or – the other dreaded possibility – that I was way off course.

I had difficulty raising the base due to interference and signal strength, but finally established that the aircraft was still flying and that they would be late arriving over my position. Why? I wasn't enlightened. It was also strange that I could not contact the aircraft direct, as I knew that they were installing a radio compatible with mine, and would by now be within range of my transmission. To make matters worse, the wind strength was increasing, which would make it more difficult to hear them approaching, or passing me to the west.

The quiet of the desert gets to you after a while. After long periods of isolation, one tends to hear noises. It had happened to me many times before but never with the frequency I was experiencing on that day. I was hearing phantom aircraft from all directions. Then at about 9.45 am I heard it clearly, but to the south of my position. The impossible had happened. Either they were searching the wrong area, or I was way off course. The latter didn't bear thinking about, or the embarrassment.

With the sun now behind me, my signal mirror was useless; I raced to the radio, but was unable to make contact with either the Flying Doctor Base or the aircraft. To make matters worse, the engine noise, which had been to the south and moving west, was no longer evident. I lit my signal fires, but did not put a lot of faith in them. The wind was flattening the smoke, which without suitable material to give off dense smoke wasn't terribly brilliant anyhow.

I don't know what made me glance to the north, as I was no longer expecting them from that quarter, but there to my amazement and relief, was a speck clearly visible in the bright blue sky and approaching me right on target. I had the signal mirror on them fast, and their wing waggle indicated that they had seen my flash. To say I was relieved would be an understatement — there would be time later to work out what had happened. The pilot did a few circles around me and, obviously happy with what I had laid out, commenced his first run.

With wheels and flaps down, and on a long low approach until right on target, the first food package tumbled out, hitting the ground only a few yards away. I couldn't help but think of the movie Dam Busters, as it bounded over the ground until pulled up abruptly by a large cane grass bush. I hurriedly retrieved the package and checked that nothing had broken. The same procedure was repeated for a second package, which I again retrieved undamaged.

Next came the water, the most vital part of the drop. It had been packed in tyre tubes as per my instructions, no more than one-third full. Too much water and they will burst on impact; the tubes must be floppy. All were dropped with precision by the pilot, enabling me to get to them quickly to salvage any that may be leaking. Of the six tubes dropped, only two burst, losing most of their contents. They were the smaller, car-type tubes, which I suspect may have been overfilled. The survivors were the truck type.

From my observation, I believe that the aircraft would have been better flown slightly higher off the ground. The tubes were hitting at almost the velocity of the aircraft. Higher up, the effect of drag or wind resistance may have slowed them down more before impact. Irrespective of this, the method was sound, and I had retrieved more water than was required.

With the airdrop over, I raced back to my radio to advise the success of the operation, and have the base ask the pilot for a position report.

Unauthorised traffic on the control base frequency made contact extremely difficult. When my signal was finally picked up, they made the now familiar request: 'Would all Aborigines transmitting illegally please keep off the air while we talk to the man in the desert'.

To their credit, most did stop transmitting, a thing they would not do for any other reason. I guess perhaps they could relate to my isolation and what I was trying to achieve.

To own and operate this type of radio equipment, you need to be licensed, have the frequencies fitted, approved, and use the set in accordance with the rules and regulations as laid out in the Communications Act. Heavy penalties apply, but are not enforced, for non-compliance, including confiscating the equipment. The frequency I was using at the time is allocated to the Royal Flying Doctor Base, Alice Springs. During normal working hours it is used with their authority to conduct normal traffic, outlying stations to base, telegrams, radio telephone and medical advice and emergency calls.

One day someone, black or white, in a remote situation requiring urgent medical assistance, will not be able to make contact to request help, due to the all-too frequent interference on this working frequency. It will be a bit late then to start enforcing regulations.

'Five Sierra Bravo Xray, this is VJD Alice Springs. Your signal is very weak, go ahead.'

'VJD Alice Springs, please advise aircraft, food and water drop okay, two containers burst, but have plenty of water, all okay.'

'5SBX message received. Your signal very weak. Check tuning of your aerial.'

I re-tuned the aerial and tried again to make contact, but nothing happened, just an ominous, unfamiliar clunk. I could hear them calling me, but obviously insufficient power remained in my battery to enable transmission.

The aircraft made a final circuit around my position, and then with a wing wag and shattering roar as it passed above, it was gone. I had a last fleeting glimpse of faces peering down on me from another domain, as they returned to a scotch and soda and a sit-down three course lunch.

And me? Well what more could a man want? I now had ample food and water, plenty of wood, and the tranquility of my desert environment had been returned. We moved again as one.

With the excitement over and adrenalin at a normal level, my immediate job was to transport all my newly acquired possessions to my base camp.

Viewed from the top of the sandhill, my campsite was idyllic. The small enclosed gully floor formed between the towering dunes was massed with gidgee trees affording good cover, and a plentiful supply of the best fuel. Gidgee burns hot and slow. The smoke from my morning fire twirled lazily upwards until caught by the wind and whipped over the dune top, while at the furthermost end of my retreat a dingo edged across one of the many small clay pans that lent a mosaic effect to the valley floor below. I named this spot the Simpson Hilton and wondered where else in the world pampered patrons would receive their breakfast delivered by air.

The running to collect packages had aggravated my knee, and the swelling had increased dramatically, so it was with relief that after many portages, I finally limped back into camp with the last of my supplies.

Before I unpacked my goodies, I set up my battery and solar panel. I had ample time now to fully charge the battery. As I had advised that I would be resting my knee for three days, and with my last message received all okay on food and water, I knew that the base would not be too concerned if I missed my radio sked for this period.

As I unpacked, I eagerly awaited the discovery of 'unasked for' extras — things like a juicy steak, fresh vegetables, perhaps even some icecream. With the exception of some honey and oranges, however, I got what I ordered — the same food I had been eating for months. They must have believed me when I said that I treated food only as fuel for the body.

I had burnt all the packaging material except for a screwed-up piece of paper before I realised that part of my order had not been fulfilled. Where in hell was the bloody toilet roll!? Smoothed out, I had two magazine pages of advertisements for house and land sales. With careful use I thought it should be enough to complete the crossing – paper sure beats using foliage, or the softer end of a bunch of spinifex, which I had been using for the last couple of days. I spent the rest of day one at the Simpson Hilton settling in for my enforced stay and sorting out my supplies.

I cleared the prickles from a sandy spot under the leafy bough of a large gnarled gidgee and unrolled my bivvy bag. Next I hung my sleeping bag out to air and catch the afternoon sun, something it badly needed. It stank! Of late I had had the distinct impression that I was sharing my bed with a dead possum. Considering I hadn't washed for about two weeks, I hoped the possum didn't mind. Then I found the annoying leak in my air mattress and patched it with a heated strip of Elastoplast. With the addition of a wood heap, my campsite was complete, and I could turn my attention to dividing up the food supplies into seventeen piles. This represented the estimated number of days I would spend in the desert.

I filled my folding plastic water containers from the vehicle tubes, and found that enough remained to have a reasonable wash, which helped my poor bottom. Grit and sand had caused abrasions in this sensitive department, and when the perspiration funneled down my spine into the area, you can guess what it felt like as my salts went to work on raw skin. The water tasted of powder, or perhaps chalk, a decidedly unpleasant vintage.

Occasionally I would reposition the solar panel so that it pointed directly at the sun. I wanted the battery fully charged before I departed on the next leg of my journey.

My work completed, I could now relax and give my knee a well-earned rest. I wanted to get the swelling down before attempting the last stage across the desert. A chemical ice pack had been included in my drop supplies, and I put this to good use on my knee. My bush method had been to pack my knee in the cold damp sand every morning and evening.

With ample water supplies, I could now continue on my planned course without detouring to the east to try to locate the native well Kilpatha. My intention was to cross the Northern Territory–South Australia border about 14 km to the west of Poeppel Corner, and then to intersect the French Track about 2 km further south. This is a well-defined two-wheel track running from the western edge of the Simpson Desert near Alka Seltzer Bore to Poeppel Corner. Once I cut this track I would follow it westward until I reached the first benchmark.

The benchmarks are survey points, each consisting of a brass plate set in concrete, and positioned along the French Track at about 5 km intervals. They are numbered and my map indicates their position. From this known point, I would then plot my new compass course to the south west to pick up the native well Beelaka.

My journey so far, and indeed until I reached the French Track, could only be described as featureless, with the exception of the west to east track crossed yesterday. However, on departing the French Track, I would encounter the numerous salt lakes of the southern Simpson, which would enable me to pinpoint my position with accuracy at any time for the rest of the crossing.

Having received the air drop, the precise position of my camp was no longer of concern to me. All I had to do was continue down dune to intersect the French Track.

I estimated that I had covered a minimum of 75 miles (120km) since leaving the Lone Gum camp, but as already mentioned, I had been informed by the pilot that he knew the position of the track cut yesterday, and that I had only covered about 65 miles (104km). Even though I was limping badly, which made it difficult to judge the distance covered per day, I still could not believe that I had not walked more than 65 miles. I wasn't consciously thinking about it when the penny dropped: we were both right. As a walker, I was thinking in terms of statute miles, and he, as a pilot, in nautical miles.

I have no explanation for what happened next. Although I needed to rest my knee I kept picturing the solar panel and thinking that I had to inspect it. 'Check on your solar panel' kept hammering at my brain. In the end it was almost as though I was propelled forcibly, unable to resist. The sun was sinking behind the dunes as I squatted down next to my battery and solar panel. Nothing looked out of place, but my thoughts were directed to a particular component in the wiring.

Before leaving Burketown, I had noticed the flimsy wires protruding from either end of this item, and had bandaged the complete unit with electrical tape to strengthen and protect it. Now, as I peeled away the tape, I saw I had a major problem: a wire coming out of one end was broken, which meant that no charge had been going into the battery. I am not electronically inclined, and had no idea what that component was for. However, I figured that if it was included in the wiring it was essential and I somehow had to fix it. The wire coming out of the plastic-coated cylinder was about the diameter of a pin, and had snapped off at the point of exit. From the copper tubing of my evaporative still, I made up a soldering iron and using the old solder coating several spare wires, I endeavoured to repair it. But I needed better equipment than I had available, and instead managed to break the remaining wire coming from the other end.

By this time the sun had disappeared and night's chill had arrived. By the warmth and light of the fire, I studied the mystery component. It was plastic coated, with what felt like a cap at either end. I could not even guess at what it contained inside.

As I could not solder or glue the wires back into their original position, I decided to open it up, even if I ruined the unit in the process. With a small length of file I carried, I gradually ground down one end, exposing a copper cap. I carefully prised this away, expecting to see a mess of intricate components, but there was only a tube of some black, carbon-type substance. The broken wires were fixed to the caps only and did not pass through this tube. I figured that if the electrical wires were in contact with the tube, the current would flow. I placed the wires through a small hole in either cap and then forced them back over the cylinder. Then I bandaged the whole lot together with strips of adhesive tape rescued from my air drop parcels. By the time I had finished, I considered that my handiwork had made the component more substantial than the original, although not as pretty.

I decided to make my next radio transmission at 12 noon on Friday. This would allow the battery one and a half days charging on the solar panel, which should be more than sufficient to enable a quick call to Alice Springs. Things now looked good at the Simpson Hilton, and that night I enjoyed my most peaceful sleep since entering the desert.

My first job on rising the following morning was to again pack my knee in the freezing sand. My bush icepack was working wonders: the swelling seemed to be going down. I spent the rest of the day just lazing around near the fire. It wasn't cold – I was wearing only shorts – but the flies were driving me mad, and I was using the smoke to keep them away.

That afternoon I was visited by a mob of sixteen camels, which filed past my camp no more than 100 metres away. Magnificent animals, they are completely at home in this hostile environment. I rated only a curious glance, a pause in stride, as they browsed their way through my gidgee domain before finally disappearing over the sandhill to the east.

By 11.45 Friday morning, I had transported my radio and battery to the top of the sandhill and rigged up my aerial. Immediately after 12 noon, there was generally a few moments quiet on the radio, and that's when I intended to make my call to the Royal Flying Doctor Base in Alice Springs. I waited in eager anticipation. The lull came and I pressed the button to transmit, but all it did was go 'clunk, clunk'. The battery was still flat.

I retreated to my camp in utter dismay. That's the trouble with a bloody radio! Not only was the weight of it a pain in the neck, but having committed myself to a reporting procedure, failure to report would raise the alarm and trigger a search and rescue party. I was alright. I certainly didn't need assistance, but they couldn't know that.

I was convinced my repair work was adequate. The wires coming from the solar panel looked okay, and that just left a small component about the size of a matchhead, which had been soldered into the leads. Again, I had no idea what function this item played in the scheme of things, but through my tiny magnifying glass, it looked sound and the solder joints at either end seemed satisfactory. I needed a way to test the whole unit. Suddenly I remembered the first time many years ago that I had seen a solar chip. It had been held up to a light bulb and I had received a small trickle of power.

Cutting all the components off the solar panel, I left only the two wires protruding from the internal part of the solar unit itself. I placed one bare wire in a cut on my finger, pointed the unit to the sun, and touched the other lead with my tongue. Instant power. The solar panel itself was working. The fault lay in the components, which I now had the means of testing. By a process of elimination, I found the problem to be in the small component: power on one side; nothing on the other. I cut it out of the circuit, rewired and tested at the terminals. The whole system worked perfectly. I didn't know at the time what damage could result from the removal of this part, but I had nothing to lose. I gave the battery two hours' charging, and then raced back to the top of the hill.

At 4.00 pm precisely, I hit the button. Sounded different, I thought, but there was no reply. I tried once again and waited for what appeared to be an eternity before my set boomed out with the sweetest man-made sound I shall ever hear in the desert. '5SBX this is VJD Alice Springs. You are coming in loud and clear. Go ahead.'

Saturday I spent preparing for the next stage of my journey. I was pleased with the appearance of my knee. Thanks to my bush medicine, the swelling had reduced considerably.

My enforced stay had been restful, but far from peaceful. I was continually kept on the move dodging the ants. Sit any longer than ten minutes in one spot and they would find and engulf you. By moving away from the gidgee trees and part-way up the sand hill I could escape, but without my smoke screen the flies then came in for the kill. I at least partly solved the problem of the little buggers trying to get into my eyes, nose and mouth: I put my hat on and then gathering a few bunches of leafy foliage, pushed the stems up under the sweat band of my hat so that the leaves hung down over my face. I must have looked a right old hobo but it worked.

Evenings were more peaceful. An odd spider or scorpion, and the occasional dingo ghosting the perimeter of my fire light became my companions. Without the so-called necessities of life, you soon discover simple pleasures and games. Trying to count the maximum number of satellites I saw in any one night became my favourite pastime.

I burnt all my water-drop tubes, and with a full pack again, departed camp with the first rays of morning light. The holiday was over. The call of the morse code birds vibrated across the valley; I am sure they were saying goodbye. I don't know their correct name, but try whistling MS in morse code – two long and three short – that's the call.

In 1977 I had made the first solo cross-country crossing of the desert from east to west by vehicle, a journey considered impossible at the time. That traverse passed within a few kilometres of my present estimated position. Its proximity brought back a flood of memories of everyday battles, constant danger and my faithful little yellow Suzuki. If I had been told then that one day I would cross the desert not once but twice on foot, and carrying my own load, I would not have believed it.

As we challenge ourselves, so we grow to stand another rung higher on a ladder as endless as our choosing.

I angled off slightly to the west to intersect what looked like a track. My original intention had been to cross the desert from north to south unaided and without using tracks — completely cross-country – but having had to accept an airdrop of supplies, it no longer mattered if I travelled for a few miles on a smoother surface. Sure enough it was a track, albeit soft and rough. I followed it until late afternoon when it abruptly terminated.

As I hadn't yet found out whether the pilot had lost his way or I had been in the wrong position, my precise location on the map was still unsure. However, I did believe that within two days I would cut the French Track. I certainly wasn't lost or worried. I considered myself to be inside a small circle on the map, not yet able to make my position into a dot.

As I travelled down an ever-winding interdunal flat covered with gidgee, the sand dunes on either side of me climbed like stairs to reach the sky. For some hours now, the shape of the sand hill to the west had been tugging at my memory. I was positive that I had seen its profile many years earlier on an easterly vehicle crossing through this general area. Possibly because it was such a high dune, I may have stopped and looked back, hence my feeling of recognition.

When I finally hit the French Track, I would have to head westward to pick up the native well Beelaka. If I knew positively where I was now, I could alter course and walk one leg of a triangle, not two, saving many miles. Therefore I took a punt on my memory and headed for the top of this enormous dune, although deep down I reckoned I knew exactly what I was going to see when I got to the crest, and sure enough, I did. The site of the native well Perlanna was clearly visible and way to the south a small clearing in the gidgee marked the native well Boolaburtinna. I knew exactly where I was. Being one of the highest dunes in the desert, the view in any direction was incredible. The circle on the map had now become a dot, and for the remainder of the journey I would be able to direct anyone to within a few hundred yards of my position. I was now in my own backyard.

Early the following day I reached Lake Mirranponga Pongunna, where Aboriginal legend tells of a bloody massacre of the local tribe by a group of Aboriginals from the north. The wind was increasing rapidly as I set out to cross the large salt lake. By the time I'd reached its middle, the far shore had disappeared – obliterated by swirling white salt and fine, cutting dust. With my visibility now limited to a few metres, I was forced to carry on by compass and was relieved to finally reach the sandhills on the other side and clear air.

As I turned down dune and plodded along quietly, the soft sand muffling the sound of my footsteps, I spotted a dingo off to one side and detoured to investigate. He had his backside to me and as I had the advantage of being downwind, he wouldn't easily scent me or hear me coming. Just for fun, I wanted to see how close I could get. He was engrossed in trying to extract something hidden in a cane grass clump, and it wasn't until I was nearly upon him that he heard me coming and almost jumped out of his skin. He took off lickity split until finally curiosity got the better of flight. After ascertaining that there was no immediate threat to his well being, he proceeded to circle me at a safe distance. This pattern, once begun, generally has a predictable finale. Finally he got downwind of me, and upon intersecting my footprints and sniffing them, he scratched a bit of dirt, gave a short howl, then lifted his leg and pissed all over them. This dingo was marking his territory, and I wasn't welcome. I resisted the temptation to go back and do a number on his.

Late in the afternoon I reached the French Track. My position now was about 1.5 km east of BM 6866 and several hundred yards from the western edge of a large salt lake. I made camp about 1 km south. It was a relief to see the bull camel that had followed me for hours continue down the other side of the lake. It was the mating season, and at this time the bulls can turn vicious towards beast and man. I was now fourteen days from the Lone Gum and expecting my first visitors tomorrow: the TV crew was coming in by helicopter to do a few days' filming. They had promised not to interfere with my daily walking schedule.

I had given them explicit instructions by radio as to my location. Imagine my surprise when they flew down the lake on time, then turned and flew away. I assumed they had spotted me but wanted to do some general filming and would then come back and land. They didn't. When I finally radioed, I was advised that they were searching for me miles away. At least they had a good look at the desert.

Just before the crew eventually arrived, I reached my cart tracks, which were still clearly visible in the salt surface. They'd been laid down the previous year on my solo, unaided west–east walk. I'd pulled my cart up the lake edge from way down south, and dropped exhausted to sleep on the salt at this very spot. I had then abandoned my cart on the top of the high dune on the other side of the lake, completing the rest of my journey to Birdsville with a backpack.

We filmed the drilling sequence, acquiring water from some three metres below the surface at Beelaka native well, and then I took the film crew to a site nearby to examine some Aboriginal skeletons exposed by the shifting sands. I had about seven more days to go before exiting the desert and the film crew made arrangements to visit me once more on the shores of Lake Peera Peera Poolanna, about the half-way point.

I also found out why they had been late with the air drop. Apparently the pilot had overflown the Plenty River, then continued a further 55 km to the east before turning down the Hay River to fly the course I had given. They had had a worrying time until they realised their error, and to make matters worse, they were then short on fuel. When they'd finally found me, they had barely had enough left to safely get back to Alice Springs. No wonder they hadn't stuck around after dropping my supplies!

Isolated rain must have fallen recently in this area, for that night I camped amidst desert splendour. The whole face of the dune I was following was massed with yellow daisies for several kilometres.

I'd first heard the noise of the big jets a few days earlier, and could occasionally see their vapour trail streaking across the sky to the south. Now I was nearly beneath their flight path, and it had been arranged that, before I left the desert proper, I should endeavour to contact the regular Sydney–Singapore Qantas Flight. I would attend to that in the next few days.

The helicopter located me as arranged on the northern shore of the lake, and we spent several hours filming there. Instead of following the lake's shoreline around, I intended to take a short cut through its middle. The flat surface would also give my knee a break from the uneven terrain. I advised that I should leave the desert in four to five days time, and as they departed, I set my compass course. My destination that night was invisible to the eye. All I could see was a straight line on the horizon marking the boundary of the white salt surface and blue of the sky.

It became incredibly hot and the glare was intense. As I sat on my pack having a lunch break, I thrilled at the visual experience, the uniqueness of my position, and my insignificance. Looking back towards my departure point of that morning, I suddenly became aware that my footprints, a thin line running as straight as a die, were all that blemished an otherwise perfectly unmarked surface. I must admit that I was pleased to see my destination gradually materialise on the horizon, and as the sun was setting, I made camp on the shore line at the northerly point of a dune that speared out onto the lake. I used the few saltbush twigs available to cook my meal and retired early to watch the night sky. How I enjoyed this period of my day, as I waited for fatigue to carry me away to another place.

I awoke startled, and with adrenalin pumping, struggled to sit upright but I was restrained by the mesh covering the exit of my bivvy bag. When I finally managed to unzip and stick my head out, I could see nothing that posed a threat. It must have been one hell of a bad dream. Morning, however, told a different story. There, not more that three metres away from my bed, were the footprints of two very large camels that had passed by in the night. I wondered what they must have thought as they gazed down upon me. I know what I would have done on awakening from a deep sleep had I looked up and spotted them towering above me!

By using the salt lake surface, I had enjoyed easier going for my knee and I now plotted a course slightly longer than my original, so I could continue to use other lakes wherever possible.

Preparing to cross a small salt lake, I noticed emu tracks, the first I'd seen so far in the desert. He was going my way and moving fast. I soon realised why. At high speed, a converging dingo track cut his and, obviously narrowly missing his quarry, turned abruptly, his splayed paws fighting for traction as he realigned himself. The next cross-over must have been even closer, forcing the emu to turn almost at right angles, his huge feet spraying out clods of the lake's surface. They played their deadly game of survival backwards and forwards across my path, each attack and counter move clearly displayed until finally the dingo trotted off, defeated. This time, score one for the emu.

Further south, curiosity got the better of me. Way out on the otherwise featureless expanse of a very large salt lake, I noticed an unexplained dark blob, so, dropping my pack, I went for a bit of a stroll to investigate. It turned out to be a camel and the poor old bugger was well and truly stuck. He was on his side lying in the sludge now exposed beneath the thin crust of broken salt. His legs were outstretched and flailed wildly as he fought to get a grip in the slime. I tried to lever his legs back underneath him with my walking stick, but it was hopeless, and also a dangerous situation for me. One kick in the head, and I could join him.

I started to walk away to leave him to the inevitable, to nature's way, when I noticed another, now recognisable, blob a long way off. It was the crows descending upon it that reminded me of my days on the farm, and of one incident in particular.

I had ridden over to investigate a downed, pregnant ewe struggling to get to its feet. The crows had pecked out both eyes, revealing gaping sockets, and had then feasted on its backside, leaving a bloody mess of flesh and trailing innards. With my sheath knife, I had quickly slit its throat, then opened up its belly to remove twin lambs. One died, but I managed to breathe life into the other's tiny form. How proud I felt as I galloped home, my tiny bundle wrapped securely in my saddle cloth. I hated crows with a passion and nothing gave me more pleasure than to blow them away with the rifle. Their call is depressing enough, but what they can do to stricken stock is sickening.

I just couldn't leave this old camel to die as nature intended.

Like a lonely gladiator out doing battle in the middle of an enormous pure white arena, I fought for dominance to maintain my grip under his jawbone. Using his immense strength he tried desperately to dislodge me and for a while I was whipped backwards and forwards like a rag doll. Finally I got my left arm around his neck, dug in my heels and then, using every ounce of my strength, I arched backwards, stretching it taut. His huge head now lay close to mine and I could smell his rancid breath. As the body of this wild thing trembled in my iron grip, a moist, incredibly soft and beautiful eye rolled backwards seeking contact with mine and it was then I saw his fear. For a moment I hesitated, questioning my right to defy nature, then I reached for my sheath knife and slit his throat.

Isolation ... a feeling of kinship with all things around me ... I don't know, but I felt really sad that this 'ship of the desert' ended life this way, and at my hand. However, as his blood spurted over the white salt, I realised that the few minutes agony I had caused paled into insignificance beside what the merciless sun and the crows would have done over the following days, until he finally succumbed.

I turned my back on the now lifeless form and as I retraced my footsteps over to my backpack, the strangest thing happened. Suddenly, all I could think about was that poor little Silver Eye that I'd killed with my shanghai when I was a kid some forty-five years ago and how I now wished I hadn't.

I grew up in the times when hunting and killing, whether for sport, food for the table or income from the fur or meat trade, was a part of life, particularly for someone in the bush. However, while I could still easily cut the throat of a ration sheep, string it up and butcher it ready for the freezer or put down any animal that was suffering without a second thought, my attitude towards killing our native wildlife just for the sake of killing certainly had changed over the years. I was no longer interested, preferring to watch and enjoy their freedom and hope that changing attitudes and habits will have them and their necessary habitat preserved and managed for the enjoyment of future generations of Australians.

The dune of soft white sand that I was following was high and gave reasonable views to either side. Away to the south, it appeared to me that the dunes were terminating against a sand mass running at right angles to them, blocking their path. This is generally indicative of a large lake or open expanse beyond and if it was what I expected, I was making good time.

The sands of the Simpson mainly originate from the Lake Eyre depression. Sand-moving winds from the south-east and south-west gradually transported these deposits northwards, forming the longitudal dunes that exist today. They run approximately north–north-west to south–south-east. Newly transported sand, i.e. that closest to the source, is almost white, however over time, the released iron oxide trapped within each grain slowly coats its surface, changing its colour to orange red and then finally to the dark red of the northern Simpson.

For several days now the diversity of bird life had been steadily increasing. Ahead I could see occasional small flocks flying an almost pre-determined course, which could mean only one thing – a water course. As I topped the dune, there it lay at my feet. I shall never forget that moment: the stunning visual impact, the complete contrast in form, texture and colour to what I'd experienced during the past long weeks as I'd moved slowly down corridors of seemingly endless parallel dunes.

The Kallakoopah Creek swept in from the north-east and turning below me raced away to the north-west, its destination Lake Eyre. Light sparkled from intermittent pools of brackish water and occasional coolabahs dotted its course, while away to the south large trees massed on its floodout country. Ducks wheeled in to land on a clay pan filled with fresh water just off the main channel, while overhead the continual movement of birds patrolled this thread of life, in an otherwise arid region.

Descending, I passed through eroded gullies carved by wind and water into the cemented sand at the base of the dune. Smaller gullies on either side ascended to create even smaller gullies, ridges, spurs and rugged peaks. Here was the formation of mighty mountain ranges in miniature.

I crossed the Kallakoopah and camped that night on the edge of a crescent-shaped depression at the southern end of a small dune. It was filled with fresh water but thick with suspended sediment. I call it milk water. With the billy boiling, drop in a small handful of the fire's white ash — let it continue to boil for a few minutes then remove. Now watch the magic as the sediment flocks to the bottom leaving a layer of clean water on top. It's an old bush trick.

I radioed the television crew and advised them that I would arrive tomorrow afternoon.

'No, don't come in then,' they replied. 'Could you make it at 9.00 am the following morning where the track crosses the huge sandhill just to the east of Kalamurina homestead?' A suspicious request, I thought, after all they had been waiting a long time for this moment, but perhaps the light would be better then for filming.

For the first time in the whole journey I slept in, reluctant to leave the confines of my bed. This was going to be a lazy day, my last in real isolation, and I was going to enjoy it.

As I set my bearing for the rendezvous point, it occurred to me that today was the last time that I would need my compass or even maps. A dirt track to Lyndhurst and then bitumen would guide me all the way to my final destination.

I started transmitting at the precise time that the Qantas flight was scheduled to cross the sky just north of my position, and immediately made contact with its skipper, Luke Visage.

'Qantas QF1, this is Five Sierra Bravo Xray, Denis Bartell. I read you loud and clear. Back.'

We chatted for a while and then he patched me through to the cabin area so that all aboard could listen to our conversation. We discussed among other things how closely Qantas was associated with my walk. It was this company, who in 1928 from their base at Longreach Queensland, donated to the Royal Flying doctor Service its first aircraft. I suggested that if those passengers seated on the left hand side looked down, they would see where I was transmitting from, just to the south of all those big salt lakes.

The captain came back rather hurriedly. 'Five Sierra Bravo Xray, this is QF1. Denis, I think you misunderstood me. We were re-routed today and are currently cruising at 35000 feet over Camooweal'.

Bugger. I must have missed that in all the excitement. This was a real thrill and something I would never have the opportunity to do again in my lifetime. Here I was, a grimy, weary desert walker sitting cross-legged in the dust, hunched over a radio and talking to hundreds of people sitting in luxury belting across the sky with one of the world's great airlines.

'QF1, this is Five Sierra Bravo Xray. Sorry Captain, however if those passengers on the right hand side would care to look out, they will see the waters of the Gulf of Carpentaria. That's where I started this journey, and at the moment I am approximately 900 kilometres due south of your current position.'

I made camp that night on the point of a rise and dragged in enough wood for a fire. Enough for a tourist fire really – that means big! As I removed my socks and stood them against a log, it occurred to me that the previous night I had had enough water available to swim in, but had not even thought to wash myself or my clothes, which hadn't seen water for the last month.

Fortunately, a small depression nearby held enough slightly green water to give my clothes and body a soapless rinse. As I stood naked, drying by the fire, I reveled in that luxury and the knowledge that I would now smell nice and fresh for my arrival the next day.

I sat late enjoying the fire and reliving my journey. The depression and anger that I had felt when forced to admit defeat in my solo unaided attempt had in time subsided, to be replaced by a fierce determination to return and conquer. I had even worked out how I would do it, using a track further to the east that would take me over half-way across the desert to the north, leaving only a small cross-country section. It wouldn't be the same, though, I knew that. Except for the day after I left the Simpson Hilton where I had used an overgrown track, by estimate about twenty-four kilometres in length, my entire crossing had been trackless — completely cross-country — compass only. But I didn't feel that I could succeed trying it that way again — not solo anyway.

That night, however, I was at peace. I wasn't going to come back to try again. There was no need. I had nothing to prove to myself, let alone anyone else. I had made a good crossing and I'd given it my all. It was in the past, and new horizons waited. A winner is not necessarily one who wins. A winner is someone who gives it a go. I think I did that.

I crossed the Warburton, a much more defined channel than that of the Kallakoopah, and almost immediately began my climb up a long dune that towered high above the flats on either side. This would carry me to my rendezvous point with the TV crew. On the way I stopped for a few moments at a patch of beautiful wildflowers and picked a bunch, which I tied together with some strands of plaited grass to form a small posy.

There had been no indication that the press might be coming. However the media have done this to me on many occasions and if they were going to fly in for a visit, perhaps bringing my wife with them to capture some sort of teary reunion, then this was the logical place and time to do it. Being prepared, however, didn't mean that I was going to arrive looking like a bloody galah carrying a bunch of flowers on the off-chance. I hid them in the side pocket of my backpack.

With about five minutes to go, I saw the TV vehicle arrive, stop momentarily, and then drive off. I finally reached the track dead on the appointed time and spotted their dust disappearing behind the sand dunes a few kilometres to the east. Well, I wasn't going anywhere. This was the point that they had designated. They could now find me.

I was surprised to see a motorbike approaching, coming cross-country, and heading straight for me. It was the son of the owner from nearby Cowarie homestead. His father had discouraged him from getting involved in our activity, but curiosity had got the better of him. He wanted to see for himself what all the fuss was about. He was a nice young bloke and a real bushie. We chatted for a while until the TV crew decided to return and pick me up and he then followed us down to the airstrip nearby where a press aircraft from Adelaide was parked. Now I knew why they wanted me to come in today. This was obviously planned.

John Ellson, our TV cameraman, informed me that he had carefully selected a site next to a huge dune of windswept sand, which he felt would make a great location to do some filming for my desert exit.

'Denis, there are a couple of reporters from Adelaide waiting over the other side,' he said, 'so I'll be set up there with them. All I want you to do is climb to the top, pose suitably for a photo, then come down and give them a quick interview, as they're in a hurry to get back'.

'Not a problem, John. I'll need about ten minutes to walk to the base of the sand hill and then I'll begin my climb, which should give you ample time to get into position. Dead easy mate.'

The vehicle taking John around to his camera took off in a cloud of dust then turned and raced back. John stuck his head out of the window and yelled: 'Hey Den, sorry, I nearly forgot mate, I have some news. The press brought up a load of mail for you and one of the reporters spoke to Rotha last night. She sends her love and says she is sorry she couldn't accept their invitation to fly up today. She's got a bad cold. But she said that there is nothing to worry about, the kids are okay and she will look forward to seeing you in a few months' time'.

Oh well, I was half right about the reporters being here, sad that Rotha wasn't, but damned glad that I had hidden those flowers. This desert walker would have looked a right goose coming over the dune holding a posy of flowers, thinking that he had out-guessed and upstaged them all.

My limpy old leg suffered on the steep climb in the soft sand, however finally I staggered to the top and as I skylined myself, I drew to my full height and paused momentarily to gaze suitably into the distance, before lowering my eyes to the press and cameras waiting below. I'd been had. It was all a bloody setup.

Rotha emerged from behind a bush and with arms outstretched, raced to greet me, closely followed by two long-time friends, Cecily and

Helen. There were women coming at me from everywhere. I couldn't believe my eyes. Well, the press got their tears — they just sort of slipped out at about the same time that I presented my wife with her flowers.

Greetings and press interviews over, we returned to the airstrip, where the ladies prepared an absolute feast while we popped the champagne corks. The station owner's son joined in with some persuasion by the girls, and I reckon he enjoyed himself. I don't know if he ever told his father, but I suspect not.

The Royal Flying Doctor representative, who had also flown in with the press, told me that the fund raising was going well and that irrespective of the final amount raised, the true value of my effort could never be calculated in dollars and cents. They were receiving unheard-of publicity and now numerous proposals were coming in from others wanting to raise money for their worthy cause. It seemed I had started a trend.

It was great to catch up on all the news from home and find out what my children were doing. All too soon, however, family and friends were away on their long flight back to Adelaide while I departed for Kalamurina station about eight kilometres to the west, along with the film crew.

The station manager just couldn't do enough for us, allowing us to sleep in the homestead and giving us the run of the property. Nothing was too much trouble. The following day he departed for his mustering camp further down on the Warburton, and we settled in. The film crew would stay for several days and I intended to rest for about a week to allow my knee to settle down.

My faithful old cart was unloaded from their vehicle pack rack and returned to me, along with several of my pre-packed food boxes, which would now give me enough supplies to almost complete my journey. How I enjoyed opening up that last package. I'd kept the best till then. Luxury items that I hadn't seen for nearly six weeks tumbled out — full-size comb, toothbrush and paste, razor, towel, soap, shampoo, torch and batteries, new tee shirts, shorts and socks. At long last, I could discard that rotten pair of undies.

Finally satisfied with their filming, the crew departed, depositing me at the manager's camp, where I spent several days enjoying the cattle muster, the branding action in the bronco yard and memorable camp fires, as well as meeting a top horseman, Eric Oldfield.

We returned to the homestead for my last day just in time to witness the coming of the pilgrims. The head honcho of Kalamurina station had arrived with mobs of hopeful relatives who, having sold everything back home, were eager to join his vision of creating an oasis in the desert — a tourist Mecca.

I listened as individuals shared with me their dreams and the segment of operations that they intended to manage. Strangely, each had a different master plan to the other, no two were the same. Blind Freddie could see that a few noses would be put out of joint before this little lot got too far down the track.

No one really knew who I was, and that night I sort of drifted into their meeting. They had plans for a caravan park, huge amenities block and possible involvement of a tourist bus company including them on their itinerary. A roadhouse was also planned near Mungeranie station on the Birdsville Track.

One young hopeful, a very nice bloke, confided in me that he intended to control operations down on the Warburton, where their flowing bore had created a water hole many kilometres long. Here he would run canoe and wildlife tours and tourists could stay in a relaxed bush camp atmosphere. His grand plan, however, was a vineyard: acres of grapes would dot the suitable slopes of nearby sand hills. I nearly fell off my chair.

'And what branch of the family do you come from?' he enquired, perhaps checking to see that I didn't pose a threat or couldn't pull rank on his piece of the action.

'Well actually mate, I'm not a relly. I'm just having a stopover on my walk across Australia and will be leaving tomorrow, but I wish you good luck with your plan.' They would want more than luck. I didn't give them a snowball's chance in hell of succeeding.

Bidding farewell to the station manager next morning, I hitched up my cart and was finally rolling again. It was now some twelve weeks and 1600-odd kilometres since I departed Burketown. The worst was behind me and the 900-odd kilometres to go seemed just a bit of a stroll really. It didn't take me long to reach the very last sandhill, which was just past the airstrip where I had met the press. Here I paused to take it all in – a complete change of scenery. From constant rolling sandhills and limited visibility, my boots would now roll on gibber-dotted plains and my eyes would once again scan distant scenery. I could see the Cowarie station homestead nestled below at the foot of the dune next to the track, and as I descended, I noticed the station owner standing in his backyard. Curiosity had got the better of him. A raised hand each was the only recognition of my passing.

My knee felt great. After an overnight stop I reached the famous Birdsville Track about midday, and welcomed an invitation to lunch by the owner of Mungeranie station. That afternoon, however, I realised that I must have done irreparable damage to my right knee, as the pain came back with a vengeance. Even though I was limping again, I made good time over the next few days, as a fierce tail wind rocketed me southwards past Mulka station and onto the wide floodout plain where the Cooper Creek crosses the track on its way to Lake Eyre.

When torrential rains fall over the north western areas of Queensland, a vast body of water slowly gravitates down the Thomson and Barcoo river systems until they finally unite to form the Cooper Creek. Spreading out over normally parched land, sometimes up to 50 km wide, filling numerous waterholes and an intricate web of massive lakes, the water can take up to seven months to finally reach the Birdsville Track. Most times it doesn't. However, a few times every century the deluge is of sufficient size, the body of water so enormous, that it finally reaches and fills Lake Eyre, and when it does, the Birdsville Track is cut for months to vehicular traffic. Fondly known only as 'The Cooper', it was named by explorer Captain Charles Sturt in 1845. When he crossed it, it was dry, hence he named it a creek. If he had found it in full flood, it would have been named a river — a mighty river — to which I would later bear testament.

I met the manager of Etadunna station and could tell that he really wanted me to stay the night if I could make it to the homestead in time. I purposely didn't, as he had also explained, I think with some embarrassment, that the owner, a city slicker, was due up any time and that he discouraged familiarity with anyone travelling the track. Visitors were definitely not welcome. It was pitch black when I passed by the homestead the following morning, but I could just make out the huge steel cross gracing its entrance.

Storm clouds gathered, and the wind that had so kindly thrust me southward now turned with a vengeance. So strong was it that I lay in my harness straining to make progress. Fortunately there was little rain and it blew itself out within twenty-four hours. Even though occasional vehicles now intruded into my space, they weren't sufficient in number to break the solitude that I had become accustomed to, and so enjoyed. My horizons were still limitless; nothing confined or crowded me. I marched past Dulkaninna, and finally friendly Clayton homestead; I was now nearing the end of this famous track.

Ahead, a vehicle kept flashing its lights as it approached. Imagine my surprise when my son David and his friend James pulled up alongside. I had no idea that they were coming. He thought he would just drive up for the night and see how the old bloke was going.

The following evening I made camp late in a large creek bed, but was on the road again well before sunup. This was going to be an exciting day, so I was getting an early start. It was still dark when I finally reached the top of a long climb, and there it was — an unforgettable sight. Away in the distance, a cluster of lights pinpointed Marree, the first town I had seen since departing Camooweal some eleven weeks and 1540 km earlier. I paused to reflect while taking in the magic of the moment. It had been one hell of a journey so far.

I spent the rest of the walk contemplating how I was going to spend my monetary wealth. A grand total of $10, which I had carried for just this occasion, was burning a hole in my pocket. I pulled up at the store just as they were opening the doors, and I had no hesitation: where was the ice cream bin?

The 80 km south to Lyndhurst was the last of the dirt. I completed this section in two days and it wasn't very pleasant. Something strange was happening to me and I was becoming extremely agitated. Numerous tourist buses and vehicles were stopping and plying me with questions, and fences now appeared alongside the road, controlling and restricting me.

I rang my wife from Lyndhurst and told her that all I wanted to do was get home, that I wished it was all over, and how I hated it now. If it wasn't for the fundraising for the Royal Flying Doctor, I'd hop on a bus or hitch a lift, and throw the bloody cart away.

When I had departed Burketown, I thought only in terms of segments of the journey, each to be conquered as they occurred; I never thought of the whole, the destination. I guess that was too difficult. Camooweal, Atula, crossing the Simpson, each was a challenge to be met and conquered, but now on the final leg, it was all too easy — just make sure I didn't get run over, and keep my feet and my mouth moving. My world was shrinking. I had reached the outskirts of civilisation and didn't like it. I was slowly losing something precious to me. The adventure had gone, and so had my solitude.

From Lyndhurst, there was another 600 km of bitumen to go. Fortunately, by the time I reached the magnificent Flinders Ranges near Parachilna, I had let go, my equilibrium had returned and I was actually starting to enjoy myself. Numerous cups of coffee, cake, hospitality and good wishes from friendly tourists and locals had finally seen to that. Sharing myself with them had enabled me to place the adventure/challenge part of my journey where it needed to go — in the past — a wonderful memory to be dusted off and savoured whenever I felt the need.

As I stood gazing up at those inspiring ridges and peaks, now in close proximity, the memory of the flight above here and my thoughts so long ago came back to me: 'Your return will be nowhere near as pleasant or as fast'. I could now add 'but it will be something that you will remember and cherish for the rest of your life'.

I'd told the Flying Doctor Service that I was averaging 32 km per day, so they had organised an itinerary for the rest of my journey based on this. Talks were lined up at numerous towns, schools and clubs for the rest of the journey. Things like having a day off, freezing cold winds or walking all day in drenching rain weren't in their calculations. I didn't let anyone down though, and on one occasion, to keep to schedule, even managed a very long, tiring 50 km day.

Just south of Hawker I was privileged to meet one of only two people who really understood what I had experienced on my desert crossing. It was Warren Bonython who, with Charles McCubbin, had also walked the desert from north to south in 1973. They had started about 120 km south of Atula station and finished near Mt Gason. It didn't take him long to hop into the harness of my cart and take it for a few laps; at the same time I am sure he momentarily relived his own crossing. I think my cart got the okay.

The signs had been there for some weeks now and it finally had to happen. My good left leg, which had borne the brunt of the journey so far, now collapsed, and the pain in both became almost unbearable, particularly for the first few hours at the start of each day. At least I didn't limp anymore.

While I was doing some shopping in the township of Quorn, a young man approached me. His knee was bandaged and he was limping badly. He had heard that I was in town and had wanted to meet me. It turned out that he was riding his push bike from the Moomba Gas Fields up on the Strzelecki Track to Adelaide, a distance of some 950 km. Apparently his mates at the camp had ridiculed his effort and told him he wouldn't make it. With only about 330 km to go, he was concerned that he might have difficulty finishing his journey because of his knee. I mentioned that old saying 'the harder the battle, the bigger the prize,' and gave him a dose of encouragement. He already stood tall for his effort. I sure hope he didn't give in. I hope he made it.

Cleared pasture and cropping land, numerous houses, the close proximity of townships plus those infernal fences finally beat me. With a lack of places to hide myself, I reluctantly swapped my nights under a canopy of stars (if it wasn't raining, which it seemed to be doing a lot lately), for motels, hotels, and other structures with slits in the walls.

The helicopter shot overhead at low altitude, executed a tight turn and landed on the edge of the roadway in front of me. Dick Smith and family had arrived in their 'airborne four-wheel drive' to take a few photos for their magazine, *Australian Geographic*. Dick had apparently been searching for me for some time; finally several linesmen working near the road pointed him in the right direction.

I was right on target. My arrival at Glenelg was scheduled for 3 pm Sunday, and I had just had my first glimpse of Adelaide away in the distance. For the last two days it had poured with rain and things didn't look hopeful for a sunny finale.

I couldn't believe the welcome as I marched in for my last night's camp at a motel on the outskirts of Adelaide. Every vehicle flashed their lights and waved. The publicity machine must have been going full bore.

I spent that night planning in minute detail the route that I would follow and exactly where I would be at any given time. I intended to turn the corner into Mosely Square, Glenelg, at exactly 3 pm as promised.

I'd only just started when a police car, with lights flashing, pulled up alongside. 'Don't walk on the side of the road, Denis,' the sergeant said. 'The whole left lane is just for you, so use it all, and I'll be right behind you for the rest of the day'. Wow!

The guards at the entrance to Government House allowed me a privileged comfort stop as I passed through a reasonably quiet city to enter Anzac Highway and the home stretch. Residents came out of houses as if on cue as I approached. I was informed that radio reports were continually updating my progress. Then a lovely young lady, Miss Glenelg 1985, took my hand. It had been arranged that she would escort me in, and was she nervous! I couldn't work out why — my family and a few friends perhaps, and some curious bystanders — nothing much to worry about there. My escort didn't enlighten me.

At exactly 3 pm, I turned into Mosely Square and couldn't believe my eyes. It was jam-packed with people! To say I was overwhelmed would be an understatement.

After the State Premier and the Lord Mayor of Glenelg, I was asked to say a few words. I really only remember saying something to the effect that I normally stand six feet one and a half inches, but carrying some of the loads that I have carried, I think I have shrunk to under six feet. However, today I stand about ten feet tall and it's all due to you wonderful people. I produced my bottle of Carpentaria Gulf water and we all headed out to the end of the jetty, where it was formally dispatched to mingle with the water of the St. Vincent's Gulf. My mission was complete, and having raised some $70,000 for the Royal Flying Doctor was, I think, very successful.

I reached the high point and turned — Adelaide was again spread at my feet and away in the distance my guiding beacons, the Norfolk Pines at Glenelg, were clearly visible but no longer beckoning. It had taken me five months and some 2500 kilometres. I'd walked across this country. I'd chased my dream and kept my promise.

Three months later I had both knees operated on. I thank God that I had found peace that night in the desert when I decided that I had nothing more to prove — that I had no need to return and again challenge the desert and myself on foot. Now I couldn't even if I wanted to. Perhaps I should say, not in the way I would want to.

What next I didn't really know, but I could swear when I looked up that I could see my name etched on a few more rungs of a ladder that reached for the stars.

Chapter 11

The Spirit of Adelaide

When Explorer John McDouall Stuart made his 1860–62 attempts to cross Australia on horseback, he had good reason to curse the sun as it beat down mercilessly on his party. In 1986 when I followed in Stuart's footsteps, travelling along a highway that now bears this famous explorer's name, I also cursed the sun during my journey — but for exactly the opposite reason. I wanted more of its rays as I attempted the first north-south crossing of Australia in a solar-powered vehicle.

Late in 1985, just a few months after I had finished my north-south walk across Australia, I had approached Trevor Berry and Peter Cannon of the Natural Energy Centre in Adelaide to see if they would be interested in building a solar-powered boat, which I could use to promote their company and solar energy in general, by boating some 1300 kilometres down the Murrumbidgee River. I was heavily into exploring our inland river systems at that time and the Murrumbidgee held a special fascination for me. As a kid growing up on the muddy banks of its headwaters I'd dreamed of travelling its length by boat, now I was keen to fulfill that dream.

We put our discussions on hold, however, when Hans Tholstrup and BP Australia announced plans for a 'World Solar Challenge' in 1987— a solar car race north-south across Australia. Peter and Trevor decided that they would like to become involved in that event, and gain experience by building a solar vehicle to test run over the course a year earlier. They figured that the knowledge they'd gain would be invaluable in their preparations for the big race. They phoned to tell me their decision and also that they had the necessary skills, both mechanical and electrical, to create a worthy contender for the big race and access to equipment for wind tunnel testing.

'Denis, instead of a boat, would you like to drive the first solar-powered vehicle to cross the continent from north to south?'

Now this question didn't need lengthy consideration on my part. Although not my usual type of adventure, I thought it would be a unique experience and an opportunity to become involved in the development of new technology.

With an enthusiastic 'You can count me in Trevor', it was all systems go and they immediately set about designing a suitable vehicle.

In 1983, adventurers Hans Tholstrup and Larry Perkins had jointly piloted the first solar vehicle to cross the continent from west to east. Their journey from Perth to Sydney had taken them 19 days in a vehicle that they had named 'The Quiet Achiever'. A team had also driven a solar-powered vehicle across America, but I didn't know the actual distance travelled, or the time taken. It was obvious that if I were able to complete our planned journey, I would not only be the first person to cross Australia from north to south in a solar-powered vehicle, but by doing it solo, I would have travelled by vehicle further on a continuous basis than any other person in the world using only the sun's rays for propulsion.

I didn't want to leave Darwin too late in the year, in case the Top End experienced an early monsoon with its attendant cloud cover – not very clever if you need the sun's rays for propulsion. However, when I visited the Brampton factory of Natural Energy early in September, the vehicle was still in skeletal form. It was a pretty flimsy looking contraption but I was assured that it was structurally sound and well engineered. Wind tunnel tests of the scale model had promised excellent stability. This was absolutely necessary given the light weight of the finished product and its need to withstand encounters with the turbulent winds generated by passing road trains throughout the journey.

Sitting in a make-believe seat that day with my bottom only inches from the ground, I couldn't help but wonder what it was going to feel like when those monsters of the highway roared by only a few metres away. They were certainly going to tower above me; I wasn't even as tall as their tyres.

The electric motor designed for the job looked more than adequate but weighed a ton and seemed out of proportion to the rest of the unit. The solar panels had been supplied by a company in Sydney and were ready to install. Because the vehicle needed to be roadworthy to secure a special permit to travel on the highway, hydraulic brakes were fitted. A flimsy-looking hand brake was installed for emergency use, and I hoped that my life wasn't going to depend on its performance. Brake lights were necessary and turning indicators; we got away without headlights as the vehicle would not be driven after sundown. A bank of batteries would be charged by the sun and supply extra power when necessary, such as when the skies were overcast or when climbing hills.

Finally it all came together. It looked great. Eighteen shiny solar panels, capable of producing some 810 watts, completely covered the top except for the seating cockpit. The sleek blue fibreglass and kevlar hull looked as though it would slip through the air with minimum resistance. As we would be travelling north to south, I didn't think that the forward sloping solar panels on the front of the vehicle would be as effective as they should be, due to their angle to the sun. However, Trevor wanted a vehicle that looked like a feasible means of transport rather than a shape designed specifically to capture maximum sun, as the ultimate race vehicle would have to be. The vehicle measured about 5 m long and 1.8 m wide, with a four-speed gearbox. Peter calculated that the top speed was about 90 kph and that it should cruise comfortably around 40–50 kph.

Testing was being carried out at a government vehicle testing circuit and I was finally invited down to have my first drive of a vehicle which I hoped would carry me safely across the continent. It was all very exciting and once the controls were explained to me I hopped in, applied power and silently slipped around the winding circuit. Everything felt great and — other than rather inadequate seating for such a long journey and my bad back — I was now really looking forward to the challenge ahead. This might be more enjoyable than I had anticipated; certainly it would be different!

A little later, taking it for another spin after some minor adjustments, I cruised down a steep section of the track and began to turn into a hairpin bend to my left. 'Strange' I thought, as I kept turning the steering wheel. 'My mind tells me I should now be going left and yet my eye tells me that the bloody car is still going straight ahead.' It sure was! The steering wheel had malfunctioned and I rocketed over the kerbing, which fortunately was sloping, and ended up stopping in a heap of bushes. No real damage was done, and thankfully it happened at the test circuit and not on the highway.

The steering was beefed up and we met again at the track for another test run. This time the steering worked fine. As I cruised down the steep slope I braked to prepare for the hairpin bend, but there was just one thing wrong. Nothing happened. My brakes had malfunctioned and again I shot over the kerbing narrowly missing a large pole that would have severely damaged our prospects, which at this late stage suddenly didn't look that crash hot.

Finally, the car was driven around the Grand Prix circuit in Adelaide for its first public appearance, and then taken back to our testing track where, with an enthusiastic press and TV media, the vehicle was formally handed over to me. It was now my job to drive it safely some 3200 km across Australia. They say that troubles come in threes, and I couldn't help but wonder with two down, what was next!

South Australia's Jubilee 150th year (1986) and my crossing was to be one of the last official events on their calendar to celebrate this occasion. To honour my State, I named our vehicle 'The Spirit of Adelaide'. My journey would also be a tribute to explorer John McDouall Stuart who opened up the way to the north so long ago, and would mark the 100th anniversary of the motor car.

With the Spirit of Adelaide securely fastened to a borrowed trailer, we began the long haul northward, which was largely uneventful, although the last night's camp before Darwin displayed the first warning signs of things to come.

We had pulled over in the late evening into a section of old, disused highway and made camp, rolling out our swags on the soft sand which lined the edge of the bitumen. Not long after, I was awakened from a deep sleep by a tremendous crack of thunder and lightning overhead, and then it absolutely poured. As the heavens opened, the sky vibrated with the most incredible rolls of thunder and lightning flashes that I have ever seen. Awe inspiring would be an understatement. Mother Nature gave a demonstration of who really is boss on this planet. It took about an hour to abate, by which time I was starting to feel decidedly uncomfortable as water was penetrating my swag. I unzipped and stuck my head out, noting with surprise that Trevor's swag, which had been tied to the trailer next to mine, was missing. We had camped in a gutter, and as I stepped out of my swag to check his whereabouts, my bed started to float away. I'd lent Trevor one of my old swags which apparently leaked badly, and rather than go down with the ship, he had escaped to the safety of the vehicle.

Our first official engagement after we arrived in Darwin was to present the solar car at the Office of the Lord Mayor. Here he handed me a scroll from the citizens of Darwin to be carried to the citizens of Adelaide, sending their greetings for the Jubilee Year. Formalities over, we retired to a large shopping centre where the vehicle would be displayed in the foyer for a day.

On 11 November 1986 I hopped into the driver's seat and eased our high-tech machine through the wide doors of the shopping centre and into the waiting arms of the police. Although I had Trevor in a back-up vehicle complete with flashing lights and a big warning sign *CAUTION — SOLAR VEHICLE AHEAD,* they had decided that they would take up the lead position and guide me through the traffic to a caravan park on the edge of the city, where we planned to spend our first night. I was glad they were there, as I found the first few kilometers a bit stressful as I endeavoured to come to grips with my unfamiliar surroundings. My total driving time in this vehicle was measured in minutes, not hours, all of it an enclosed, secluded driving track. Now here I was in a world of hustle and bustle, suddenly mixing it with steel monsters that towered above me, while I plodded along silently in my little blue dinky toy. I would be lying if I said I wasn't thinking about failed steering, failed brakes and if it happened now, how I could easily end up as dead meat.

I was glad when that first day's driving was over and we were safely off the road. However, instead of an overnight stop, we were forced to spend several days at the park as Trevor tried to fix a rear axle that had developed quite a wobble. This concerned me, as it had occurred after only a few hours of travel. The axles were hollow tube; to my untrained farmer's eye, they were not strong enough. I didn't feel that a replacement was satisfactory, considering the distance we had to go and lack of repair facilities along the way. I thought they should have been solid and also not have had an overhung bearing. Trevor, however, was adamant that all the mathematical calculations were in order and it would stay as designed.

The locals were marvellous with their willingness to help and finally we rolled out of the caravan park's rear gate and headed back to rejoin the highway. We didn't make it: the incline proved too much for my drive chain. As I changed gear, the shear pin snapped, and I had to be towed back to the park. The pin was too soft and installed into a sloppy hole. I convinced Trevor to acquire extra shear pins of suitable strength and size, as the chance of purchasing them through the remote area ahead was practically nil. The following day we again set forth and this time made it to the highway.

Although I hadn't covered many miles, I was already becoming accustomed to the noises emanating from my almost silent machine. This one, however, really did sound strange, and was occurring once on every revolution of a wheel. It was coming from somewhere behind my seat, so I figured that it had something to do with the axle and slowly pulled over. Trevor came to inspect and, so that he could also hear the sound that was alarming me, we slowly rolled the vehicle forward. I watched in amazement as the rear driver's side wheel and axle slowly extended out from the vehicle to finally part company altogether. This time the axle had snapped completely. What if I'd been in front of a huge road train? The ramifications didn't bear thinking about!

We loaded the 'three-wheeler' up onto the trailer and beat a hasty retreat to the safety of the caravan park and the workshop for Trevor to have a re-think and seek advice from his mate in Adelaide. Finally, new axles were made, this time from solid steel, and days later as we again rolled out of the workshop for the highway, I silently prayed that I would not be returning.

Clouds had been rolling in every day since our arrival in Darwin, and it was very hot and humid. Sitting in the cramped cockpit was like sitting in a steam bath with your clothes on. Now, when I needed every bit of sun available to make up lost time, sunshine was spasmodic, and I soon flattened the reserves carried in my bank of batteries. As I wasn't getting enough continuous sunlight on to my solar panels, the power available from these alone was insufficient. While the Spirit of Adelaide could crawl along occasionally on level ground, the slightest rise forced us to a halt. We were spending more time waiting for the sun to top up our batteries than we were driving.

I didn't really mind — I knew that it was going to be a long journey and had already settled in to enjoy the experience. I didn't care how long it took, just as long as we got there. There's nothing worse than failure. Every stop brought an enquiring public seeking details or photos, and I pointed the technically minded in Trevor's direction. I handled the light-hearted, more mundane stuff, like the second day out, when a minibus stopped and disgorged a full complement of nubile, scantily clad young ladies. They were all Miss Australia entrants who had just finished a photo shoot taking a dip in an outback waterhole.

Would I consider being photographed with the bikini-clad beauties draped over the vehicle? Hell, someone's got to do it — life's tough on the road!

I'd wanted to be well south by the time the monsoon season arrived to deluge the top end. We didn't make it, for the wet had arrived early and we'd left late, so now I spent most afternoons in the back-up vehicle out of the rain. Finally we made it to Adelaide River and managed to get the solar car under cover for repairs. Perspiring freely, I sat on a pile of discarded tyres in a ramshackle shed enjoying the tropical downpour. At least for a change we would have a dry place to camp for the night.

The previous year I'd departed Burketown to take a walk across Australia and I couldn't help but make some comparisons. At a constant 32 km per day, I had covered more distance in four days on foot, than for the same period in my solar-powered vehicle. The lack of sun, the rain, continuous mechanical repairs and the hills through Hayes and Pine Creeks were all taking their toll and we continued to slip further behind schedule.

When the sun went down, so did we. Where we stopped we slept, even though we might be only a few kilometres from a town or roadhouse. Due to the solar car's low ground clearance, we were unable to go any great distance from the side of the highway, so our sleep was always shattered by the roar of the semis. Occasionally we fluked a roadside rest area with a smooth entry surface, enabling us a measure of escape.

We were getting close to Katherine, and as the sun went down we could see the lights of the town away in the distance. As we could never leave the solar car unattended by the side of the road, Trevor would drive into town to send and receive messages while I stayed and looked after the baby. Tonight it was late when he finally returned and I could see he was agitated.

'Trevor, what's happened mate?' I asked. 'I hope no one is sick in the family.'

'I have just had a long discussion with my partners back in Adelaide,' he blurted, 'and they're not very happy'. He paused as if to let it sink in before continuing: 'They want to wind up the venture now, call it quits and bring us home immediately.'

The enormity of his statement took a moment to sink in and when it did I felt as though someone had just kicked me in the guts. I had entered into this venture using my background to promote their solar energy company and in return I would get to drive a futurist vehicle across the continent. Weeks of my time had already been given freely to achieve this goal. I had suffered the embarrassment of numerous mechanical breakdowns forcing us to hide from the press, together with poor vehicle performance and failed brakes. I had melted while driving in the tropical heat and humidity, survived on junk food, when we had any, and slept rough on the edge of the bitumen, all without complaint. Now here was someone telling me that they wanted to terminate the venture. More than that, they wanted to drag me down with them as failures and quitters. Well they didn't understand me very well and I had difficulty controlling my anger.

'Okay buddy, what's the problem?' I asked, needing to get to the bottom of this quick smart before I blew a fuse.

'Denis, it's as simple as this. My partners are upset that our company name is hardly ever mentioned in newspaper articles or television interviews. It is all about an adventurer named Denis Bartell, your past exploits, what you are doing now and your future plans. We don't feel that we're getting publicity value for money and time spent or the recognition.' He was visibly agitated by the time he'd finished.

Now I'm not stupid. The vehicle wasn't living up to their grand publicity hype and expectations and rather than face the distinct possibility of further disappointments and ultimately, perhaps, egg on their faces, they wanted to bolt down the nearest hole and pull me in there with them.

'Trevor, it doesn't work that way.' I explained. The only reason we had received more than just a cursory glance from the media was because of my past exploits. 'You know as well as I do, that that's the reason I'm driving this vehicle and not you.'

I couldn't understand why it wasn't evident to them at the beginning that this was the way it would have to be. They had tried to get the media interested in their company project but had failed. I'd deliberately kept out of it until they officially handed the vehicle over to me. Only then did I take charge — I was able to immediately get the interest of television stations and newspapers in the project.

The vehicle didn't yet have a character or a history, but if it could complete the journey to Adelaide, they would have a machine that had accomplished something. A first. Their publicity would then come from static displays in shopping centres, etc. and their own company advertising. I'd be long gone and forgotten as they generated their own personal and company recognition and started to recoup their promotional investment.

What they needed now was to have the guts to stick with it. Sure we'd had a rough trot, but as we moved further south out of the monsoon, things should improve as far as sunshine was concerned. The car's mechanics was another matter, but we had managed to keep the vehicle mobile so far and there was no reason to believe that we couldn't continue to do so.

Trevor didn't have anything else to add to the conversation so it was over to me and I wasn't going to stuff around. I pulled out the big guns.

'Okay mate, this is the deal. I have a message to deliver from the Mayor of Darwin to the Mayor of Adelaide and I am going to deliver it come what may.' I was damned if I was going to accept defeat and travel home with him with our tails between our legs. I could easily change the very nature of this challenge and make it into an interesting personal adventure for me while still delivering my message to the Lord Mayor in grand style.

'Trevor, if your company decides to quit, then you can leave me by the side of the road. I have my HF radio and will contact one of the radio stations down south to see if they can find a retailer to lend me a push bike and send it northwards on the first available truck. If I can't get a bike I'll buy a wheel barrow in Katherine and bloody well walk to Adelaide … trust me!'

I could see the headlines. After 3240 km pushing a wheelbarrow, Bartell finally arrives at the Adelaide Town Hall to deliver his bi-centennial message. Would I do it? You bet. I knew if that occurred their solar car and their company would get more publicity than they could handle. Tough.

Conversation came to an abrupt halt after that. I knew if they were going to pull the plug it would be tomorrow in Katherine after Trevor could get to the phone for another pow-wow. That night, tucked in my swag, I dreamt of push bikes and wheel barrows.

We were early into Katherine and parked in the main street, where a mob of interested onlookers quickly gathered. Trevor was soon into full swing explaining the workings of a solar-powered vehicle while I took the opportunity to escape my capsule, do a bit of shopping and phone home. I wanted to prepare Rotha for the idea that this journey could take a little longer than planned. There was also a matter of satisfying my cravings: I needed an ice cream.

I was standing by the side of the vehicle deftly fending off questions when Trevor finally returned.

'Okay Denis, whadya reckon? Are you ready to roll?' he said. 'We've got a long way to go yet.'

'We sure have, mate,' I replied, and with that I slid behind the wheel, fed in a trickle of electricity and silently eased the shiny blue Spirit of Adelaide out into the southbound traffic. The door to defeat slammed shut and would never be reopened, at least not on this journey.

Our hydraulic foot brakes, which had failed some time ago, still hadn't been fixed and I anxiously waited for the replacement which had been promised as soon as possible by head office. My safety depended entirely on that flimsy handbrake lever. Our brand new CB radios for inter-vehicle communications had also failed just out of Darwin: I could hear Trevor but he could not hear me. Because he needed to know the condition of my instruments and any concerns or queries I might have, I soon became proficient in passing all information through some thirty-odd hand signals.

The journey was now over less hilly terrain and we were able to pick up speed, although cloud was still prevalent. Despite the heat and cramped conditions, I handled the long days well as we continued to proceed ever so slowly across the outback landscape which I so love and enjoy. This was the land of a special hero and my thoughts were never far from John McDouall Stuart and his companions as I relived his journey and pondered over the difficulties he encountered as he fought for every mile in this arid land. Long periods of isolation were only broken by the few small towns and roadhouses that we encountered, or motorists requesting a photo and a chat.

The vehicle felt secure and handled well on the highway, and other than an occasional annoying flap from the hinged nose cone in severe turbulence, it was largely unaffected by the massive trucks that continually fly up and down the highway. Aerodynamically the design was sound. Not that I felt that secure — I could handle the trucks coming head-on, but as they towered above me from behind, there was always the thought that I could end up like a squashed bug.

We stopped for the mandatory photo at the Devil's Marbles, did some further repairs, and then topped up our supplies at the gold mining town of Tennant Creek. When Central Mount Stuart loomed large on the horizon, we only had about 200 km to go to reach our half-way point.

🦎 🦎 🦎

The year was 1860 and the race was on. The South Australian Government had offered a prize of two thousand pounds to the first to cross the continent from south to north. They wanted to know if this uncharted region had the potential for expansion.

John McDouall Stuart, a draughtsman, had cut his teeth on exploration when he accompanied Captain Charles Sturt as he attempted to reach the centre of Australia in 1845. Sturt had been defeated only 150 miles from his goal. Ahead of him lay a wasteland of parallel sand ridges, while to the east a stony desert was just as impenetrable; he had been forced to beat a hasty retreat.

Stuart, now an experienced bushman, tried his hand at gold prospecting and farming and carried out general exploration in the vicinity of the Flinders Ranges. He accepted the Government challenge; financed by friends and accompanied by two companions, he headed north to a land never before penetrated by white man. He discovered and named Chamber's Pillar and on 22 April reached the centre of Australia. He scaled the nearby hill and, planting the flag, named it Central Mount Sturt as a sign of respect for his one-time leader whom he so much admired. The Government later changed it to Central Mount Stuart. We pulled over to read the roadside plaque and reflect for a moment on this great explorer.

At Attack Creek, just north of our present position, Stuart was forced to retreat back to Adelaide due to hostile natives, lack of food, scurvy, and the constant lack of water.

Learning that Robert O'Hara Burke had departed Melbourne with one of the greatest caravans ever assembled to conquer the inland, Stuart didn't waste any time. He re-equipped — this time with Government help — and set off with ten companions post-haste. They followed his old route to Attack Creek and then pressed on for a further 100 miles, until an impenetrable barrier of scrub and low supplies again forced a retreat to Adelaide.

On 26 October 1861 Stuart again departed Adelaide and, finally breaking through the scrub barrier, was soon crossing a tableland of lush grass, to reach the ocean on 24 July 1862.

Their return trek to Adelaide was a nightmare for all. Stuart suffered from scurvy and nearly went blind. No longer able to ride, he was carried on a stretcher slung between two horses. His right hand was useless and he was completely blind after dark. He commented that 'he felt in the grip of death'. When they finally reached the sanctuary of Adelaide in December 1862 they were given a heroes' welcome, while at the same time, the funeral procession of Burke and Wills, who had died on Cooper Creek, moved towards their final resting place in Melbourne accompanied by their mourners. After his mammoth effort, Stuart was denied the ultimate prize, for Burke's diary recorded that they had reached the tidal waters of the Gulf of Carpentaria in February 1861.

Defeat was never in John McDouall Stuart's vocabulary — he gave his all and pushed himself to the absolute limit. His was an epic of Australian outback exploration, of incredible hardship, and an inspiration to all who have the guts to aspire to loftier heights.

🦎 🦎 🦎

The paper came whistling through the air and landed next to the solar vehicle. This was an early morning ritual that had been going on for some time now. Every morning I awoke, and there it was, kindly tossed out by the newspaper truck as he raced northwards. Thanks mate — it was most welcome.

On 2 December, we rolled into Alice Springs, the half-way mark, and while displaying the vehicle at a shopping centre, we received a warm welcome from the Lord Mayor, Leslie Oldfield. I was entrusted with another official congratulatory message to be handed to the Lord Mayor of Adelaide.

As we rolled out of Alice Springs into marginal weather to complete the last leg of our odyssey, the Spirit of Adelaide underwent a name change. Its signage, once so proudly displayed, was now obliterated by a large Natural Energy Centre sticker, hurriedly forwarded from headquarters. That will teach me to be a romantic!

I took time off to visit a friend, Noel Fullerton, at his camel farm on the highway just to the south, and he brought over a few of his charges to inspect my mode of transport. The old and the new met, and I couldn't help but wonder if we wouldn't have been better off on one his 'ships of the desert'.

Electrical problems persisted and overcast skies still dogged our progress, severely restricting daily mileage. If I managed 100 to 110 km in any one day, I was doing well. In fact, the largest distance that I had driven in any one day since departing Darwin was 140 km. We certainly hadn't broken any speed limits.

Long stretches of isolation were broken only by the occasional roadhouses until we finally reached Coober Pedy. I vividly remember the first time that I had visited nearly 30 years ago. I had been returning home after spending a year in the Gibson Desert looking for minerals. There were only two buildings standing above ground and they were on either side of a wide dusty track near where the present-day hotel stands. To share my patronage, I purchased fuel from one store and food from the other. I understood that they were not on speaking terms!

Numerous business premises now line the main street and a variety of above-ground dwellings dot the surrounds. Underground houses, originally conceived due to the cost of building materials and also as an ideal way to escape the searing summer heat, were cut into all available slopes and hills. Coober Pedy had become a thriving mining town, not only unearthing fortunes from its famous opal diggings, but also generating wealth from the thousands of tourists who stay to enjoy a unique experience amongst a multicultural society. A frontier town had come of age.

As Trevor and I passed through the vast sheep station country on our way south, I was reminded of an incident that now makes me shudder, although at the time it was absolutely normal, particularly if one aspired to get anywhere in the world.

I was about 20 years old and employed by the large pastoral firm of Elder Smith & Co., fondly referred to by its employees as 'Uncle Elder'. I worked in their factory at Mile End with windmills, pumping equipment, tractors and other farm machinery. I had been sent north to repair a pump supplying water to a remote station homestead. I left Adelaide by train with a tool box and suitcase, suitably dressed in a suit, white shirt and tie.

At Port Augusta I waited for hours in stifling heat, wet with perspiration, until finally I could board the cab of a mail truck, which would drop me off at my destination while doing its rounds. I'll never forget the dust and the heat in that cabin. Finally, I was forced to remove my coat, but the tie stayed put. Appearance and a proper dress code were important in those days. I changed into my work clothes after I arrived, but ended up not fixing anything. They told me that the parts hadn't arrived, but over the years I often wondered if they had decided not to trust the 'city slicker' – not that anything was ever said.

I continued to do all the company's windmill and pumping equipment installations throughout the state, however, after that incident, I felt that conforming to tradition amidst the dust and flies was rather ridiculous, so I gave convention the flick and never again wore a suit out to the start of a job.

At about this time I also threw away the useless, continually saturated singlets that my mother and convention insisted I wear. She had told me that they were absolutely necessary to protect me from 'catching my death', or at the very least, a chill in the back. I had also been warned against sitting on cold concrete as it did something nasty to one's backside, but I can't remember what – maybe it was so delicate an issue that I was never told!

At last the magnificent profile of the northern Flinders Ranges came into view, and as we crested a rise I had my first glimpse of the blue waters of Spencer Gulf. Memories of this sight from thirty years ago flooded back. I'd had a year in the desert, and in all that time it had only rained once. How I had longed to see the sea and a volume of water of such magnitude that I could actually immerse my whole body in it!

We rolled into Port Augusta and stayed for a welcome break overnight. Trevor carried out some urgent repairs and rearranged the electrical system as directed by head office. He was hoping to speed our progress over the final 320 km into Adelaide. However, something went horribly wrong. I only made about 10 km the following day before we ground to a halt. My gauges indicated to me that some form of cross-draining between the batteries was occurring. Trevor said that this was impossible due to the way they were wired, but he was unable to rectify the problem. Finally, I suggested that the time had arrived to seek help. We needed an auto electrician or electronics whiz complete with test equipment; otherwise we were going to spend the night just on the outskirts of town.

Trevor drove back to Port Augusta and several hours later returned with the local expert on all things electrical. After agreeing that short circuiting was indeed the problem they set about trying to fix it. Our expert was as amazed as I had been to discover that the wiring was all coloured red, which made it extremely difficult to trace individual leads through the tangled mess. They must have done a deal on a 'job lot'! Finally we were on the move; I couldn't afford much more lost time. Arrangements had already been made to roll up to the Adelaide Town Hall on Friday at 12.30 for an official welcome by the Lord Mayor, Mr Jarvis.

For our last night on the road, Trevor had the evening with his family at home, while I stayed with the solar car and slept in a nice, clean, comfortable cabin near Two Wells on the outskirts of Adelaide. This had been donated by my generous hosts, who operate one of the most immaculate parks that I have ever stayed in. It certainly made a change from my swag on the side of the highway.

For my last day on the road, I was granted an almost cloud-free sky. I had started off with full batteries, so made good time and wasn't inconvenienced by the delays caused by the press and television interviews. As I rolled past the motel at Gepps Cross on the outskirts of the city, I re-lived my departure by foot from there the previous year, as I had headed for a reception at Glenelg and the termination of my five-and-a-half month walk across Australia.

I was feeling apprehensive now, having to contend once again with busy city traffic, but all went well and finally I cruised over the River Torrens bridge, complete with my police escort, and up the hill to enter into King William Street right on time. It was 19 December 1986.

Adelaide's main thoroughfare was packed with people going about their daily activities — all turned to witness this strange, colourful, futuristic, noiseless vehicle making its way slowly through the centre of their city. The TV cameraman hung out of the back of his vehicle capturing the moment as I waved to the crowd and to the wife I hadn't seen for such a long time. It had been a magnificent journey and one I wouldn't have missed for quids.

Ahead lay the Adelaide Town Hall and as I silently slipped The Spirit of Adelaide into the space reserved at its entrance, I breathed a sigh of relief. We'd finally made it. The Lord Mayor of Adelaide was waiting to welcome me and I formally handed over the letters of greeting that I had carried across a continent.

With my official duties over, we parked the solar car for a short time on the grass in Victoria Square so that it could be viewed by a large crowd of interested citizens. It was also an appropriate spot to officially finish, as this square is home to a statue of the great explorer, John McDouall Stuart, who had blazed the route that we had just covered, but on horseback, some 125 years earlier.

Finally, I drove my vehicle to the headquarters of the Natural Energy Centre, pulled on that skinny little handbrake for the last time (my main brakes had never been fixed), thanked my guardian angel and handed over my charge. My commitment to this solar energy venture had now finished, and after nearly six weeks away, I was returning home to my family and preparations for a gold mining expedition back into the Northern Territory. Unknowingly, I was also into the countdown for an event that would soon knock me for six and change my life forever.

I realised full well that our effort would be rated puny, almost laughable, when compared to the million-dollar plus machines, with their well-equipped and catered-for back-up crews, who would race over the same course the following year. There were even reports that some entrants had requested that the speed limit on the South Australian section be lifted above 110 kph. We were, however, the first. We had blazed a trail for others to follow and with what we had available to us completed our mission, despite the challenges that faced us.

Crossing Lake Alexandrina after boating 3500 km down the Mole, Dumaresq, Macintyre, Barwon, Darling and Murray Rivers to reach Goolwa and the Murray mouth in a record time of ten days, two hours and seven minutes –1983.

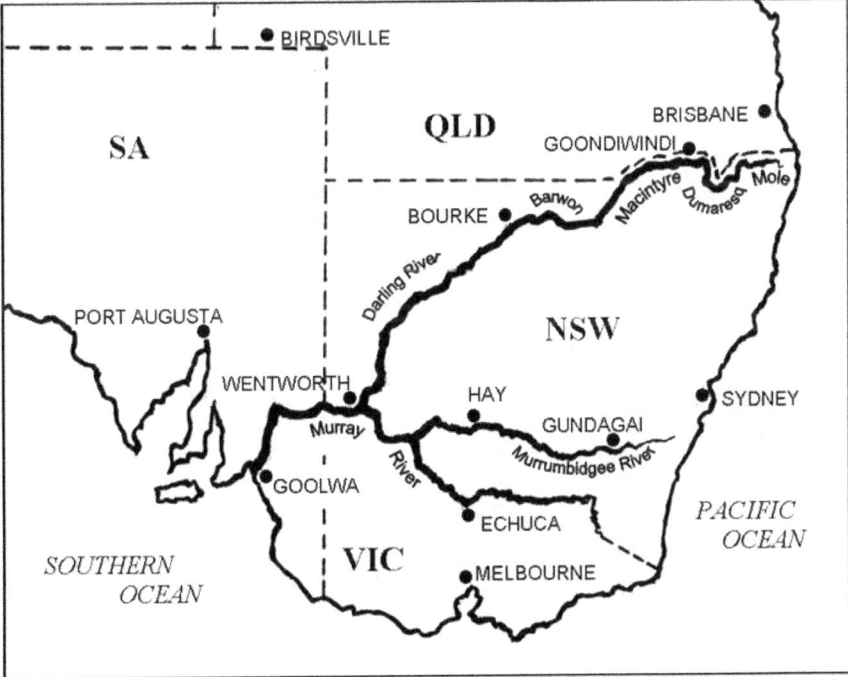

Steep Point, most westerly point of mainland Australia –1977.

Journey's end: Byron Bay NSW to Steep Point WA and back through
Australia's desert heart. An isolated crossing of over 8000 kms –1977.

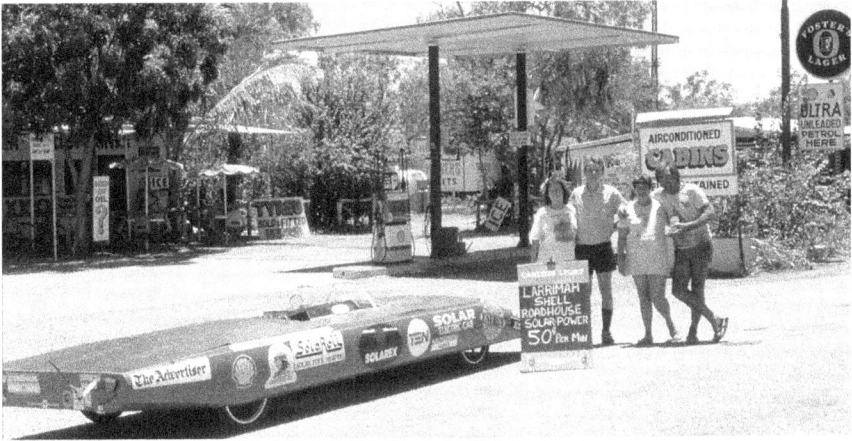

My fuel from the sun is free, but I did buy an ice cream!

Eighteen shiny high-tech solar panels producing some 810 watts completely cover the vehicle top except for my cramped seating compartment.

Not even as tall as their tyres! Giant tankers tower above my light weight solar vehicle.

Located near Wauchope, the Devil's Marbles, some balanced precariously, is a scattered formation consisting of thousands of naturally rounded and oval granite boulders—believed by the aborigines to be the eggs of the rainbow serpent.

Noel Fullerton's camel farm—an ancient mode of transport meets the futuristic.

Roadside stop.

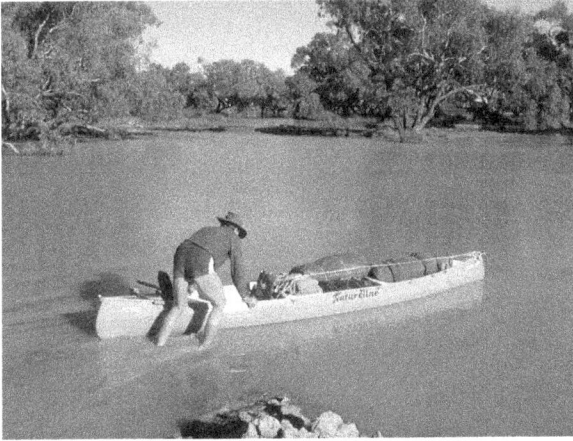

From Burke and Wills famous Dig Tree in Queensland, my goal was to ride the slowly moving floodwaters of the Cooper Creek over 600kms to Lake Eyre in South Australia.

Numerous aboriginal rock carvings estimated to be around 30,000 years old lie at the eastern end of Cullyamurra Waterhole.

When in full flood, the Cooper can spread, in places, to over 40kms wide.

THE DB SWAG: I designed and manufactured a snake and insect proof swag which was the forerunner of all the modern day swags.

Idyllic days on The Cooper.

Only a cairn now remains above water where the road from Innamincka to the Birdsville Track crosses the Cooper Creek —erected by the workers from Moomba as a memorial to their mate, Sid Walker, in 1987.

Left: Road signs in the swamp. This track will be closed for many months.

Below: Small solar panels maintain power for my HF radio.

Left:
The Yawarawarrka aboriginals who lived in this region until about the 1880's used stones like these to grind the seeds of the Nardoo and other plants into a flour-like paste. Numerous fresh water mussel shells litter their feasting sites.

Right: Many birds' nests like this one, probably that of a yellow-billed Spoonbill, were threatened by the rising water.

Abandoned by her dingo mother, the rising flood waters were rapidly covering her tiny island and when I rescued her, death was only hours away. I named her Cheater.

With the flood waters now up in the tree tops, it was necessary to continually break a path through the branches. With visibility down to zero, navigation in many areas became extremely difficult.

Shaken free, spiders of all descriptions fell by the hundreds into my canoe.

The ever present majestic pelican is just one of the dozens of water bird species including seagulls, ducks, stilts, avocets and swans that arrive in their thousands to breed in the flooded waterways.

Another great camp.

My swag rolled out on top of the canoe—another night trapped in the swamp.

Cooper reflections.

Left: Now about 100kms from the Birdsville Track, I have outpaced the floodwaters. I arrange a lift to Adelaide where I spend a month before returning to retrieve my canoe from its hiding place and continue my journey.

Right: Spiders and lizards were popping out of the cracked earth ahead of the flow as Cheater inspects the very front of a mighty deluge that fell six months ago in central Queensland.

The seldom used famous Birdsville Ferry.

I rescue a young eagle found floating in the water.

On October 8th 1989 Cheater and I finally reach the Birdsville Track and journey's end as the flow can carry us no further.

In 1990 floodwaters again roared down the Cooper. On October 4th I continue my journey as I cross the 10km wide expanse of Lake Kilamperpunna heading once again for Lake Eyre.

Left: Me and Cheater just cruisin'.

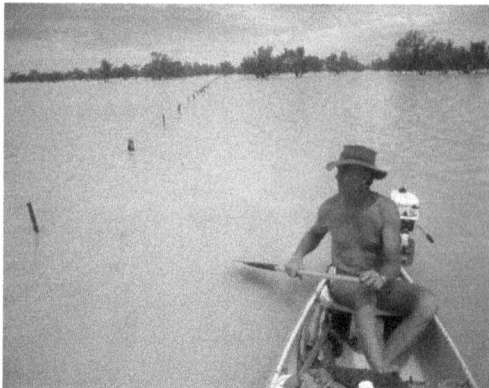

Above: Although many kilometres wide, the shallow depth of the water is shown by the fence posts.

Right: I steer well clear of eroded sand cliffs where huge chunks continually crash into the water creating large waves.

Left: Journey's End. On October 7th I enter Lake Eyre to fulfil my dream.
Behind me the Cooper now lay majestic, unique, memorable and conquered.

Below: Muffy, my riding camel, drinking from an improvised water trough.

Above: Noel Fullerton's Oshkosh delivering camels to Bloods Creek Bore.

This is where we commence our journey retracing the route of Danny's father, Ted Colson, who became the first white man to cross the Simpson Desert back in 1936.

Right: Our camel train– mere specks on the vast plains near Mt Dare Station.

How good is this? Able to ring anywhere in the world and fondly called "my camel phone". Our journey formed part of the official launch of the Optus Satellite phone system in Australia.

The views are forever.

The Knolls are two small hills. They feature in aboriginal legend and are notable landmarks in an otherwise sea of rolling sand.

Ted Colson rested his camels on this exact spot back in 1936.

Lost in thought. Atop the Approdinna Attora Knolls which stand on the shores of Lake Tamblyn, Danny connects with the spirit of a father he never knew and reflects sadly on a love denied him.

Remains of the old rabbit proof netting fence first erected over 100 years ago to halt the devastating rabbit invasion sweeping across the country.

Two desert mates camped at Big Red remember the pain and the pleasure of a desert now crossed.

Arriving into Birdsville after nearly 500kms of desert travel.

The monument to Ted Colson and his aboriginal mate Peter stands in front of the Birdsville Pub. Danny's childhood dream of following in his father's footsteps across the Simpson Desert has now been fulfilled.

Chapter 12

Gold Fever

There was absolutely no doubt; I was riddled with it. And once you get it you're stuck with it until you die. I caught gold fever early in life from my best mate. We were farming together in the south east of South Australia near the township of Keith. Bert Pexton, who was nearly twice my age and passed away many years ago, had been a hard rock miner in his younger days. With his father and brothers, he had worked underground extracting minerals from the hills to the north of Adelaide. It was a damned hard life and a dangerous one, but he thoroughly enjoyed it. He always talked of the thrill of following a thin vein and wondering if the next blast would open up that long-awaited bonanza. He talked of having gold fever.

I became well and truly hooked when metal detectors were invented and I took off to explore the old gold workings scattered around Australia. I will never forget the very first piece of gold I found, in Western Australia near the town of Leonora. It was smaller than a match head, but under a large magnifying glass it assumed gigantic proportions. Around the camp fire that night in a sandy creek bed I shared my find with new-found acquaintances who had never seen alluvial gold before. We handed it back and forth as we each let our dreams run riot – dreams of the yellow riches that would surely come our way as we waved our magic wands.

Two of that group departed after a few days to go their own way and were never seen again. The other, a city bloke unfamiliar with the bush, decided to team up with me. I had a feeling that he was frightened of being alone in that environment for he never drifted far from my side. Sometimes I felt that I was more a guardian than a leader. One day in another sandy creek bed he would die in my arms, ultimately setting me on the path to the greatest mental and physical challenges I've ever faced. I have already recounted his story. His name was Len.

Prospecting the old gold fields led me into some exciting areas! I enjoyed Western Australia the most, for it was there that I seemed closest to the early prospectors and the challenging life they chose to lead. They endured enormous hardships just getting to some of the remote areas, let alone maintaining their existence once they arrived. They came in their droves — bank managers, shop keepers, husbands, ordinary people and crooks. They travelled by horse, camel, push bike, or on foot with all their worldly goods stacked high on a wheelbarrow. They pushed out along ill-defined tracks for hundreds of kilometres to get to the latest rush or set out through trackless wastes to be the first to locate new auriferous areas.

Working in the searing heat or freezing cold amidst the dust and the flies using primitive hand tools, while back breaking, must also have been character building. In a harsh, barren and for the most part waterless land, they pitted their wits and strength against an unforgiving adversary that would just as soon take their lives, and frequently did. Many returned penniless, some very wealthy, while others stayed on in unmarked graves. They had all wanted more out of life. They had all dared to dream and had the guts to challenge themselves and follow their dreams.

That was the exciting part of detecting around the old alluvial fields, particularly the more remote ones, where there had been very little disturbance to the scenes of long-gone gold rushes. Artefacts unearthed by the metal detector or just lying scattered around bore testimony to their owners' makeshift, hardworking and frugal lives. In my early days, most of the gold found by detectors was that which had been wasted by the old-timers through inefficient extraction means. In time, however, we broadened search areas around the main workings to locate the scattered golden plums, while completely new areas would be discovered, some with huge financial benefit.

One day I came upon a recently abandoned camp that showed signs of a pitiful existence. Hung up on the limb of a tree by a home-made coat hanger was a large pair of tattered overalls. Perched on top was a battered hat and tied to each leg, a worn-out pair of boots. Pinned to the chest was a note that read: 'Arrived a pauper clad in rags … left in top hat and tails'. I would love to know how much he had found. Its effect on me? … well, I just worked a little harder, with an unshakeable conviction that the big one was only just around the corner.

There were interesting characters galore, many of whom you bumped into time and again. It didn't matter what gold field or what state of Australia you were in, every so often someone would just materialise out of the scrub and we'd spend time over a smoke and a billy reminiscing. We would discuss other areas we'd visited, the gold we'd found and where we'd found it. It was always great to catch up. I really enjoyed meeting these prospectors. Some were very intelligent, others mildly so and there was a good sprinkling of deadbeats and alcoholics. Irrespective of this, they all had interesting stories to tell around the camp fires.

There was the Yank, Kiwi, Goldfinger, The Pom, The Weasel, Stretch, Spear Chucker, Cat Killer, Hooker, The Shaker … the list goes on and on. I don't think I ever knew a surname. It didn't seem to matter. Goldfinger is self-explanatory: he's one of the best detector operators in the business. He mainly worked the top end of Western Australia and the Northern Territory. The Cat Killer was once a cray fisherman who found cats made good bait for his cray pots and cleaned a certain West Australian town out of cats — well, that's the story that was told to me.

I prospected a lot with Dave, the part-time disc jockey, old Pete, and young Pete and Sue. They were all pretty normal, although each was afflicted with the same dread disease: gold fever. I must admit, however, that when I first spotted Dave, he didn't look too normal. In fact, he looked a bit suspect. It was at the Goanna Patch in Western Australia. I stood still in the shadows of a thin belt of trees for a moment and watched as this young man strutted his stuff. He cut a dashing figure as he strode along clad only in his underpants and a pair of very, very oversize thongs while swinging his detector with great determination and concentration. Here was a man on a mission and a real professional in the making if ever I saw one. He bolted when he first spotted me, but this was only to advise his female companion that nude sunbathing would be off the agenda for a while. Damn!

Over the years we detected a lot together. Incidentally, just beneath my feet in that belt of trees where I had first spotted Dave were scattered over half a million dollars' worth of nuggets. We had all detected over the area but they were just out of reach of our equipment; it wasn't until years later that someone put a tractor blade cut through it and they were brought within reach.

On my numerous trips I really didn't make a fortune; mostly I just covered traveling expenses, good wages and a few thousand dollars over. However, I never tired of working daylight to dark and occasionally well into the night. The head of the detector swinging backwards and forwards was hypnotic and there was this optimism that at the end of the next swing a whopper was waiting to be unearthed.

Not long after my solar car journey, I found myself back on the Stuart Highway, this time heading north. Living within the confines of a city was becoming more of a struggle as the lure of the outback drew me with increasing intensity. It wasn't really the people or the towns that drew me, it was the incredible scenery and the isolation of inland Australia. It was the utter freedom I always felt when I immersed myself in it.

Back in the mid-1950s I couldn't wait to get to Alice Springs. Now, once I have refueled, I can't wait to get out. To me, it's no longer a desirable place to even visit. The same goes for a few of the towns further north.

Just south of Wycliffe Well I left the bitumen and headed for the hills to the east. I had heard on the grapevine that a couple of the characters I knew were working in the area, and thought I'd drop in and see how they were going. One retained remnants of a very good social life and our discussions were always interesting, the other, was just a deadbeat. Both were alcoholics and used their isolation out in the bush as their drying-out clinic. When I tracked them down they were around their campfire demolishing the last of their grog supplies, so I knew that for the next two to three weeks they would be into clinic mode.

We decided to team up and search out previously untouched ground in the hope of finding a new gold-bearing area. Within a few days we did just that. On an area no larger than a house block, we unearthed one of the best finds that I had ever encountered. We worked non-stop and at the end of two weeks we had accumulated over $70,000 worth of gold.

There wasn't much left, just the occasional small piece, and I was now finding it increasingly difficult to keep them motivated. They kept reminding me that we were nearly out of food, but that wasn't their real motivation to head for town. They would each have enough gold in their pockets to hit the pubs big time where they would stay in an alcoholic stupor for many weeks. When they did a number on themselves, they sure didn't mess around, and I knew that this time it was going to be a big one. Finally we were completely out of food and there was no alternative but to depart. We stopped on the way at a waterhole for a swim and a wash and to dolly up the specimens before weighing and dividing our gold into three equal packets.

My first job when we hit town was to race to a phone box to share my excitement with my wife. It really was a lot of money for a few weeks' work and probably amounted to a year's wages for some people.

Gold, however, barely rated a mention throughout my numerous phone calls that night. The topic of separation and divorce reigned supreme. My official notification came by post. I really don't remember much of the next few days, but ultimately found myself back in the bush. I tried to concentrate, to regain my enthusiasm for work. It was impossible, so I headed back to Adelaide to face the music.

What can I say? I have always believed that in most marriage breakups, there are faults on both sides. Small things grow and multiply over time to ultimately destroy if they are not tackled and resolved early on. With us, I was the major contributor to our problems. I had just blundered on. I didn't learn because I didn't listen. I had always been too busy working, trying to make money and selfishly living my dream. I was now getting what I deserved. In my way I still loved Rotha and deep down I hated myself for having caused so much pain to a wonderful person, a fabulous mother and someone who had sacrificed so much to allow me to live and achieve my personal goals. We had three beautiful children and had achieved much in our years together, but now it was time to say goodbye. I don't think I could have ever left — I needed to be pushed and I commend Rotha for having the guts to do just that.

The house was painted and ready for sale and our assets were divided equally, just as they should be when someone has been a mainstay in your life for 29 years. The solicitors weren't going to have a field day with us, although they tried. We invited our friends around for one last party together. If you have got to go, you might as well do it with style and I think we did it with dignity. We told them of our decision to separate and it was all very sad.

When our house was sold we said our final goodbyes, sitting on the floor in the middle of the huge family room now devoid of relics of our life together. Years earlier I had visited this exclusive, leafy Adelaide suburb of Springfield and thought how exciting it would be to live there. In moving there I had fulfilled another dream. As I paused at the gate for one final look at our charming old-English style home nestled in its enormous garden fringed by huge trees, I realised just how special it had been to me.

Sir Robert Menzies, one-time Australian Prime Minister, used to stay there when visiting Adelaide. His favourite room overlooked a tranquil, vine-covered corner where a gnarled silver birch stood proud, casting filtered light over the moss-covered herringbone brick pavers below. I often wondered what affairs of the nation were discussed and decisions made as tea was taken. In those days silver service was supplied at the press of a button. We called it 'The Menzies Room'.

I turned my back on my past — my future looked rather bleak. I couldn't even cook, so I would probably starve to death. I remember a young bloke telling me once how he came home from work to find that his wife had left him and taken the kids and all their furniture. He said he spent several days sitting on the floor in a dark corner of the empty house trying not to go crazy.

I was lucky that I didn't have to do it all alone in the very early stages. I now understand and feel truly sorry for those in a similar situation with no-one to turn to. My youngest sister looked after me, fed me and kept me going through the hard bits. I owe her a debt of gratitude.

Rather than hang around like a bad smell, I soon decided it would be better for all concerned if I was to start a new life in another state. But where? Childhood memories and a desire for a warmer climate led me back to Queensland. Noosa, a few hours' drive north of Brisbane, appealed to me although I really had no idea what to expect. I had heard it was supposed to be a fabulous place and Melbournians flocked there to escape the winter months, although that in itself is not necessarily any recommendation! Any place would be better than a winter in Melbourne.

A stopover in Brisbane with my brother had me in a real dilemma. His retired engineer neighbour told me that Noosa was situated on reclaimed land and he wouldn't consider building on it in a fit. He suggested that I couldn't go wrong if I settled on the higher ground of Buderim, about 35 km to the south.

Continuing my journey north, I didn't particularly like Caloundra or Mooloolaba and by the time I had stopped for lunch at Maroochydore, I was beginning to doubt the wisdom of moving to Queensland. A chat with those in the know quickly knocked out the highly recommended nearby town of Buderim which I could now see sitting on a hill in the distance. Apparently it was full of retirees and known locally as 'God's waiting room'. This was definitely not the place or image for a young man like me. I was only 55 and I wasn't about to tempt fate.

Travelling on, I found the coastal drive becoming more interesting, but it wasn't until I reached the crest of the hill after Noosa Junction that I had the first real inkling of what was in store for me. The view over the small town nestled below looked exciting. There were lakes and waterways aplenty, while in the distance over Laguna Bay, the ocean swell broke against multi-coloured sand cliffs and rippled along a beach that ran unbroken and uninhabited for as far as the eye could see. Westward the green hills of the hinterland looked cool and inviting, and before I had even completed my drive down Noosa's famous Hastings Street I knew it was all over. I had arrived.

I bought a three-bedroom apartment on the waterfront on that 'reclaimed land', hibernated on my balcony for a while and shed a few more tears. It wasn't long, however, before I realised I needed some outback therapy.

Chapter 13

Journey to an Inland Sea

When I first heard that the Cooper River crossing at Innamincka was closed due to flooding, I was in Adelaide, South Australia. Full of optimism, I called Mike Steel of the Innamincka Trading Post, but he told me that the eight feet of water over the causeway represented only a minor flood that would soon peter out. I switched back to my original plan to ride the flooded Murrumbidgee River, and began to prepare for that venture.

Several years earlier I had boated 2350 km down the Murray River, from the Hume Weir in New South Wales to Goolwa in South Australia. The following year I had ridden the floodwaters of the Mole River in Queensland into the Dumaresq, McIntyre, Barwon, Darling and finally Murray River to terminate where it empties into the sea, a distance of some 3500 km. With the Murrumbidgee now in flood, it was a good opportunity to ride another tributary of the enormous Murray–Darling system, and at the same time, follow the path of Captain Charles Sturt, one of Australia's famous early explorers.

I had just arrived home in Noosa to complete my preparations for the Murrumbidgee venture when I saw the following newspaper headlines: 'Central Queensland isolated by floodwaters. Towns marooned in Channel Country's worst floods for fifteen years. Devastation, loss of stock, and hardship to thousands of people, with some lucky escapes'.

In the Quilpie district, one man had spent the night clinging to a tree after being swept away while trying to cross the five-kilometre wide Bullo River. Helicopters and rescue services were pushed to the limit plucking people to safety, organising food drops to towns and pastoral properties and ultimately to starving stock. Homesteads would be isolated, cut off for weeks to motor transport, as flood waters submerged some and left others perched on saturated islands.

Engulfing streams of muddy water would converge from over a vast area to inundate enormous tracts of land before racing away on their long journey, seeking to reach and perhaps fill Australia's inland sea, the normally dry salt bed of Lake Eyre. The means of fulfilling my dream to ride a desert waterway, the Cooper, were now in the making.

Through the Bureau of Meteorology Flood Operations Centre in Brisbane, I plotted the position, progress and level of the floodwaters, and as rain continued to deluge various sections of the catchment area, there was no doubt in my mind that this was going to be a big flood. Staff at the Flood Operations Centre was most helpful and were about equally divided as to whether they thought the floodwaters would reach Lake Eyre. All seemed to agree, however, that the water would reach the famous Birdsville Track.

The Thompson and Barcoo Rivers join just north of the township of Windorah, and their unification is then known as the Cooper Creek. This is rather strange, as creeks normally flow into rivers, however, the reason is simple. Our early explorers habitually named channels without water in them as creeks, and channels with flowing water as rivers. Obviously the Cooper, when named, was dry.

On 15 May 1989, the river level at Windorah reached its peak of 7 metres, with the peak then reaching the cattle stations of Durham Downs on 27 May at 3.5 m and Nappa Merrie on 8 June at 6.9 m. The Cooper reached its peak at the little township of Innamincka on 11 June, making 25 feet (7.6 m) over the causeway, and at the same time, I committed myself to a canoe journey down the Cooper, to depart from the Dig Tree in Queensland about mid-July.

Fortunately, most of the equipment that I had chosen for the Murrumbidgee River trip would suit the Cooper challenge. I had selected a canoe because I thought it would make an interesting change; my other river trips had been in a ten-foot aluminium punt. Maybe deep down I just wanted to play Indians. The canoe was a 16 foot (nearly 5 m) fibreglass Canadian, manufactured by Natureline, and I felt it was a suitable craft for this journey.

Well, that's how it all started. This big flood had the potential to reach Lake Eyre and would give me perhaps the only chance in my lifetime to ride this waterway. There was no way I intended to miss out on this opportunity, and I spent the next weeks in eager anticipation as I prepared my gear.

I decided to carry two single-blade paddles in case one broke or got washed away, and a Johnson 1.2 hp outboard motor with several fuel containers. The outboard was mainly intended for the long haul down Lake Eyre, should the flood carry me that far, but it would give an extra margin of safety overall. An accident could leave me unable to paddle, and with most of my intended journey accessible only by helicopter — a costly exercise — at least with an outboard I may be able to stay mobile and perhaps get myself out of trouble.

I packed spare parts and tools for the outboard, and a pot of resin and fibreglass mat for repairs should I be unlucky enough to get a hole in my canoe. For storage, I selected two large blue plastic watertight drums with wide screw-on tops, and a selection of red plastic bags made for canoeists, which, when sealed properly, are completely waterproof. For safety I included my HF radio transmitter to enable contact with the Royal Flying Doctor Bases at Port Augusta and Alice Springs, and a 12-volt motor bike battery to power it. To charge the battery, I would use my small solar panel, which had proven itself on previous adventures. I found this unit gave adequate charge provided the radio was not used for prolonged conversation and I made a point of topping up the battery at every opportunity. In good sunlight, the charge rate of the panel was about .5 amps per hour.

The journey down the Cooper would be during winter, and although rain is not generally a problem in the outback, nevertheless it can be windy and bitterly cold. Obviously it would be even colder messing about on or in the water, so I included a diver's wetsuit, without sleeves, and a pair of rubber boots. Other clothing included shorts, windcheater, jeans, waterproof jacket and a pair of boots, in case it became necessary to abandon all and walk out to safety, provided of course that I could get to dry land. Tie-down eyelets were placed around the canoe so that in the event of a capsize my load would stay securely confined within the hull. Other small items were a compass, maps covered in plastic, a sun signal mirror, a life jacket, torch and spare batteries, and a small first aid kit, which included a broad bandage for snake bite, antiseptic, burn cream, antibiotics and sunscreen.

My food for the journey consisted of eighty-four individual day packs, each identical. Breakfast was a cereal I had prepared and roasted myself, with banana chips, dried fruit, full cream powdered milk and Sustagen (a high protein nutritional supplement which contains a range of vitamins and minerals); lunch was dried fruit and nuts, plus Weetbix, powdered milk and more Sustagen; and the evening meal was rice, instant potato, dehydrated vegetables, soup and Ryvita biscuits. Peanut butter, honey, tea and a few vitamin pills rounded it off. All that would be needed to prepare and enjoy this gourmet's delight was a small billy, cup, spoon, knife and matches.

The big choice was deciding what type of bedding I would carry — a lightweight backpacker's tent, or a heavy, bulky swag. I arranged my gear in the canoe and came to the conclusion that I could accommodate my DB Swag. I preferred it anyhow, as after years of use I considered that I had designed a very practical unit.

For those who don't know, a conventional swag consists of a flat piece of canvas. You place your bedding down the middle then pull one side over the top of you, then the other over on top of that. Very waterproof and allowing a quick exit if necessary. It also leaves ample room at the top and bottom for all sorts of creepy crawlies to wander through at will. Rolled and buckled with a couple of leather straps, it also doubles as a seat or back rest around the campfire. That was back in the days when swags were for ringers and bushies and unchanged in design since early settlement.

However, in my lifetime a new type of swag had been born – it all started in front of the reeds surrounding Purni Bore on the western edge of the Simpson Desert …

I was up early and having a wash in the hot pool when I noticed this very large King Brown snake, at least six feet long, coming across the flat towards my campsite. He didn't detour, and when he got to my swag and food boxes he gave them a thorough going-over: looking in my bed and checking everything out in minute detail before finally continuing on his way, disappearing into the reeds. I'd been lying there only moments earlier; the thought of waking up and stretching or eyeballing him just as he arrived alongside me didn't bear thinking about. I hate snakes anyhow.

So I designed a modern swag with zips and mesh to defeat the early morning flies, mosquitoes, bugs, creepy crawlies and the likes of the Purni Bore King Brown. I also wanted the canvas cover to stay clear of my face. It needed to be tough, waterproof, green, and suitable for future gold fossicking ventures in the hot tropical north, or exploration in the cold of the desert interior. Above all, it must look like a conventional swag when rolled and on the back of a truck.

The DB swag is ready for use after tying one end up to the bullbar or a tree, and then it only needs a kick in the middle to unroll it. No pegs, no poles, no hassles – and there were no comparisons at that time. After designing and spending months at a time in this 'home away from home', it is flattering to note that my new concept created so long ago is now available in a range of great new swag designs and look-alikes and even a few blatant copies of the original DB Swag. First marketed by a company in Adelaide about 1979, demand has steadily increased amongst the 4x4 fraternity, who could see the benefits of 'swagging it', and acceptance has continued to grow with station people and exploration groups. I was glad to be able to use mine for this trip.

The flooding of the Cooper dates back into the Dreamtime, a gift of rebirth to the Australian bush through which it moves, providing food for native animals and Aboriginal tribes as they travelled near its path. In 1989, the flood was a pastoralist's dream – with waterholes full, the channel country would burst with feed as the floodwaters subsided — an adventurer's challenge, and a canoeist's delight. But one man's meat is another man's poison: the flood spelled despair for the tiny township of Innamincka, a small and remote frontier settlement on the banks of the Cooper. It is situated in the centre of an extensive pastoral lease known as Innamincka Cattle station.

Before white men arrived, the Yandruwandra and Yawarrowanga Aboriginal tribes lived here. Explorer Captain Charles Sturt first ventured here in 1845, and the area was traversed by Burke and Wills on their journey across Australia in 1860. In 1882 a Police Camp was established at the site, and by 1886 a store and hotel had opened for business. The townsite was declared in 1896 and named Hopetown in honour of the Governor of Victoria. However, local pressure restored the original name, Innamincka, a corruption of an Aboriginal word meaning 'you go into a hole there', referring to a legend in which a totem hero ordered a rainbow snake to go into a water hole. The township thrived until 1952, when it became a ghost town, and was revived in 1970 when the Gidgealpa gas field was developed. In June 1986 the South Australian Government declared 1318 square kilometres of Innamincka station a National Reserve under the protection of the National Parks and Wildlife Act.

These days, the remote township thrives and survives on the tourist trade. With the area inundated and access by road limited, the hotel, together with Mike Steel's Trading Post, would suffer financially for many months. Mike and his business partner, Andrew Gassner, have been trading here since 1974 and have become modern-day custodians of the area.

Peter Young, a four-wheel drive equipment businessman in Adelaide, was intending to visit the area to promote his products, so I was fortunate to be able to hitch a ride. With my gear securely stowed on board his vehicle, we departed from Adelaide, concerned only with which access tracks were open, and which had already been cut off by the flood waters. However, the Strzelecki Creek was dry when we crossed at Merty Merty station, and we used the Tippaburra Road to gain access through Toolachee and Dullingari oil and gas fields, arriving at Innamincka on 3 July.

As we broke out of the sandhills on to the Innamincka Nappa Merrie Road, I expected to see a vast body of water. But not a drop did we see. As we came down over the hill and into the township itself, I was again disappointed: all that could be seen was a normal sort of river and miles and miles of trees. I had obviously retained the image of Mike Steele's vivid description a few weeks before my departure, when he told me the flood waters were up to 30 km wide just to the south of Innamincka. Even though I knew that the water had since dropped 13 feet (4 m), that graphic description had stayed with me.

However, when I finally reached the water's edge, I began to feel the volume and power of this mighty flood as it raced away to sundown. At the Innaminka crossing, the marker posts indicated a depth of 15 feet (4.6 m) over the causeway.

Driving back into the township, it was evident that no one was going anywhere in a hurry. At the Trading Post, Mike's pet dingo got up and scratched himself, and so did Mike. The publican surfaced mid-morning with bleary eyes, the result of trying to reduce his stock almost single-handedly, and bemoaned the fact to his partner, who was hanging her head in shame and embarrassment, because some nasty local had told Dick Smith, an Australian adventurer who had dropped in the night before, that she really didn't like him.

The following day I was invited to take a flight over the floodout, and accepted without hesitation, as it would give me the opportunity to inspect what I already suspected would be the main problem area of the whole journey. We followed a very impressive river, lined with massive red gums for about 35 km downstream from Innamincka. Then the

Cooper fans out into a vast swamp, laced with a maze of lignum-choked inter-connecting channels stretching as far as the eye could see. I called it the Spaghetti Bowl.

There were two main waterways into the area, and I decided that I would use the most northerly one, which passes the Goonabru Yards. How I would find my way through the torturous maze was anyone's guess, and to stray to the north or south of the main thrust would have me boating into receding waters. While I had been disappointed visually with the river on my arrival, from the aircraft I could see the enormity of the floodout created by its peak, and although the remaining water was draining away rapidly, it was still most impressive. I thought that this section through to Merimelia and on to Gidgealpa would prove to be the most difficult of the whole journey as far as navigation was concerned.

The real question now was when to depart: too soon and I would quickly catch up with the headwaters, then spend weeks going nowhere. An advantage, however, would be that if I missed a channel the water would be deep and wide enough to navigate. In other words, I would have more scope of movement to correct any navigational errors. If I left too late, the receding waters in tricky channels and lakes might be too shallow to canoe easily, and naturally I would encounter more snags. I came to the conclusion that I would not let the water over the causeway fall below 9 feet (2.7 m) before my departure from Innamincka, although there was no real reason for arriving at this height, just guess work.

A film crew from EVP Television Adelaide was due to arrive on 10 July to film my departure. Watching the steady rate of fall in water levels, I thought they would not want to leave it much longer.

I would rate my experience in canoes as about nil. Apart from a few casual encounters since boyhood years, such as paddling the placid Noosa River waterways in Queensland, my canoe experience was limited to childhood adventures in a home-made model constructed from a sheet of flattened corrugated roofing iron. Now it was time to revive those childhood skills and to build up a few paddling muscles, so each day as I waited for the film crew to arrive, I spent some time paddling on the Cooper near Innamincka. By getting into the flow, I soon started to become accustomed to the feel and to the ways of this mighty creek, to be at ease with it, to be at one; however, I never felt complacent.

Standing on the bank and looking at the thrust of the water as it sped on its long journey, it was impossible not to ponder on the dangers

I might encounter on the way, especially in the tree-choked sections. A capsized or sunken canoe could break up or be physically irretrievable, should it become wedged with that weight of water behind it. A 5–10 km swim in frigid water would not be pleasant.

The days were now cold and windy; the water freezing. The sandflies at the water's edge were diabolical. If they were there all the way down the Cooper, it would be a miserable trip. But as yet there were no mosquitoes, and the cold weather had put paid to the flies.

Despite the floodwaters pouring in from the north, there had been no local rains in this area and the landscape surrounding Innamincka was as dry as chips. There would be no spectacular wonderland of wildflowers and greenery, as some of the southern press articles suggested. Certainly the flooded area and channels would green up, but unless local rains fell, there would be nothing else.

It was now 9 July. The water over the causeway was 12 foot 9 inches (3.9 m) and islands were appearing where previously I had canoed. There was plenty of water left, but the river was shrinking dramatically. I was anxious to begin my journey.

As the width of a river decreases, the speed of the water increases, and where I had easily been able to paddle upstream along its edge, it now required a major effort on my part. The flow in the middle of the river was so fast that any attempt to paddle against it was impossible.

On 10 July the film crew arrived, and with the ever-enthusiastic Mike Steel at the wheel, canoe and gear securely lashed to his trailer, we headed off into Queensland to my planned launch site, where the Nappa Merrie homestead road crosses the Cooper. We were also carrying a boat for the film crew, who wished to spend a few days and nights on the water with me at the beginning of the venture.

On 11 July my canoe slid into the mirror-calm murky waters for the start of its long journey down the Cooper Creek. Its destination would be determined by my ability, and the water itself, or lack thereof. I was hoping to reach Lake Eyre, but would be grateful to reach the Birdsville Track.

First port of call was the Dig Tree a few kilometres downstream. Standing only metres above the water level, it is not impressive in its own right – just another coolabah. However, its significance in terms of early colonial Australian exploration creates a powerful attraction, to me at least. It was here that the stage was set to create a tragedy that will live forever in the history of this country.

Without rehashing the well-known events, suffice to say that Burke and Wills, departing from their base camp at this tree on 16 December 1860, became the first white men to cross the continent, and after returning to this point, died several months later just downstream on the banks of the river.

My first day's run was down a well-defined river, and my first camp was an idyllic one on a sand island surrounded by coolabahs. The morning light, however, showed a thick coating of ice on all the equipment: that's how cold it can get this time of year.

I had allowed two days to get back to Innamincka, with several planned stops for filming on the way. The flatter country either side now started to squeeze and lift, and distant hills could be seen approaching on the northern side.

Finally I arrived at the eastern end of Cullyamurra waterhole, where I eased my canoe out of the racing current and stepped ashore. Rocks covered the southern bank, and among them the object of my visit: carvings abound in these rocks. Modern Aboriginals do not know their meaning; it has been lost in their Dreamtime, or perhaps beyond even that. Experts are equally at a loss to explain their origins, but estimate the age of the carvings at about thirty thousand years. Sitting where ancient people once sat patiently chipping rock away to leave their mark, one can easily feel rather insignificant in the overall scheme of things.

I canoed back to the main channel and lined up for the run through the rock choke, aiming to keep to the northern side. The other half of the river roars and pounds over huge boulders and certainly wasn't the place for me, especially with a fully laden canoe. Once committed, there was no turning back and after a short, fast, thrilling ride, I was thrust into the deepest water hole in inland Australia. The Aboriginals call it Cullyamurra. This magnificent waterhole is some 9 km long, in excess of 30 metres deep, and to my knowledge has never dried up.

With the river in flood, Cullyamurra forms just another section of a continuous body of rushing water — a jewel submerged, in competition with a thousand other visions. However, when normality returns and the river dries up, this waterhole remains to greet the traveller as a beautiful oasis nestled in a remote and arid landscape.

Beneath its murky surface, Cullyamurra teems with life. There are tortoises, water rats, callop, bream and catfish. Because of this, and its permanence, it is normally home to large numbers of pelicans. I expected to encounter them all the way along, but passed just one small group, about thirty in number, sunning themselves on the bank. I guess the others had departed to the rapidly filling lakes and waterways to the west, and fresh feeding grounds.

The sluggish flow of Cullyamurra waterhole meant I had to paddle all the way, but as I made my exit, the river narrowed and the speed of the water increased. I was again swept along, covering distance with little effort on my part. Majestic tall river red gums continued to line the banks of the main channel, while the coolabahs spread over the floodout country off to the sides.

So far the bird life had consisted mainly of corellas and galahs. With their breeding season close at hand, they were all busy selecting homes from those existing, or gouging wood away with their beaks to reach some invisible hollow and create a new home.

I revisited Burke's memorial, which is situated under the leafy canopy of a twisted old coolabah. In this idyllic setting I couldn't help thinking that with all the trouble Robert O'Hara Burke went to in reaching and choosing this as his place to die, surely he wouldn't have been too impressed with his final resting place in the city of Melbourne. Marks on the trees indicated that at the height of the flood, the water had covered the monument by about two metres.

Stony hills encroached on the northern side, and soon the homestead of Innamincka station came into view. Their road access to the south had been cut now for several months, and they faced many more months of isolation before the crossing at Innamincka would again be open for traffic. Wisely, they had positioned a vehicle on the southern side of the crossing before the flood arrived, and now commuted the 3 km by boat for supplies or a beer.

I arrived back at the tiny township right on schedule, and spent the next two days rethinking my provisions and requirements, and – when the service was working – making last-minute phone calls before committing myself to the weeks of isolation that lay before me. I was also called upon to do some river filming sequences for the two television channels that had flown up from Adelaide especially for the occasion.

The massive tower on the hill was Telecom's (now Telstra's) beacon of progress. However, some residents grumbled that they had been better serviced by the old Royal Flying Doctor radio network, as their hi-tech phones were out of order most of the time. In a night-time medical emergency, rescue aircraft could not land on the town airstrip as the height of the tower was considered a hazard, so close to the circuit area. Apparently no-one wanted to accept the cost, or perhaps the responsibility, of installing a warning beacon on the tower; the only airstrip available for use at night was across the river. One could only hope that for the next few months night-time evacuation of a sick or dying person would not be required.

On Saturday 15 July, the water level over the causeway measured 11 feet (3.4 m) and once again I eased my canoe back into the floodwaters to continue my journey. This is what I had been waiting for and it was great to get started. The journey so far had been a warm-up — now I was into the real thing! From now on I would be on my own for a least a month – or until I reached the vicinity of Waukatanna waterhole, some 300 km distant – as vehicle access to the intervening section would be impossible. If I needed help it would have to come by air.

With little effort on my part I covered about 8 km within the first hour, travelling down a wide waterway lined with river red gum. About midday, rain and wind forced me to make an early camp some 25 km from Innamincka, and 7 kms downstream from Wills' grave. The falling river levels had left the steep banks covered in knee-deep mud, making it difficult to clamber up to a suitable dry campsite.

Rabbits were in plague proportions. Meanwhile, up in the trees, the corellas and galahs kept up a deafening racket, no doubt showing their displeasure at having to share their prime real estate with an intruder. At sunset the wind dropped, the full moon shone in a cloudless sky, and an almost unbelievable quiet descended over the area.

As I didn't wish to be caught next night in the swamp area ahead, miles from dry land, I left at daybreak, with the intention of making it to Merrimelia waterhole, which curves around the northern tip of a large sandhill.

There were two major channels into the difficult section ahead and I chose to enter down the second, or most northerly, one. At this point, the northwest branch of the Cooper fills a maze of waterways, swamp land and lakes before swinging back southwards to rejoin the main channel at Deparanie waterhole.

My direction was now south-west down a much narrower river, with a defined bank on either side. However, just past Goonabru Yards I entered the floodout plains and found most of the land still inundated.

What was not was covered with a knee-deep layer of putrid mud. Just weeks earlier, this whole area had been an unbroken sheet of water, in some parts 30 km wide. This was now the most critical stage. I had to choose the correct channel to get through.

About two hours later, with the water level only just sufficient to float the canoe, I realised that I had come too far north, and to continue would be courting disaster. I could see the tree line of what I assumed to be the main channel over to my left, but it was too far away to even contemplate pulling a heavy canoe through the mud to reach it. I had to retrace my route, but I soon found this to be almost impossible, as I could barely paddle against the flow of water.

My last night at Innamincka I had seriously considered leaving behind the outboard motor and fuel to save space and weight. I was really only carrying it for when I reached Lake Eyre. Fortunately I hadn't, and now, with the little motor sounding like a demented bee, I was able to boat my way back to the main channel.

My second choice of exit ended up the same way, only this time kilometres to the south of the main channel. I climbed a large gum tree and thought I could see the tree line of the main water course away in the distance so I decided to head directly to it. I couldn't use the paddle, so, knee-deep in slimy mud and water, occasionally dropping into holes up to my armpits, I tried to pull and swim my canoe northwards through a dense thicket of lignum, but it really was mission impossible. I was again forced to retreat.

Night fell and I was still trapped in the swamp, but with a full moon I decided to carry on in the hope of reaching the main channel, and finding a dry bank to camp on. With so many narrow, silvery passageways only metres wide ripping through the trees, twisting and turning, it wasn't surprising that after about an hour of constant battle I lost the main flow and ended up in a shallow backwater of stinking slush. The scene was eerie and depressing; the Spaghetti Swamp was proving much more difficult to penetrate than I had expected and had defeated me twice in a day. Well, tomorrow was another day. Now, I was utterly exhausted. With great difficulty I managed to roll out my swag on top of all the gear in my canoe and sleep.

The following morning, I had just about made it back to the main channel when I saw Mike Steel's aircraft fly over. He was obviously looking for me, so I raced to get into a wide expanse of water and then waited. If he returned by the same route and I could attract his attention, I might be able to convey my need for help in selecting the correct exit. I had only one known possibility left, a small channel just a few hundred metres away from the one I had used to get me into yesterday's predicament. A lucky glance backwards as they were heading home had them banking towards me. I hurried to the exit of my last option and pointed with a paddle to the three alternatives, two of which I had already followed to no avail.

They dropped a map with my position marked on it, which was useless as I already knew where I was. What I wanted to know was — which exit? I continued to point with the paddle and Mike's final pass over and wing wag seemed to indicate that my last alternative was indeed the correct one. They were pointing the way.

Rejuvenated in spirit, I headed off down a small channel some fifteen metres wide and then in utter disbelief, watched as it slowly curved towards the exit I had used previously then rejoined it. I recognised trees blocking my way that I had encountered before, and could see where I had broken my way through. However, somewhere in that twisted labyrinth I must have chosen the correct channel, for slowly I was starting to curve towards the north-west. Finally I was on my way.

It was late afternoon when I entered a magnificent waterhole of fast-flowing water. I judged by the speed I was travelling that Merrimelia waterhole and a dry camp were a certainty until I suddenly faced another choice: a reasonable-sized waterway broke off the main channel and seemed to head more to the west, the way I wanted to go, so I decided to follow it. However, after about twenty minutes its already choked condition had deteriorated significantly, making it almost impossible to continue, so I decided to retreat back through the tangled growth while I was still able. I certainly didn't want to be trapped in there for the night.

The sun was slowly sinking and it was becoming quite dark under the dense canopy of leaves. It was also eerily quiet. I was unable to see more than a few canoe lengths in any direction and there was a constant threat of jamming the canoe in the fork of a tree, and then not having the physical strength to extract it against the force of the water. I was also concerned about tipping over and filling with water. The canoe wouldn't sink and all my gear was tied securely to it, however, I would never be able to manoeuvre its dead weight out of this tangled maze to safety. It would quickly become wedged and probably break up. I'd be unable to use my HF radio to call for help and no one would bother looking for me for weeks. Even if they did, they would never spot me from the air. Man and canoe could easily disappear for a very long time in the middle of this swamp. One mistake and this section had the potential to be lethal.

Ever mindful of the hazardous nature of this solo journey, I was wearing my dive suit, which covered my legs to my chest. This would protect me long enough from the freezing cold water while swimming the several kilometres or so to shore and I had on my tight rubber dive boots which I would ultimately need for walking. I was also wearing my knife. I had committed to memory my map of the swamp area and also the overland route I would take to reach help. All I needed now was my watch, the sun and the Southern Cross at night. I wouldn't even need food for four to five days and water to drink certainly wasn't going to be a problem. Fast, light travel was the way to go.

In an emergency I was mentally and physically prepared to abandon ship within seconds and need nothing more than what I was wearing to escape the swamp and reach safety.

Dozens of spiders shaken loose from the branches cascaded down upon me. I didn't know if any were poisonous, so I refrained from slapping those on my face or in my hair, preferring to let them scurry off unmolested to find hiding places amongst my belongings. I was working on the 'I won't hurt you if you don't hurt me' principle!

My real concern in there was snakes. I had to continually break away foliage with my bare hands to clear a passage. But I couldn't see anything amongst the foliage. It only wanted one large angry King Brown snake which had been forced to take refuge in the branches to latch onto me and it could all be over.

I returned with difficulty and carried on in the main channel until it too abruptly terminated. I knew that I was not going in the direction I wanted, but kept hoping for a change.

My route once more deteriorated, and it was a continual battle to find a way forward. Handling the canoe in these conditions was extremely difficult due to its length – 16 feet can be a lot to manoeuvre! Finally, just before dark, the trees of the main channel petered out. My direction was now marked by an occasional large tree along a gutter a few metres wide. I was surrounded by a sea of tall, almost impenetrable, lignum.

A break in the trees had previously given me a glimpse of sandhills approaching on my right, which by their proximity, indicated that I was several kilometres to the east of where I should be. It was now obvious that I wasn't going to make dry land tonight either, and while I didn't look forward to a second sleep atop my wobbly platform, I had survived last night's mess and somehow I would survive this one also.

On the main waterways, wildlife noises generally ceased at sunset, but here in the middle of the swamp, the night noise was incredible as the abundant bird life carried on with the business of communication and survival. Water hens and ducks splashed and cavorted only metres from the canoe, while the plaintive meowing of a starving feral cat, trapped up a nearby tree by the rising water, continued until dawn.

All in all I had another sleepless night. I wasn't overly worried about the hundreds of spiders that now infested my canoe, or the occasional ones that crawled across my face, waking me up. I had no alternative but to live with them until I could get to dry land and unpack. What really concerned me that night was the threat of a snake on a forced move using my canoe as a dry camp for the night. I had already spotted several big ones swimming along earlier in the day, so I guess it was fresh in my mind. I hadn't dared zip up the mesh on my swag in case I rolled over the edge in my sleep and ended up disorientated and face down in the water.

With the visibility of daylight, the situation still looked bleak. I climbed a large gum tree and, from my vantage point, with the curvature of the sandhills once more visible, could get a fairly accurate position fix.

There was no point in going back, and I certainly could not penetrate the sea of tall lignum which surrounded me for even a few hundred metres, let alone the 2 km I now estimated would be necessary to get me back on course. I had no alternative but to doggedly pursue the little channel that I had been following, though it was now not much wider than the canoe, and was leading me away from my goal, deeper into the heart of the swamp.

Then came my salvation. Just in front of me and running at right angles to my direction of travel, I spotted the wire of a fence, and a post protruding out of the water. It wasn't so much the sight of a fence that gave me the surge of excitement, but what should go with it. As I squeezed the canoe under the top wire there it was: an access or maintenance track following the fence all the way to the other side giving me a beautiful clear path of water on my left to where I wanted to go.

After two days of living on a handful of dried nuts and biscuits, and a few sips of slimy water, I used the track to head for the nearest shore, which was on my right. I needed a hot meal and to boil the billy to get some clean fluid into my system. A quick climb to the top of the nearest sandhill then confirmed my general location. By using a back bearing on to the sandhill at Merrimelia, which was now clearly visible, I was able to fix my precise position on the map.

I called Mike Steel on my radio to let him know that I had finally broken out of the swamp, and would shortly depart via a fence track to reach the major channel several kilometres away. I confidently predicted that I would reach Merrimelia waterhole that night. Mike decided that he would fly over and check out the scene, so I jokingly suggested that perhaps a bottle of Scotch and a packet of smokes would be in order.

I had only travelled about half-way along the fence line when I heard the aircraft approaching, and used my sun signal mirror to flash him into my position. On his first pass he held a package up to the window indicating that he wanted to toss it out.

I quickly tied the canoe to a bush, hopped overboard and waded away a few metres as he lined the aircraft up. He came in very low and very slow and I hoped I could reach whatever it was before the current floated it away. There was no need to worry. With an accuracy of which he could feel justifiably proud, a foam-covered package left the aircraft and landed at my feet. If he had flown any closer, he could have handed it to me. They departed for a quick circuit of the area to check out Merrimelia waterhole and then, after one final low-level pass, they winged their way back to Innamicka.

That night, sitting by a warm fire with a mug of scotch diluted with a dash of the Cooper, my swag spread out under the leafy canopy of an ancient bean tree, I voted this to be the best camp that I had ever spent in the bush. No doubt this feeling was enhanced because I was out of the swamp, and didn't have to spend another night on my waterbed.

I did, however, have a major dilemma to deal with. Instead of the packet of cigarettes I had suggested, Mike had delivered a whole damn carton and here I had been using this journey to give up — once again I might add. Now I had enough smokes for weeks.

I poured another scotch, double strength this time and undiluted, then grabbed another smoke from my already-open packet, inhaled deeply, filling my lungs, and, coughing madly, consigned all the other packets in the carton to the fire. I didn't know till then that it was possible to feel both proud and stupid at the same time. I did keep the open packet – just in case I met a fellow traveller who was desperate for a nicotine fix — well, that was my excuse!

I had considered spending twenty-four hours resting at this idyllic waterhole, but awoke to such a beautiful day, that I decided to use the perfect conditions to head for Embarka waterhole, an estimated two to three hour journey. As always, uppermost in my mind was the water level. Signs on the bank indicated it was still falling, and ahead lay the enormous Embarka swamp, which I still had to negotiate.

The struggles of the last few days had blotted out all thoughts of personal comfort, but now I realized what a fool I had been not to have worn my gloves. The hours I'd spent breaking a path through the trees with my bare hands had cut them badly, and they were obviously poisoned, swelling rapidly. I had great difficulty even holding a spoon to eat my cereal.

I eased back into the flow and had a fast run down a wide waterhole for about one kilometre, at which point it started to narrow and deteriorate. It wasn't difficult following the main thrust — just a matter of keeping an eye on the types of trees that line the deeper sections, watching the speed of water, and a bit of guess work. For the next 5 km, the river became a twisted, choked waterway and I was again thankful that I had chosen a canoe for the journey. It enabled me to slide through narrow passages.

Finally I pulled into Gidgealpa homestead, on the magnificent wide Embaka waterhole, only to find the station deserted. They had apparently abandoned the homestead when vehicle access was cut by the rising waters. Starving rabbits, oblivious to my presence, foraged in every nook and cranny seeking non-existent grass blades, while the station goats climbed the trees, stretching to reach the lowest leaves.

Ahead now lay an enormous open swamp choked by lignum over the southern and western areas, with mainly open water covering the remainder. I set off down a main tributary, which, although it aimed for the middle of the swamp, should lead me closer to the open water. I didn't make it. After several hours breaking my way through a tangled maze, unable to get clear due to insufficient depth of water either side, I retreated and took another major channel leading to the western side of the swamp. Several hours later, with dense lignum slowly closing in all around me and my position again looking hopeless, I spotted a clear path, obviously a roadway, which led me directly towards a tower sitting on a sandhill, and the Tirrawarra Oil and Gas field base camp.

This unscheduled stop gained me vital information which enabled me to locate the passageways they used to get through the lignum to the clear water. They also gave me a thrilling ride on a recently acquired air boat, brought down in desperation from Darwin, so that they could continue to service their outlying equipment. They were having great difficulty servicing the oil and gas installations dotted in and around the swamp, and the addition of an air boat, as well as enhancing their current operations, would ultimately play a vital role in the difficult transition period as the flood waters receded, and the ground dried out sufficiently to enable the use of four-wheel drive vehicles.

It was interesting to listen to their stories of animals trapped by the rising water, and of the many they rescued. Lizards and snakes were clinging precariously to slowly disappearing islands or bushes and numerous feral cats, the scourge of the bush, were seeking shelter in the tallest trees. Hopefully the cats would starve to death. A cow, its calf still hanging out undelivered, its head chewed off by the dingoes, graphically illustrated the struggle to survive. One of the staff, on noticing my wetsuit, mentioned that his wife worked in Adelaide making that particular brand. It's a small world.

Following their cleared lines through the sea of lignum, I passed many gas and oil installations to finally break out into the northern end of the swamp, and clear water for the final 6-km run to where the sandhills again squeeze the Cooper into a more defined channel. I camped the night at Moonari waterhole.

Next day I climbed the nearby sand dune and got a commanding view of what lay ahead: nothing but a green sea of trees as far as the eye could see.

I spent 21 July as a rest day, washing, charging my battery, and cleaning out the hundreds of spiders that infested my canoe. I was still riding the back of the flood, as my marker stick stuck in the bank indicated that the water level had dropped about 4 centimetres in 24 hours.

Mike advised by radio that the river was now 9 feet and 6 inches (3 m) over the causeway at Innamincka, and also that a group of canoeists had been 'rescued' from the flooded Diamantina River, while crossing Goyders Lagoon just south of Birdsville. From what I could gather, a very expensive search had been instigated by the local police that the canoe party hadn't requested, as they weren't in any trouble. It sounded as though the over-zealous Birdsville publicity seeker was at it again. I was also given to understand that the organiser of the search had mentioned that Bartell was down on the Cooper, and that he would be the next in line for rescue. I thought, 'Thanks for the vote of confidence mate — you don't know me very well — but I'll be damned if I'll make *your* day!'

I arrived at Walkers Crossing after having spent several hours tied to a large tree in the middle of open water, as violent storms whipped through the area. Walkers Crossing, on the track between Tirrawarra and the Birdsville Track, was named by the Moomba workers after a mate who died in the area, and is marked by a monument which, when I arrived, was just sitting out of the water.

At the end of Darby waterhole, I finally broke out of a choked maze of waterways, a normal hazard to be encountered on arriving and departing each major waterhole, and entered Boggy waterhole. Here I squeezed the canoe under the top wire of a brand new fence marking the boundary of Innamincka station and the National Park, and paddled down Moonlight Flat. This day was to be the most memorable I had spent on the water since departing the Dig Tree in Queensland.

A magnificent vision unfolded beneath a clear blue sky. Broad floodlands stretched to the horizon, dotted with patches of newly invigorated green lignum, and a thick, intermittent tree line meandered over a mirror surface, marred only by the ripple of my canoe and the movement of numerous water birds.

Boggy Lake, some 3 km wide and 4 km long, was devoid of all vegetation except for the coolabahs wetting their feet at the northern end. It was surrounded on three sides by high terminating ridges of sand, and nestled amongst the blue and the red its surface glistened in the sun like a highly polished silver plate.

Towering red sandhills lined the northern shore of Moonlight Flat, while on the southern side, long fingers of sand penetrated deep into the swamp and died, their bare sand noses blunted by the passing water. I also saw for the first time a dingo mother and pups, and watched their curiosity and then their running, tumbling flight, as they sought to escape the unknown intruder paddling by. Gulls I'd not seen before wheeled over the area, while a variety of duck, many with ducklings in tow, graced the waters.

At Parachirrinna waterhole I made camp for two days, which I spent wandering the dunes, stalking and trying to photograph dingo pups, and studying the numerous signs left by Aboriginal groups. Shell middens (Aboriginal garbage dumps) and other artifacts are scattered all though this country. Clear skies during the day led to freezing nights, and I was glad that I carried top-quality sleeping gear. My rough calculations indicated that I had travelled about 235 km since leaving the Dig Tree, and that I was 142 km from Lake Hope, and 235 km from the Birdsville Track.

I departed on 26 July into a wide, fast-flowing river, and in the first hour made 7 km with very little use of the paddle. In the following hour, however, I covered only 1 km. The water was up in the tree tops and the density of growth made passage very tough, as I was forced to break a pathway through the branches for most of the way. Arriving at Deparanie waterhole, I climbed a huge dune on the southern side to view the joining of the waters. It is here that the northwest branch of the Cooper rejoins the main Cooper channel after having filled Coongie, Tootoowaranie, Apamburra, Kanbakoodnanie and numerous other lakes on its long journey. What a sight it made in this arid, sandy landscape as it surged in from the north. Combined with the view to the south as it headed on down the Kanowana Channel, it formed an unbroken sheet of water some 30 km long.

About 6 km to the south west I could see where the main Cooper Channel departed from the Kanowana Channel through a gap in the sandhills, and, paddling over a sea of glass to that point, I made camp as the sun fired up the sky to create a brilliant display. Pink-eared ducks drifted lazily by as avocets waded along the sandy shore. Overhead, flights of birds wheeled along the waterway, and for the first time I heard the call of black swans.

Climbing a sand spur next to the cattle yard at Mollichuta, I could look 12 km down a saturated interdunal corridor to see Lake Coogiecooginna, a magnificent sheet of water some 7 km long. At the southern end of this lake, in 1861 McKinlay had made a base camp as he explored the area, searching for the explorers Burke and Wills.

Passing weird sections of bubbling water – maybe the result of air or gas, I do not know – I reached Murra Murrina for a day's stop-over before making camp near the stockyard at Cooroomunchena waterhole. From the sand spur to the east, I noticed a fast flow of water travelling northwards, which confused me somewhat until I checked my map. At the northern tip of that sand ridge and about two kilometres from my camp, the waters of the Kanowanna Channel rejoined the main Cooper Channel. Due to the tangle of trees at this point, I had missed its entry as I passed by.

Near the new stockyard, partly covered by drifting sand, lay the ruins of the old one. Nearby I spotted the remnants of an early model Ford, while all around this area were midden heaps, mostly of freshwater mussels, and other Aboriginal artifacts.

My 2 August radio sked with Mike Steele revealed that the water level was now 7 feet (2.1 m) over the Innamincka crossing. Information he had received from the pilot of a light aircraft indicated Lake Hope to be about five-eighths full, and the Cooper from there to the Birdsville Track to be completely dry.

With only about 90 km to go to Lake Hope, I was fast catching up with the frontal surge, as my marker stick on the water's edge had indicated a slight rise in level. I should now be close to the crest of the flood.

I departed Cooroomunchena waterhole and almost immediately headed out across the top of a large lake to rejoin the main channel on the far side. Numerous little islands slowly being inundated swept by, and on one of them sat a dingo pup. I just managed to cut the canoe out of the raceway, and then crashed to a stop on top of her sinking domain, where for a moment we sat and stared at each other. She had her back to the swirling water, which, if she went in, would sweep her to certain death in the broad expanse of lake ahead. I obviously was the more terrifying of her options, for finally she turned and departed terra firma, flat out. I raced from my canoe, but by the time I had her by the scruff of the neck, I was in over my waist and then fell into a bottomless hole.

The hunter and the hunted, now both in the drink, were being swept away. Things weren't looking too good until I was able to grab an overhanging bough, and with some difficulty, hauled us both to safety. She didn't put up much of a struggle, but you could tell she would have just loved to get my hand in front of the end with the needle-sharp teeth. Locating a bag, I dropped her in, leaving only her head protruding, pulled up the drawstring, and lowered her into her floating home.

I rejoined the main channel as it turned southwards down a flooded, but not heavily timbered, interdunal corridor some twenty-six kilometres long, to make camp near the stockyard at Narrawalpinna waterhole.

I made a collar for the pup from a strap taken from my life jacket, and extracted her from her bag. She showed no interest in the food I offered, and spent the night curled up in a hole I had dug under my swag, probably petrified.

The following morning I noticed that the water level had risen a little over a centimetre as I pushed off for Eagle Hawk waterhole. It was an interesting run through a forest of trees and occasional dense patches of lignum, with prolific bird life and one large flock of black swans, about forty in number.

On my climbing a sand ridge, the view down the Cooper showed a massive wide avenue of trees flanked on either side by an arid landscape of sand ridges, and occasional bold domes of barren, windswept sand.

I had christened my companion Cheater, as I felt that she had avoided certain death, but if she didn't hurry up and eat, she wouldn't be able to cheat it much longer. I had only managed to force feed her a few spoonfuls of powdered milk.

On 5 August, I departed Keenaweena waterhole for Waukatanna waterhole, where I intended to spend a few weeks. This would be the first place since leaving Innamincka that the film crew could get vehicle access to me, so they were coming up in about a week's time to do some more filming. I couldn't go much further anyhow. The water was still flowing into Lake Hope and the main channel beyond that was dry.

I was now well ahead of the flood's peak. The water had speeded up, and spilled out of the main channels to spread over the surrounding low-lying land and up into interdunal flats. A network of channels was creating numerous, soon to be devoured, islands, and trapping a variety of wild life. There were rabbits, dingos, large feral cats and bearded dragons, all waiting to take the inevitable plunge.

Finally I swept into the Waukatanna waterhole and made camp near the stockyard. That night Cheater dined like a queen. As soon as she smelt the blood of the rabbit that I had plucked from the limb of a tree, there was no stopping her. Obviously a steady supply of underground mutton would solve this lady's eating problem! Our growing friendship, however, was stretched to the limit when early the following morning she set up an incredible howling from her hole beneath the edge of my swag. No sooner would I shut her up than off she would go again, a performance that lasted for several hours, while she chatted with every other dingo in the area.

Just over the main sand ridge to the west of my camp, I located a reasonable-sized clearing of sufficient length to create an aircraft landing strip. After several days' hard work chopping down bushes, and filling in holes using my paddle as a shovel, then marking out the base and centre line with toilet paper, I was ready for my first visitor.

There is a large S-bend in the river here, so when I moved my camp 8 km downstream, I ended up 1 km west of where I had started, and about 100 metres from the official parking bay of my airstrip.

I spotted Mike Steele's aircraft coming in right on course, and after a precautionary approach, and a few helpful hints by radio from me, he dropped his Cessna in for a perfect landing. For a month now I had wandered a wilderness, seeing only part of the enormity of this flood. Today I was granted my wish for a bird's eye view, when Mike offered to take me for a run downstream to locate the headwaters.

I knew the river had changed dramatically in the last 4 km, with dead trees and samphire flats now prevalent, but from the air it was even more dramatic. To the north I could see the dense forest of trees that I had canoed through; to the south a more open, desolate looking channel awaited me.

About 22 km from my base camp we reached the headwaters of the Cooper, which were now spreading out over Red Lake Yard. Beyond, only a dry channel snaked off to the horizon and the Birdsville Track, some 80 km distant.

Just upstream, a narrow channel departing the southern end of Lake Appadare was the reason the water had not already reached the Birdsville Track and beyond. Heading down dune for 16 km, this fast-flowing stream entered Lake Hope, an enormous depression some 13 km long by 4 km wide, and this was draining most of the water out of the Cooper. It was a jewel of sparkling water set in an arid landscape of rolling sand dunes, and it would need several more months' intake to fill it.

I remembered calling in here many years ago while retracing explorer John McKinlay's footsteps as he searched for Burke and Wills, and seeing about 5000 pelicans just in one flock standing on its shores. Once the lake filled, they would be back again for the abundant fish life.

Mike flew back to Innamincka and as I once more settled into my solo ways, life slowly returned to a peaceful coexistence with nature and the elements. I made a home for the next couple of weeks in a cubby hole deep under the canopy of a large leafy tree, where I could retreat to escape the chill winds that occasionally roared in. At my doorstep the Cooper flowed relentlessly onwards, while birds, particularly big mobs of pelicans, came and went in a never-ending procession. Still water mirrored the huge red sandhill forming the opposite bank perfectly, its splendour only outdone when the sky also doubled up its act with clouds fired brilliantly by a setting sun.

Hunting rabbits for Cheater's tucker and taking long walks in the sandhills occupied most of my time. For an upper body workout on sunny days, I'd paddle my canoe a few miles upstream, have a quick swim and then just settle back with my feet up and let the current carry me home.

My life was uncomplicated and stress free — until the TV crew arrived to set up their home away from home amidst my serenity, and fired up their smelly little generator to cast unnatural light over my starlit domain.

I dragged lizards out of holes, just like Harry Butler, television's famous naturalist, caught rabbits, discussed Aboriginal artifacts, tip-toed through the wildflowers and paddled numerous miles backwards and forwards. My offer to do a nude bathing scene, however, was flatly rejected! At the end of a week they had captured enough and were ready for the city lights.

As the water was only just starting to exit Red Lake Yard and would be weeks before reaching the Birdsville Track, I decided to return to Adelaide with them. On 23 August, I paddled down to Lake Appardare and hid the canoe back in the sandhills. We found the headwaters of the Cooper a few kilometres further on and what a fascinating sight it was. Lizards and spiders were popping out of cracks and holes ahead of the flow as it inched its way slowly along the dry channel. I knelt down and with my finger reduced the headwaters of this mighty flood, which had inundated vast areas of Queensland and caused such devastation, filled numerous lakes and waterholes as it created a sea along the Cooper Channel, into a thin line drawn in the sand. That's power!

While Cheater and I waited patiently in Adelaide for news of sufficient water to enable the continuation of our journey, she just kept growing. She was rapidly developing into a magnificent-looking dingo. It would be sad to ultimately see her go, but with her temperament and the fact that, after all, she was still very much a wild animal, she would never suit city life.

On 12 September I contacted Mungeranie station, on the Birdsville Track, and was advised that the floodwaters had now covered the base of Lake Pandruannie. When I called them again on 25 September, the water had finally reached the site of the Cooper Creek Ferry and was spilling out over Lake Killamperpunna.

When the floodwaters of the Cooper Creek cut the Birdsville Track the only access north or south along this famous Australian track is via a 50 km detour to the east, where an outboard-powered ferry waits to transport vehicles across a narrow section of the Cooper.

Finally, Cheater and I returned to the Cooper, and on 3 October dragged my canoe from its hideout in the sandhills and began a two-day dash down the floodout to meet with a film crew, who would be waiting for me at the ferry. They wanted to document my arrival by canoe on to the Birdsville Track.

My timing was a little out, and it was frustrating waiting and watching the water slowly inch over the surface of Lake Killamperpunna. It took several days for it to conquer the last few hundred metres and reach the famous Birdsville Track.

I departed the Cooper ferry on 8 October for my final run down this magnificent waterway. It was glassy calm as I paddled the 10 km stretch of open water, and finally found access through the trees to pull my canoe up on to the Birdsville Track, and, sadly, journey's end. The thrust of the water was now weakening, and with the high temperatures of summer, and an increased evaporation rate just around the corner, it was obvious that the Cooper was not going to make it to Lake Eyre, and neither was I. My dream of riding a flooded inland river into Lake Eyre would remain unfulfilled, as the chance of another flood of sufficient size to reach the lake during my active lifetime seemed remote.

With the canoe securely strapped to the roof rack, I headed back to spend time in Adelaide before returning home to Noosa. Travelling down the Birdsville Track, I passed through a high fence near Clayton station, and it occurred to me that I had just travelled down one of the tributaries that makes Lake Eyre the largest drainage basin in the world. At the same time, I'd passed over the largest artesian basin in the world, and now I was passing through the Dingo Fence, the longest fence in the world. That's impressive!

As for the young pup rescued from the swirling floodwaters just a few short months ago, Cheater had now grown into a fine young bitch. With me she was fine, but as soon as strangers approached she was in flight mode and had great difficulty coping. The city would never be her home and it was with relief that I was finally able to relocate her to a country property in New South Wales, where she would be used in a breeding program.

My three-month ride down the floodwaters of the Cooper Creek fulfilled part of a long-held ambition. While I was elated to have reached the Birdsville Track, I was also disappointed. 1989's big flood could carry me no further, and now within a few kilometers of the Birdsville Track, its waters would disappear into the cracked earth now being baked by the onslaught of summer.

However, I had travelled down a magnificent waterway on a fascinating journey through an arid landscape and I felt truly privileged. I had watched as it conquered all before it, extracting a heavy toll on the wildlife, but at the same time paving the way for the land's rebirth, maintaining the rhythm of life exactly as nature intended it.

Considering the time the floodwaters had taken to reach the Birdsville Track, the vast area of inundation that occurs, the shallowness of the whole system, and its intrusion through an inhospitable desert, it truly is a unique and special creek. My Cooper.

🦎 🦎 🦎

Based on past performance, I would have rated the chance of another big flood occurring in my active lifetime at about nil, but early in 1990 an even greater deluge descended on outback Queensland, and the Cooper was in full flood once again. I waited patiently until the water had reached Lake Eyre before preparing my canoe and then setting out to complete my dream.

I departed the Birdsville Ferry on Thursday 4 October 1990 and again entered Lake Kilamperpunna. The eagle's nest was still there, now occupied by this year's young, which reminded me that it was almost one year to the day that I had rescued a drowning fledgling eagle from this very spot. He'd obviously tried to fly too soon and crash landed in the milky water. The wind started to whip up the waves as I set out for my second crossing of this 10 km lake. Wisdom dictated that I take a longer route, closer to the shore, as I headed for the Birdsville Track, my termination point of the previous year.

There would be no gravel rash now for my canoe! With a metre of water under her keel, I soon left the track behind, its position marked only by the occasional white guide post protruding a few inches above the water. For the rest of the day I navigated a tree-covered, flooded landscape some 30 km long and up to 15 km wide by compass. I crossed several fences by sliding the canoe under the top wire, which gives an indication of the average depth of this vast body of water. Black swans were prolific and I passed several mobs of cattle standing trapped on small islands.

The following day I pushed northwards to intersect the main channel again, and at times had barely enough water to float the canoe. This was a very difficult area to negotiate with nothing to see but trees. I turned westward at Tinkarmoorakoo waterhole and by the time I had reached Cannatalkaninna waterhole, I was being swept along in a wide, defined river that remained tree-lined until I reached Cuttupirra waterhole late the next day.

There were numerous nesting eagles and hawks, several mobs of camels and the occasional dingo, while on the water were the ever-present pink-eared ducks, which had been with me in large numbers on this waterway almost from Queensland.

From Cuttupirra waterhole the country changed completely. The tree line disappeared, leaving only stunted growth to dot the sandhills that crowded the river on both sides. I was now in the heartland of the Tirari Desert. On some of the bends, picturesque high cliffs had formed and all were pock-marked with nesting holes, from which screeching corellas voiced their disapproval of this intruder, while the mud homes of swallows clustered in crevices and overhangs. I didn't dare boat too close as I saw and also heard in the still of night, huge sections of cliff breaking away to come crashing down into the water.

Numerous islands, only inches above the turgid grey waters, had already been claimed and settled by thousands of stilts and avocets. They set up a frantic pretence of injury as they endeavoured to draw what they considered to be a threat away from their nests and young.

Standing on a high dune overlooking the racing river, I marveled at the contrast of desert and water in this infrequent event. What an incredible sight! Towering lines of almost-barren dunes glowing in the setting sun raced away to the north and to the south, their heart wrenched apart. A chasm created thousands of years ago was now being reworked by an unstoppable force: the flood that had originated in central Queensland some seven months earlier.

This creek that had filled a thousand waterholes and numerous lakes had brought rebirth to its water inhabitants, the fish, the birds and all animals that rely on it for their existence. It had also sent moisture deep into the soil so that the trees can survive while they await its next coming.

The river was shallow now as it meandered, split and rejoined, carving and cutting the white river sands. Finally, months after it fell as droplets in a far-off land, it reached its destination and its death bed, Lake Eyre.

On 7 October, I fulfilled my dream as I entered this magnificent lake, completing my journey from Queensland to Australia's Inland Sea.

Behind me the Cooper lay majestic, unique, memorable and conquered, while ahead, the hypnotic sparkling of the lake shivered my very soul as it danced with images of challenges yet to come.

Chapter 14

Jeanne

Life moves in mysterious ways.

Several years had passed since my relocation to Noosa and I had not found the woman of my dreams. I knew that there was a need in me to have a soul mate. But where might she be? How would I know her? Did this dream woman even exist? This might be the most difficult journey of all for this solitary desert walker.

The balconies of my Noosa apartment had just been tiled in preparation for sale. The tiler was about to walk out the door with his cheque in hand and I was preparing to drive south to join my daughter in the ski fields prior to returning to my recently purchased home in Adelaide. I happened to mention to him by way of idle conversation that Noosa could be quite a lonely sort of place if you don't have a companion.

Little did I know my world was about to change dramatically. This innocent comment would open one of the most important doors in my life; and my angel waited on the other side.

'Strange that you should mention it,' he said. 'I just happen to know this fabulous blonde unattached lady who owns a swish continental deli in Hastings Street – I have just recently tiled her townhouse. She's into aerobics and fitness things I think. Why don't you stop by and say hi.'

Well, my tiler was tattooed all over, and at one time I suspect he had owned a Harley Davidson and belonged to some notorious motor cycle gang down in Sydney, where he hailed from. Maybe he was even on the run! Images of what he considered to be a 'fabulous blonde' flashed into my mind, conflicting with the vision I had already conjured up. Mine was better!

Not that it mattered much one way or the other. Fate had already prearranged this meeting. Provided I took that first little step, two people were about to be manoeuvered on to a collision course.

The password was 'I hear that you make the best pies in Noosa,' and he would tell her that afternoon when he was in town, to expect me. I was to learn later that he did just that and she nearly had a fit: how dare he try to match-make! She didn't need a man in her life and 'how old is he anyway?' He said he thought about 50 and copped another earful. She was only just 41 and certainly wouldn't be interested in an older man! With this big bad bikie now in full retreat, he had completely forgotten to mention the password in his haste to escape the tirade.

With my curiosity aroused, I fronted up next morning at the deli and purchased a pie, but there wasn't a blonde woman in sight. I tried again the following morning with the same result. This lady was now on borrowed time — you know, three strikes and you're out. The next day, I bought my third and last pie and delayed my departure as long as I could by studying the numerous exotic goods displayed. 'What the hell is schwartzvelder schinken?' I asked myself. This sure was up-market stuff. I could see her assistant was starting to wonder why I was hanging around, so I headed for the door.

This is where seconds can change the direction of your life, for once outside, that's all it would take. A left or a right turn and I would disappear forever. I wasn't coming back.

Captivated by her beauty, I was stopped dead in my tracks. Confronting me now was this lithe blonde woman coming my way with the speed and grace of a gazelle in full flight.

I stepped aside to let her pass but before she could get behind the counter I had cornered and complimented her on having the best pies in Noosa. She thanked me shyly without a sign of recognition and I got the feeling that she either hadn't received the message or this was regretfully the wrong person. Damn, I quite liked this one. Furthermore, her year of manufacture looked about right.

I wasn't one to miss an opportunity, so with flashing eyes and slightly rusty youthful charm in full swing, I fumbled with a bit of small talk about the goods on display. I then mentioned how I would miss the great Noosa weather as I was on my way to the cold south for a break in the snow, then on to my other home in Adelaide now that the tiling in my apartment was finished. Bingo! At the mention of tiling she blushed madly, lighting up like a poker machine when you hit the jackpot.

Fate must have breathed a sigh of relief.

Well, obviously my clumsy attempts at charm had worked, as she joined me for a cup of coffee, and then again the following morning before I departed. We certainly seemed to be on the same wavelength and never stopped chatting the whole time. Looking back, I think I loved her almost at first sight. She came over to the carpark to see me off and I gave her a very casual peck on the cheek then turned to put some gear into my vehicle. When I turned back thinking I might try for something a bit more substantial, she had gone, leaving me deflated to say the least. I don't know, but she had a strange look on her face when I had mentioned earlier that morning that I was 57. Perhaps she thought this was a problem?

I didn't stay in Adelaide for long. With my phone bill to Jeanne having risen to astronomical proportions, I high-tailed it back to Noosa. The age difference hadn't been mentioned and now I was dreaming of her sitting next to me in my four-wheel drive as we headed out into the unknown. Over a couple of cups of coffee, was it possible that fate had really worked some sort of magic over two people in such a short time? I was about to find out.

Well Jeanne turned out to be a dream come true — strong, intelligent, independent and with a kind heart and a loving, caring nature. And above all she loves me. She had been in business for herself and had spent the past twelve years raising her son on her own, so independence was natural, I guess. I had a few barriers to break down before I earned her trust and love and I knew early on that I would have my time cut out in handling this one. She was a thoroughly modern woman so maybe I could change my old ways and we could both wear the trousers, so to speak. Perhaps I could become one of those new-age, you know, fifty-fifty people. Obviously that wouldn't include housework, cooking, washing, or ironing, however I felt that I could change enough to make a sizeable contribution with whatever was left!

The magic was there, so we soon started planning a life together. Jeanne sold the deli and, with her full real estate license, we opened Noosa Destinations – a dedicated property management office. After a slow start, we grew rapidly into a large and respected business, due I must say, to Jeanne's people skills. We were also incredibly fortunate that we managed to gather around us a small team of absolutely loyal, delightful and dedicated young women who were as excited and proud as we were of our growing business.

Finally, with such great support, I was able to reduce my involvement significantly and Jeanne asked if I would like to take some time off and go bush. I am sure it had nothing to do with the fact that hardly a day passed without some mention of the outback on my part. I didn't hesitate.

Chapter 15

Desert of Dreams

The Simpson is not the biggest desert in the world, nor does it fit the generally conceived pattern of what a desert should look like, but it is the largest parallel sand dune desert in the world. From the air one sees a grid of vast proportions running away to the north and south, many lines unbroken for hundreds of kilometres, while to the east and west some eleven hundred ribs stand like motionless waves of a frozen sea. Located in the dry, hostile interior of Australia, it spreads its ridges across Queensland, Northern Territory and South Australia. It is some 400–500 kilometres wide and its area is slightly smaller than Victoria, about the size of England and Wales together.

In 1845, explorer Captain Charles Sturt became the first white man to penetrate this unique area as he attempted to force a path to the centre of Australia. His journal records: 'The sand was of a deep red colour and a bright narrow line of it marked the top of the ridge amidst the sickly pink and glaucous coloured vegetation around'. The desert proved to be insurmountable and Sturt was forced to retreat.

In 1880, Augustus Poeppel completed the survey and marking of the border between South Australia and Queensland to the point where it joined with the south-east corner of the Northern Territory. However, due to wear on the chain used to measure his distances, this corner peg was located too far west and in 1884 Larry Wells re-surveyed the boundary and relocated the corner peg of the three states to its present position. He then continued to mark the Queensland/Northern Territory border.

In 1886, a superb explorer and bushman named David Lindsay set out from Dalhousie on the western side of the desert and made a successful crossing to a point on the Northern Territory–Queensland border about 32 km north of Poeppel Corner. His initial goal had been to proceed only as far as Queensland.

However, hearing from the local natives that white men were camped at a nearby well called Yelkerie, he decided to continue his journey eastward to investigate. Then, when another band of roaming Aboriginals informed him that all the white fellas had left, Lindsay decided to return to Dalhousie as there was now no reason to proceed further. About three more days' ride and David Lindsay would have been the first white man to cross the Simpson Desert. Lindsay, however, was for exploration, not firsts, and knowing that Poeppel and Wells had traversed this eastern area, he felt it was rather pointless continuing into known lands.

The desert now lay dormant and still unconquered other than by its Aboriginal inhabitants until that historic journey in 1936 when a stocky, no-frills South Australian pastoralist named Ted Colson set out from his home at Bloods Creek to cross the Simpson Desert from west to east and back again. Ted reasoned that with the heavy rain falling out over the desert, there would be an abundance of feed in a few weeks to afford a safe crossing. I have no doubt in my mind he wanted to be the first white man to completely cross this area, as he knew that a bloke called Madigan was planning just such a venture.

Early in 1994 I happened to find a twelve-year old newspaper cutting that I had retained relating to Danny Colson, Ted's Aboriginal son. In the article, Danny talks about how he was forcibly removed from his mother and her tribal lands — the custom at the time — and put into a home at Quorn for part-Aboriginal children. Years later he heard that his father was coming to Adelaide, and believed that he would collect him from the home and take him back to his mother and the outback he missed so terribly. Unfortunately Ted was killed and Danny was quoted as saying, 'All my dreams were shattered'. Ted had been on his way to Adelaide to collect a vehicle in which, I understand, he intended to make the first motorised crossing of the Simpson Desert, when he ran off the road and died, possibly of a heart attack.

I had always wanted to do a solo camel journey, although not necessarily in the Simpson, and was contemplating where I would venture when I chanced on that article about Danny. Re-enacting Ted Colson's journey was not important to me, as I'd visited all his prominent landmarks on numerous occasions, but it was Danny's words ('All my dreams were shattered') that would finally dictate where I would enjoy my camel experience. Instead of one of my solo adventures, perhaps this time I could make someone else's long-held dream come true by giving him, at this late stage of his life, a close association with his father's exploits. There was some urgency for me due to deteriorating back and knee problems, so that if I wanted to ride a camel, it had to be soon. I wasn't getting any younger!

I finally located Danny, who was now living with his family on their homeland north west of Mintabie, and he had no hesitation in accepting my offer. He wrote that he had planned a Simpson Desert crossing with his sons by vehicle, but was excited about a crossing as his father had done, by camel. Pinned to Danny's letter was a hand-written note from his daughter.

> My father has always helped others to try to
> reach their goals — this is the first time someone
> has reached out to help my dad reach a very
> personal goal. My dad's memory of his father
> is precious and something he doesn't talk about
> enough. Thank you for giving my father this
> opportunity to follow in his father's footsteps.
> Grandfather would have been very proud of my
> father as I know I am. Thanks. Rosslyn Moore.

There's only one place to ring if you want camels and the best advice available, and that's the old camel man and father of camel safaris in Australia, Noel Fullerton. He was also a friend of long standing so it was only natural that I sought his help. 'Would I be able to borrow four camels instead of the three I previously asked for? I now want to take someone with me across the Simpson Desert. Don't make a decision yet, I'll drive over and see you.'

During this journey, many of the people I met on the western edge of the Simpson cast doubt on the relationship between Danny and Ted.

'Uncle Ted was not like that,' said one, 'and in any case the Pitjantjarjara women did not visit the Blood's Creek area'.

Or, 'I doubt it. A lot of Aborigines took on the names of white people and in particular, their white bosses. He is just someone capitalising on an important person's name'.

Noel agreed to lend me four good camels and then, my curiosity aroused, I returned home to do a bit more research on Ted Colson.

Ted Colson had married Alice Jane Horne at Kalgoorlie in 1904 and moved to Victoria in 1917. In 1927 he moved to South Australia and was involved in the construction of the railway line from Oodnadatta northwards. In 1928 he explored the area around Goyder River and Mount Irwin station, and then had an extensive association with the Musgrave Ranges, the Ernabella areas and later the Peterman Ranges. He roamed the Pitjantjatjarra lands until 1931, when he took over the abandoned pastoral station of Bloods Creek, and settled there with his wife, Alice. Danny Colson, I learnt, was two years older than me, which meant he was born in 1931. Ted Colson was in Pitjantjatjarra lands during the time Danny would have been conceived so it was certainly possible that Ted was his father. It was too late, anyhow, for me to have second thoughts. I was now fully committed to taking Danny on his dream journey.

I made another trip over the Simpson, back to Noel Fullerton's camel farm to spend a few weeks familiarisation with the camels before our departure. As my total camel experience to date had been a seven-day trip with Noel on one of his safaris, I had a lot to learn in a hurry. Noel's main concern, repeated many times, was not my general stock ability – as he knew I had spent time on the land – or the fact that we would be crossing hostile terrain (I knew that area too well), but that I would lose his camels through accident. Not only were the animals selected for my journey valuable, but being his favourite camels, they were irreplaceable at any price.

What a burden to carry! I must say that there were several times that I nearly gave the idea away. Years ago I had wanted to buy my own animals so that I would have them available when I was ready for just such an event as this. Noel had talked me out of it, suggesting that if the occasion arose, he would lend me some of his. Now we both had to deal with the results of that decision.

The boss of my string was Muffler, Muffy for short. Not that tall, but a powerfully built bull camel with big teeth who, as Noel said, would keep walking until his feet wore down to his knees. Not fast, but a good leader and one that would control the others, particularly coming down the sandhills. With several tons of camel above me on a steep descent, this sounded like a good idea. A gentle camel normally, Noel's favourite, and a pet to all, but he came with the warning 'Never trust a bull camel when he is in season' — and guess what, Muffy was well and truly in the mating mood, and would stay that way until the weather warmed up. Suddenly I wished it was summer.

When in season, a bull camel displays several distinct signs: frothing at the mouth, arching of the neck as he sniffs the females on heat, displaying his dulaa, a pink sack of skin attached to the roof of his mouth which, when inflated, hangs out like a balloon, and standing with his hind legs apart swishing his tail backwards and forwards. He also exudes a dark, oily substance from a gland on his neck at the base of the skull.

Peter Pan, number one pack camel, and a gelding, was huge. Noel had used to ride him but found that he was too temperamental and difficult to control; he really didn't like anyone on his back. But as a pack animal he was superb. Grong Grong, another gelding, was my number two pack, and appeared to be a reasonably quiet beast. Where Peter Pan complained constantly and had a nasty and dangerous habit of jumping up when being loaded, Grong Grong just seemed to accept his lot placidly. The other riding camel, to be used by Danny, was yet undecided.

During one of my early training rides on Muffy, I had dismounted to open a gate and ended up walking home with a frothing, bubble-blowing, teeth-grinding monster behind me. It was a freezing cold day and he could still smell the females upwind at the farm. There was no way that he was going to hoosh down for me to remount and continue our journey. He wanted to get back to the ladies! Muffy had beaten me and bluffed me, and this was the camel that I had been hand feeding and trying to make friends with. It was several days before I tackled that gate again.

Grong Grong, compared to the others, was just perfect. He made no noise and did everything he was told. How I wished the others were just like him. He became my favourite until one night Noel related to me how he had intended to keep Grong Grong as a bull, but was finally forced to give him the unkindest cut of all. A pet donkey had shared the yard with Grong Grong and was continually running up to him, kicking and biting and teasing him in general, all of which was accepted with placid indifference, until finally one day he could take it no more. D Day had arrived for this donkey! Grabbing the insignificant pest with his huge neck, Grong Grong thrust the now startled donkey under his chest pedestal, and dropping to the ground, squashed the life out of him. For the rest of the day Grong Grong prowled the yard like some victorious but demented gladiator, frequently visiting the dead animal to kick and toss it around like some rag toy, and allowing no one near to remove its carcass. Beneath the hump of this giant beat the heart of a monster.

With Noel's experience, and in particular his intimate knowledge of his camels, surely he couldn't have made a mistake in choosing the three beasts most suited to my lack of experience and the journey ahead. He hadn't, but it was to take me at least another week to gain the experience to approach all my charges with something resembling confidence. I was nearly the boss and just as well, because it was time to go.

The gear was double-checked and loaded, and my charges were led up the truck ramp along with Danny's camel, Charcoal, who had only just arrived back from safari. Then it was away, the Oskosh roaring into the night to arrive at Bloods Creek very early the following morning. We only managed a couple of hours' sleep before unloading and saddling up the camels, then all too soon Noel was on his way home, in my hand his parting gift — my cameleer's learners permit. Thank goodness he hadn't given me L plates to hang on Muffy!!

I'll never forget that sudden feeling of total isolation as the desert quiet descended, broken only by the occasional breeze that stirred and creaked the huge sails of the now disused windmill. As the nearby floodout was thick with the acacias known as 'dead finish', I moved the camels over there so that they could feed on it as I settled down to wait.

It was late that afternoon before Channel 9, who were doing a documentary on Danny, arrived, followed by Danny and his family, and then Australian Satellite Services, who were installing my camel phone. Optus were about to launch their new satellite phone system, and with NEC, the equipment manufacturer, they thought it was a good idea for me to give the system a trial run out in the desert. What better place than the middle of the Simpson on the back of a camel?

Muffy was rigged to carry the phone, battery and aerial, and I had intended Peter Pan to carry the solar panel and spare battery. Peter, however, did his usual trick of jumping up suddenly, and the spare battery flew out of its pack and landed heavily, damaging one of its terminals. So the donkey killer got the job of carrying this fragile and important piece of equipment.

Danny was introduced to Charcoal – it seemed to be love at first sight. I heard him telling his camel: 'We gotta be good mates, that's what we gotta be. That's if you don't get funny ideas'.

The biggest day of the whole journey was the following morning, with the flurry of people and activity, last-minute adjustments to the phone, and the whirring of cameras. It wasn't until about 9.30 am that my caravan finally rolled out and headed the kilometre or so down the track to the ruins of Bloods Creek station. It was 12 August 1994.

This was where Ted Colson had waved goodbye to Alice and departed on his epic journey. This was Danny's father's home and a very emotional moment for him, and his daughter, Rosslyn Moore. I remember the tears in her eyes as she strolled amongst the relics of the past, and her comment to me, 'You know Denis, Grandfather would've been so proud of Dad if he could see him now.'

Our next stop was Mount Dare station, about 30 km away, and while I am not certain that Ted called in there on his outward journey, he certainly did on his return. It was to be a long day in the saddle, but it did give me time to chat with Danny and learn a little of his past.

Danny Colson was born in 1931. His mother was from the Pitjantjatjara people near Ernabella, where he went to school. At that time, a policy existed where part-Aboriginal children were taken from their parents and brought up in institutions to integrate them into white people's ways. At the age of ten the police came to collect Danny. He remembers his mother hiding him under a blanket and sitting on him to conceal him from them. When he was finally found and taken away, he was terrified. With him was a young girl; on their way south to Colebrook Home at Quorn, they discussed the fact that they were probably going to be eaten. On leaving school at fifteen, Danny worked on a number of outback properties and finally married Gloria Warren from Finnes Springs station.

Over the years he worked on the railway from Marree to Alice Springs, and it was during this period that he was finally reunited with his mother at Ernabella. He was never to meet his father. Moving to Port Augusta he was offered a job as a field officer with the Prisoner's Aid Association, and spent many years working in Adelaide with prisoners.

In 1977 he was sent overseas to work with the American Indians and learnt a lot from their rehabilitation centres. Danny has, over the years, been Chairman of the Port Augusta Aboriginal Sporting Committee, Community Welfare Consultation Committee, Aboriginal Community Affairs Panel and Department of Further Education and Legal Rights – a tireless worker for his people, and still continues to be so.

The policy of separation caused great grief and dislocation to many part-Aboriginal children when they were removed from their families and tribal ways. Without condoning the practice, it also gave many of them another choice, another direction, if they wanted to take it, for how their lives could develop. Danny told me how he appreciates today the opportunity forced on him so long ago, as he can now have a better lifestyle for himself and his family. He said that many of the childhood friends he left behind are now dead or living in total confusion, poverty and degradation.

We departed Mount Dare station and the warm hospitality of our hosts, Phil and Rhonda Hellyer, at 10 am the following morning. Mount Dare was formerly a cattle property owned by Rex Lowe, which was then purchased by the SA Government to create the Witjira National Park It's a last-stop shop for travellers crossing the desert. They offer fuel, food, accommodation and a chance for that last beer in their licensed premises.

We pushed on into a stiff breeze that occasionally lifted the dust from our arid surroundings. Ahead, I noticed on the track a large section of bull dust; in the middle of it I received one hell of a surprise – Muffy suddenly dropped to his knees and started to wallow! One moment I was sitting ten feet tall, and the next I was down in the choking fine dust, unable to see, and astride a beast who was having a whale of a time and could roll at any minute. With hefty encouragement from the whip and a fair bit of yelling, we finally surfaced intact, but from there on, we gave anything that looked like a camel dust bath a wide berth.

We turned eastward and paralleled the southern side of the Finke River floodout to camp at an old holding yard and dam about nineteen miles from Mount Dare. Here the film crew and their chopper would say goodbye and we would at last be able to get down to the serious business of crossing the Simpson, which lay ahead. Our ridiculous starting time of around 10 am had to go, and I felt sure that without outside interference we would be able to settle into a better routine. We certainly needed to.

We had a rather pleasant journey now, with the thick trees and vegetation of the Finke cutting down the violent cold wind. Feed for the camels was plentiful: mainly flowering wattles There were numerous fresh camel tracks, which meant we had to keep a careful watch, as I didn't wish to be surprised by a wild mob. We camped that night in the remnants of an old yard at Arina waterhole.

With the stark, picturesque beauty of Mount Alinerta to the south, we finally turned north-east, arriving at Dakota Bore mid-afternoon. The sight of the athel pines brought back a flood of memories. This is where I had found water at the completion of my successful solo vehicle journey across the Simpson in 1977. It was a real haven then for wildlife, but a few years later when I returned the stench of death had stalked Dakota and surrounding areas. Parked out of sight, full of somewhat surprised warriors, was a helicopter gunship. I'd spotted it from a high hill, and gone to investigate.

They hadn't wanted to talk much about what they were doing, probably thinking that I may be an animal liberationist or something. It was Brucellosis eradication time for the cattle industry and to help control the disease, they were shooting all the wild, unfenced cattle and anything else that could contribute to its spread. Rotting donkey, brumby and cattle carcasses lay everywhere.

Now there was even less life, as the bore had been capped, its gushing waters terminated. I decided to use the old cattle yards to hold our camels and made camp early. I wanted to show Danny the large Aboriginal rock placement site nearby with its huge serpent that I had located many years ago and also Ritchie's Ridge, but we really couldn't afford the time to detour. Yarning around our campfire that night, I told Danny about the South Australian Government's expedition to Ritchie's Ridge back in 1938 and how, accompanied by Noel Fullerton, I had relocated their campsite.

In the early 1930s, a story, circulated in the Black Bull hotel in Adelaide by a station owner, a Mr Lowe from the far north of the state, was picked up by eager reporters. They told a sensational tale of how the Lowes had located the bones of some six to seven people lying on a sandhill at the edge of the Simpson Desert about sixty miles to the east of Abminga rail siding.

It wasn't long before the bones were associated with those of Ludwig Leichhardt's 1848 expedition, in which, while endeavouring to cross the continent from east to west, he and his party disappeared forever. There had been never-ending speculation as to Leichhardt's final resting place, and this find out in the sandhills fired imaginations to such an extent that the Government decided, in 1938, to fund an expedition to retrieve the remains. A surveyor, photographer and an anthropologist were included in the retrieval party and they took with them seven coffins.

From Abminga rail siding, they travelled by truck, then horse and camel, to reach the site, which they named Ritchie's Ridge. Instead of human bones, they were disappointed to find that the white material scattered along and down the ridge was actually calcified roots of trees. As the party had brought sieves and digging tools with them, they decided to excavate a large area where they had noticed a few teeth and Aboriginal grinding stones, which indicated that at one time the site had been occupied. They found some harness leather, badly rusted steel, and bone and teeth fragments, but most surprising of all was the discovery of two coins. One was a Maundy threepence dated 1841 and the other an 1817 half-sovereign.

Leichhardt had departed England in late 1841 and it is possible that the Maundy threepence, of which only 2904 were minted that year, was given to him as a keepsake. Nothing else was found to even remotely link Leichhardt with the site and if the threepence had belonged to him, then how did it get there, when all evidence points to his demise at Wantata waterhole on the other side of the Simpson Desert, some 400 km away?

Greenstone for axe heads and shells, amongst other items, had travelled vast distances along the Aboriginal trade routes that criscrossed the continent, and it would have been relatively easy for a coin to have travelled the same way. We will never know if the coins had in fact belonged to Leichhardt, but it certainly lent a measure of intrigue to the Government's Bones Expedition.

A few years earlier Noel Fullerton had asked me if I had been to Ritchie's Ridge, as he was intrigued by the story of the bones and would like to visit the site. I hadn't, but I had all the references needed and considered that I could easily get us into the vicinity. To locate the actual site of the dig after such a long time was highly unlikely.

Noel had spoken to two of his friends before our departure and they had each given him different directions as to the whereabouts of the site, both of which I knew to be incorrect. I suspect that they may have got their information from Rex Lowe of Mt Dare station, in which case I am sure that he deliberately misled them. Rex was a young lad when he went with his father and the Government expedition to locate the bones and clearly remembered the incident.

The site had been surveyed by the expedition, but as I suspected when I plotted the location on my map, it was incorrect. They were out in their longitude, which put them well into the sandridges and not, as reported, on the slope of the first sandhill forming the western boundary of the desert proper. I considered that their latitude was more than likely accurate. Noel and I had pushed our way over a large floodout covered with regrowth to reach the first sandhill and parked in front of it, and there I marked a tree as a reference point with the blaze facing to the east.

About 300 metres south of our position, in the sandy valley immediately behind this frontal dune, we located the dig site. The mounds of sieved sand were still clearly visible and the ridge pole and timber pegs used for the team's shelter were lying just as they had dropped them when they abandoned their search some 56 years earlier. I spent some time with my metal detector, but all that I could locate were a few nails and the foil covering of a roll of film.

As they wouldn't have camped here with their horses and camels, we crossed the ridge back on to the gum-tree-shaded flat on the other side and soon located some wire and a large fallen tree trunk, on the underside of which we could feel a blaze mark. This was obviously the main Government campsite – exciting to locate after it had lain undisturbed for so long.

😾 😾 😾

Today, Danny and I would confront the desert. While we were still rather slow in packing and getting underway, we were showing signs of improvement. Just to the north of Dakota lies Mt Etingimbra. Ted Colson records that he camped just to the south of this, which was then the last charted hill, before entering the unknown sandhill country that lay to the east. We set a course to parallel his. We hadn't been going long when I spotted a bull camel in the undergrowth. As he hadn't smelt us yet I altered course to skirt him and to keep us downwind of him. This manoeuvre took us to higher, exposed ground from where we could see in the distance a mob of some 20–30 camels. Spotting us, they bolted and disappeared from view, however their smell, which carried downwind to us, excited Muffy so much so that I had to apply a heavy continual left rein to force him to proceed in our required direction.

Sometime later we spotted the mob heading towards us en masse.

Leading the rush was the largest bull camel that I have ever seen, a magnificent sandy specimen. I pulled out my rifle, loaded up and waited for the unknown. Muffy was now really agitated and becoming harder to control, fighting the rein as he no doubt became excited by the scent of the females in the mob, and perhaps the threat of a physical challenge by their leader, who was now closing rapidly.

Sticky beads of exuded black scent formed rivulets down his neck. Curiosity would bring these wild camels in, and probably once satisfied they would go, but we couldn't be sure. I certainly wasn't looking forward to some form of fracas. With two camels tied on behind limiting my manoeuvrability, and the chance that we could end up with nose pegs wrenched out or wild camels tangled in my lines, there was room for concern. With Danny yelling, trying to deter them, I waited until I could see the whites of the big bull's eyes before firing a warning shot over their heads ,which brought the charging mass to a hesitant stop. Another shot sent them on their way; our camel experience had grown another notch.

For the rest of that day, we continued east through low sandhill country sparsely dotted with bushes, and distinctly lacking in feed for the camels. I wasn't too concerned as I knew the wattles would start soon, possibly by early the next day. During the day I had noticed a slight tingling in my feet and a feeling that my legs were frozen. I attributed this to a lower back problem and wasn't so much concerned about completing this journey, more the long-term ramifications. Danny, on the other hand, had severe pain in his lower abdomen in the vicinity of a recent operation. That was a more immediate worry, and he was also enduring what I suspected was sciatic pain down his leg.

As both our symptoms had occurred for the first time that day, on our first cross-country section, it seemed to me that the jarring and twisting created by uneven terrain had contributed significantly in aggravating underlying health problems. I therefore decided to alter course southwards to intersect the French Track, which would give us smoother going; we would then follow it to intersect Ted Colson's track near the Knolls. If we were to have medical problems, access to help would also be more readily available.

Mt Etingimbra had long faded from view by the time we made camp in a small clearing surrounded by spinifex clumps. Nearby there were enough strong bushes to leg-rope the camels for the night and sufficient wood for a small fire. We had entered the desert proper at last, and while we slept the parallel dunes would cocoon us in their tight embrace for the first time. That night the heavens shone with a brilliance denied to city dwellers as a million stars frolicked in their cloudless arena. It felt good to be back, and even better to have the promise of a great journey ahead.

Stiff and sore, Danny headed for his swag early. After a last check to make sure our camels were secure, I settled down to play with my new-fangled toy. I had finally succumbed to modern technology and purchased a GPS (Global Positioning System). I really didn't know how to use the damn thing, however, as I only wanted my position in latitude and longitude, all I had to do was press 'on' and then 'pos' (position). When the light stopped flashing up came the numbers! Then it only took me a few minutes with the aid of a ruler to mark our campsite with a dot on my map. It was now a simple exercise to get the distance and compass bearing for Purni Bore on the French Track, which was to be our next objective.

I was up before dawn, and sunrise found me sitting on a nearby high sand dome intently studying the southern sky with my binoculars. I didn't have long to wait. Intermittent faint smudges travelling erratically just above dune height moved from west to east and always at a certain point on the horizon, they disappeared from view. Shortly afterwards, the process was repeated, but this time the smudges were travelling to the west. If I were doing this exercise solely as a bushman, then where the smudges disappeared is where I would go to find water, in this case, Purni Bore. The smudges were flocks of birds wheeling in for their first drink of the day.

Now we would put my years of bush experience to the test with this hi-tech equipment. I took a bearing on the site with my compass and then compared it with the one derived from my GPS calculations the previous night. They were identical. It was obvious to me that with sophisticated tools like this available at such a reasonable price, you wouldn't travel remote isolated areas without one. However, my advice would be to not rely on it completely. One day it may decide to have a hissy fit and you need to be armed with a bit of extra old-fashioned back-up knowledge.

We finally reached the Rig Road turnoff about 30 km east of Purni Bore. We were making good time now. Both of us felt better physically, so the smoother going along the track had helped as I had hoped it would.

Danny was saying goodbye to a friendly group of desert travelers who had stopped us for a photo shoot, when another unrelated vehicle pulled up nearby. From it jumped a rather puffy, unfit-looking character who seemed to be in an almighty hurry to catch us before we departed. He looked like a classic heart attack candidate. He was yelling something unintelligible in a foghorn of a voice that was an assault to the ears. I rode over to meet him and our conversation then went something like this:

'You and Hans Tholstrupp get publicity whenever you do anything! I have also driven across the Simpson Desert from east to west,' (obviously referring to my solo desert crossing some eighteen years ago in my little yellow Suzuki) 'and I didn't get any publicity for what I did,' he yelled, 'but you two always do'.

His voice and expression left me in no doubt that he was starting to lose the plot. As for me, I had a creepy feeling that something not very nice had intruded into my personal space. I had never met this man before to my knowledge, so unless this was his normal behaviour with everyone, he obviously disliked me intensely and there appeared to be no love lost with Hans Tholstrupp either.

When I asked him what track he had used for his crossing, it was a bit of a trick question. He told me that it was out through Poeppel Corner, to which I replied:

'Well, mate, I didn't use a track. I crossed about 60km north of there as that was the purpose of the exercise — to see if the desert could actually be traversed cross-country, no tracks.'

He exploded again. 'How could you?' he shot back, cutting me off. 'I had a big motor in my Suzuki and also large tyres like yours, and I couldn't climb the dunes off the track.'

Somewhere in his garbled monologue, I also gleaned that he'd had a mechanical problem and got bogged in one of the many salt lakes that lay across his path. He was well and truly agitated by now and, I suspected, bordering on out of control.

I could feel the hot, prickly flush of anger and hear the warning bells signaling it was time to get out now before it was too late. He was obviously calling me a liar by inference and I knew if he continued any further and actually said so, then I would hoosh Muffy down and rearrange a few things to his detriment. Sometimes I amaze myself. I wheeled Muffy around and disappeared over the dune top without further comment leaving him behind. I still didn't even know his name.

Over the next few days my anger slowly subsided to something more akin to pity. I finally came to the conclusion that I had met a very sad and angry under-achiever who had, not a chip on his shoulder, but a bloody great log, the weight of which would kill him sooner rather than later. Somewhere in his life, or perhaps all through it, he hadn't received the recognition he considered his due and he was obviously extremely jealous of anyone who had. Hans and I were probably just two of many.

The encounter, however, had left me with a nagging thought, which I commented on to Danny. 'You know, something about that bloke and his Suzuki bogged on a salt lake, rings a bell – I have a feeling that the township of Innamincka is involved, but I can't think how.'

The thought wouldn't let me rest though, so when I finally got home to Noosa, I called Mike Steel of the Innamincka Trading Post.

'Hi Mike. Denis Bartell here — just wanted to pick your brains, mate. Did you ever tell me a story about a bloke with a voice you could never forget and a Suzuki bogged in a salt lake?' I also gave him a brief physical description.

He thought about it for a while before replying, 'No Denis, I can't say I remember that, however we did have a character wandering around here some time ago who had an irritating voice and a physique to match your description. But that's it … no bogged Suzuki … sorry'.

Well it was close, but not close enough. 'Thanks Mike, but I need the vehicle to tie it all in together. Catch up again one day.'

My next call was to a retired policeman. I had first met him at Innamincka and subsequently stayed overnight at the Leigh Creek Police Station as his guest, while on my north–south walk across Australia. Great bloke — he owned an Auster aircraft which he absolutely loved. He was a very active person until one day on duty he became involved in a high-speed chase with a stolen motor vehicle, the driver of which, when finally stopped, purposely ran him down, seriously crushing his knees. It finished his career, leaving him in agonising pain for years and ultimately destroying his marriage.

Finally I tracked him down. 'Hi Peter. Denis Bartell here. Remember me?' I am never sure if it's a good or a bad thing when people reply, 'How could I forget?' I just hope for the best and plough on.

'Peter, it's probably a silly question, but did you ever tell me anything about a voice and a person you could never forget, and a Suzuki bogged out on a salt lake?'

It only took seconds for a reply. 'Bloody hell mate. You haven't had the misfortune to bump into that idiot, have you? Hell, I would have thought that someone would have done him in by now!' Peter was having a good old chuckle and obviously I had hit the jackpot. 'There wouldn't be two galahs like him in all of Australia, that's for sure!'

'Okay Peter, tell me the gruesome details once again, because yes, I did run into him on a recent trip crossing the Simpson Desert by camel.' I briefly filled him in on my encounter, poured a scotch and settled back to hear his story unfold without interruption.

'There were two of us on patrol duty out at Mount Davies near the Western Australian border when we received a radio call from our base at Oodnadatta. We were instructed to rescue a bloke in a Suzuki who was bogged on a salt lake in the middle of the Simpson Desert. His transfer case was also apparently broken. Police Headquarters in Adelaide had been advised by Sydney police who had received a call from a CB operator who had taken this bloke's mayday call for help over the radio. We took it in turns driving non-stop through the night and I covered about a thousand kilometres before we finally reached him. We met up with another two officers from Oodnadatta at Mokari airstrip on the western edge of the Simpson and travelled on together to search for this bloke. On the last leg of the journey we had been guided into his position by one of our police aircraft and I can tell you, by the time we arrived, we were well and truly stuffed.

'I lost the toss of the coin and my offsider and I drove our Land Rover out into the middle of the salt lake in which we could see him bogged. It was pretty hard going because of the extremely soft under-surface of the lake and I was a bit peeved that he made no attempt to walk over to us, let alone acknowledge our presence. Now you're not going to believe this Denis, but his very first words to us when we finally got to him were not g'day, thanks, or apologies for the inconvenience and the long drive, but "Have you got my spare parts?" Even "kiss my arse", would have been better than that!

'We explained that we were only here to rescue him, and not act as a delivery service, or tow his vehicle from its up-to-the-axles bogged state. What he did with his vehicle was his problem — our job was to look after his safety. He had a young Blue Heeler pup with him that he had recently bought from Rex Lowe at Mt Dare station and it was sitting under the Suzuki. By this time, mate, I was feeling more sorry for the dog than I was for this character. Take it from me Denis, he carried on like an idiot, although nothing compared to what was to follow. When we pulled out a couple of coldies, thinking we deserved them after our ordeal, and after offering him the same, or a soft-drink or cold water, he went right off, threatening to report us to the police commissioner for drinking on the job. I seem to recall that he mentioned something about being a reformed alcoholic.

'Anyhow, we loaded him and his personal gear into our vehicle, left his Suzuki and took off. But by the time we had reached the Colson Track, we couldn't put up with him any longer. We had been swapping him backwards and forwards between the two police four-wheel drives because none of us could put up with him for much longer than 15 to 30 minutes — he was a total pain in the bum. There was an oil drilling rig camp operating just up the track so we decided to divert and drop him off there, although that hadn't been our original intention. As my mate said when we left: "Thank God they took him because I was ready to cut his throat; there's no way we could have put up with him all the way to Oodnadatta".

'Then a week or two later I had to fly out to the drilling camp. I was using Peck's aircraft from Ooodnadatta to deliver their weekly food, mail and other supplies. Well, he was still there, standing with the Rig Boss when they met me at the nearby airstrip. It was obvious that he didn't recognise me out of uniform and again there was no such thing as a greeting, just, "You'd better have my parts". Later the Rig Boss jokingly said I was a bit of a mongrel for not telling them what sort of a goose we'd landed them with. You see Denis, the whole bloody camp, each and every one being hard-working, hard-drinking types, were ready to kill him! You know, take him out and lose him behind a sandhill somewhere, and I'm not joking! I asked what their next move was with this bloke and was informed that their mechanic was going to head out to his vehicle the same day to repair it and get him out of their hair — that's how keen they were to be rid of this bloke. That's about it mate, and I hope it answers your questions, and personally I hope I never have the misfortune to meet up with him again.'

By now I was feeling totally vindicated. The resentment I'd harboured towards a person who I considered to be an aggressive, belligerent loudmouth appeared to be completely justified. I'd slipped in another icecube, drowned it with scotch — double this time — and was starting to thank Peter when he cut in.

'Oh by the way Denis, he carried out his threat and did indeed report us for drinking on the job. I had considered at the time advising him that as Officer In Charge of the two patrols in attendance, I had the authority to permit drinking, within limits, whilst on duty. He was such a pain though that I didn't want to spoil the good fun he thought he would have by reporting us. In the end we got a report from the Commissioner's Office congratulating us for a job well done under such trying conditions. His letter of complaint was simply attached for our information. The top brass decided to thank him for his trouble by sending him an invoice for his rescue. What goes around comes around. Whadya reckon mate?'

'Well, that's it then Peter. Thanks for solving a mystery for me. Unfortunately we don't know his name, so once again the poor old bugger misses out on his recognition!' I laughed.

'Not a problem Den,' he replied. 'One thing's for sure, talking to you has brought back a flood of memories, not only of my beaut time at Oodnadatta, but also Marree, Leigh Creek, Marla and so on. Thankfully though, my time at Oodna and Marree was before four-wheel drives became as popular as they are today. I caught up with a mate of mine from my police days a couple of years ago — he'd just returned from a trip to Innamincka and told me that you can't just camp anywhere on the banks of the Cooper as we used to. Apparently there are public dunnies everywhere and the National Parks and Wildlife have rebuilt the old AIM hospital ruins as their headquarters and run around as if they own the bloody country. Worse still, the four-wheel drivers are everywhere, and of course the real beauty of that country was the solitude. I guess I'm just getting old and unwilling to change, but at least I've had the absolute privilege of seeing it all and been on just about every track on a line east/west north of Leigh Creek from one side of the State to the other. If I haven't driven on it, I've at least seen it from the air. I miss it all! Thank heavens I still get to go to Arkaroola and the northern Flinders Ranges every couple of months. Take care and thanks for the walk down memory lane.'

🦎 🦎 🦎

Reading Ted Colson's diary, the country so far had conformed well to his description. The major difference for us was the lack of succulent feed. In a good season our camels would have obtained most, if not all, of their water requirements for the entire crossing from the plant life. However, due to the shocking conditions existing now, water would be our major problem. We were carrying 110 litres on each pack animal, and a further 30 litres between the other two. As Phil and Rhonda from Mt Dare were meeting us at the corner of the Colson and French Tracks, I decided to get them to bring a 44 gallon drum of water, about 200 litres. Although it was only four days since the camels had consumed 50 litres each, when we reached that drum they demolished it all quick smart. Boy, can they drink!

Eleven days into our journey and we were camped near BM 6853 on the French Track, about 10 km south of Ted's track. Although the going had been a slow slog for the camels, at least we had found enough food for them: flowering wattles and bullock bush. We had slowly changed our 10.00 am starting time to around 7.30 am, were averaging about 23 km per day and generally stopped to camp around 4 pm. We had both settled in well to our venture and although still suffering from our physical problems, we were much improved. We worked as a team, each one complementing the other — a set procedure, everything in its place, nothing left to chance.

I had no favourites now: we had a great team of camels, each with its own personality. You couldn't fault our tireless leader, other than being so pitifully slow. How I hated to use the whip to keep him moving, but the desert at this time was not a place to linger. Peter Pan just plowed ahead. I don't think anything would have stopped him. The few times that we met tourists on the track he would come alongside, and resting his huge head on my lap like a shy old softie, eye off the intruders.

Danny and Charcoal had developed a special kind of bond. If he didn't dismount quickly enough when we stopped, Charcoal would be biting his foot in the stirrup to hurry him up. When Danny unwrapped a lolly, or had a drink, he would hear the noise and around would come his head demanding his share. I think he had Danny pretty well sorted out, and if he wanted a special bush to eat away from our chosen path, he usually got his way. They were good mates, so much so that it wouldn't have surprised me if Danny had made Noel an offer to buy him.

On day twelve, the country changed dramatically and my diary states:

'Only occasional wattle and bullock bush, the driest I have seen the Simpson in 20 years, rabbits five feet up the trees ringbarking the boughs, all ground cover cut to pieces by the drifting sand, camels very tired, hard slog, desolate'.

When you move at the pace of the desert, you see the prints left each night: the life of the desert. This section was lifeless except for the occasional dingo hugging the track. For one, though, his harsh life had been terminated by man's intervention. He wasn't mangy, tempting a bullet from kindness; it looked like he'd just been shot for fun. More disturbing, a hundred yards away, was the carcass of a wedge-tailed eagle, the spent 22 cartridge — its ticket to death – lying on the track nearby.

Finally we crested a high dune, and away to the south-east I could make out the familiar shapes of the Approdinna Attora Knolls. I headed in their direction. These were first seen by David Lindsay in 1886 and I had passed them in 1980 as I re-enacted his crossing. Ted Colson had also visited the Knolls, and using one of his photos as a guide I was able to hoosh our animals down exactly where he had and then, climbing the southern-most knoll, we viewed a scene largely unchanged since his visit. Ted named the salt lake before us Lake Tamblyn after his school master who, next to his father, had the greatest influence on his life. Lake Warrabulla is its Aboriginal name.

'Okay Danny, I want you to stand just here,' I said as I handed him a copy of a photo taken by his father showing a large salt lake. 'This is where your dad stood, mate, when he took that shot.'

I could see his hand tremble as he held the photo up to compare it with the view ahead. When he finally spoke, there was a huskiness to his voice that I'd never heard before and then I glimpsed the shimmer of tears in his eyes. 'Den, nothing much has changed in the last fifty-eight years has it. It's almost identical.'

'You're right mate. It's timeless out here. That's precisely why it's so special.'

As I watched Danny standing in deep thought, I knew that for the first time in his life, with the help of the desert, he was now finally and totally connected to the spirit of the father he had never really known. I could feel Ted's presence around us as I uttered words that I believe he wanted me to say. 'Danny, you might be here to relive your father's glory, but I know your dad would be mighty proud of you and your own achievements. You stand tall, mate. You've come a long way. You have risen above all obstacles and most importantly, you have done it without hate.'

As I left Danny gazing out over the salt lake and the gidgee-massed valley, I had no doubt he was longing for a voice or a touch denied him so long ago. A child's dream was now being fulfilled in the only way possible. His face displayed his emotions. Perhaps it was the angle or the play of light, but suddenly I was struck by the similarity in appearance to the photograph of Ted that I had. I no longer had any doubt that this was Ted Colson's son.

We were well and truly into gidgee country now and I was rather concerned that, because our camels were so hungry, they might eat its green leaves. Noel had pointed out from his book on poisonous plants that gidgee could be a problem. It had something to do with their ability to absorb arsenic from the soil and store it in the leaves. I also remembered some time ago being told that cattle were dying from gidgee poisoning on Argadargada Station, and that they were trying to eradicate the trees. Perhaps it is only poisonous at certain times of the year, or if stock has nothing else to eat — I didn't know. However, I couldn't take the chance, so we leg-roped the camels at night so they would be unable to reach the trees.

This particular night, to get the camels closely grouped near to us, we had only been able to find three solid dead trees in our vicinity, the other camel being tied by Danny to a huge log.

Early in the morning, I was awoken from a deep sleep by Danny making a hell of a racket, and yelling out that we were surrounded by wild camels. 'Denis, get up quick! We're being attacked.' I came out of my swag stark naked, surging with adrenalin, in full flight-or-fight mode like some primitive from the past, and, grabbing my rifle, tried to sort out what was happening to us. My worst nightmare, that of a confrontation with wild camels while we were asleep, had apparently come true.

We were camped in a hollow, and the first thing I saw towering above me, bathed in the glow of a brilliant moon, were two huge camels confronting each other. By their stance, they were ready to do battle. I realised one had to be Muffy by his location and could just make out his leg-rope stretched taut behind him as he endeavoured to get to this intruder.

We were in no immediate danger that I could see, but my thoughts were racing as I tried to rationalise the situation, to assess if, when and how I had to dispatch this interloper to another place. Strange, but I thought I could see something hanging from its neck, and the torch that I had finally located soon confirmed that this was the case. It was our Grong Grong, the donkey killer, out on the prowl. Grong Grong obviously hadn't fully forgotten that he was once a bull, and had dragged his massive log all the way over so that he could have a bit of a 'dust-up' with Muffy. We managed to find a dead tree some distance away and relocated Grong Grong to it.

Our next stop was Poeppel Corner and we pushed on into marginally better country. Ahead lay a series of large salt lakes to cross, but due to the dry conditions, these would not present a problem. The weather was warming up now and rather pleasant compared to the cold at the start of the journey. It was good to get the sun on my body and the start of a tan after the winter hibernation.

In my sixty-odd trips across the Simpson, there are many places that will forever stir memories of the past. We were approaching one such place now, so I stopped to show Danny a rather insignificant tree. It stands on the southern side of the track about two hundred yards from the lake edge and 1.25 kilometres east of BM 6866.

During my solo gulf to gulf walk, I passed through Atula station then turned southwards into the desert, crossing the French Track at this very point. On this tree, I had removed some branches to clearly display a message hung there for the next passing vehicle. Continuing down the lake, I had then crossed a set of tracks still visible in the salt crust. These were from the two-wheel cart used on my solo unaided walk across the desert from west to east the year before. I could point out to Danny the very sand dome where I had abandoned my cart after hauling it up from the valley floor, before proceeding on with my back-pack to Birdsville.

That west–east crossing was without doubt the most physically difficult journey that I had undertaken. Through lack of water and nutritionally insufficient food, I had completely stripped my system — there was nothing left. I moved like a mechanical man motivated only by a will to conquer, a feeling so intense, so powerful that I would readily push myself to my death attempting to achieve my goal, still upright and still walking. It took months of good food and rest before I felt remotely well again.

Many times sitting on Muffy, watching my charges slowly slog up the seemingly endless sandhills, and forcing them ever onwards, I felt sorry for these beautiful animals. However, I had pulled my heavy cart up similar dunes for two weeks straight, then lumped a pack with all the necessities of life on my back for hundreds of miles through this desert — I knew exactly what it was all about. I was asking no more of my camels than I had asked of myself. This was my turn to take it easy, and what an effortless way to see this area. I had all the advantages of walking, namely the closeness with my surroundings, but without the physical burden.

Finally we reached Poeppel Corner, now marked by a modern concrete post designating the junction of three states: NT, QLD, and SA. The original post was moved many years ago and now rests in the Art Gallery of South Australia. There is, however, a wooden replica nearby, officially positioned on 4 July 1989. Ted Colson was unable to locate this point on his outward journey, positioning himself instead on a boundary peg located in the middle of the second salt lake to the east. On his return, he found Poeppel's peg and records that he only missed it by three hundred yards on a compass shot of over one hundred and forty miles.

In no way detracting from his effort, I nevertheless believe that this statement was not strictly accurate; I think more that he was lucky to have stumbled so close to it. Ted himself placed the Approdina Attora Knolls astride the twenty-sixth parallel and from there states in his log that he continued his journey east. As the Knolls are approximately eight kilometres south of the twenty-sixth parallel, by continuing east as stated, he should have then passed eight kilometres south of Poeppel's peg, not three hundred yards. The answer, I believe, lies in the seasonal conditions at that time. Big rains had fallen over the desert and some of the numerous salt lakes to the east of the Knolls could have been wet, and therefore slippery for the camels to negotiate. I think he would have rounded many of them at their northern extremity, which would have slowly forced him back towards the twenty-sixth parallel.

From Poeppel's peg, we followed the remnants of the old French Track eastwards; I estimated that we would take about three days to reach the Eyre Creek floodout. We led the camels over the second and last salt lake, due to occasional slippery patches, and I was able to point out to Danny one of the border survey pegs spotted and recorded by his father.

Passing the end of the French Track, we then followed a faint track, in parts almost obliterated. I had first passed this way some eighteen years earlier, and as it is the most direct route to exit the desert, had also used it for my west to east solo walk.

We had made 27 km that first day out of Poeppel's and I noted that the country was as bad, if not worse, than that we'd encountered so far. The few odd little bushes that the camels could eat were descended upon by four hungry mouths, and demolished in short time. I guess that you could say it was a bush's worst nightmare to spot us coming.

My mobile satellite phone was working perfectly, so I called to advise that we were on schedule and would enter Birdsville as planned on 2 September. This coincided with the start of race fever in the remote town. The only problem I'd encountered with the phone was with the second battery, which had been damaged at the start. This had finally given up the ghost, which really restricted our ability to make non-urgent calls. The solar panel was charging okay, but not quickly enough to allow unlimited use. I did, however, make a quick call to Australian Geographic to show off my high-tech phone.

While still bulky and very heavy, what a change from the HF radio I have carried and used for so many years! No waiting, no verbal interference, no static, no repeating, just crystal-clear private communication. The only difference was a slight delay for the signal to return from the satellite. Riding along, it was as simple to use as a phone in your own home. This 'camel phone' was a definite winner and now no place in Australia need have second-rate communication. Optus had arrived.

The second day from Poeppel's was just as depressing as the first. We departed at 7 am – the earliest start we'd ever made – as I wished to make good mileage early in the day. It was now very hot, which further enhanced the desolate appearance of our surroundings. The camels managed one good feed from the mistletoe growing on a small stand of mulgas. They were in fruit and the glistening moisture-laden clusters of berries were devoured voraciously. I can vouch for their great taste.

In a cloudless sky, the ever-present eagles circled effortlessly above us. They were using us to hunt, as our movement disturbed an occasional rabbit foraging far from the safety of home. We could always hear the eagles coming by the incredible noise they made, as with wings folded, they arrowed out of the sky before flaring and with talons out-thrust, struck at their terrified prey.

Generally speaking, the sand dunes of the west Simpson are smallish and close together and are well clothed with spinifex, cane grass and bushes. Near the eastern side they increase in height, have less vegetation and the interdunal flats grow considerably, some up to one mile wide.

The following day we made another early start at 6.45 am, proceeding into ever-widening flats and high ridges from which we could see forever. How we enjoyed those early morning vistas and marvelled at the magnificence of this land. Many times we stopped, overawed by the vision of distance and the ever-changing movement of suspended ridges and domes, as they magically floated and distorted. Green rivers of gidgee cut the landscape, swirling like ribbons fluttering in a breeze.

Wild camel tracks were appearing now, and we spotted one large mob away to the south. There were occasional grassy patches, the remnants of isolated rain, but too dry to be of any use to us. The camels were in conservation mode due to the lack of water, and would not consume anything that did not contain moisture. The only feed available was an occasional wild plum.

We stopped for lunch and sheltered from the burning sun beneath some scrappy wattles. The animals were feeling it now, needing constant urging to get them one small step at a time over the high dunes. When it was time to go Grong Grong refused to budge, despite enthusiastic encouragement from both of us.

I backed Peter Pan in and, hooking up the lead rope, endeavoured to pull Grong Grong upright. All I did was stretch his neck. He wasn't going anywhere. I didn't want to annoy him too much — I was thinking about the poor old donkey and what he did to him when he got mad! I finally encouraged him to his feet by offering him some of the remaining water I was saving for an emergency. This he eagerly devoured and I decided to split up the remaining water between the other three. It was pitiful to see the agitation of the others as they waited for their turn to arrive. They were all very thirsty and wanted more.

Although we would have made it now, I wasn't prepared to let them suffer when help was so near. I made a phone call to David Brook at Birdsville, and was able to arrange a 44 gallon drum of water to reach Eyre Creek at 9 am the following morning. Although we could have travelled at night, I wasn't prepared to risk a broken leg down a rabbit hole. I had just about made it safely through with Noel's favourite camels and didn't want to blot my copy book at this late stage. We rested for a few more hours and then pushed on to reach the water drop on time.

Birdlife was increasing – magpies, crows, plovers, plains turkey and occasional small flights of finches – sure indicators that we were leaving the desert and close to water.

Late that afternoon we reached an old fence, just as Danny's father had done, but about 4.5 miles north of his position. Ted records, 'We came upon the remains of the old rabbit-proof fence, which was erected over fifty years ago by the Vermin Board in an attempt to repel the fast-invading army of rabbits then migrating northwards. From the skeletons of the rabbits that are visible today in the trap yards of the fence, I realised that the rabbits must have invaded this country in their millions.'

We soon climbed to the top of a ridge and there at our feet saw the first of the coolabahs: we had reached the floodout country of Eyre Creek. We made camp at 6.00 pm — it had been a long, hot day.

With the promise of water to motivate us, we were mobile at 5.45 am and then, swinging north-east, we reached the QAA line at 7.15 am, followed it to arrive at Eyre Creek by 8.45 am and then met the vehicle carrying our water at 9.30 am. What a surprise to see Joey, an Aboriginal acquaintance from long ago, who was now head stockman for David Brook. They were moving cattle out here and were checking on conditions. The 44 gallon drum of water disappeared like magic.

We had stopped for lunch just past the first station fence and less than fifty yards from the track, when two vehicles approached.

I said to Danny 'Looks like we are going to have company,' to which he replied, 'They probably won't see us, they're just tourists'. I watched their faces as they drove past. They hadn't noticed us, and I wondered what they would see for the rest of the journey.

Finally we crested a high dune, and there before us was the unforgettable face of an even higher dune, Big Red, as I had named it many years earlier. As we came over the top of it, I could see Nappanerica Stock Yard where we would rest for a day, but more importantly, through the gap in the sandhills, a well-filled dam. There would be another big drink for the camels and our first wash in nearly two weeks. It was now twenty days since we had departed Bloods Creek, and we had covered nearly 500 km.

Later that afternoon a film crew arrived, closely followed by the prime mover of a refrigerated truck up from Adelaide carrying a full load of hangovers for the Birdsville Pub.

Optus was celebrating the launch of their satellite phone and a promotion was being held that night over at Ayers Rock to mark the occasion. As part of their entertainment, they had organised a live TV hookup with several of the trial users of their phone system who were scattered around the country in remote areas. The beer truck had been fitted with a phone for his run up the Birdsville Track and had then been sent out to meet me for a joint live transmission. I heard later that Muffy and the camel phone were the star performers.

Around the campfire that night while we were chatting about the desert's original inhabitants, Danny paid me what I considered to be a great compliment.

'You know Denis, you've been across this desert dozens of times in all different directions, driving, walking, riding, seeking to unlock its mysteries and promoting its beauty. You absolutely love it out here and it is obviously so much a part of your soul that from now on I name you the Wangkangurru Man in honour of the people who once lived and roamed this region.'

The journey across the gibber-strewn plains to the outskirts of Birdsville was uneventful, slowed only by the constant photo shots of the numerous travellers heading out to see Big Red. It was hard to believe that a story I'd written about fourteen years ago about a place that was special to me had now become a must-see for all who visit this remote area.

It was the start of the famous Birdsville Race Meeting, so we arrived early in the morning to avoid the crowds, and hooshed our camels down in front of the Birdsville Hotel. This was journey's end and as I shook Danny's hand in front of the monument erected to commemorate Ted Colson's journey of 1936, I sincerely hoped that his dream had come true, that this close association with his father's journey would in some small way help compensate him for his loss, that of a father denied him.

There was no sign of Noel's truck, which was due to collect me, so I got out of town as fast as possible. This was the last place I wanted to be after the peace of the desert.

Danny departed after lunch to join his relatives, and suddenly I was alone again, forced to camp my final night watching the lights of the town, and listening to the racket created by the loud-mouthed sprulker drumming up business for his boxing troupe.

It was with relief I welcomed Noel the following afternoon, and as the doors of the truck slammed shut that evening, my venture terminated and along with it, my burden of responsibility to Noel and the magnificent animals that had carried us safely across a desolate terrain.

Chapter 16

Ghost of Sturt

As a private pilot myself I always feel disappointed when, after fluking a window seat on a commercial flight, all I see is cloud, especially when the flight path is over something special. However on this trip home to Noosa I was fortunate as the cloud band terminated at just the right moment and there it was some 30,000 feet below. A green belt sparkling intermittently as the sun mirrored light on the surface of its spine which twisted like some giant snake as it made its way towards the horizon – the Murrumbidgee.

As I gazed down, I couldn't help but think of the first white man to boat its waters. In 1830 Captain Charles Sturt and his seven companions had pushed off by whale boat down the Murrumbidgee River into the unknown. Their voyage down to the mouth of the Murray and back was a heroic epic of endurance that ranks with the greatest feats of early Australian exploration.

For years now I had wanted to re-enact this section of Sturt's voyage, but somehow other journeys had taken precedence. I had boated the Murray's northern tributaries: the flood waters of the Mole, Dumaresq, MacIntyre, Barwon, Darling and then the Murray itself for some 3450 km, and also the Murray from the Hume Weir for 2350 km. Both journeys ended where this huge river system disgorges its contents into the southern ocean. Now, inspired by the vision below, I made an instant decision to ride the Murrumbidgee, dependent on water conditions, naturally. Hopefully this was the year to conquer another leg of the mighty Murray River.

On my return home, a quick phone call to the Water Resources Board at Leeton NSW confirmed that there would be sufficient water in the system over the entire length for at least the next five to six weeks.

They did advise however that most locks would be closed, necessitating some portage and also that the river levels would fluctuate as irrigators along its length withdrew large volumes of water.

With Jeanne's blessing I dusted off my canoe, last used on the flooded Cooper Creek, added a simple outrigger, threw in a small 2 hp outboard with my paddles, prepared my maps, selected a menu, and was on my way. First stop was Gundagai, where I off-loaded my canoe and provisions, then Mildura, where I left my vehicle with friends for safekeeping. This beautiful river town would be journey's end. I didn't feel the need to continue further downstream as I had already boated that section several times before.

I took the overnight bus from Mildura to Gundagai, and after a long and tiring journey, arrived just on daybreak to begin my adventure. It was 15 July 1996, and light rain was falling as I slipped my canoe's green hull into a gravel-lined, rapidly flowing waterway just below the old bridge at Gundagai.

Stage One to Wagga Wagga, although not that difficult or dangerous, did require considerable care. Many canoes have been destroyed by losing directional control in tight, fast-flowing bends filled with dead trees or snags. The canoe can end up wedged in the timber, where it fills with water, and is then snapped by the tremendous pressure.

For this journey I had decided that I would make my canoe a bit more stable, as I intended to use my outboard motor to the full. The outrigger I'd made for one side of the canoe was 4-inch PVC pipe with aluminium cross-bars to attach it. I had tested and adjusted the unit in our swimming pool. While the outrigger had many advantages, I learned quickly that first day that it could easily create disaster, and very nearly did. There were lots of dead trees and limbs protruding from the swirling waters, with eddying currents ever ready to thwart my intended line of travel.

I couldn't alter course quickly enough and the forward beam connecting the outrigger to the canoe slid straight up an angled log leaving about half of my canoe out of water and the rear end starting to fill. I sprang to the front end as ever so slowly we pivoted, before slipping back into the drink to continue our mad race, now backwards and definitely out of control, around the rest of the bend. Without the outrigger I would have hit hard, bounced off and continued on my way with little loss of direction or control.

Shallow gravel beds abounded and played havoc with my propeller; small pebbles continually lodged in the water intake of my motor, causing overheating. I knew as the hills started to disappear in the vicinity of Wagga, so too would the gravel, so opted to paddle through the worst of it using the motor only for the good sections. I needed to protect the outboard and the speed that it would give for the long journey ahead, as I had limited time.

A friendly group of people, one of the few I sighted on the whole journey, shared their morning catch of Murray crayfish with me, and offered a welcome cup of coffee. Their crayfish were boiled in a huge pot of water liberally laced with rings of orange, and I voted this crustacean the best ever, vowing one day to return and catch my own. It was day two and still raining.

On day three I passed a mansion so grand that at first I couldn't believe my eyes. It was positioned prominently on a rise with a commanding view both up and down a delightful section of this waterway. I didn't pop in for a cuppa, however, as warning signs displayed in profusion along the fenced bank proclaimed dire consequences for any trespassing mortal!

I made a quick stop under the road bridge at Wagga to get a few forgotten supplies from a handy service station in the main street, then made camp in a hollow on a grassy bend on the outskirts of the town, far enough to be away from prying eyes. Not that anyone would be wandering around, as it was still raining intermittently.

In the morning I left Wagga behind, and as I moved out of the hilly country the gravel beds slowly disappeared and the segmented river that I'd been following opened to a more defined deep channel with sandy banks.

Berembed Weir was to be my first man-made obstruction on the river and I wasn't looking forward to the encounter, as I had heard that it was closed. Fortunately, however, a section of the lock was raised and I rocketed through on a one-way ticket. It was just as well, as the high bank would have made for a difficult and tedious portage.

Yanco Weir was a different kettle of fish. It was off to my right and I could see that it was closed to river traffic. Around a bend to my left, I could glimpse and clearly hear the water roaring over a concrete spillway wall. This was the obvious way to go but I wasn't game to approach too closely until I could size up the situation and weigh up the danger.

I pulled in to the left bank, tied up the canoe, then managed to struggle through a swamp to finally reach the southern corner of the spillway wall. If I could canoe around to this point, then I could remove my canoe from the water and drag it past the end of the weir structure, then keep dragging it another 200 metres downstream until I reached a cutting in the steep bank. This would allow me good access back down into the river.

I needed to hug the thick bushes lining the river's edge as they curved around to where I was now standing and use the calmer water they created in a small section just behind the wall. At the last moment, I would have to gun the motor to turn and push the canoe through the bushes and on to the bank. This manoeuvre would require split second timing. My rear end would only be metres away from the tumbling water and a motor failure at the wrong moment would see the whole kaboodle hurtling over the edge.

This really turned out to be the easy part, as it then took me several hours to slowly portage all my gear back to the river. Both knees, which had only recently been operated upon, suffered. I could hardly walk by the time I'd finished.

Golgeldrie Weir was open and I camped just downstream, high up on the bank. Across the river, a noisy two-stroke chainsaw motor shattered the silence, and later the owner's dogs made a racket well into the night. Even though I'd travelled through a fairly densely populated section of the river, nearly all camps had so far been well secluded and strangely quiet. How quickly I'd slipped back into bush mode and the peaceful solitude that it brings. This was camp number seven, about 320 km from Gundagai, in Jurambula, one of the numerous state forests that line this waterway. It was still raining.

A beautiful sandy beach jutted out from the inside corner of a wide bend and I quickly pulled over. It was time to camp and this looked a great site. I dragged my canoe out of the water and tied it to a large limb protruding vertically out of the sand for about three quarters of a metre. I was tempted to camp on the clean soft sand near the water's edge, and also save my aching knees the haul up the bank some distance away. However, ever wary, I ended up camping in the trees on the bank and dragged my canoe further up the beach so that I could tie it to one of the bushes nearby. Just as well, for morning light illuminated a vastly different scene. The huge sandy beach of the night before had completely disappeared, covered by still-rising water, and the limb that I had originally tied my canoe to had vanished. Obviously a flush of water had come through overnight. You can never be too careful.

At Darlington Point, I replenished my fuel supply for the long run to Hay and was pleasantly surprised when they gave me some shear pins for my propeller. Those had been forwarded by the supplier, who had been informed by Alan Cox of Hay that I was running short due to damage sustained by hitting submerged logs. When I reached him, Alan would have more pins waiting for me. Great people out this way.

Camp nine, which was up a steep bank, was reached after an exhausting day's run of about 70 km. I was now about 440 km from Gundagai. It had been raining solidly all day and was very cold. Sitting for long hours cramped in the rear corner of my canoe, wet, with numb legs and a cold wind forcing its way through my clothing, had taken its toll. My knees were so painful that it was only by digging steps in the bank with my paddle that I was able to haul the meagre gear I needed overnight up the slippery slope to the campsite. A few years earlier I would have bounded up there carrying everything I needed in one hit. Coming back down was worse.

I boated into Hay on the eleventh day, having covered about 570 km since Gundagai. It was still raining and I sheltered under the bridge while I called Alan Cox on my mobile.

He arranged to meet me on the river a few kilometres out of town and after much effort in the mud, we finally stowed my canoe and gear securely in his trailer, and headed to his home for a most welcome hot shower. I hadn't met Alan before, but had spoken to his daughter, who works at the *Australian Geographic* magazine office in Sydney. It was through her that Alan and his wife had taken on responsibility for my welfare whilst in their home town. I spent two days with them and was shown their extensive vegetable growing operation and large packing shed, which was in full swing weighing and boxing broccoli.

We did some urgent welding work on the engine bracket, topped up my food supplies, then took a quick run out by vehicle to inspect the Hay Weir about 20 km out of town — river distance that is! The weir gates were closed and the water thundered down the spillway, causing massive eddying at its base. I wasn't going to be able to portage around this one by myself.

A local TV crew wanted to do a story and film my departure. I agreed, provided that they then came down to the Hay Weir where I assured them that they would get some excellent footage. They were also going to get a good workout!

The Coxes organised a dinner party for my last night, and I spent an enjoyable, informative evening at their massive red gum dining table. Alan had located a huge fallen red gum on his riverfront property and had retrieved, sawn, and then stored the large slabs to fully dry over a period of several years. After shaping and polishing, the end result was truly spectacular. I understand that it took six men just to lift the top on to its base.

The rain had become intermittent during my stay, but as I departed Hay, the weather forecast predicted increased activity and some storms heading our way. In all Alan's years living in this remote area, he had never experienced such continuous rainfall as that which had beset their normally dusty township over the last few weeks.

I bade farewell to my most generous hosts, and later, with the help of the film crew, portaged my canoe up and over the Hay Weir.

I quickly slipped back into my daily river routine which, due to the almost continual rain since my departure, consisted of not much more than sitting huddled up, damp and shivering, in the rear of my canoe without moving for hours on end, getting out only for meal breaks and toilet stops. No wonder my knees were seizing up.

While this journey wasn't in any way a record-breaking attempt, I was ever mindful of the limited time I had allocated to complete my mission. Nonetheless, several times a day I would kill my outboard motor and get stuck into paddling. These were magical moments – with little effort on my part due to a strong current, I glided silently and swiftly down a twisting, ever-changing waterway where tall gums crowded the banks on both sides and housed a variety of birdlife. My maps told me that I was never at any time more than a few hours' walk away from help, but for the most part I felt totally isolated. Other than the occasional irrigation suction pipes which dangled over the river bank into the water, there was little to remind me of human activity.

Camp thirteen out of Gundagai was made in the rain. The ground was absolutely saturated and the near constant deluge made it almost impossible to find suitable firewood. This stretched my fire lighting capabilities to the limit. My camp would have been magnificent without the rain, situated as it was amongst some of the largest river red gums I'd seen so far.

I had help over the Maude Weir before proceeding into the most isolated section of the whole journey. For the most part, the river had been bounded on one or both sides by a network of roads which were never any great walking distance away. Now I was slowly heading away from the Sturt Highway and minor tracks were almost non-existent. The river level was low and I encountered more snags, necessitating constant vigilance. My supply of shear pins was starting to dwindle.

The surrounding countryside had changed distinctly and it was near here that Captain Charles Sturt, who had followed the river to this point by foot, had decided, due to the inhospitable nature of the swamp lands, that he would launch his boat. He thus commenced an epic voyage that would take him to Lake Alexandrina in South Australia and back again.

In Sturt's day, the tiny settlement of Sydney was hemmed in, and it was the general feeling in the colony that settlement beyond the coastal area was impossible. Many attempts had been made to penetrate the mountain barrier to the west — all had been beaten back.

In 1813 Blaxland, Lawson and Wentworth departed Blaxland's farm at South Creek heading westwards. With them were four convicts, five dogs and four horses. They became the first white men to see the breathtaking grandeur of the Jamieson Valley and follow the plateau rimming the Megalong and Kanimble Valleys. They reached the bare rock top of Mt York, and a few days later considered that they had conquered the mountain barrier. They had travelled for twenty-one days and covered about 93 km. They had not, in fact, crossed the main range, but they deserve their fame, as they had found the way through the obstacle created by the Blue Mountains.

George Evans was sent by Governor Lachlan Macquarie to check that the barrier had indeed been breached. He crossed the main range and went as far as the present-day town of Bathurst. In 1814 William Cox began building the first road across the mountains and the scene was then set both for the rapid expansion of the colony westward, and for inland exploration.

In 1817 John Oxley explored the western plains and followed the course of the Lachlan River until further progress was prevented by marshes. He also followed the Macquarie River, only to be stopped again by marshes and swamps. He was convinced that the eastern part of Australia was separated from the western half by a sea. He concluded that New South Wales was a long island and that its western half ran into vast swamps.

History could not forget Hamilton Hume and William Hovell, whose journey in 1824 ranks with the most important. Departing Hume's property at Lake George, near where Canberra now stands, they travelled southwards, crossed the Murrumbidge River, then continued along the western side of the Great Dividing Range. Finally they reached Port Phillip Bay, where Geelong is now situated, then returned home. They had travelled more than 1900 km and discovered millions of acres of fertile land on their way to Port Phillip Bay.

Captain Charles Sturt followed the Macquarie River and proved that there was no inland sea just beyond and he also named the Darling River. He did believe, however, that somewhere in the vast interior lay an inland sea. In 1829 at the age of 34 Sturt set out to follow the Murrumbidgee River. He ultimately reached the marshes near the Murrumbidgee's junction with the Lachlan River, and with some difficulty, managed to find the main channel of the Murrumbidgee. Here he assembled a boat, carried on the off-chance that he would locate that elusive inland sea, and with seven companions set off into the unknown. The swift current gave a reckless ride in parts as they rushed through rocks and down treacherous rapids, and in about five days, they entered the Murray River, which they named after the Secretary of State for the Colonies.

Where the river narrowed and a sand bar partially blocked the way, a large party of Aborigines gathered and it seemed inevitable that a massacre was about to take place. Rifles were readied but a lone Aboriginal sprang from the opposite bank and, swimming to the war party, managed to calm them down. They passed the entrance of a fresh water river and Sturt wondered if it was the Darling, which he had named some 900 km to the north. It was.

Sturt's party reached and named Lake Alexandrina, and on 13 February 1830, they started back on what can only be described as a horrific journey, finally reaching Sydney on 25 May. So ended an epic of such magnitude that it will forever occupy a place in the history books of this country.

The bends in this waterway become very apparent when isolated homesteads pop up and you can peer into the front door as you pass. Sometimes, up to 2 or 3 km away, you come around another bend and there is the same homestead – only this time you are looking at the rear door.

Camp fourteen was a few kilometres upstream of Willowgrove homestead. My mobile phone, which had worked for most of the journey, was now out of range, so I missed my usual two-minute nightly call to Jeanne back in Noosa. Even though I was now about 28 km away from the Sturt Highway, with the flat terrain and a slight wind I could still faintly hear the roar of the big semis as they charged through the night to their destinations.

About 35 km further on a seemingly insignificant river entered on my right-hand side, just prior to my taking a hairpin left-hand bend. This was the Lachlan River: with its headwaters up near Cowra, it was probably as long as the Murrumbidgee to this point. I made a mental note that I would also like to boat it one day.

The water level was higher now, no doubt backed up by the Redbank Weir, which was obviously closed. Occasionally the river spilled over its banks to run into swamp or irrigation land on either side — interesting for me as it gave a nice change to being below the level of the surrounding country, as I was for much of the way.

I camped just below Redbank Weir which, as I had suspected, was brim full. I'd managed to portage with the help of two elderly residents, but we had to trailer the canoe about a kilometre downstream to allow me access again as the banks were so steep.

I had about 80 km to go to Balranald and I think that this was one the most isolated sections of the whole journey. Being flood land on either side, the few station homesteads in this area were well back from the river, and out of sight. The water level was low, the banks steep and high, and with the width of the river remaining almost constant, it was like travelling down some man-made gutter. My notes say: 'No rain! — saw some swans, no human beings — beautiful gums all the way — defined river — lots of snags!' And snags there were, particularly as I got closer to Balranald. In parts, huge gum trees had fallen completely across the river blocking the way.

Flowing water indicates the presence of underwater obstructions by turbulence, but here the river was very sluggish and it was really a matter of luck whether I hit anything. Every so often I had to replace a shear pin.

I made camp sixteen at Balranald Caravan Park and the nearby service station owner drove me a few miles out of town to have a preview of the last man-made obstruction across my waterway.

The gates of the Balranald Weir were in place, blocking my path, however, the water level on the upstream side was within a metre of the top, and with only a few metres to drag my canoe and gear to a re-entry point on the other side, this was one that I could handle easily.

At camp seventeen the river was most sluggish. There had been lots of snags for the day, although they seemed to be easing, and I had another rain-free period. Things were looking up, though this was to be my last night on a magnificently forested waterway.

My journey had been peaceful and undisturbed by other river users, until negotiating a tight bend I was suddenly confronted by a revving outboard and a flat-bottomed tinny going like a cut cat! I think he got as big a shock as I did. He turned out to be a licensed fisherman who was checking a few nets that he had in the vicinity. We drifted and chatted for a while and I learned that he had been in the business a long time and wouldn't trade places with anyone else. He absolutely loved his occupation but now felt that it was under threat as other people with a larger collective voice considered their rights had priority over the fish stock that he was endeavouring to manage on his licensed reach of the river. He had to be rather cunning in disguising the location of his nets, as if found, they would be cut and destroyed. This is not a conflict that will be easily resolved, as throughout Australia huge numbers of anglers and professionals fight for a share of a dwindling resource.

When I asked if he was catching much, he reached almost lovingly into his fish tank and produced a large specimen that lay placidly in the palm of his hand. He didn't go goofy with hugs and kisses like some people on TV, but when he described its intended destination, I could understand his care. The fish he caught were taken home and put into a large tank, and every Wednesday they were despatched live to an agent in Sydney, who freighted them to Japan for consumption that weekend. We said our goodbyes and I headed off to conquer the last few bends of a river that I had now canoed for some 900 km.

I couldn't believe my eyes when suddenly the junction appeared before me. How pitiful the Lachlan had seemed as it had entered my wide domain. Now my river was being dwarfed by the mighty Murray, and I couldn't help but wonder how Captain Charles Sturt felt as he too burst into this grand waterway nearly 160 years before me.

It was a broad river now, encompassed on either side by state forests with numerous picturesque campsites and no steep banks to struggle up. There was also a good flow of water, which helped increase my speed, and I soon arrived in the huge fruit growing areas of Robinvale and Euston. The rain now set in again.

At the Robinvale lock the gates stood ready to be operated at set times throughout the day for oncoming traffic from either direction. Boats signaled their intention to the lock master by several blasts from their air horn. However, the lock master had already been advised of my coming by the locals further upstream and he was waiting for me. It seemed such a lot of water to let go just to lower my minuscule craft to the downstream level, but I was most grateful for the assistance. I was invited to the office for a cup of coffee and to dry out, which was also truly welcome, although the feeling of comfort didn't last too long.

As I waved farewell, the rain absolutely bucketed down and soon a fierce wind ripped down the long straight sections and I was buffeted by white-topped waves that threatened to swamp me. Cold and miserable, I didn't last too long – about 10 km from the weir, I pulled over to the right and made camp where the water had cut through a narrow neck of land, cutting off a big bend and about 2 km of river travel. The wind finally died and the rain eased to occasional light showers. I needed to dry out and get warm in a hurry. With only soggy wood available, I sacrificed my considerable fire lighting talents just this once for a liberal dose of petrol — way to go!

It rained all the following day and when I finally headed for camp just upstream from Colignan I felt like a miserable water rat. The ground was absolutely saturated and squelchy underfoot. I gathered large quantities of bark and made myself a platform to lay my swag on out of the mud. Town and traffic noises reminded me that journey's end was near at hand.

The rain did finally clear up overnight and the following day was rather pleasant. This was day 21 out of Gundagai and by my reckoning it had rained for about 17 of these. On the right hand side I passed a group of prominent residences that have been nicknamed 'Millionaires Row' by the locals, and just on dusk pulled my canoe out of the water on the Mildura Ski Club lawns. This was journey's end. In 21 days I had travelled some 1300 km, about 800 miles in the old language, from my departure point, Gundagai.

The ghost of Captain Charles Sturt would now continue on his way alone and I would return to Jeanne and our home in sunny Queensland — I hoped that sunny was the operative word!

I had enjoyed my journey immensely, despite the cold and rain — and had fulfilled another dream. While I had conquered another leg of the massive waterways that make up the Murray Darling system, and ridden the silver serpent that I had gazed down upon as I travelled the skies' highways, I didn't want to feel wet or cold again for a long, long time.

Departing Gundagai for Mildura 1300kms away.

Numerous sandy beaches make pleasant camp sites.

Murray River crayfish.

Portage around the Yanco Weir.

Paddle steamer near Mildura.

His catch will be in Tokyo *live* in 5. days.

Majestic red cliffs of the Murray River.

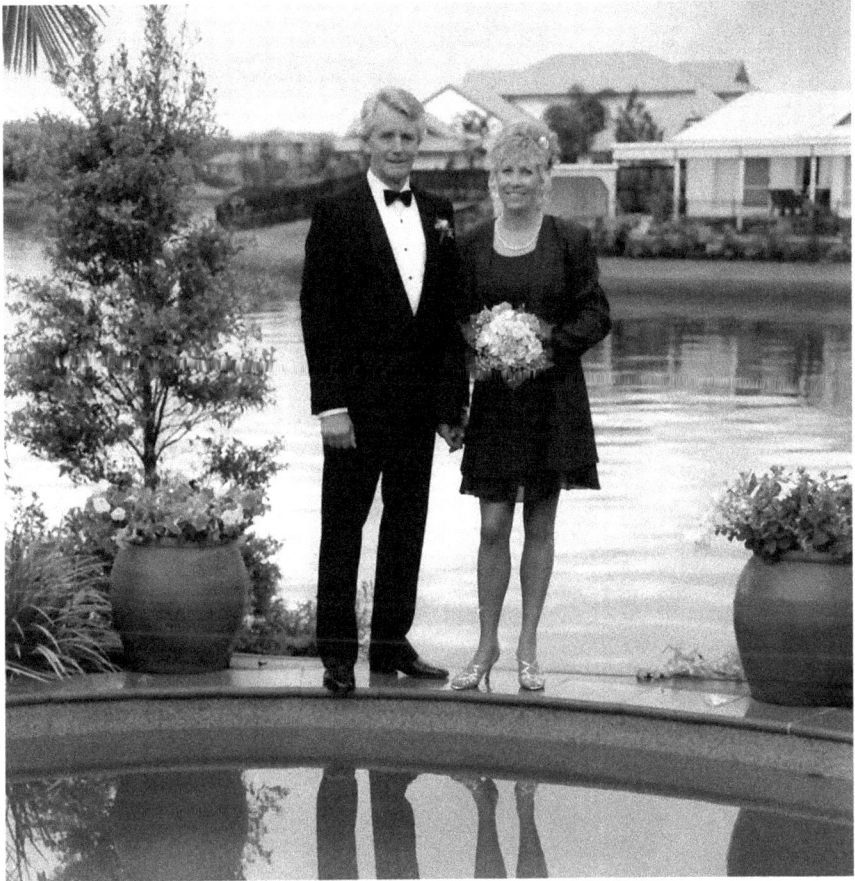

Our wedding day at our home in Noosa.

Our family: Left to Right: Richard, Damien, Susan and David.

With Jeanne in Noosa.

In uniform and on the job
Coral Sands Resort Trinity Beach

Receiving The Order of Australia at Government House Adelaide in 1989.

Dick Smith presenting me with the Australian Geographic
Society's Adventurer of the Year Gold Medallion 1994.

Arriving at Dalhousie Springs: Left to Right: Carolyn, Margot, Susan, Catherine, Debbie and the Alice Springs Aero Club pilot Ingrid.

Left: Dalhousie Ruins.

Below: On the track.

Left: Departing from the first sand hill on the western edge of the Simpson Desert.

Cold early morning starts.

With a hand auger, we drill and strike water at 12ft. Susan lowers a bailer on a string to bring it to the surface.

Climbing Big Red.

The Desert Mums on Big Red.

Inflating balloons at the base of Big Red. All were hand tied—no string or plastic and 100% bio-degradable latex.

Ready for release.

Set free: Representing the average number of lives lost to breast cancer each year in Australia (including 80 blue for the men), we release 2500 balloons from the top of Big Red.

Entering the township of Birdsville.

Susan with her dad at Big Red.

Birdsville Pub: Raising over $120,000 for breast cancer research, four jubilant Desert Mums celebrate the completion of their mission.

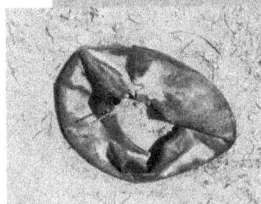

Ron and I finally locate the ashes of my camp fire last used over 9 years ago while on my north to south walk across Australia.

Insert: Air drop tube.

Richard still has a long way to go on his west to east walk across the desert.

The desert in bloom.

Richard taking a welcome break.

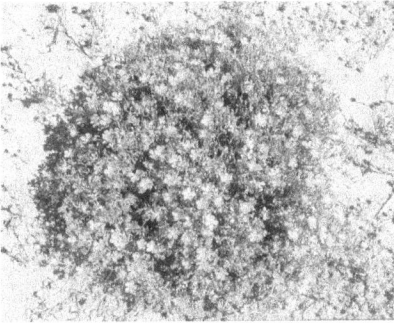

Desert flowers.

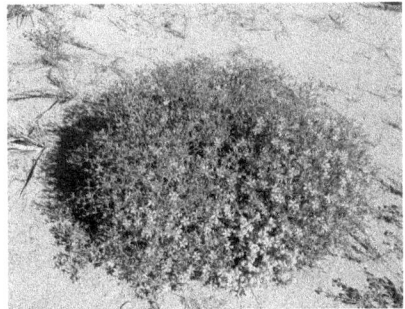

The desert in bloom.

A unique way to cross the desert.

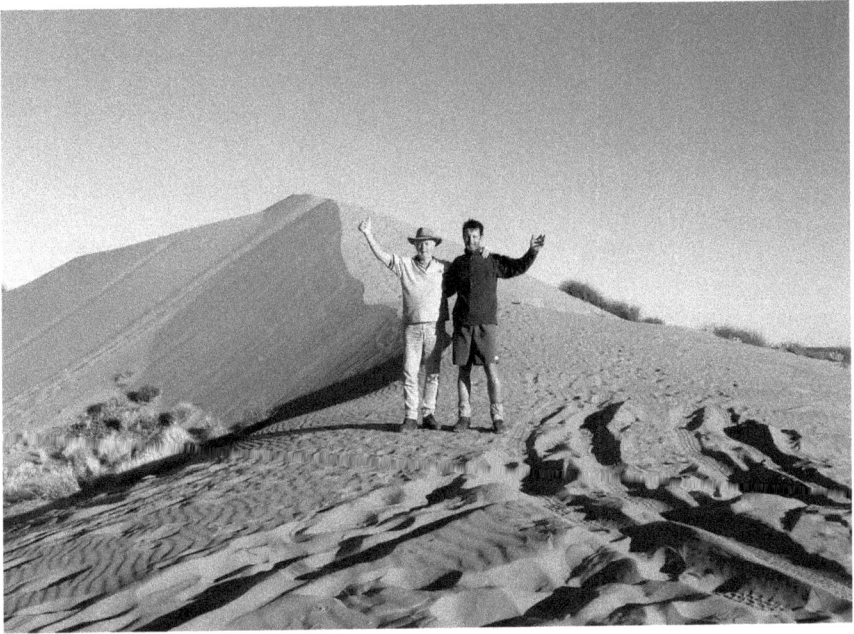

Father and son on Big Red.

Tractor convoy crossing Little Red. Lake
Nappanerica on the right is full to the brim.

Little Red: I had to detour 12kms—Richard just swam across.

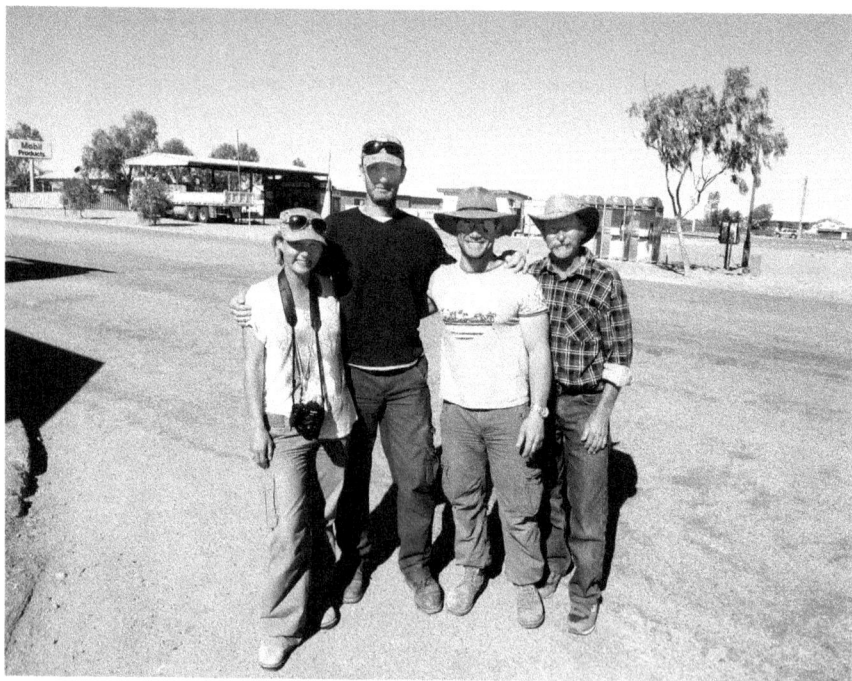

Desert travellers welcome Richard into Birdsville at the end of his walk.

Chapter 17

Retirement

Meanwhile, we'd built Noosa Destinations into a successful property management business, then sold and settled into retirement. After having lived in harmony for about seven years we decided to make our union official and – lucky me – I got to marry a truly wonderful person who looked every bit the princess on our magic day. Jeanne was a beautiful bride and I'll never forget the moment when she looked up at me with misty eyes and stated quite clearly 'to love honour and obey'. I certainly remember the 'obey' bit, which Jeanne continues to this day to dispute and disregard.

We bought a caravan, rented our home out and then took off to join the grey nomads travelling around Australia doing, as they say, 'the big one'. I enjoyed most of it, Jeanne loved some of it, but at the end of the year we were glad to get back home with our marriage still intact. Although living in paradise at Noosa, we soon became restless, realising we were still young and needed further challenges. Jeanne also reminded me that I was only 65 and she could get a few more years' work out of me yet!

I had always wanted to live where the mountains meet the sea and a lucky glance at a magazine led us to just such a place. We sold everything and moved to Trinity Beach on the outskirts of Cairns in far north Queensland in 1998. Here we purchased the management rights to Coral Sands Resort, a magnificent beachfront property of sixty luxury holiday apartments. We once again lived in paradise and the coral reefs, mountains and rainforests absolutely lived up to their world class status.

Cyclone Steve whirled through in February 2000, knocking the hell out of the area, particularly the local pub. The wind roared, and before the street lights went out I could see debris flying everywhere. The noise was unforgettable and more frightening than anything I had ever experienced. It battered everything in its path before dying to a deathly quiet, as the eye of the storm passed overhead. With the electricity gone, it was so black outside you could not see your hand in front of your face. We took this window of opportunity to check on our guests and the building; our torchlight showed the grounds to be littered with small debris.

A few of the in-house guests appeared on their balconies, alerted by the waving light of our torches, and assured us they were all okay. In fact, one group was partying by candlelight. Obviously the wine had taken their minds off the gravity of the situation. The floor of their apartment was awash with about half an inch of water, but they didn't seem to mind. In the harsh light of the following morning, though, they blamed us for the cyclone and for ruining their holiday. Conversely, we had a lovely family from the UK who saw the whole thing as an exciting adventure that added to their Australian experience – to the point where both young children spent hours helping us clean our huge lagoon pool of debris. These lovely people actually left a $100 tip for our staff. Every building manager has a million stories to tell … but that is another book!

The streets around our property were covered with fallen trees and branches, making them impassable to vehicles. Across the road, the corner shops looked like a bomb had hit them. Occasionally a subdued voice would break the eerie quietness.

The silence didn't last for long. The cyclone came back as a puff that barely rustled the leaves, but as we sprinted back to the shelter of our apartment, we could hear the roar approaching as the wind now blasted in from the opposite direction. The cleanup was horrendous. Our swimming pool looked like a big bowl of vegetable consommé and the outside walls and ceilings of every balcony were splattered with vegetation. Overall it was an incredible experience and gave us both an appreciation of what the people of Darwin went through when Cyclone Tracy came to their town for Christmas.

Unfortunately, physically I was on borrowed time; slowly my knee joints, which had already been operated on twice previously, had deteriorated so much that I wobbled from side to side like a drunken sailor when I walked. When each 100 metres dictates a rest stop, things are not looking good, particularly as work required continual journeys up and down the nine three-storey stairwells of the complex. When my knees first gave out during my Flying Doctor fund-raising walk across Australia, I knew that ultimately there would be price to pay if I continued. However, it was non-negotiable for me then; I would finish what I had started no matter what. Fifteen years later it was time for major surgery.

I flew to Adelaide in 2001, where the orthopedic surgeon rammed home my shiny new titanium joints. While I cannot say that having a full replacement done on both knees in the same day is a lot of fun, it wasn't all that bad. I'm glad that I didn't do them one at a time, as a lot of people I know have done: they all dreaded going back for seconds.

As the years rolled by, the outback and adventures became a distant memory relived only in my dreams. Our lives were totally committed to our business, which is how it should be if you wish to succeed at anything in life. However, working 24/7 does ultimately take its toll, both mentally and physically, especially when dealing with the increasing demands of the travelling public. It was especially draining for me as I am not really people orientated.

I'll never forget the day. I was standing at the seaside entrance to our complex. Across the road was a magnificent sandy beach and I couldn't resist the uncontrollable urge to take time out to go and just sit on it for a few minutes. As I casually mentioned to Jeanne later, that had been my fifth time in six years. So at 72 years of age, now well and truly grey — although Teresa, my hairdresser, said I had natural highlights that some men would kill for — Jeanne finally relented and decided I should be turned out to pasture. Just so that I wouldn't be lonely, she would retire as well.

We built our waterfront dream home on the canals at Bribie Island in Queensland about one hour's drive north from Brisbane, sold our business and settled in to enjoy our retirement. I assured Jeanne that as I was now a little worn-out old geriatric man, any thoughts of desert and adventure were well and truly in the past. A rocking chair, a good book and the telly was for me. I lied, and she knew it!

Chapter 18

The Desert Mums

Two were okay, and barring accident, would complete their mission. The remaining two were in real trouble, each suffering incredible pain as hour after hour they staggered on. They carried their burden without complaint, but distress was clearly evident in their faces and gait. To give in now would bring bitter disappointment to haunt them for the rest of their lives. Failure plodded along just one step behind like a vulture waiting for the moment when one step more is a step too far.

The tears that flowed that day out on the white salt crust were, however, not for their anguish, but for others. Word had just been received by satellite phone that another of their friends had lost her battle to live. They cried for them all: mothers, wives, sisters, daughters; black, white or brindle. They were walking for them, their personal pain insignificant when they thought about the greater pain and fear faced by others fighting for their very survival. In honour of all women worldwide who had lost their lives, The Desert Mums dubbed the area upon which their tears fell, Lake Courage.

🦎 🦎 🦎

'Dad, do you remember when we were teenagers and you gave my brother a car and you gave me, your only daughter,' (heavy emphasis on only daughter) 'a lovely pink hairdryer instead?'

Susan's voice on the other end of the phone line purred like a well-tuned BMW, however, years of experience had taught me that when my daughter starts a conversation this way, it's with the express purpose of achieving victory without lengthy negotiation. Before I could think of a suitable reply, she struck with the speed of a King Brown snake.

'I've still got it packed away somewhere as a treasured memento, you know, something special to remember you by!'

Now I knew for certain that this conversation was going to cost me big time. Cool was the way to go. 'And how is my beautiful daughter this morning?' I enquired.

'I'm fine Dad. I just wanted to ask you something. Have you got a moment?'

I felt like a rat in a trap, but what could I say. 'For you, Angel, I have all the time in the world.'

Over the next five minutes I was to learn a lot about breast cancer, pink ribbons, self-awareness programs and medical research. I must admit I was a bit staggered to learn that worldwide about 375,000 women die yearly from this dreaded disease. In Australia some 85 men and 11,000 women will be diagnosed with breast cancer, and of that number we will lose about 2500 a year. All are going to go through hell. I certainly hadn't realised that men could also have this problem and should be on the lookout for symptoms. I also couldn't make out where this conversation was taking us, so while still on guard I was starting to feel that I may have misjudged my daughter's intentions. I had ascertained early on that she didn't have breast cancer, so we just appeared to be having an informative chat.

'Dad, do you remember when you were preparing to do your solo unaided walk across the Simpson Desert from west to east and I asked if I could come along, but you fobbed me off by saying that the desert was no place for a young lady.' Susan paused to let this sink in and my defence mechanism went into overdrive. 'Well, I'm forty-two now and I want to challenge myself mentally and physically just like you have done all your life. I want to walk the Simpson Desert for me, and I want to walk it with two other friends. So what do you think about that?'

Now while it may have been a question, Susan wasn't waiting around for a reply and I instinctively knew that crunch time was near. 'I want you to be our guide and drive the back-up vehicle. I want to walk in your footsteps and I don't want your reply now. Just take all the time you want Dad. Think about it and give me a call back in a few weeks.'

I was, metaphorically speaking, just picking myself up off the floor when she really made sure of my acceptance. 'Oh, and by the way Dad, if you don't want to, or if you feel too old, that's okay. I'll just ask that young adventurer, you know, Hans Tholstrup. I am sure he would.'

'Bloody hell Susan,' I shot back, 'There's no way I am going to allow him to take my daughter across the Simpson Desert. In your dreams sweetheart! In any case, it is now thirty years since my Suzuki battled it out with Hans Tholstrup's Daihatsu through the centre of Australia, so there's no way he could still be young. He's more likely grey, carrying a bit too much weight, perhaps even flabby, retired with six kids and a demanding wife who won't let him out of her sight.' Without overdoing it, I thought I'd painted a rather bleak picture of Hans as an alternative however I wasn't going to take any chances. 'Well Susan, you win. When do we go? And by the way, Angel, I'd retire that pink hair dryer if I were you. It's reached its use-by date.'

Once Susan had made up her mind that she wanted to challenge herself by walking the Simpson Desert, there was no stopping her. A quick phone call to two former school mates, Carolyn and Margot, left them with little alternative. 'You're doing this with me.'

Not long after, Debbie heard about it and said 'Count me in. I'm coming too.'

That's how the Desert Mums came about. Four city women with children deciding to remove themselves from loved ones, familiar surroundings, their comfort zones and their security — it was about facing tough times, discomfort and challenging their fears in a place far removed from any previous experience. It was about mateship and the growth of the human spirit.

The Simpson Desert, the largest parallel sand dune desert in the world, was about to become their teacher. While I didn't know how, of one thing I was certain: they were all going to undergo a life-changing experience.

Like most families in Australia, the Mums had all been touched by knowing someone who had had breast cancer. By the time Susan called me, the Desert Mums had realised that their walk could be made even more meaningful for them if they could link it to a worthy cause. The National Breast Cancer Foundation was the obvious choice and they were soon on board, fully endorsing the Mums' walk.

For every $35,000 the Desert Mums could raise, a one-year research scholarship could be set up. The National Breast Cancer Foundation (NBCF) would select the recipient of this scholarship through a peer review process involving researchers across Australia. The Mums reset their personal goals to include a three-year scholarship of $105,000, awareness-raising about breast cancer and research, and promotion of the importance of breast self-examinations and regular mammograms.

The venture was planned to start on 5 May 2006 from the first sandhill on the western edge of the Simpson Desert. Heading east, they would then cross some 1200 sand dunes, finally to end their journey in that most famous of all outback towns, Birdsville. Their start date was almost 22 years to the day since I had commenced my solo walk and they wanted to follow closely the route that I had taken.

I was rather excited at the prospect of returning to a landscape I love so much. For someone who has, at a rough guess, crossed the Simpson Desert well in excess of 70 times over the last 30-plus years, it had been an unbearably long time since my last visit. When Danny Colson and I rode our camels out of the desert and into Birdsville in 1994, I wouldn't have believed it if someone had said, 'Denis, you won't be back for over twelve years!'

Just to make things difficult, it wasn't long after our discussion that Susan, Ian and our granddaughter Milli moved from their home in Mt Beauty, Australia, to Canada, where Ian took up the position of CEO of the Silver Star Mountain Ski Resort, near Kelowna. Thanks to the internet and Skype we were enabled to make unlimited free video calls to organise our venture. We couldn't have managed without it.

By the time we had started serious planning I had accumulated a party of seven: four Desert Mums, Susan, Carolyn, Margot and Debbie, who would do the walking; Katherine, a videographer and Susan's new-found friend from Canada, who would film the journey; and Carolyn's husband Andrew, who would drive the second back-up vehicle. Working on a maximum of 21 days for the crossing, seven people equalled a lot of food, camping, survival and personal gear and especially water. It was evident that my two-vehicle convoy would have difficulty carrying the load.

For my walk, I had just subsisted – perhaps I should say, just managed to stay alive – on about 3.25 litres of water per day. If I now allowed a more realistic 5 litres per day, this would equate to about 36 jerry cans of water to be carried. I obviously needed to tow a trailer or create several dumps along the way. As I have never been a fan of trailers in the desert, I finally chose the latter option.

The Desert Mums were to set up a website, liaise with the National Breast Cancer Foundation, organise the media coverage, chase up sponsor and product support and push the fund raising. They were going to need a mighty effort if they were to achieve their goal of $105,000.

I was in charge of all the logistics that needed to come smoothly together to generate a safe and successful desert crossing and the fulfilment of their dreams. They were in for a real treat, as I was also going to choose the food and cook the meals, which they would probably think very boring – every third night would be a repeat of the same. And they thought that walking the desert was going to be the hard bit! I'm a terrible cook!

With design help from Balloon Magic of Tasmania I manufactured two very large nets to contain 2500 pink plus 80 blue balloons (for the boys). Made from fully biodegradable latex, the balloons would be inflated, hand tied so there would be no string or plastic, then set free from the top of Big Red. This release would honour all the Australians who lose their lives to breast cancer each year.

Finally, after months of planning, I left Brisbane towing a trailer full of helium gas cylinders, empty water containers and food, and headed for Birdsville. I couldn't go via the direct route, as the Cooper was in flood again, and had cut the road at Windorah. Instead I drove down through Innamincka and on to reach the Birdsville Track via Walkers Crossing.

The proprietors of the Birdsville Caravan Park looked after my trailer while I made two dashes into the desert to create water dumps. Taking 12 five gallon (22 litre) plastic jerry cans at a time, I buried one lot on the WAA Line, one of the desert's major tracks, and the other near Poeppel Corner. I found the desert to be drier than at any other time I could remember, even worse than when I crossed by camel, and that had been bad enough. People who first cross it under dry conditions such as these need to revisit so they can also experience its amazing transformation to a garden land after a good rain. It's all there, buried, just waiting for the deluge when it bursts forth to continue its never-ending cycle of life and death.

Andrew joined me at Birdsville and we loaded the two vehicles from the trailer with our food requirements for the crossing. By way of variety, I headed for Dalhouse Springs via Marree and the Oodnadatta Track. Andrew hadn't been into the Simpson Desert before so I wanted to keep it as a surprise that he could experience with the Mums. We were heading up the track north of Oodnadatta, crossing the odd sand dune, when Andrew asked me if the track across the Simpson would be similar to this. I said, 'Yeah, just like this mate, with perhaps a little bit more sand'. Boy was he going to be in for a surprise!

We made our base in the camping grounds at Dalhousie Springs with its elaborate toilet and shower block, designated fenced-off little parking lots, rules, regulations and a decent hike to the pool for a swim. I shouldn't complain, I know – restrictions are necessary if this fragile area is to survive the ever-increasing numbers of tourists. I have seen it deteriorate over the years and the regrowth that is now occurring due to control measures is commendable. If you haven't been there before, you'll probably love it just the way it is, but don't forget to pack the Aeroguard; I can't help remembering the way it was — deserted.

Andrew manned the fort while I made a 50 km dash down to where the walk would begin to deposit food and water. I now needed all the seating space I could muster to transport the Mums, who were due to arrive after lunch. From Canada, New South Wales and Victoria they had all co-ordinated their flights to meet en masse in Adelaide for the final stage of their journey to Alice Springs.

The Alice Springs Aero Club confirmed that the Mums had been collected from the main terminal and were now boarding its six-seat Saratoga for their flight to Dalhousie. It was a warm day, so if the pilot came in low as I had suggested, to allow a good view of the countryside and ample photo opportunities, then they were in for a bumpy ride.

Finally the big moment arrived; I've never seen so many green-faced people exit an aircraft so quickly, all offering silent thanks to the gods that they were finally safely back on terra firma. They wasted no time, however, in stripping off and heading for the hot springs. It is marvelous what a few hours' soaking and swimming can do to rejuvenate tired bodies and minds.

The excitement around the campfire that night was clearly evident. After months of planning, the Mums were now only one day away from beginning a journey, a dream conceived so long ago. Their adventure of a lifetime was about to begin.

Pre-dawn starts would be the order of the day for the actual crossing, and I wasn't about to ease them into it gently. When my call went out the following morning, there was a fair bit of moaning and groaning. While Andrew and I broke camp and loaded the vehicles the girls set out to walk towards the Dalhousie ruins. I know it's not towards Birdsville, but I had decided that rather than sit around and twiddle their thumbs, they could do a few warm-up kilometres. By the time we finally got to them, they had about 7 km on the clock and were going well. Just to prove I'm not a slave driver, we bundled them all into the vehicles for the short run into the ruins. I just love that place and its history. The date palms are not native, but to remove them, as has been suggested, would seem to me to be destroying an attractive and visual link to its fascinating past. I had to drag the girls away but we had a rather tight schedule to adhere to.

We were fortunate that the track down through the middle of the Spring Creek delta had been reopened after recent rain, as it allowed fast travel compared to the alternative. There were patches of high country to the north and south, but ahead a featureless, flattish horizon loomed ever closer until finally we reached the first sandhill of the Simpson Desert. After a quick bite of lunch, the girls donned their pink cowboy hats and, amid wild cheering from their support crew, the Desert Mums were on their way at last. It was 5 May 2006 and their next stop was Purni Bore, 18 km away. Once we had repacked our vehicles from my nearby cache, we only just had enough room for Katherine and her camera equipment in the Land Cruiser. Andrew's Pajero was absolutely full to the brim.

We set up camp at Purni Bore, which had been drilled in 1963 as part of an oil exploration program. While unsuccessful in finding oil, the bore gushed hot water (80° C) at the rate of 2.5 million litres per day. It was abandoned uncapped and left to flow freely, creating an artificial oasis in the desert. In 1987, as part of a tri-state agreement to cap wild flowing bores in the outback, the SA Government decided to terminate its flow. This was met with such vigorous opposition by so many diverse groups that finally they relented and agreed to allow it to continue, but at a reduced flow rate.

Purni is the last permanent surface water supply until Birdsville. Instead of the reed-encircled pool we used to soak in long ago, there was now a shower and toilet block, which was put to good use by the Mums when they finally arrived. There was every possibility that this would be their last wash for eighteen days, and they made the most of it. At best they could expect a small wash using up whatever water remained, if any, when we reached each of the two dumps that I had deposited.

While the Mums sat around the fire that night excitedly reliving their adventure and the incredible scenery encountered so far, I allowed my mind to drift back in time. It had been pitch black when I finally pulled my cart over that last sandhill and arrived at this bore. Although it was

22 years ago, I could relive that moment as if it was yesterday. For the Mums, as for me, it all started out as a dream. Now theirs was about to become a reality.

It was inevitable that over the coming days I would continue to relive my own journey. But more important to me was how proud and privileged I felt that through my daughter, a ghost from the past would be able to walk the desert in her boots step by step one last time.

I had planned on a 31 km per day walking average and they would have to religiously adhere to this. They had all trained hard, broken in their boots, and were very fit. Barring some sort of physical damage or accident, they were more than up to the task ahead. Several rest days were allocated at Big Red to prepare for the balloon launch, then we were due to arrive in Birdsville at 10 am on 22 May for a series of connecting flights back to the big smoke.

The rules were set early on. Anyone unable to continue, even if just for a day, was out of the challenge permanently. While I was hopeful that all would finish, I was also determined that after so much time had been given to this venture, nothing was going to stand in the way of success. I needed to get at least one Mum over the line to fulfil promises made to sponsors and the Breast Cancer Foundation, and if the dreams of others were sacrificed to achieve this end, then so be it.

We soon settled into a routine that would have us all camping together at night and meeting during the day only at their morning and afternoon snack breaks and for lunch. Other than that, I wanted to keep the vehicles out of sight as much as possible, as I knew it would lift their awareness of this remote wilderness landscape to another level, something unachievable other than by walking in quiet solitude through it. I wanted them not only to conquer a desert, but to retain a memory far deeper than that of a mere physical challenge. Safety wasn't compromised, however, as they carried a satellite phone enabling immediate contact with me if needed.

Day 2 was again along a firm track and we achieved 28 km, which was acceptable. Debbie acquired a very bad blister, which surprised me; I thought she would be the last one to have problems. The following day they had a sneak preview of the French Track before turning south for Mokari Airstrip and then continuing east along the clay-capped Rig Road.

The days continued to be hot and still. Flies were in plague proportions, driving them mad, and by the time we made camp after 31 km, they were all done in. Everyone now had large blisters, and I think for the first time they were starting to realise just what they had taken on.

Departing the Rig Road, we continued our easterly direction along the WAA Line. This is just a two-wheel sandy track, and of all the tracks in the desert, I have probably enjoyed it the most over the years. Once hardly ever used, which I guess was its main attraction to me, it has lately become popular as an alternative to the much shorter French Track. The reason we were using this longer route was simply because it's the way I had walked the Simpson and my daughter's desire was to follow in her father's footsteps.

While pre-dawn starts had become more tedious with the temperature dropping to around 3º C, the cold snap was at least bringing some early morning relief from the flies. Susan's blisters didn't seem to worry her, however her knee was very painful, particularly while descending the dunes, and needed to be strapped. Although Carolyn's blisters were massive, she still managed to put one foot in front of the other. Margot, on the other hand, had twisted her back and was in a lot of pain. She had bent to pick up something heavy and in doing so, drastically rearranged her spine. Debbie was on top of things with well-plastered feet and going great. Barring accident, I was confident she would make it.

Despite the soft sand, at the end of day 6 they had picked up the few kilometers lost and were on target. This was where I had buried my first water drop and the likelihood of a special treat had probably encouraged the extra effort. There was enough water remaining in the vehicles to enable us all to have a quick bush shower and, although cold, it certainly put a smile on the Mum's faces. While I was slaving over the cooking, Andrew, who had just finished giving his wife Carolyn a tender hug, leant over and whispered in my ear, 'Hell Denis, they sure smell great now, don't they?'

Unfortunately, wildlife had been rather sparse. While continually on the lookout for camels, the best the girls could find so far were footprints, fresh droppings and a few large piles of bleached bones. A variety of birds, a couple of lizards, several dingoes and a snake completed their tally. The most notable change in vegetation was the large stands of corkwood trees that had now appeared. For the next day, however, I had a few surprises in store for them.

Just before lunch I stopped the girls and took them for a walk along the edge of a small dune to visit an area I had first located many years ago. They come and go depending on the movement of the sand and today we were lucky: there was one human skeleton completely visible. How many more lay covered nearby waiting their turn to be briefly exposed would be impossible to guess, but I am sure it would cover an Aboriginal occupation of hundreds, if not thousands of years.

For my next trick we unpacked my hand-operated aluminium drilling rods and set off at a brisk stroll to a special site. When I had pulled my cart into this spot 22 years ago, it had been a make or break situation. I needed water badly, for without it my journey would have come to an abrupt halt, wasting all the mental and physical energy I'd expended up until then, not to mention shattering my dream.

The Mums were excited at the prospect of finding underground water in this hostile terrain. When we started drilling, I crossed my fingers that at about twelve feet I would strike water once more. The ground was incredibly dry, which made screwing the auger down very difficult. At about 9 feet it became increasingly difficult and I started to wonder if it was worth the effort and particularly the time, as the Mums still had a long walk ahead to complete their daily quota. I would also have expected some moisture on the drill by this point and was concerned that it may have dried up due to the lack of rain over so many years.

Suddenly the bit broke through, dropping about 2 feet. I could tell by the sound it made that we were there. They all crowded around as I dropped my small bailer tube into the hole and drew up a quantity of water for them to taste. The look on the Mums' faces made the effort worthwhile – I knew that they would remember this moment as one of the highlights of their journey.

For days they had been following a sandy track and climbing a seemingly endless procession of dunes, so when they spotted their first salt lake, it was a welcome visual change. It also meant 2 km of easy going over a firm, flat, salt-encrusted surface.

From this point I had proceeded easterly by compass to cross a few more salt lakes before finally heading for Poeppel Corner. Now, due to the Mums' health issues, I chose to follow the track northwards to the Knolls and join the French Track near there.

The girls were enjoying the easy going up the interdunal flats until they hit the dense stand of gidgee trees. I had radioed back that they could continue straight on or turn left and follow my wheel tracks which would lead them along the bottom of a nearby dune. They chose to take my first option as they didn't want to walk one more step than necessary.

There was no wind, and outside the air-conditioned comfort of my vehicle, the heat was intense. For the Mums, it must have been like walking in an inferno, and I knew that in the stillness the hordes of flies would be driving them mad. To top it all off, there was this stinking smell given off by the gidgee trees, which they told me later reminded them of rotting carcasses.

By the time they struggled into base that night they were a miserable, cranky bunch. I'd left them happy, but now they seemed to have developed kinks in their personalities. They likened the section of the walk through the gidgee as their 'walk in hell' and labeled it Death Valley. I was chastised because I had made camp about one kilometre further on than I had advised they would walk for the day. I retired quickly to the solitude of my kitchen where I knew I could redeem myself by cooking up a storm. Tonight was canned stew atop instant mashed potato laced with dried beans – a gourmet delight delicately sprinkled with dried parsley.

Over the past few days Margot's back problem had continued to worsen. Her spine had developed a distinct curve, forcing her to walk in a twisted, unnatural way. It was evident that she was in a lot of pain and needed urgent physiotherapy. She never complained — I don't think it is in her makeup. Now unable to sleep lying down, she intended to try sitting up in the front seat of the vehicle for the night. I knew she would fight to the bitter end, however, we were only just over the half-way mark and still had about 210 km to go.

Carolyn, though she was suffering with huge blisters on both feet and developing ankle problems, refused to slow down. She was generally first on the track leading the way. How difficult it must have been for Andrew, her husband, watching her shuffling along in pain and be powerless to do anything about it. However, this was her dream and she was living it under her rules, and quitting wasn't an option in her mind. She had the guts to push herself to the limit and he must have been very proud of her.

Susan still had the odd twinge in her back, but I was confident that, along with Debbie, she would also make it. I had two positives and two doubtfuls, and we were still on schedule.

Finally we reached the French Track and turned east once more, heading for Poeppel Corner. The scenery now changed dramatically. All vegetation had been cut to pieces: shredded then obliterated by abrasive sands driven by fierce winds which could now rampage unobstructed over its surface. The desert was on the move once more, cutting, re-shaping, forking, and all the while following in the footsteps of previous sands that had once occupied this space before drought or fire had liberated them to continue their relentless march northwards. I have seen its many moods, enjoyed them all, but this must have been the most desolate, fiery face that the Simpson Desert had presented in the last thirty years.

The Mums were finding it tough now, with steep, soft sandhills to climb, excessive heat and incessant flies plaguing them. They walked, limped, hobbled and shuffled, each with their own individual aches and pains, but they put it into perspective for me: 'Our pain is nothing to what women with breast cancer go through'.

I was waiting for them 200 metres west of the edge of the first salt lake to be encountered since departing The Knolls, about 29 km from Poeppel Corner. It's the southern extension of Lake Mirranponga Pongunna and holds special significance for me. This was the lake that I had pulled my cart up some twenty-two years earlier while on my solo west-east walk, and I was able to point out the high dune away to the south-east where I had abandoned it before throwing on my backpack for the last stage of my walk to Birdsville. They were also standing on the French Track at the exact spot where I had crossed it on my five-and-a-half month gulf to gulf walk from Burketown to Adelaide.

It's not all doom and gloom on the track. Knowing the Desert Mums were just ahead, two lovely couples we'd met the day before had cooked an apricot layer cake in their camp oven as a special treat for the girls. When they finally caught up with them and made their presentation, the girls were absolutely thrilled and couldn't stop raving about their treat.

Ahead of us lay numerous large salt lakes and I knew that their wide, firm surfaces would be a welcome relief for the Desert Mums, who had been doing it tough in the soft dunal sands. At 12 kms from Poeppel Corner I made camp amongst a large stand of gidgee. These desert trees have extremely hard wood which burns long and hot, ideal for fires. Margot limped in last to spend another night sitting upright in the vehicle's front seat, while Carolyn was in a lot of pain with her ankles and blisters. Tomorrow it was Mothers Day and a flood of warm wishes for them all poured in from family and friends via the satellite phone; while it lifted their spirits, there were a few tears.

The firelight dancing on the walls of the Mums' tents woke them to a special treat. Normally we departed so early that I didn't bother to light a fire, however, today was their day. A sleep-in and then a warm fire to defrost over before departure was my gift to these wonderful ladies, who I knew would be missing their children terribly. I heard later that they had discussed requesting breakfast in bed, however, my daughter had talked them out of it. Susan is smart. She assured them all they had 'Buckley's chance'!

Extreme temperatures plagued them again. Whenever I stopped alongside, they crowded in for a chat. I didn't wake up to what was going on until someone asked if perhaps I could wind the window down a little further. They were all after a few gulps of my refrigerated air.

The Mums reached a milestone of significance on Mothers' Day and called in on the satellite phone so that we could all share in the moment. 'Dad, our pedometers indicate that we've done 375,000 average steps since we started.' They were all very excited, as this represented one step for every life lost worldwide every year due to breast cancer.

Where the Australian states of Queensland, the Northern Territory and South Australia meet stands Poeppel's peg, marking the spot, and reaching this monument was another highlight of their journey.

The Mums now headed due east by compass to intersect the next salt lake before turning northwards to follow a track along its shores. Queensland National Parks had discouraged us from taking my original cross-country route from here on, so we were committed to the QAA Line to exit the desert.

Andrew and I dug up my last supply cache and then, passing the girls on the track, we made camp on a high point overlooking the lake and awaited their arrival. This was definitely a low point for me as I had almost convinced myself that I was about to lose one, if not two, of the Mums. They were also now discussing this possibility seriously amongst themselves. We had a time schedule and if anyone couldn't keep up, they had to drop out and not sacrifice the chances of the others. The mission was more important than the individual.

Over the last few mornings, as was my usual practice, I was up before dawn and had spotted Margot, obviously in pain and unable to sleep, wandering around the perimeter of the camp in the dark. She shuffled along like an old lady, her back was twisted and her feet were sliding along barely making one foot in front of the other. I don't know how she managed to warm up enough to start her daily routine, let alone finish. Straight out Aussie guts would be my guess. I had expected her to go first, now this afternoon, I decided it was going to be Carolyn. My personal dilemma, if they both went, how I could make enough room in the two grossly overloaded vehicles to carry them.

By the time they arrived in camp that night we had the fire going, the tents up and a very special treat prepared. The bush shower was hung off the side of the vehicle and, with enough water left over from this leg of the journey, everyone was able to enjoy another quick wash, our second since Purni Bore. Then as a finale, we carried chairs to the top of the sand ridge overlooking the huge salt lake, and consumed, in plastic glasses, a small portion of champagne carried for a special occasion such as this.

The Mums proposed a toast to departed friends and family members whose lives had been cut short by this insidious cancer of the breast. There wouldn't be too many people in Australia who don't know at least one such person. They talked of husbands who had lost their best mates, children who'd lost their mothers and of Carolyn's friend – word had just been received by satellite phone of her passing. They shared intimate stories and, with tears streaming down their faces, stood and symbolically named the lake at their feet in honour of all those brave mums worldwide who didn't make it, Lake Courage. So ladies, you have a special spot in the Simpson Desert; if you are ever fortunate enough to drive or walk by, then pause for a moment to reflect the passing of so many of your sisters.

As the sun set on our prime piece of lakeside real estate I knew for sure that they would remember this particular Mother's Day for a very long time.

Surprisingly, they all fronted up next morning ready to go. Setting off by torchlight they followed a firm, flat track a further 12 kms north, before turning east to cross the lake. They were now on the QAA Line and about four days out from Big Red dune.

Every time the Mums topped a dune, they would scan the valley floor below looking for camels. That's all they seemed to talk about lately and, truth be told, it helped drive them forward to the next one, in anticipation. Well, we finally encountered our one and only mob. All the Mums got were footprints and fresh poo, while Katherine and I, being further in front, got the real deal. After a fast run, I was able to head them off and force them to climb the steep face of a nearby dune.

What I was hoping for happened. It was as if, once halfway up the climb, they all suddenly realised they had me beat, for they came to an abrupt halt when I switched off the motor and stood staring at us with what could only be described as aloof disdain. One raised his tail and I wondered if that was the camel equivalent of 'the finger'. Katherine shot out of the vehicle as I came to a stop and then, dropping flat on the deck, got her long-awaited camel footage. I now had one very pleased Canadian videographer on board and Chloe, her four year old daughter, had been granted her special request: she would see a wild Australian camel.

The dunes were higher now, and as we progressed eastward, they grew further apart. Some interdunal flats were over 1 km wide, and their firm base gave the Mums welcome relief from the soft sand of the dunes. The mornings had been very, very cold and the afternoons horrendously hot. Such are the extremes of the desert temperatures. As always, the flies were abundant, driving everyone mad. The Mums were sticking well to my 31 km daily target, and when we finally reached the dry bed of the Eyre Creek to make camp, I knew that, barring accident, they would all walk into Birdsville. The night was full of excitement as they looked forward to the morrow and a very special place that they had pushed so hard, conquered so much, to reach. Margot, as usual, slept sitting upright in the car.

Standing anxiously on top of Big Red with a bunch of tourists, Andrew, Katherine and I finally spotted the four dark specks, momentarily skylined on the dune to the west, before they commenced their descent. From our towering vantage point, the magnitude of the surrounding scenery dwarfed them until eventually they crossed the wide interdunal flat and slowly grew to more lifelike proportions as they tackled the long climb up the face of this well-known sandhill.

There were cheers and tears, yelling and screaming, as they came over the top, with lots of hugs thrown in for good measure. What a special moment for the Desert Mums! One remarked later, 'the experience was too special for words — such an awesome, overpowering feeling to have arrived after so many days of continuous walking'. My four girls had made it and I was overwhelmed with pride.

I had climbed this sand dune so long ago and now here I was reliving my journey while witnessing my daughter Susan following in my footsteps. I'll leave it to you to work out how this old dad felt, but if you need a clue, I had a very large handkerchief in use.

We had a day off camped at the base of Big Red while I did a trip to Birdsville to collect our trailer, the gas bottles, more water to give them another shower, and also to do a bit of laundry.

At 4 am I woke the Mums with less than my usual enthusiasm. The wind had howled all night, threatening to blow us away, and it didn't look like it was about to abate. I wanted to cancel the balloon launch and go back to bed, thinking it would be almost impossible, however, Susan put her foot down. 'Dad, we've waited a long time for this moment and we're at least going to give it a go, so let's get into it'. I guess I shouldn't have expected anything less from my daughter.

We had been joined by Ed and Janice from Toowoomba and now, working furiously as a team, we somehow managed to fill two huge nets with 2500 pink and 80 blue balloons, representing one for every life lost on average per year in Australia to breast cancer. The helium-filled balloons were biodegradable latex, hand tied with no strings or plastic.

The wind was so strong that the sand-covered valley floor was literally moving and our two bouncing nets, instead of floating majestically above us, lay almost horizontally as they strained on their moorings. By 9.30 am I'd positioned my vehicle on top of Big Red to use as an anchor and then, one net at a time, the team walked them up to the launch site where they were again tethered to await their freedom.

My wife Jeanne had stayed at home to be our liaison person with the outside world, ready day and night to receive our calls and fulfil our numerous requests. She had done an incredible job helping to put the total package together and we all would have been lost without her. Jeanne was thrilled to have played a part and formed a close association with the Desert Mums via the web. As she said, 'It has been a huge task that these four friends have given themselves and taken on together. They have all done a wonderful, unselfish and courageous thing and I am proud of them beyond words.' Well, they were proud of her too. As for me, I just wished she could have been there with us all for this special moment.

At 10 am the blue sky above Big Red burst into life with an awesome display of colour. What an incredible sight as nets were opened and thousands of balloons turned loose! Against the fierce wind whipping overhead, they fought to rise skyward in celebration — a symbol of honour to the lives of those who are no longer with us. Spirits set free, now racing away on the wind.

Then it was back to business doing what Desert Mums do. After a quick lunch, while Andrew, Katherine and I packed the vehicles and trailer, they set forth to conquer the next 25 km section. Strong headwinds, swirling sands, dust, flies and gibbers underfoot made for a tough afternoon. Gibbers are smooth, irregular-shaped stones unique to parts of Australia's deserts. Walking on these can roll an ankle in a flash. Carolyn at least didn't have to worry, as both her ankles had collapsed inwards long ago – this just added an extra measure of agony.

At 25 km I made camp. Birdsville was in sight, and with only 15 km to go to complete their mission I knew that the next day they would easily arrive at 10 am, right on schedule.

This was the most desolate campsite I had ever chosen in my entire life. The best I could do on this barren, flat, almost treeless landscape was to try to group us behind a few dozen sparse 'dead finish' bushes to help break the incessant wind.

Sore and tired from an extremely long day, the Mums finally trudged into camp. To mark this milestone and also to dull their aches and pains, Andrew produced a few bottles of red wine. It didn't take long for them all to settle back and enjoy this last night camping under the desert stars. Reminiscing was the name of the game; away in the distance the blinking lights of Birdsville, oh so close, continually reminded them all that the next day their journey would come to an end.

Well the desert got down and dirty later that night and put on a first class tantrum. The wind howled through the camp, swirling the soft drift sand into everything, including tents and sleeping bags, coating their occupants with a gritty layer. Sleep was almost impossible, except perhaps for Margot, who was in her usual spot sitting up in the front seat of the vehicle. Still, by 9 pm the next night they would all be in a hotel in Melbourne, enjoying a real bed with crisp sheets, steaming hot showers, maybe seafood for dinner, cold wine, no dust, no wind, no flies, no more early morning starts and no more of my cooking.

Next morning, although still dark, everyone was glad to escape their sandy confines and I could sense their excitement. After a leisurely breakfast, the Mums took off on the last leg of their journey. In Susan's pocket she carried an old newspaper photo of my own arrival into Birdsville. This time father and daughter would walk in together. While we packed, I received a call from Jeanne updating us on the fund-raising effort and we hurried to catch up with them to relay the good news. They were now over their target of $105,000 and still climbing, which meant that a three-year research scholarship could definitely be offered to one lucky graduate.

The Mums had reached their target thanks mainly to Debbie's fundraising skills. She had worked from the beginning with enthusiasm, imagination and total commitment to the project, and deserves a huge pat on the back for such a successful financial outcome. Now all they had to do was walk into town so that further financial pledges, reliant on them successfully completing the crossing, could be honoured.

This day belonged to them, so from the shadow of the pub verandah, I watched discreetly as they began their journey down the home stretch, and for a moment my vision clouded. I saw this tall solitary bearded figure carrying a backpack emerging out of the heat haze — then it was gone — to be replaced by four lovely Mums striding it out, their dream close to fulfilment.

At 9.47 am, after walking 430 km, climbing some 1200 sand dunes and enduring a great deal of physical pain, four dirty, sweaty, extremely tired but very proud women knocked on the door of the Birdsville Pub and so ended their amazing journey across the Simpson Desert.

Susan, Debbie, Carolyn and Margot, The Desert Mums, eventually settled back into their daily lives away from the adrenalin-filled escapades of those weeks, but no doubt, they will never ever forget their time 'on the track'.

There was a lump in my throat as all too soon the chartered aircraft whisked Susan away to fulfil her last commitment to the National Breast Cancer Foundation and the cause that had benefited from so much of their time and energy. Back in Canada, Milli, her four-year-old daughter was now anxiously waiting her return, and while it was sad to see Susan go, I had shared something with my daughter that very few fathers will ever do. It was unique and wonderful.

My job was now finished and I returned to 'retirement' and my beautiful Jeanne, who had given so freely of herself and contributed so much to the project. As for the Desert Mums, I love and miss them all, and the tears I shed on several occasions were tears of pride. They all did a mighty job and I am so thrilled that my daughter gave me the opportunity to lead them across a special place I call the 'Desert of Dreams'.

Early in the trip, I had told Andrew that the DVD player in my brand-new vehicle was broken — selfishly, I didn't want the peace of my desert destroyed by blaring music night after night — the desert silence is, in itself, magical. However the night before the Mums walked into Birdsville, I relented, admitted my fib, and we all awoke in the morning darkness to the sounds of an Andrea Bocelli – Sara Brightman duet: 'Time to Say Goodbye'. The dance I had with my daughter on the windblown desert sand under a starlit sky was a special moment that will remain with me for the rest of my life.

Susan wrote:

Having time to reflect and digest the enormity of what we did, I believe this was the hardest challenge I have ever undertaken. Logistically pulling it off was difficult to say the least (four states and two countries involved for 18 months) and then to have such a dream run to the finish ... wow! Walking alongside the most determined and committed team was such a pleasure and honour. I now know what 'inner strength' means and admire my friends now more than ever for being such powerful women.

> Dad — bloody hell – what can I say here? You are
> one hell of a father and human being. I have walked
> away with such an appreciation of your kindness, love,
> generosity and humour. I had no idea you were so
> well respected out in the desert and it blew me away
> to hear the Aboriginal park rangers talk of you with
> such high regard and respect. There is not one inch of
> the desert you do not know and to walk it with you
> was mind-blowing for all the girls. You put your heart
> and soul into sharing your desert with us and we are
> eternally grateful. You are my hero. Love you Dad.

The Desert Mums' lives have all been enriched by their experience and normal living will never be the same to them again. They had all accepted the challenge and dared to climb another rung higher on life's endless ladder.

I believe in giving life all you've got. When you think your tank is empty it's probably not even sitting on half. If we really want to live a dream, then it's waiting to start just one short step away.

Chapter 19

My Mate Ron

I first met Ron McHendry in 1994, when Danny Colson and I crossed the Simpson Desert by camel. From the top of a high dune Danny and I could see a lone vehicle straddling the track ahead of us, while its sole occupant waited patiently in the shade of the one and only nearby bush. It was hot … real hot; even the camels were feeling it as we slowly descended the steep face of the dune to reach his position. As I drew Muffy to a halt, Peter Pan moved up alongside then reached over and rested his huge sandy head almost in my lap as he gave this intruder the once-over.

This was more than just a chance meeting with a couple of grey-haired, sixty-somethings out in the Simpson Desert living life to the full. Ron had heard that I was coming over the desert by camel and had driven out from Birdsville specifically to meet me. It was obvious at that brief encounter that we shared a similar love of the desert, and in time, that he had entered my life for a reason.

Once back in civilization we maintained regular phone contact, and when a few years later I mentioned to him that I was going out into the desert on a special mission, Ron decided to join me. I wanted to do a quick search for the actual site where I had received my airdrop while walking north–south across Australia some ten years previously.

We met in Birdsville and then headed out together into the Simpson. Without a precise dot on the map to aim for this wasn't going to be easy; it would push my skills to the limit. At my best guess the site was somewhere inside a rectangle of around 3 by 6 kilometres. That still left an almost impossible amount of rolling sandhill country to search with the limited fuel and time we would have available on this trip. However, I had retained a vivid visual memory of the landscape off to the west. All I needed to do was close my eyes and up it would come like a photograph, so I was easily able to describe the scene to Ron. If I could get us into the near vicinity I was sure that I could locate the actual drop site.

Using the French Track, we went west from Poeppel Corner until finally I turned us up a wide interdunal corridor. There were no tracks now, and by my best calculations we had about 60 km to go in a northerly direction. We would be following the strike line of the dunes all the way to the airdrop search area that I had marked on my map.

That night we had one of those memorable campfires. Our swags were rolled out on a small, smooth, almost circular claypan, the fire's light flickered over the dense stand of gidgee surrounding us, while above the jewels of the heavens shone out of a cloudless sky. There wasn't a breath of wind to dislodge the thin spiral of smoke from its upward journey, and off to the side, at the very edge of the fire's glow, a solitary dingo prowled silently.

We chatted for hours – mainly about the desert, remote areas and past adventures – and I deeply enjoyed this moment in the company of someone who had found in himself a complete love of the outback. Most of my journeys have been solo affairs. To spend time with a like-minded bloke is something very special indeed.

It turned out to be a slow but pleasant drive north, and just before midday we arrived in the vicinity of the search area. We had been continually climbing, and for the last kilometre or so high sandhills on either side had restricted our view of the surrounding country until finally the one on my left ended abruptly. Rolling away to sundown there now lay exposed a succession of parallel dunes, the middle area of which seemed to be sinking into a valley or depression as they headed southwards. This was my mental photograph, exactly as I remembered it.

We now turned east across a wide interdunal corridor towards another very high dune and I confidently predicted to Ron that on the other side we would find my old campsite at its base. I turned out to be slightly off course; it wasn't until I had driven south along the ridge line for about 500 metres that I radioed Ron to follow me down the face of the dune. I thought I now recognised some small clay pans and was positive we had arrived.

I was tremendously excited as we finally pulled up in front of the group of gidgee where I'd spread my bivvy bag and spent three unforgettable days recuperating so long ago. As if for final proof to Ron,

I scraped away the sand with my boot from the area where I'd lit my fire and exposed its ashes. At that moment, however, the thing that stirred me the most occurred: I heard again the call of my 'morse code birds'. How well I remembered that sound. It was as though they were welcoming me home.

Some distance away, Ron found the remains of one of my water-drop tubes, which still had the valve stem attached. Obviously, the moment I'd departed the dingoes must have dragged it out of my fire before it had time to burn, thinking that they could eat it. Ron recorded the site with his GPS at S25°28'56" and E137°39'57".

We split up in the desert a few days later, each to go his separate way, but not before we shared one final memorable moment. We were standing on the top of an extremely high dune. Ron had also been there before and I gathered that this was his favourite place.

'Den,' he said 'This is a lot bigger than Big Red, don't you reckon?'

'Well Ron, it is and it isn't,' I replied. 'It depends on how you look at it mate.' I went on to explain that as I see it, Big Red is a solitary long sandhill rising from a hard valley floor on either side. It is a defined single item, and certainly most impressive in its proportions. By contrast, to reach the top of the one we were now standing on, you started on the valley floor and then climbed a series of individual parallel dunes, each taking you progressively closer to the top: a bit like climbing stairs. However you look at it, he was certainly correct about it being big, and the view was incredible. We stood way above the surrounding landscape and for 360 degrees the desert stretched to the horizon, seeming to go on forever.

Sadly, this would turn out to be our last visit together to this unique area.

🦎 🦎 🦎

I remember the day I got the phone call with the dreadful news. Ron hadn't been feeling well and a series of tests had confirmed that he had Non-Hodgkins Lymphoma. Cancer.

We continued making phone contact at least several times a year and I would listen and give encouragement as best I could. I'm always left feeling desperately inadequate at times like these. There were moments of highs and hope and then moments of despair as he worked his way through the numerous treatments.

We seemed to have this strange thought connection. If I was thinking about him, invariably within a day or so, or even within hours, he would phone, and if the same occurred in reverse, I would ring. We commented on it many times.

I felt an urgency to contact Ron on one particular occasion, and when I did, I was shocked at the sound of his voice. It was evident that he was at an extremely low point; his speech was laboured like I had never heard it before. We had a conversation for far longer than I deemed wise considering the difficulty he was experiencing in just breathing, but I just went with the flow as he seemed anxious to talk. Naturally, we reminisced about the desert and past journeys and he commented that there was little likelihood of his ever going back to the sandhill country west of Birdsville. I could tell he was really sad about that.

Well, I made a promise to him there and then. One day I would go back and camp a night on that high sandhill and he would be with me, by my side all the way. Apparently I was the last person he ever spoke to, and early the following morning, after battling his cancer for seven long years, he finally slipped away.

Chapter 20

One Last Camp

It was early 2009, and I would soon turn seventy-six. Ron had passed away four years earlier, aged 57, and I figured it was about time I honoured my promise to him before I also went walkabout to that other place.

My destination lay in the Northern Territory section of the Simpson Desert, about 42 km north-west of Poeppel Corner. I purchased a Desert Parks Pass for the sum of $107.00. This would allow me access into the Territory via Queensland so that I could then go by compass the rest of the way, as well as access to some other places I wanted to visit.

I remember the days when desert travel was free and unrestricted. Come to think of it, so was most of Australia. I suppose if you were just starting out to explore the great outback now, you'd more easily accept the vast areas denied to you. It would be normal. But having seen so much of it over such a long time I find it difficult, like so many from a past era, to accept the ever-increasing restrictions.

When I first ventured into the bush and then the large cattle and sheep stations some fifty-odd years ago, arrivals were always greeted with open arms. A cuppa or an invitation to stay the night was the norm, not the exception. This was due to their isolation and their thirst for knowledge of what, to many, was almost another world beyond their nearest town. Gradually, better cars, roads, communications and light aircraft allowed even the most isolated station-dwellers to escape more frequently to larger centres and cities. Attitudes slowly started to change.

The advent of the four-wheel drive vehicle accelerated this change. Nothing now was remote. The outback was shrinking rapidly. With this 'conquer all' vehicle came numerous tourists from the urban areas and bush hospitality started to decline noticeably in the face of increasing demands by ill-prepared travellers and the growing intrusion on bush people's privacy.

How would you like to have twenty four-wheel drives suddenly appear in your backyard, form a defensive circle like the wild west wagon trains of old, then disgorge a mob of people all ready for a chat and a photo shoot? Especially if these visitors had ignorantly damaged your private place with deep wheel ruts cut into recently saturated soil. How could you blame the outback folk for not taking to them? Finally the ratbags arrived: shooting water tanks, cattle and horses for sport, leaving gates open, breaking down fences to gain access and pinching any equipment that they could lay their hands on. 'Keep Out' signs started to appear, along with legislation restricting entry to properties.

I consider myself privileged that I was able to explore my country and experience its hospitality and mateship with a freedom all but gone nowadays. Check out how much of Australia is now regulated, with restricted access and permits needed if you can get one. National Parks, station properties and enormous chunks of Aboriginal land have thousands of 'Keep Out' signs denying access to the majority of Australians.

After I took the South Australian Government expedition across the Simpson Desert in 1986 to show them the native well sites I'd located, they asked me to submit my recommendations on the existing tracks that should be made available to the public so that they could enjoy a unique and varied experience through this magnificent area. I got the feeling at the time that they were contemplating restricting a crossing to the French Track only. I suggested the French Track, the WAA (my favourite) and the Rig Road. They had formed the basis of a story I'd written for a magazine some time previously called *Three Tracks across the Simpson*. These, together with about four interconnecting tracks, I felt should satisfy all needs in terms of safety and variety of scenery and these were ultimately accepted by the powers that be. I guess we should be thankful that we have as much desert access as we do.

I was preparing for my desert journey when flooding rains fell over the huge catchment areas of the Diamantina and Georgina Rivers. This effectively blocked access into the Simpson as their floodwaters raced down its eastern perimeter heading for Lake Eyre and forced me to delay my departure. The flood turned out to be fortuitous – saving me from what could otherwise have been a significant desert drama. I ended up spending a few weeks in hospital undergoing major bowel surgery, and then, before I'd fully recovered from that, I went back in for a second operation. All this knocked the stuffing out of me, and it was many months before I felt well enough to travel.

After such a long dry spell the deluge brought joy to the station owners whose cattle properties straddled its path. It didn't take long for the birdlife to locate this massive body of water from thousands of miles away and flock there in huge numbers to breed. How they manage this feat I do not know.

We must never, ever allow the diversion or damming of any of the normally dry rivers that make up the Lake Eyre Basin. It is one of the largest in the world where life hangs by a thread, waiting sometimes years for the next rejuvenating flood to arrive. It's too valuable an asset. Look at what we have done to the mighty Murray River system, where over allocation of water for irrigation, greed, and failure by the different States to agree to a unified management approach, combined with a severe run of droughts, has finally brought it to its knees.

The Diamantina had stopped flowing by the time I finally arrived in Birdsville and made my way to its historic pub for a quick beer. My last drink in that pub had been back in 2006 as I celebrated journey's end with the Desert Mums after their charity walk.

But I wasn't just remembering their success. At that time I'd casually asked the publican if he happened to have seen a friend of mine around lately — someone I hadn't bumped into for over twenty years. I was shocked to learn that she and three others had been killed about ten years earlier in a horrific head-on vehicle accident that had devastated the small township of Tibooburra in north-western New South Wales.

Dinah was a special person who loved life, the desert, the outback and its people all with a passion. As co-author of the book *The Fence People*, she left a lasting memorial to her short but adventurous life.

The publican also told me that a group of her friends had scattered her ashes over Big Red. I was absolutely dumbfounded. I don't know why they would have chosen that particular site. Maybe it's because she had frequently worked in the area and had expressed such a love of the desert that they thought it would be a fitting place.

A long time earlier I'd mentioned to Dinah, amongst others, that when I died, I wanted my ashes spread over Big Red. Then when I met and married Jeanne, I changed my mind: half for Big Red and the other half with Jeanne's, if she would have me, which would mean somewhere near the sea, or even in it. I wanted a foot in both camps. One thing is for sure, Dinah will have lots of visitors to this most famous of all the Simpson Desert sandhills.

I refuelled, double-checked my gear, and then departed this well-known outback town. It sure had grown since my first visit well over thirty years ago.

I paused long enough at Big Red to pay my respects to Dinah and lay a bunch of flowers I'd picked from the roadside. Then, lowering my tyre pressure to 20 psi and attaching a very large flagpole to the bull bar, I was away into the sandhill country I so enjoyed.

Crossing Eyre Creek and its floodout country proved not to be an obstacle. Due, however, to the dramatic growth in tourist numbers, I crested the top of each dune with extreme caution, hoping that all oncoming vehicles were also fitted with high flagpoles. The risk of a head-on collision increases yearly. Motorbikes worry me the most, due to their speed and small size. In many places, they wouldn't be seen until it was way too late. A plaque on the QAA Line once marked the site of a motorcyclist's death.

Situated in the remote south-eastern corner of the Northern Territory, the top of a very high sandhill, my destination, and the purpose of my journey finally appeared. In a few hours I would fulfil the promise I had made to a dying friend.

First, however, I had to detour to check on a special tree. It had been blazed by explorer David Lindsay in 1886 when he stopped to water his camels at the nearby native well. Lost after the Aboriginals departed the area in 1900, I had found the tree in May 1980 alive and well, but on a visit in 1992 the old gidgee had appeared to be dead.

My visual memory of the area was crystal clear, and to say I was excited about returning would be an understatement. With unerring accuracy I headed towards the site, with the rusty old chisel I'd found there and thought might be Lindsay's nestled on the seat beside me. It was coming home, but only for a visit.

The tree was nowhere to be found. My guess is that having been dead some seventeen years, it had fallen over and been buried by the continually shifting sands. Dead and weakened, it wouldn't have stood a chance against some of the severe winds I have experienced in the desert.

When they arrive at night it is not a pleasant experience. You hear them coming, faintly at first, then suddenly it's a mighty roar, like a runaway locomotive on steroids bearing down on you. In the pitch black, all hell breaks loose as it cuts its destructive path across the landscape. Trees are annihilated and everything in its path is blasted with cutting sand and flying debris. Tucked up in your swag it feels like a giant hand is trying to carry you away as it shakes you like a terrier would a rat.

Lindsay's tree, once it hit the ground, would have shattered and then very quickly backed up the sand to cover itself. Like the human skeleton I could now see exposed nearby, it will occasionally re-emerge for a period, but sadly not today.

I had more success with the Aboriginal wiltja, or humpy, where I had found the chisel so long ago. Its structure, while collapsing badly, was still recognisable and it's amazing to think that this home was built and last inhabited over 109 years ago.

Now I had satisfied my curiosity it was time to go if I were to reach the top of the sandhill and make camp before dark. I took this last opportunity to collect enough wood for a small fire. There was none where I was going. Then, with the shadowy fingers of night creeping across the valley floor, I started my climb determined to beat them to the summit.

Finally I stood high above it all, my feet planted on grains of sand that rested, but only momentarily, on their relentless, wind driven northerly march.

Years of desert crossings have not numbed my senses to the stark beauty of the unique arid region that surrounded me. I stood captivated as deep emotions overwhelmed me. I felt totally at peace and at one with the landscape. I was glad to be back.

A lone wedge-tailed eagle arrowed out of the sky to circle effortlessly above me before dropping to the valley floor below. We eyeballed each other as he passed gracefully by, almost within reach. Then as the sun slowly slipped over the horizon, one by one the high domes shed their glow until finally it was our turn and darkness once more fell over the land.

My cooking fire, which until now had danced images around me and limited my vision to the immediate vicinity, finally died to a pile of red-hot gidgee coals. Slowly my eyes adjusted to a landscape now dimly lit by a million stars. Brooding and immense, it seemed to go on forever and it took little imagination to feel that you were completely alone in this universe. There was no wind. The silence was deafening.

I settled down to savour the warmth of my fire and to drink a toast or several to Ron McKendry. I had finally kept my promise, and hoped that he had enjoyed the journey as much as I had. He had returned once more, through me, to our special place. Rest in peace old mate.

I unfolded and re-read my tattered copy of George Lindsay Jones's letter, written back in 1896 to his parents as he lay thirst-ravaged and dying out in another desert away to the west. He was just 18 years old. It's something I occasionally do when alone in remote areas. I think it keeps me connected to all the explorers: people like Hume and Hovell who started me off as a kid on my personal journey of outback discovery. It reminds me of the hardships endured by the early pioneers that I so admired and also all those souls who down through time have lost their lives out in this magnificent, harsh and unforgiving landscape that we call the outback.

George Lindsay Jones had attached his letter to the outside of a notebook. When he was found some six months later, it was lying next to his head intact. His companion, Charles Wells, lay a short distance away. How incredible after all that time that the Aboriginals, who had removed other items, didn't touch it, and that it hadn't been burnt by a fire which had come very close to their bodies.

I feel that it was meant to survive as a lasting testimony to his courage and his beliefs, and his last words would have meant so much to his grieving parents – giving them comfort, closure and an immense feeling of pride.

His death at the age of eighteen reminds me of how fortunate I've been to have had the opportunity to have witnessed so much of life. I've lived from the final stages of the horse and cart days, through the end of World War II to the emergence of modern transportation and unbelievable advances in aviation, medicine and technology. Who could forget Sputnik, man's first steps on the moon, Cyclone Tracy, terrorists, the Twin Towers and those brave individuals who willingly and knowingly gave their lives when they brought to earth the flying missile that zealots were endeavouring to use to destroy the White House?

Now we have Barack Obama, the first African–American president of the USA coming into power as the whole world sinks into its deepest recession. And then there is the big unknown, global warming. At least when things go wrong, we can blame it on that – rightly or wrongly. Take, for example, the struggle of the Murray–Darling river system to survive, the forecast demise of the Great Barrier Reef or the tragic bushfires that raced across southern Australia, claiming some 173 lives and making it one of the worst natural disasters in Australian history from a human perspective.

In my view, those mammoth fires were made far worse than they should have been by legislation pushed through by the 'Greenies', who had not only saved the roadside rubbish as a habitat for a few native lizards, ants and sundry small crawlies but also allowed massive tracts of forest to build intolerable levels of undergrowth fuel. When the inevitable happened, roads became death traps for fleeing vehicles, and houses, no match for the towering infernos that roared unrestrained to their very front doors, turned to ash.

The Aboriginals used fire for hunting, and as the animals in each area were depleted, moved on to newer pastures and repeated the process. When they finally returned, it was to a land revitalised and the process was repeated once again.

I remember one station owner way out towards the Kimberleys who, when his kids were giving him a hard time, gave them the keys to the ute, a box of matches and told them to go away and light a few fires. His station, due to their patchwork burning, was forever protected from total disaster as areas in various stages of regeneration stopped or slowed any chance of a massive wildfire.

Let us learn the lessons this time so that in future the animals and the forest we all so enjoy will never again be decimated in total. We are the ones who, in our stupidity, are trying to upset a balance that nature had learnt to live with. It uses fire for its very survival.

Above, the Southern Cross, which had guided me unerringly on so many occasions over dark and featureless terrain, continued its never-ending march across the night sky, ready as always to point the way. On this night, it turned my thoughts in different directions.

I've always encouraged the young to get out and experience our great outback and our heritage and to challenge life in general. For the not-so-young, I have endeavoured to show by example that age is not a barrier, merely an excuse, and that dreams can become reality if one is prepared to give it a go. If you haven't already been, may the Southern Cross one day guide you on your own personal journey of outback discovery.

I rolled out of my swag before dawn, stoked up the fire to boil the billy and packed my vehicle. My mission was complete. While I had now honoured my promise to a dying man, I knew deep down that there was another very personal reason that I was now standing on top of this magnificent sandhill way out in the middle of nowhere. The unthinkable had happened. I was here willingly to say goodbye to a desert I had enjoyed for so many years, knowing I wouldn't be back.

It is not that my adventuring days are finished, mind you. Perish the thought! Locked inside is this barefoot kid with the skinny legs who still wants to run like the wind, to wander, to explore, to challenge and to dream. I don't think we need ever grow up — we do however grow old, grey and wrinkly. Bugger!

A magazine once credited me with more knowledge of the Simpson Desert than I possess. I can claim, however, that my association with this area has been prolonged and varied when compared to the norm. During the last thirty-plus years I have walked it twice, ridden camels over it, unlocked some of its lost Aboriginal history and retraced paths trodden by its early European explorers. By vehicle, I have travelled extensively over its surface on mostly solo journeys – well in excess of seventy – and with the exception of the odd occasion where I received partial financial support, it's all been at my expense. I wasn't paid to be there, I was drawn back time and again by forces beyond my control to immerse myself in the magic of a unique and beautiful landscape.

Over the years I have seen the Simpson Desert become a garden land after good rains have fallen, its surface clothed with a magnificent array of wild flowers and abundant green growth all pulsating with energy as they busily set seed, preparing for life after death. Normally dry, where life is a continual struggle and only the hardy survive, it occasionally descends after years of prolonged heat and drought to the depths of despair. Driven by fierce winds, the abrasive sand easily shreds everything in its path, uncovering another face of the desert – completely different, but in its own way just as fascinating.

I have been left with a soul enriched and memories to last a lifetime. I read somewhere that the secret of a life well lived is not counting the years, but making the years count, and I've had more than my fair share of good ones. I had driven 1900 kilometres just to get here to spend a night alone on top of a sandhill. Was it worth it? You bet. Life doesn't get much better than this.

Then, as the sun's fiery ball once more burst over the horizon, my outlook slowly expanded, enabling me to locate the native wells of Boolubootinna and Perlanna away in the distance.

My vivid imagination recreated the scene: from the cooking fires of a dozen humpies, columns of smoke spiralled lazily upwards, only to flatten then smudge the valley floor as they drifted and slowly dissipated in and over the dense stands of gidgee. Dark bodies moved gracefully as they went about their daily business, just as their ancestors had done; kids played and screamed as kids do.

They heard them coming from the south long before they could be seen. White fellas riding camels had finally arrived into their sanctuary. They camped by an old gidgee tree upon which they left their mark and drew water from the nearby well. It was 1886.

Their arrival didn't change lives that day, but they were the forerunners. They opened a window into another civilisation that had long since moved from the stone age hunter-gatherer existence. The lure of change would ultimately prove irresistible to these desert dwellers. Stationary for thousands of years, their next leap forward had finally arrived. Fourteen years later, a chisel was thrown into a dying fire as every man, woman and child, gathering only the possessions needed for a long march, departed their desert home never to return.

All around me bare domes and sawtooth peaks of golden sand gave irregularities to the rolling waves of ridge tops, while the valley floors below flowed with green rivers of gidgee.

Then, after one final long lingering look, it was my turn to move on. I said my last goodbye to a very special place, then heading towards sun-up, I turned my back forever on my Desert of Dreams.

Five Sierra Bravo Xray — off and clear.

Post Script

I thought I had well and truly put the Simpson Desert behind me – so what happens when a very special person in your life says, 'Dad, I want to walk the desert as you and my sister have done. I would like to do it over about six days and I need your help'.

In August 2010 I was privileged to act as backup for my 43-year-old son Richard, who walked the desert along the French Track from west to east (Freeth Junction to Birdsville) in seven and a half days. For three days straight he easily averaged 61 km per day and was ahead of his self-imposed target. Unfortunately, he developed painful shin splints in both legs and was forced to reduce his pace to just over 42 km per day. He never complained, and I realised once again that I have a son of whom I am immensely proud. It appears that desert walks have now become a family tradition.

What a great year for the Simpson Desert, with widespread rains drenching most of it! At the foot of Big Red we camped on a sandy spit at the water's edge and I have never seen Lake Nappanerica so full. Eyre Creek was flowing, and with its floodout channels now green and vibrant, played host to an abundance of bird life, while way out in the desert the lake at the eastern end of the WAA Line was full to the brim.

Above all, a desert which for so many years had battled to survive was now bursting with energy. Past visions of parched red sand were now softened as a covering of green embraced all, while a variety of wildflowers created a garden-like landscape of incredible beauty.

For so long the sand's surface, the true indicator of desert life, had been depressingly sterile. Now it carried the footprints of life: millions of them crisscrossing the sand dunes; creatures scurrying from bush to bush leaving tracks that told of a desert in rejuvenation.

I have seen the many moods of the Simpson Desert over more than thirty years. Perhaps this journey with my son was meant to draw me back to view my beloved desert one more time. A desert after soaking rain is a rare and beautiful thing and something not to be missed.

Out there the desert lies waiting, ever changing and yet never changing, for other Desert Walkers with their own dreams to live.

To All My Readers

50%

Special Discount Offer on

"OUTBACK ADVENTURES"

My DVD COMBO – Duration 115 mins

It's a stunning visual appreciation of the vast Australian Outback and will bring my story DESERT WALKER to life.

1. DESERT WALKER (An Australian documentary — Duration 45mins)
This is an account of a solo journey by foot across Australia from Burketown on the Gulf of Carpentaria to Adelaide on the Gulf St Vincent, a distance of some 2,200 kilometres. This five and a half month epic walk would pass through the very heart of the Simpson, the largest parallel sand dune desert in the world—a daunting place with an average rainfall of less than 130mm and temperatures ranging from 60º C to near freezing. Departing Camooweal en route, the next township was Maree, 1487 kilometres to the south. Imagine no towns, no support vehicles and only a handful of station people living

in a vast emptiness. It could only happen in Australia. Denis's courage and determination to succeed fired the imagination of the Australian public who donated $80,000 to his favourite cause, The Royal Flying Doctor Service. Their aircraft and personnel provide a MANTLE OF SAFETY over Australia's outback for the people who live in it, or the traveller just passing through.

2. JOURNEY TO AUSTRALIA'S INLAND SEA (**An Australian documentary — Duration 50mins**) After two attempts over 15 months, Denis Bartell's epic journey by canoe followed the normally dry Cooper Creek from "The Dig Tree" in Queensland to Australia's Inland Sea, Lake Eyre In South Australia - a distance of some 700 kilometres. As the flood waters from the vast Queensland catchment areas of the Thompson and Barcoo Rivers joined, then flowed slowly into the Cooper, Denis was able to paddle his canoe through one of the driest regions in Australia until the waters dried up upon reaching the Birdsville Track. An even bigger flood the following year enabled him to complete his journey as the waters reached and almost filled the magnificent Lake Eyre basin.

3. THE DESERT MUMS (**A four part news item screened on Global BC News Canada — Duration 20mins**) Guided by Denis Bartell, his daughter Susan and three of her closest friends set out to walk across the Simpson Desert just as her father had done 22 years before. This is their journey as recorded for Global BC News Canada. Through the highs and the painful lows these four ordinary Australian mums always remained focused and at the end of their journey their effort had raised well over $130,000 for breast cancer research.

Don't Miss Out!
go to: www.desertwalker.com.au

Preview my DVD Combo, **Outback Adventures**, and if you would like to purchase a copy at your special discounted price,

Email me:
denis@desertwalker.com.au
To arrange payment and shipping details.

DVDs are forwarded by regular mail at your risk to minimize costs. Should you require the extra protection afforded by Registered Mail, please advise me so that I can price your postage and handling accordingly. Goods damaged in transit should be returned in their original packaging for a replacement item.

Thank you for purchasing
DESERT WALKER

Acknowledgements

After nearly eighty years, there are so many who have contributed to my life's journey that it is impossible to individually thank them all here.

So to those who nurtured me, tutored me, inspired me, challenged me and helped me along the way, I thank you all and express my deepest appreciation!

BIBLIOGRAPHY

I have always had a great interest in, and empathy with, the early explorers and of the hardships and disappointments they endured during their exploits to open up our magnificent country. Having personally retraced the footsteps of many of these courageous men using information gleaned from their journals and archival material, their ventures have been woven into some of my own adventure stories. Although generally brief, it is hoped that readers will be encouraged to delve more deeply into their lives and our past Australian history as a whole, both Aboriginal and European.

Recommended Reading Books:

Australia Twice Traversed Vol 1 & Vol 2 by Ernest Giles - Sampson Low, Marston, Searle & Rivington Ltd. London

To the Great Gulf – The Surveys and Explorations of L.A. Wells by Wilfred and Christopher Steel - Lynton publications Pty Ltd, South Australia

Spinifex and Sand by Hon. David W. Carnegie - C. Arthur Pearson Ltd. London

The Explorers by William Joy - Rigby Limited, Australia

Great Australian Explorers by Marcia McEwan - Bay Books Pty Ltd, New South Wales

Crossing the Dead Heart by C.T. Madigan - Georgian House Pty Ltd, Melbourne, Victoria

Burke and Wills – The Dig Tree by Sarah Murgatroyd - The Text Publishing Co. Melbourne, Victoria

Coopers Creek The Story of Burke and Wills by Alan Moorehead - Nelson Publishers, Melbourne, Victoria

The Mystery of Ludwig Leichhardt by Gordon Connell - Brown Prior Anderson Pty Ltd. Melbourne, Victoria

In Leichhardt's Footsteps by Bruce Simpson - Australian Broadcasting Corporation, Sydney, NSW

Where the Seasons Come and Go by Eric Bonython - Published by Illawong Pty Ltd SA.

Dune is a four-letter word by Griselda Sprigg with Rod Maclean - Wakefield Press, SA.

The following book is a great reference for all those who are contemplating a vehicle crossing of the Simpson Desert:

The Simpson Desert – Natural History and Human Endeavour by Mark Shephard, Royal Geographical Society of Australasia and Giles Publications, Adelaide, South Australia

It covers in detail the land forms, plants, bird and animal life, Aboriginal occupation and early European exploration. Heightened interest in gas and oil exploration led to the formation of the South Australian and Northern Territory Oil Search Company (SANTOS) who in the late 1950's carried out extensive air and ground exploration into the desert regions. In the early 1960's the French Petroleum Company drilled a well at Purni Bore near the western edge of the desert and soon after cut the now famous French Track from there to Poeppel Corner. Ultimately this track, along with numerous others cut by various exploration crews allowed easier access into and across The Simpson and paved the way for a recreation boom which has grown from just a handful of crossings per year to hundreds, perhaps by now, even thousands.

PUBLICATIONS AND JOURNALS

Reference was made to the following:

Nine Simpson Desert Wells by Hercus L.A. and Clarke P. 1986.   Archaeol. Oceania 21 (1986) 51-62

E.A. Colson 1936 Royal Geographical Society of Australasia, South Australian Branch, Adelaide.

Lindsay D.L. 1886 Royal Geographical Society of Australasia, South Australian Branch, Adelaide

McKinlay J. and Hodgkinson W.O. Royal Geographical Society of Australasia, South Australian Branch, Adelaide

The reproduction of a letter in Chapter 1 from George Lindsay Jones to his parents: Image courtesy of the State Library of South Australia. SLSA: PRG 1011/?: Jones, George Lindsay—Letter "To my dearest Mother and Father", 18/6/1897.

The collection of photos and material over such a long period of my life has meant that the origins of some have been lost in time and I may have unintentionally failed to give recognition where it was due. If so, I apologise and request that you please notify me so that acknowledgement may be included in the next print run.

www.ingramcontent.com/pod-product-compliance
Lightning Source LLC
Chambersburg PA
CBHW062356090426
42740CB00010B/1302